Women's Life in Greece & Rome

Women's Life in Greece & Rome

a source book in translation

second edition

Mary R. Lefkowitz &
Maureen B. Fant

Duckworth

Reprinted 1995, 1997, 1999
Second edition 1992
First published in 1982 by
Gerald Duckworth & Co. Ltd.
61 Frith Street
London W1V 5TA
Tel: 0171 434 4242
Fax: 0171 434 4420
email: enquiries@duckworth-publishers.co.uk

A catalogue record for this book is
available from the British Library

ISBN 0 7156 1641 2

Photoset in North Wales by
Derek Doyle & Associates, Mold, Clwyd.
Printed in Great Britain by
Redwood Books, Trowbridge, Wiltshire

Contents

Contents

Men's words in women's mouths

II. MEN'S OPINIONS

Praise

Contents

IV. LEGAL STATUS IN THE GREEK WORLD

Crete

Athens

Amorgos

Sparta

Egypt

Roman Egypt

VI. PUBLIC LIFE

Women's bravery in legend and history

Women and men

Babies

Parents and children

The home

Celebrations

Epitaphs

VIII. OCCUPATIONS

Apprenticeship

Self-employment

Prostitution

Women gladiators

The arts and entertainment

Skilled labour

Sales and services

Other records of women's employment

IX. MEDICINE AND ANATOMY

Philosophers observe nature

Writings of practising physicians

Contents   xvii

X. RELIGION

Dionysus/Bacchus

Hera

Demeter

Athena

Artemis

Aphrodite

Asclepius

Serapis

Vesta

Bona Dea

Witchcraft

Priestesses

Plates

(between pp. 166 and 167)

1. Relief. Maenad. Metropolitan Museum of Art, New York
2. Black-figure hydria. Women at a fountain. Museum of Fine Arts, Boston
3. Pyxis. Women doing wool work. British Museum, London
4. Wall painting. The citharist, from Boscoreale. Metropolitan Museum of Art, New York
5. Terracotta figurines. Two women (girls?) playing knucklebones. British Museum, London
6. Sarcophagus. A woman and the Muses. Nelson-Atkins Museum of Art, Kansas City, Missouri
7. Coin. Julia Domna with Caracalla and Geta. American Numismatic Society, New York
8. Terracotta figurine group. Two tambourine players on a camel. Emory University Museum of Art and Archaeology, Atlanta
9. Black-figure lekythos. Women working wool. Metropolitan Museum of Art, New York
10. Red-figure kylix (interior). Mother and baby. Musées Royaux d'Art et d'Histoire, Brussels
11. Relief. Gladiatrices. British Museum, London
12. Red-figure kylix (interior). Two women walking. Metropolitan Museum of Art, New York
13. Relief. Midwife delivering a baby. Museo di Ostia (Fototeca Unione)
14(a). Epitaph of a midwife. Kelsey Museum of Archaeology, Ann Arbor
14(b). Papyrus recording a dowry payment. University of Michigan, Ann Arbor
15. Mosaic. Saints Perpetua and Felicitas. Archbishop's Palace, Ravenna (Photo Anderson)

To our mothers, Mena Rosenthal and Nancy Brown

Preface

When, ten years ago, the first edition of this source-book was published, there were only a few scholarly books and articles describing the lives of women in antiquity. Since then many new studies have appeared, and courses about women in antiquity have been taught in many schools and universities. This expanding interest in the lives of ancient women has encouraged us to produce an expanded second version of our collection, with new translations and additional notes.

This new edition, like the first, is intended to make accessible to people who do not know the ancient languages the kinds of materials ancient historians work with. Such a collection by its very nature is not meant to be a substitute for a text book or a comprehensive treatment of the subject. To begin with, the materials at our disposal themselves come from whatever happens to have survived antiquity. Because the surviving documents come from many different types of sources, scattered over place and time, it is impossible for us to give the reader a coherent impression of chronological development, even within categories, or to describe every aspect of women's life even in those cities that we know most about, Athens, Oxyrhynchus and Rome.

A further restriction is imposed by the nature of the materials in this collection, many of which are not the sort of documents one would expect to find in a modern history book. Some are taken from works of literature or philosophy, others from lawyers' formal speeches or from public documents inscribed on stone. Only a small number of the texts surviving from the ancient world were written by women, and even some of these, such as the women in Pythagoras' family, or the alchemists Mary and Cleopatra, may never actually have existed. A few texts written for or about women by men, such as speeches from Greek drama, attempt in some way to represent a woman's point of view. But all the other documents in this or any such collection necessarily present the voices of men, speaking with varying degrees of sympathy and sensitivity to the conditions of women's life.

The selection we ourselves have made from the materials that chance and scholars in the distant past have selected for us, imposes yet other limitations, to which we have tried to call attention in our notes. Many selections come from larger works that are not primarily concerned with women. Satires exaggerate women's defects, gravestones their virtues. Since the full context of many documents is lost, we cannot know how much trust should placed in the allegations they present. There are annoying gaps in some texts, and questions about date and authenticity. We have tried to provide the necessary background information, but we urge our readers to look, whenever possible, at the whole of a work from which we have taken excerpts, and to consider documents of the same type and from the same times and places about the lives of men.

Although certain ancient myths, such as stories about the Amazons or legendary heroines, have direct relevance to the lives of women, we have chosen here to concentrate on documents that describe the lives of women in specific historical contexts. We have further narrowed the field by choosing documents that can speak for themselves, with a minimum of editorial comment. We have omitted many other documents, more fragmentary or more difficult to interpret, that would have helped to make our account of women's lives more comprehensive; for these our readers should turn to general histories of women in antiquity, and the many more specialised studies that have appeared in the past decade.

But the greatest constraint was probably space. When we began collecting ancient sources on women's lives, in the late 1970s, we, and our publishers, expected to cover the field in a single medium-sized volume. We now know that an enormous quantity of ancient material on women's lives exists; but long and patient labour is required to discover and make sense of it. Thus inevitably, while this collection attempts to be representative of the available sources, it cannot claim to be complete. In the few months allowed us to prepare this new edition, we realised that we could easily spend the next several years not only on papyri and inscriptions but also reading with new eyes old friends, such as Tacitus or Pausanias.

Virtually everything that appeared in the 1982 edition has been retained in this edition. Along with the medical texts that appeared in English there for the first time, the majority of documents in other categories now also appear in our own translations. We hope that the new translations will make the book easier to use, since readers will no longer need to adjust to sudden changes in English style and vocabulary.

We have abandoned the division into separate parts on Greece and Rome. The documents are grouped by topic, and chronologically under each topic. The letters 'G' and 'L' indicate whether the original text was in Greek or Latin. This arrangement, although inevitably somewhat arbitrary, should offer some guidance to less experienced readers, who can thus see how attitudes or practices changed over time. Since the later sources tend to provide more explicit detail about women in all walks of life, development is evident in every category, and especially in public life, occupations and the law. But for readers who would prefer to read the texts in an order of their own choosing, we have again provided a concordance of sources.

We have added many documents in almost every category. In response to our colleagues' suggestions we have included selections from extant Greek tragedies (as well as some additional fragments). We also offer for the first time in English epigrams by women preserved in inscriptions. We have added more papyrus letters describing women's legal problems (including some criminal acts committed by women), and reorganised the section on Roman law. We now offer more information about working women, such as prostitutes, wet-nurses, gladiators, musicians and lecturers. There are more documents describing priestesses and women's roles in religious rites, both in pagan cult and in the early church. We have added readings about holy women, such as the Christian saints Thecla and Macrina, as well as the pagan clairvoyant Sosipatra.

The illustrations, new in this edition, were chosen for their relevance to topics covered in the text, rather than as sources in themselves to provide additional information about women's lives.

Mary Lefkowitz is primarily responsible for the translations of documents written in Greek, and Maureen Fant for those in Latin. We both have many debts.

For the enthusiasm with which they greeted news of the revision, and the generous spirit with which they gave criticism, valuable information, suggestions and material help, friends and colleagues in Oxford, Rome and much of North America have earned our most heartfelt thanks. We are particularly indebted to John D'Arms, Clayton Fant, Tony Honoré, Nicholas Horsfall, David Lewis, Sir Hugh Lloyd-Jones, Thomas McGinn, Susan Martin, Richard Saller, Thomas Sienkewicz and Ute Wartenberg. We are also grateful to Charlayne Allen, Ewen Bowie, Alan Bowman, Roger Brock, Roberta Capasso, Robert Cohon, Caroline Dexter, Dominic Monserrat, Carolyn Osiek, Sarah Pomeroy, Lucilla Rodinò, John Sullivan and Bonna Wescoat.

The individual scholars who kindly provided translations for this book or who gave their permission to use existing translations are named in the text. We thank the following publishers for permission to reprint: Harvard University Press and the Loeb Classical Library (nos. 339, 384-6, 389); Penguin Books (74, 242, 341); Johns Hopkins University Press (355, 357, 375, 380); AMS Press (114-19, 123-9, 133-7, 139-47, 352); University of Texas Press (107-8, 388); Duckworth (112-13, 132); Cambridge University Press (407); Oxford University Press (445-6); Cornell University Press (351); University of Illinois Press (39, 276, 418); University of Chicago Press (343).

Wellesley and Rome   M.R.L.
April 1992   M.B.F.

I. Women's Voices

'This stone has heard much lamentation'

Female Poets
'She entered into rivalry with Pindar'

It is only fitting that the first speakers in a book about women should be women. Their words give some sense of the importance of women in women's lives, of the pleasures of owning and giving, of participating in festivals and in household games. But we must wait for men to tell us about the social, legal, and physical environments in which ancient women lived, since the course of women's lives, from birth to death, was set by men, fathers, husbands, brothers, uncles, by the male citizens by whom governments were formed and armies raised. It is men too who – selectively, we may presume – tell us most about women's achievements.

Aside from poetry, women's writing survives only in private letters written on papyrus, preserved, by an accident of nature, only from Hellenistic and Roman Egypt.[1] Students of the ancient world are always acutely aware that only a fraction of the writings of antiquity has survived. Much of what remains was preserved because men in late antiquity and the Middle Ages felt it to have enduring value. It is thus both logical and poignant that we should have so little of what women wrote. Surviving fragments and references in the work of male authors are tantalising indications that the intellectual efforts of women were, at least occasionally, committed to writing.

That women in all periods of antiquity could write sophisticated verse indicates that at least some women were educated. But the fact that from all antiquity only a few female authors' names and a few fragments of their poetry survive suggests that such intellectual attainments were at best exceptional. If all women had gone to school and had been able to record what they felt about their world, a very different, and surely less self-congratulatory, picture of ancient life would have emerged. As it is, what little remains of women's writings offers eloquent testimony not so much of an informing literary inheritance, as of a potential never realised.[2]

The poetry of Sappho, in the sixth century BC, had a profound influence on both the content and the form of subsequent lyric. The emphasis on emotion and on the action of the mind that distinguished her poetry from that of her male contemporary Alcaeus set the pattern for the concerns of all later love poetry. The sensual appeal in her poetry of the natural world reappears in the careful landscape of Hellenistic pastoral. By imitating her stanza-form and metre, later poets could instantly convey the stance of the isolated lover

1

and the pain of a friend's departure or loss.

Many of these poems describe a world that men never saw: the deep love women could feel for one another in a society that kept the sexes apart and the intense excitement of rituals in which only women could participate. Later women poets occasionally write of this other world: Erinna's *Distaff* speaks of a girlhood friendship lost through marriage and through death. Anyte's epitaphs describe the special offerings women leave goddesses at shrines. But in the Hellenistic age, when women gained new privileges and freedom, women poets began to write about men's subjects and for the same occasions for which male poets wrote. In many cases, if we did not know names, there would be no way to tell the author's sex.

Sappho (Lesbos, 6th cent. BC)
'Release me from my cruel anxiety'

1. *To Aphrodite (Fr. 1. G)*

Aphrodite on your intricate throne, immortal, daughter of Zeus, weaver of plots, I beg you, do not tame me with pain or my heart with anguish

but come here, as once before when I asked you, you heard my words from afar and listened, and left your father's golden house and came

you yoked your chariot, and lovely swift sparrows brought you, fast whirling over the dark earth from heaven through the midst of the bright air

and soon they arrived. And you, O blessed goddess, smiled with your immortal face and asked what was wrong with me, and why did I call now,

and what did I most want in my maddened heart to have for myself. 'Whom now am I to persuade to your love, who, Sappho, has done you wrong? For if she flees, soon she'll pursue you, and if she won't take gifts, soon she'll give them, and if she won't love, soon she will love you, even if she doesn't want to.'[3]

Come to me now again, release me from my cruel anxiety, accomplish all that my heart wants accomplished. You yourself join my battle.

2. *When I look at you (Fr. 31. G)*

The man seems to me strong as a god, the man who sits across from you and listens to your sweet talk nearby

and your lovely laughter – which, when I hear it, strikes fear in the heart in my breast. For whenever I glance at you, it seems that I can say nothing at all

but my tongue is broken in silence, and that instant a light fire rushes beneath my skin, I can no longer see anything in my eyes and my ears are thundering,

and cold sweat pours down me, and shuddering grasps me all over, and I am greener than grass, and I seem to myself to be little short of death

But all is endurable, since even a poor man ...[4]

3. *Anactoria (Fr. 16. G)*

Some would say an army of cavalry, others of infantry, others of ships, is the fairest thing on the dark earth, but I say it's whatever you're in love with

It's completely easy to make this clear to everyone, for Helen, who far surpassed other people in beauty, left behind the most aristocratic

of husbands and went to Troy. She sailed away, and did not remember at all her daughter or her beloved parents, but [Aphrodite] took her aside

(*3 lines missing*) which makes me remember Anactoria[5] who is no longer near,

her lovely step and the brilliant glancing of her face I would rather see than the Lydians' chariots or their infantry fighting in all their armour.

4. *Parting (Fr. 94. G)*

'The truth is, I wish I were dead.'[6] She left me, weeping often, and she said this, 'Oh what a cruel fate is ours, Sappho, yes, I leave you against my will.'

And I answered her: 'Farewell, go and remember me, for you know how we cared for you.

'If you do remember, I want to remind you ... and were happy ... of violets ... you set beside me and with woven garlands made of flowers around your soft neck

'and with perfume, royal, rich ... you anointed yourself and on soft beds you would drive out your passion 'and then ... sanctuary ... was ... from which we were away ...'

5. *Remembering the girl Atthis (Fr. 96. G)*

... you, like a goddess renowned, in your song she took most joy. Now she is unique among Lydian women, as the moon once the sun sets

stands out among all the stars, and her light grasps both the salt sea and the flowering meadows

and fair dew flows forth, and soft roses and chervil and fragrant melilot bloom.

Often as she goes out, she remembers gentle Atthis, and her tender heart is eaten by grief ...

6. *The wedding of Hector and Andromache (Fr. 44. G)*

'... Hector and his comrades are bringing a girl with dark eyes from holy Thebes and ... Plakia, soft Andromache in their ships across the salt sea; many curved bands of gold and purple robes and intricate playthings, countless silver cups and ivory.' So he spoke. And [Hector's] beloved father quickly got up, and the story went out to his friends throughout the city [of Troy] with its wide dancing places. Then the Trojan women led mules to wheeled carts and a crowd of women came out, and also of ... -ankled maidens, and separately the daughters of Priam and men brought horses with chariots (*unknown number of lines missing*) ... and the sweet-sounding *aulos*[7] was mixed with the noise of castanets, and the maidens sang a sacred song and the holy sound reached heaven ... bowls and goblets ... perfume and cassia and incense were mixed and all the older women shouted out, and all the men cried out a fair loud song, calling on Paean, the far-shooter, the lyre player, to sing of Hector and Andromache, who were like gods ...

Corinna (Tanagra, Boeotia, 5th cent. BC?)
'They hid the holy goddess's baby'

7. *The contest of Cithaeron and Helicon (654 P. G)*

This fragment from a much longer poem concentrates more on the feelings than on the tangible rewards of victory and defeat.

'... They hid the holy goddess's baby in a cave, a secret from Cronus the crooked-minded, when [his mother] blessed Rhea stole him away and won great honour from the immortals.' So he sang. Straightway the Muses got the blessed gods to bring their voting pebbles to the golden bowls, and then all together arose. Cithaeron won more. Hermes proclaimed with a shout that he had won the victory, and the gods decorated him with wreaths, and there was joy in his heart. But Helicon was overcome by harsh grief ... and he tore out a bare rock and from the height dashed it into countless stones.

8. *Reflections on a woman poet (664 P. G)*

I blame clear-voiced Myrtis, because – though a woman – she entered into rivalry with Pindar.

Praxilla (Sicyon, 5th cent. BC)
'Maiden from the neck up'

9. *Two fragments (747, 757 PMG. G)*

These lines, from a speech by the dying Adonis, were proverbial for their silliness.

(747) The most beautiful thing I leave is the light of the sun, and after that the shining stars and the face of the moon, and then ripe cucumbers and apples and pears.

From an unknown context:

(757) You look prettily through the windows, maiden from the neck up, but below it a woman.

Erinna (Telos, 4th cent. BC)
'Dolls in our bedrooms'

10. *Childhood (GLP 3.120 = Suppl. Hell. 401. G)*

The surviving fragments of Erinna's three-hundred line *Distaff* appear to describe the girlhood of the speaker and her girl-friend Baucis and a separation caused first by Baucis' marriage and finally by her death.[8]

... into the sea, with mad running ... from white horses ... I shouted ... you as tortoise, leaping through ... the garden of the great courtyard. These ... poor Baucis ... I weep for you ... these traces lie still warm in my heart ... now embers ... of dolls in our bedrooms ... at dawn your mother, for the workers; she came to you ... about the salted meat ... When we were little girls Mormo[9] brought panic ... her ears on her head; she ran on

all fours ... she changed faces ... But when ... you forgot all that you
heard as a child from your mother, dear Baucis ... forgetfulness ...
Aphrodite. So weeping for you I leave aside ... my feet do not ... from my
house permitted, nor to see ... or to lament with bare head; but blood-red
shame tears me ...

11. *Two epigrams for Baucis (AP VII.712, 710. G)*

I am the tomb of Baucis the bride. This stone has heard much
lamentation. As you pass by, tell this to Death beneath the ground: 'You
are jealous, Death.' As you look, the fine inscription on the tomb tells you
of Baucis' savage fate: how her husband's father lighted her funeral pyre
with the torches they carried while they sang to Hymenaeus, the
marriage god. And you, Hymenaeus, transformed the wedding dances
into cries of lamentation.

Column and my sirens, and mourning urn, you hold my death, these few
ashes. Tell all who pass by my tomb to greet me, be they from this city or
another country: 'The tomb holds a bride, my father called me Baucis, I
came from Tenos,'[10] so they will know. And tell them that my friend
Erinna inscribed this epigram on my tomb.

Anyte (Tegea, 3rd cent. BC)
'We were three maidens'

Poems on a variety of topics by four women poets were included in the
Byzantine collection of Greek epigrams known as the Palatine Anthology.
Hedyle's mother and son were also poets; Moero, whose father was a tragic
actor and husband a grammarian, also wrote epic poetry. But only Anyte
and Nossis wrote epigrams on women's life.

12. *Miletus (AP VII.492. G)*

We leave you, Miletus, dear homeland, because we rejected the lawless
insolence of impious Gauls. We were three maidens, your citizens. The
violent aggression of the Celts brought us to this fate. We did not wait for
unholy union or marriage, but we found ourselves a protector in Death.[11]

13. *Antibia (AP VII.490. G)*

I weep for Antibia, a virgin. Many suitors wanted her and came to her
father's house, because she was known for her beauty and cleverness. But
deadly Fate sent all their hopes rolling away.[12]

14. *Thersis (AP VII.649. G)*

Instead of a bridal bed and holy rites of marriage, your mother set here on your marble tomb a maiden, like you in size and in beauty, Thersis. So now we can speak to you although you are dead.[13]

15. *Philaenis (AP VII.486. G)*

Often here on her daughter's tomb, Cleina in her sorrow cried for her dear child who died too soon, calling back Philaenis' soul. Before she could be married, she crossed the pale stream of Acheron.

Nossis (Locri, 3rd cent. BC)
'Deliver Alcetis from her hard labour pains'

16. *To Hera (AP VI.265. G)*

Sacred Hera – since you often come down from heaven to see Lacinion with its fragrant incense – take this linen cloth. Theophilis, daughter of Cleocha, and her noble daughter Nossis, wove it for you.

17. *To Aphrodite (AP VI.275. G)*

I think that Aphrodite will be happy to receive as an offering this band from Samytha's hair, since it is intricate, and smells sweetly of the nectar that Aphrodite herself uses to anoint fair Adonis.

18. *To Artemis (AP VI.273. G)*

Artemis, goddess of Delos and lovely Ortygia,[14] set down your sacred bow in the Graces' laps, wash your skin clean in the Inopus, and come to Locri to deliver Alcetis from her hard labour pains.

19. *Polyarchis (AP VI.332. G)*

Let's go to the temple of Aphrodite to see how her statue is intricately worked from gold. Polyarchis set it there, with the great wealth she won from her own body's splendour.

20. *Thaumarete (AP IX.604. G)*

This picture captures Thaumarete's form – how well he painted her pride and her beauty, her gentle eyes. If your little watch-dog saw you, she would wag her tail, and think that she saw the mistress of her house.[15]

21. *Callo (AP IX.605. G)*

This picture – the image she made of herself, Callo set here in blonde

Aphrodite's house. How gently she stands there. Her charm blooms. I greet her: there is no blemish at all in her life.

Sulpicia (Rome, 1st cent. BC)
'Venus kept her promise'

Though other Roman women are known to have written poetry – Melinno (2nd cent. AD) composed sapphic stanzas (in Greek) in praise of Rome – Sulpicia is the only Roman woman of whose work we possess more than fragments. She was the ward of M. Valerius Messala Corvinus, writer, politician and patron of the arts during the Augustan age. Among his circle was the poet Albius Tibullus, who seems to have befriended the young Sulpicia. The identity of her love, whom she calls 'Cerinthus', is unknown. The poems are preserved in Book 3 of Tibullus' works. The work of another Sulpicia is described by the poet Martial (no. 224).

22. *To Messala (Tibullus 3.14. L)*

My hated birthday is coming, and I will have to spend it in sorrow in the nasty country without Cerinthus. What is nicer than the city? Or is a farmhouse a fit place for a girl – or a freezing river near Arezzo? Now, Messala, calm yourself; you take too good care of me, and a trip can often come at an awkward moment. Here I leave my heart and soul – while I am carried unwilling away – though you will not let me make my own decision about them.

23. *To Cerinthus (Tibullus 3.15, 17, 18, 16, 13. L)*

(15) You know that that tiresome trip now has been lifted from your sweetheart's shoulders? I am now allowed to have my birthday in Rome. Everybody should celebrate that birthday, which now by chance catches you unawares.

(17) Have you no solicitude, Cerinthus, for your sweetheart, because a fever is tormenting my exhausted body? Oh, I would never want to conquer the miserable disease unless I thought you wanted me to. After all, what good would it do me to vanquish my illness if you could bear my woes with a steady heart?

(18) Light of my life, may I be no longer your love's fire – as I seem to have been a few days ago – if I ever again do such a stupid girlish thing that would make me sorrier than leaving you alone last night, in my desire to keep from you my desire.

(16) It is a fine thing this – that you are so sure of me now that you take

liberties, lest I, incapable, should suddenly take a foolish spill. Let a
toga'd whore and her wool-basket be of more importance to you than is
Sulpicia, Servius' daughter. There are those who care about me, and their
greatest worry is that I might lose my place to a nobody's bed.

(13) At last a love has come of such a kind that my shame, Gossip, would
be greater if I kept it covered than if I laid it bare. Cythera, implored by
my verses, brought that man to me and gave him into my embrace. Venus
kept her promise: let anyone talk about my joy who – it's said – never had
any of his own. I would not want to send anything to him on sealed
tablets, lest anyone should read it before my own love does; but my sin is
a joy, though it's tiresome to keep a straight face for gossip's sake. Let it
be said that I was a worthy woman, with a worthy man.

Claudia Trophime (1st cent. AD)
'You tend the eternal flame of fire from heaven'

24. *Two epigrams. Ephesus, AD 92/3 (Inscr. Eph. 1062. G)*

Claudia, priestess of Hera in Ephesus, appears to have written these poems
to celebrate her term as *prytanis*, or chief priestess, of the cult of Hestia.[16]
Both poems make use of ingenious comparisons. In the first, the point is
that the goddess ensures that the gods had enough of their food and drink
and provides the fire that enables mortals to cook their food; in the second,
that as a mountain retains rain, so the goddess preserves fire.[17]

(*In prose*) Claudia Trophime the *prytanis* wrote this song of praise to
Hestia: (*in verse*) she [the goddess] both gave satisfaction to the gods in
their feasts, and tends the blooming fire of our country. Sweetest divinity,
flower of the universe, you tend the eternal flame of fire from heaven on
your altars.
　　(*In prose*) The same priestess wrote this: (*in verse*) The [mountain] Pion
secretly drinks[18] within himself the moisture from the mist and draws it
into his sides towards the vast sea. How then can one describe you
[goddess], who keep and hold within yourself the god-sent fire, a remnant
of the harmony [of the universe]?

Inscribed on the Colossus of Memnon
'I heard the voice of the divine Memnon'

Greeks and Romans treated the Colossus at Luxor in Egypt as a
representation of and shrine to the hero Memnon. Among the 107
inscriptions carved on the statue's legs are poems by three Roman
poetesses.[19]

25. *Caecilia Trebulla.* AD 95 *(Bernand 92-4. G)*

Three poems in iambic trimeter.

(92) (*In prose*) When I heard the holy voice of Memnon, (*in verse*) I longed for you, mother, and prayed that you might hear it.

(93) (*In prose*) Caecilia Trebulla wrote this after I heard the voice of Memnon a second time. (*In verse*) Although we had heard his voice only once before, now Memnon, son of Dawn and Tithonus, greeted us as old friends. Has Nature who made the universe given feeling and voice to a stone?

(94) (*In prose*) I, Caecilia Trebulla, wrote this after I heard the voice of Memnon. (*In verse*) Cambyses shattered me, this stone which is the image of the king of the East. Long ago I had a voice that could lament, which wept for Memnon's sorrows, but Cambyses took it away from me. Now my cries are inarticulate and unclear. I grieve for the remnant of my past fortune.

26. *Balbilla, a member of the court of Vibia Sabina, wife of the Emperor Hadrian.* AD 130 *(Bernand 31. G)*

(*In elegiac couplets*) I, Balbilla, when the rock spoke, heard the voice of the divine Memnon or Phamenoth. I came here with the lovely Empress Sabina. The course of the sun was in its first hour, in the fifteenth year of Hadrian's reign, on the twenty-fourth day of the month Hathor. [I wrote this] on the twenty-fifth day of the month Hathor.

27. *Damo. Uncertain date (Bernand 83. G)*

(*In elegiac couplets*) Hail, son of Dawn. You spoke to me favourably, Memnon, for the sake of the Muses, whose servant I am, Damo lover of song. And my lyre has come to my aid and sung always of your power, holy one.[20]

Men's words in women's mouths
'Of all creatures, we women are the most miserable'

From Greek tragedy
'I would rather serve three times as in battle than give birth once'

28. *Medea's complaint. Athens, 431 BC (Euripides, Medea 230-51. G)*

Medea, who has learned that her husband Jason plans to leave her in order to marry the princess of Corinth, wins the sympathy of the chorus of Corinthian women by describing their common lot.

Of all creatures who live and have intelligence, we women are the most miserable. First of all, we must buy a husband by vast expenditure of wealth, in order to obtain a master for our body. This is a greater misery than the dowry, because everything depends on whether we get a bad husband or a good one. Being divorced harms a woman's reputation, and she cannot refuse her husband. She must be a prophet when she arrives among new habits and customs, which she did not learn at home, to deal with the sort of husband she has acquired. And if when we manage all this well our husbands live with us not bearing the yoke [of marriage] unwillingly, our lives are enviable. But if not, it's best to die: a man, when he becomes unhappy with the people inside his home, goes out and puts an end to the ache in his heart ... (246) but we must look to that one man alone. People say that we women lead a life without danger inside our homes, while men fight in war; but they are wrong. I would rather serve three times as in battle than give birth once.

29. *Andromache's ideal behaviour. Athens, 415 BC (Euripides, Trojan Women 643-58. G)*

After Achilles has killed her husband Hector, and Troy has been taken by the Greeks, Andromache observes that her fine reputation resulted in her being made the prize of Achilles' son Neoptolemus.

I aimed at a fine reputation and got more than my share of good fortune. For everything that has been found proper for a woman I did in Hector's house. First, here – whether women deserve to be blamed for it or not – since what causes women a bad reputation is not remaining inside, I put aside my desire [for going out], and remained within the house. I did not bring women's bragging talk into the house, and since I had my intelligence as a good teacher I was self-sufficient. I offered my husband a silent tongue and a calm appearance. I knew when I ought to win out over my husband, and in what instances I ought to allow the victory to him. But my reputation became known to the Greek army and has been my ruin ...

30. *How a wife ought to behave. Athens, 5th cent. BC (Euripides, Andromache 205-27. G)*

Andromache was brought to Neoptolemus' home in Scyros and has borne him a son. When Neoptolemus' wife Hermione accuses her of having used magical charms to prevent her from having a baby, and wants to have her put to death, Andromache defends herself by explaining that Hermione is too possessive of her husband.

Your husband doesn't hate you because of my drugs, but because you don't provide what he needs to cohabit with you – that's the magic spell you want: it isn't beauty but virtue that gives pleasure to one's consort. If you suffer some annoyance, the Spartan city is an important city and you place Scyros nowhere. You are a rich woman living among the poor; you think your father Menelaus is a greater man than Achilles. That's why your husband hates you.

(213) For a woman must love her husband, even when she has been married to an insignificant man, and not provoke a contest of pride. If you had had a tyrant in frozen Thrace for a husband, where one man shares many women and sleeps with each in turn, would you have murdered the other wives? Then you would have been exposed as bringing on all women your own lust for bed. Your behaviour is disgusting. Our problems are more difficult than our husbands', but we know how to make things work.

(221) Dearest Hector, I went along with you in your love affairs, if Aphrodite gave you any trouble, and I gave my milk to your bastard children, so that I might not betray any bitterness to you, and by so doing I drew my husband to me by virtue. But you, Hermione, are so afraid that you won't allow even a drop of rain to fall on your husband.

31. *Deianeira contrasts women's childhood with life after marriage. Athens, 5th cent. BC (Sophocles, Women of Trachis 141-52, G)*

Deianeira was glad that it was Heracles rather than the river god Achelous who won her as a bride, but her marriage has brought her less happiness than anxiety, because Heracles is always away fighting, as well as considerable loneliness: 'We had children whom he sees from time to time, like a farmer who has a remote field, who sees it only at sowing time and at harvest' (31-3). She addresses these remarks to the young women in the chorus.

You have come, it seems, because you heard of my sorrow. I hope that you will not learn by suffering of the nature of the misery in my heart, because now you have no experience of it. For a young life grows just so in its own place, and the heat of the sun-god and rain and winds do not strike it, but it uplifts its untroubled life in pleasure until she is called a wife instead of a girl, and takes on her share of worries in the night, because she is afraid for her husband or her children. Then you might see for yourself, judging from your own experience, what sorrows weigh me down.

32. *The lot of women: Procne. Athens, mid-5th cent. BC (Sophocles, Tereus, Fr. 583 Radt. G)*

Procne's husband, Tereus, has seduced her sister; in revenge she plans to murder their son.

But now outside my father's house, I am nothing, yes often I have looked on women's nature in this regard, that we are nothing. Young women, in my opinion, have the sweetest existence known to mortals in their fathers' homes, for their innocence always keeps children safe and happy. But when we reach puberty and can understand, we are thrust out and sold away from our ancestral gods and from our parents. Some go to strange men's homes, others to foreigners', some to joyless houses, some to hostile. And all this once the first night has yoked us to our husband, we are forced to praise and to say that all is well.

33. *Pasiphae. Athens, mid-5th cent. BC (Euripides, Cretans, Fr. 11 GLP. Tr. H. Lloyd-Jones. G)*

Pasiphae, condemned to death for having had intercourse with a bull and having given birth to the monster Minotaur, speaks in her own defence. In Euripides' *Trojan Women* 914-51, Helen puts responsibility for her adultery on Paris' mother Hecuba and the goddess Aphrodite.

If I were to deny the fact you would never believe me; it is clear enough. Now if I had prostituted my body in clandestine love to a man, you could have rightly said I was a whore. But as things are, it was a god who drove me mad; I am sorry, but it was not my fault.

It makes no sense; what is it about the bull that could have stirred up my feelings with such a shameful passion? Did he look so splendid in his robes? Did his auburn hair and his eyes flash brilliantly? Was it his dark beard? It can hardly have been the symmetry of his form! This is the love for which I got into the skin and went on all fours; and this makes Minos angry! I could hardly wish to make this husband the father of children; why was I afflicted with this madness?

It was Minos' evil genius who afflicted me with his curse; the one human being who bears all the guilt is Minos! It was he who broke the promise he had made to sacrifice the bull that came as a portent to the sea god. It was for this that Poseidon's vengeance came upon you, and it is on me that it descended! And then you cry aloud and call all the gods to witness, when the doer of the act that put me to shame is you yourself!

I who gave birth to the creature have done no harm; I kept secret the god-sent affliction of the curse. It is you who publish to all your wife's disgrace, handsome as it is and proper to display, as though you had no part in it, maddest of madmen!

You are my ruin, because the crime is yours; you are the cause of my affliction! Well, if you wish to drown me, drown me! You are expert in bloody deeds and murder. Or if you lust to eat my flesh, then eat it, feed to your heart's content! I shall perish free and guiltless, for a crime for which you are guilty!

34. *In defence of women. Athens, 5th cent. BC (Euripides, Melanippe Captive, Fr. 13 GLP = Fr. 499 Nauck. G)*

A fragment from a debate in a lost tragedy. The first three lines were quoted out of context in ancient biographies of Euripides, to counter allegations of misogyny based on out-of-context quotations from his other dramas.[21]

Men's criticism of women is worthless twanging of a bowstring and evil talk. Women are better than men, as I will show. (*Five fragmentary lines*) Women run households and protect within their homes what has been carried across the sea, and without a woman no home is clean or prosperous. Consider their role in religion, for that, in my opinion, comes first. We women play the most important part, because women prophesy the will of Loxias in the oracles of Phoebus.[22] And at the holy site of Dodona near the Sacred Oak, females convey the will of Zeus to inquirers from Greece.[23] As for the sacred rituals for the Fates and the Nameless Goddesses [i.e. the Furies], all these would not be holy if performed by men, but prosper in women's hands. In this way women have a rightful share in the service of the gods.

Why is it then, that women must have a bad reputation? Won't men's worthless criticism stop, and men who insist on blaming all women alike, if one woman turns out to be evil?[24] Let me make the following distinctions. There is nothing worse than a bad woman, and nothing better in any way than a good one, but their natures differ.

35. *A fragment of a comedy. Athens, 4th/3rd cent. BC (Anon., in Menander, ed. Sandbach, p. 328, GLP 185-7.[25] Tr. H. Lloyd-Jones. G)*

A daughter tries to persuade her father not to make her marry a man richer than her present husband.[26]

Father, you ought to be making the speech that I am now making, because you ought to have more sense than I have and to do any speaking that is needed. But since you have given me permission, maybe all I can do is to say what is right myself, since I must. If my husband has done great wrong I am not the one that ought to punish him. If he has offended against me, I should take note of it. But I know nothing of it; perhaps I am stupid, I couldn't deny that. Yet, father, even if a woman is a silly creature when it comes to judging other matters, about her own affairs perhaps she has some sense.[27] Explain to me how by whatever he has done he has done me wrong.

There is a covenant between man and wife; he must love her, always, until the end, and she must never cease to do what gives her husband pleasure. He was all that I wished with regard to me, and my pleasure is his pleasure, father. But suppose he is satisfactory as far as I am concerned but is bankrupt, and you, as you say, now want to give me to a rich man to save me from living out my life in distress. Where does so much money exist, father, that having it can give me more pleasure than my husband can? How can it be just or honourable that I should take a share in any good things he has, but take no share in his poverty? Tell me, if the man you now want me to marry – may that never happen, dear Zeus, nor shall it ever happen, at least if I can help it – if this man in turn loses his property, will you give me to another husband? How long will you go on tempting fortune in the matter of my life, father? When I was a young girl, you had to find a husband to whom to give me, when the choice was yours. But once you had given me to a husband, from that moment this responsibility belonged to me, naturally, because if I make a mistake in judgment, it's my own life that I shall ruin. So in the name of Hestia don't rob me of the husband to whom you have married me; the favour that I ask of you, father, is just and humane. If you refuse it, you will be enforcing your will and I shall try to bear my fate properly and avoid disgrace.

II. Men's Opinions

'Zeus was angry in his heart'

Praise
'She kept the house and worked in wool'

Inscriptions
'This stone marks a woman of accomplishment and beauty'

36. *Archedice. Athens, 5th cent. BC (FGE 786-9 = Thuc. 6.59. G)*

This dust hides Archedice, daughter of Hippias,[1] the most important man in Greece in his day. But though her father husband, brothers, and children were tyrants, her mind was never carried away into arrogance.[2]

37. *Aspasia. Chios, c. 400 BC (CEG 167. G)*

Of a worthy wife this is the tomb – here, by the road that throngs with people – of Aspasia, who is dead; in response to her noble disposition Euopides set up this monument for her; she was his consort.

38. *Dionysia. Athens, 4th cent. BC (IG II².11162. G)*

It was not clothes, it was not gold that this woman admired during her lifetime; it was her husband and the good sense that she showed in her behaviour. But in return for the youth you shared with him, Dionysia, your tomb is adorned by your husband Antiphilus.

39. *Claudia. Rome, 2nd cent. BC (ILLRP 973 = ILS 8403 = CLE 52 = CIL I².1211 = CIL VI.15346. Tr. R. Lattimore. L)*

Friend, I have not much to say; stop and read it. This tomb, which is not fair, is for a fair woman. Her parents gave her the name Claudia. She loved her husband in her heart. She bore two sons, one of whom she left on earth, the other beneath it. She was pleasant to talk with, and she walked with grace. She kept the house and worked in wool. That is all. You may go.

40. *Eucharis. Rome, 1st cent. BC (ILLRP 803 = ILS 5213 = CIL I².1214. L)*

[The tomb] of Eucharis, freedwoman of Licinia, an unmarried girl who was educated and learned in every skill. She lived 14 years.

Ah, as you look with wandering eye at the house of death, stay your foot and read what is inscribed here. This is what a father's love gave his daughter, where the remains of her body lie gathered. 'Just as my life with its young skills and growing years brought me fame, the sad hour of death rushed on me and forbade me to draw another breath in life. I was educated and taught as if by the Muses' hands. I adorned the nobility's festivals with my dancing, and first appeared before the common people in a Greek play.

'But now here in this tomb my enemies the Fates have placed my body's ashes. The patrons of learning – devotion, passion, praise, honour – are silenced by my burnt corpse and by my death.

'His child, I left lamentation to my father, though born after him, I preceded him in the day of my death. Now I observe my fourteenth birthday here among the shadows in Death's ageless home.

'I beg you when you leave, ask that the earth lie light upon me.'

41. *Amymone, housewife. Rome, 1st cent. BC (ILS 8402. L)*

Here lies Amymone wife of Marcus best and most beautiful, worker in wool, pious, chaste, thrifty, faithful, a stayer-at-home.[3]

42. *An accomplished woman. Sardis, 1st cent. BC (Peek 1881. G)*

An inscription set up by the municipality of Sardis in honour of Menophila, daughter of Hermagenes.

This stone marks a woman of accomplishment and beauty. Who she is the Muses' inscriptions reveal: Menophila. Why she is honoured is shown by a carved lily and an alpha, a book and a basket, and with these a wreath. The book shows that you were wise, the wreath that you wore on your head shows that you were a leader; the letter alpha[4] that you were an only child; the basket is a sign of your orderly excellence; the flower shows the prime of your life, which Fate stole away. May the dust lie light on you in death. Alas; your parents are childless; to them you have left tears.

43. *Murdia. Rome, 1st cent. BC (CIL VI.10230 = ILS 8394. L)*

The funeral eulogy for Murdia, delivered by her son by her first marriage, was inscribed on marble. Before praising his mother's personal virtues, the speaker approves of the provisions of her will.

(*The first part of the inscription is lost*) She made all her sons equal heirs, after she gave a bequest to her daughter.

A mother's love is composed of her affection for her children and equal distribution to each child.

She willed her husband [the speaker's stepfather] a fixed sum, so that his dower right would be increased by the honour of her deliberate choice.

Recalling my father's memory and taking account of it and of the trust she owed him, she bequeathed certain property to me. She did so not in order to wound my brothers by preferring me to them, but remembering my father's generosity, she decided that I should have returned to me the part of my inheritance which she had received by the decision of her husband, so that what had been taken care of by his orders should be restored to my ownership.

In such action she determined to maintain the marriages given to her by her parents to worthy men, with obedience and propriety, and as a bride to become more beloved because of her merits, to be thought dearer because of her loyalty, to be left in greater honour because of her judgment, and after her death to be praised in the estimation of her fellow-citizens, since the division of her estate indicated her grateful and honourable intentions towards her husbands, her fairness to her children and the justice shown by her sincerity.

For these reasons, praise for all good women is simple and similar, since their native goodness and the trust they have maintained do not require a diversity of words. Sufficient is the fact that they have all done the same good deeds that deserve fine reputation, and since their lives fluctuate with less diversity, by necessity we pay tribute to values they hold in common, so that nothing may be lost from fair precepts and harm what remains.

Still, my dearest mother deserved greater praise than all others, since in modesty, propriety, chastity, obedience, wool-working, industry, and loyalty she was on an equal level with other good women, nor did she take second place to any woman in virtue, work and wisdom in times of danger. (*The rest is lost*)

44. *Pythion and Epicydilla. Thasos, 1st cent.* AD *(Pleket 10. G)*

Pythion son of Hicesius set up this common memorial to himself and to his wife Epicydilla daughter of Epicydes. He was married at 18 and she at 15, and for 50 years of life together they shared agreement unbroken, and were fathers of fathers [*sic*] of fathers, twice archons of their city, happy among the living and blessed among the dead. If anyone places another body here, he must pay to the city 12,000 minae.

45. *From the tomb of the Statilii, Rome, 1st cent.* AD *(CIL VI.6593 =
CLE 1030. L)*

When I was alive I pleased my husband as his first and dearest wife and I
left my soul in his cold mouth.[5] Weeping, he closed my eyes. That's
enough praise for a woman after death.

46. *Epitaph for a little girl, Politta. Memphis, 2nd/3rd cent.* AD *(Peek
1243. G)*

A good plant from a holy root – citizens, weep for me. I was pleasing to all,
blameless in my mother's eyes, faultless in my father's. I lived 5 years.

47. *Allia Potestas. Rome, late 3rd-4th cent.* AD *(CIL VI.37965 = CLE
1988. L)*[6]

This unusual inscription is not easy to classify, and its extravagant praise
has been taken by some scholars for irony. The deceased, a freedwoman,
who was at some point owned by two men (as was Neaera, jointly owned by
two men, who contributed towards the cost of her manumission; cf. no. 90,
section 29). The epitaph attempts to make her sound like a proper *matrona*,
chaste (two lovers notwithstanding) and diligent at her wool work, but then
goes too far and praises her physical attributes. The encomia to Murdia and
'Turia' (nos. 43 and 168) have a very different tone.

To the gods of the dead, [the tomb] of Aulus' freedwoman, Allia Potestas.
   Here lies a woman from Perugia. None was more precious than she in
the world. One so diligent as she has never been seen before. Great as you
were you are now held in a small urn. Cruel arbiter of fate, and harsh
Persephone, why do you deprive us of good, and why does evil triumph,
everyone asks. I am tired of answering. They give me their tears, tokens
of their good will.
   She was courageous, chaste, resolute, honest, a trustworthy guardian.
Clean at home, also clean when she went out, famous among the
populace. She alone could confront whatever happened. She would speak
briefly and so was never reproached. She was first to rise from the bed,
and last to return to her bed to rest after she had put each thing in its
place. Her yarn never left her hands without good reason. Out of respect
she yielded place to all; her habits were healthy. She was never
self-satisfied, and never thought of herself as a free woman.
   Her skin was white, she had beautiful eyes, and her hair was gold. An
ivory glow always shone from her face – no mortal (so they say) ever
possessed a face like it. The curve of her breasts was small on her
snow-white bosom. And her legs? Such is the guise of Atalanta upon the
stage.
   In her anxiety she never stayed still, but moved her smooth limbs,
beautiful with her generous body; she sought out every hair. Perhaps one

may find fault with her hard hands. She was content with nothing but what she did for herself. There was never a topic she thought she knew well enough. She remained virtuous because she never committed any crime.

While she lived she so guided her two young lovers that they became like the example of Pylades and Orestes – one house would hold them both and one spirit.[7] But now that she is dead, they will separate, and each is growing old by himself. Now instants damage what such a woman built up; look at Troy, to see what a woman once did. I pray that it be right to use such grand comparisons for this lesser event.

These verses for you your patron – whose tears never end – writes in tribute. You are lost, but never will be taken from his heart. These are the gifts he believes the lost will enjoy. After you no woman can seem good. A man who has lived without you has seen his own death while alive. He carries your name in gold back and forth on his arm, where he can keep it, possessing Potestas.[8] As long as these published words of ours survive, so long will you live in these little verses of mine.

In your place I have only your image as solace;[9] this we cherish with reverence and lavish with flowers. When I come with you, it follows in attendance. But to whom in my visiting can I trust a thing so venerable? If there ever is anyone to whom I can entrust it, I shall be fortunate in this alone now that I have lost you. But – woe is me – you have won the contest – my fate and yours are the same.

The man who tries to harm this tomb dares to harm the gods: believe me, this woman, made famous by this inscription, has divinity.

48. *Athenodora. Athens, Christian period (Kaibel 176. G)*

Good Athenodora of Attica, wife of Thaumasius, filled with God's influence. She bore children and nursed them when they were infants. Earth took this young mother and keeps her, though the children need her milk.

49. *Urbana, housewife. Rome, 3rd cent. AD (CIL VI.29580 = ILS 8450. L)*

Sacred to the gods of the dead. To Urbana my sweetest, chastest, and rarest wife. Surely no one more distinguished ever existed. She deserved honour also for this reason, that she lived every day of her life with me with the greatest kindness and the greatest simplicity, both in her conjugal love and the industry typical of her character. I added this so that those who read may understand how much we loved one another. Paternus set this up in honour of his deserving wife.

50. *Macria Helike, a Christian. Rome, 2nd/3rd cent.* AD *(Greek verses in Kaibel 727 = Peek 1164. G)*

Her husband, who is still alive, has in his heart a memorial to his own wife after her irrevocable fate. Wayfarer, I have written this on a stone tablet, [a record] of what she was like. She had looks like golden Aphrodite, but she also had a simple soul dwelling in her breast. She was good, and abided by all God's laws. She absolutely broke none of them. She has brought joy to her survivors. She began as a slave, but now has won the crown of freedom.[10] She bore three live children, and she was the mother of two sons. After she had seen the third, a female, she left her life painlessly, on the eleventh day. She had an incredible beauty, like an Amazon's, to inspire passion more when she was dead than when she was alive.[11] She lived simply for 20 years. This dark tomb conceals Macria Helike.

Literary sources
'A woman who never had women's defects'

Daughter of a hero, wife of an aristocrat and mother of champions of the Roman people, Cornelia was admired for her virtue, fidelity and, not least, her intelligence. She was the standard by which Roman matrons were measured and has been remembered as the ideal of Roman womanhood for two millennia. For other texts on Cornelia, see nos. 259, 260.

51. *Cornelia's noble nature. Misenum, 2nd cent.* BC *(Plutarch, Life of Gaius Gracchus 4.3, 19.1-3. G)*

(4.3) The people of Rome honoured her not less for her children than for her father, and in later times set up a bronze statue of her with the inscription, 'Cornelia, Mother of the Gracchi'.

(19.1-3) Cornelia is said to have borne these and all her misfortunes nobly and magnanimously, and to have said about the shrines where they were buried that their bodies had received worthy tombs. She herself spent her days in the area called Misenum, and did not change her customary way of life. She had many friends and entertained her friends, and there were always Greeks and learned men in her company, and all the kings exchanged gifts with her. She particularly enjoyed discussing with visitors and friends the life and habits of her father Scipio Africanus, and she was most admirable because she did not grieve for her sons and talked to her audience without weeping about their sufferings and their accomplishments, as if she were telling stories to them about the ancient heroes of Rome.

Some thought that she had lost her mind because she was old and had suffered so greatly, and that she had become insensible because of her misfortunes, but these people were themselves insensible of how much nobility and good birth and education can help people in times of sorrow, and that for all the attempts of virtue to prevent it, she may be overcome by fortune, but in her defeat she cannot be deprived of the power of rational endurance.

52. *Tiberius chooses to die in place of Cornelia. Rome, 2nd cent.* BC
(Plutarch, Life of Tiberius Gracchus, 1.2-5. G)

[Tiberius and Gaius Gracchus] were the sons of Tiberius Gracchus, who had been censor and twice consul in Rome and had celebrated two triumphs, but derived the greatest honour from his virtue. Because of this, Scipio, the general who fought against Hannibal, offered Tiberius his daughter Cornelia in marriage, even though he had not been Tiberius' friend, but rather the opposite.

A story is told that Tiberius once caught a pair of snakes on his bed; the soothsayers considered the omen and did not let him kill or free both of them, but instead offered him a choice, that if the male were killed it would cause Tiberius' death, and if the female, Cornelia's. So Tiberius, both because he loved his wife, and because he thought that it was more fitting for him to die since he was older, and she was still young, killed the male snake, and let the female go. And not long after that he died, leaving twelve children who had been born to him and Cornelia.

Cornelia took over the children and the household, and proved herself so sensible and motherly and generous that it seemed that Tiberius had made a good decision when he chose to die on behalf of such a woman. When Ptolemy[12] offered to share his kingdom with her and proposed marriage, Cornelia refused. She remained a widow, and of her children, only a daughter survived, who married Scipio the younger, and the two sons, the subjects of these biographies, Tiberius and Gaius. After they were born she raised them in such a laudable manner that, although they were generally agreed to be the most naturally gifted of all Romans their virtue was regarded as having come from their education rather than their birth.

53. *Womanly virtue (Valerius Maximus, Memorable Deeds and Sayings 6.7.1-3. Rome, 2nd-1st cent BC. L)*

The the historian Valerius Maximus chooses three examples of womanly virtue. Loyalty to a husband appears to have been the highest excellence a woman could attain (cf. Arria, no. 170, and Fannia, no. 172)

Tertia Aemilia, the wife of Scipio Africanus and the mother of Cornelia,[13] was a woman of such kindness and patience that, although she knew that her husband was carrying on with a little serving girl, she looked the other way, [as she thought it unseemly for] a woman to prosecute her great husband, Africanus, a conqueror of the world, for a dalliance. So little was she interested in revenge that, after Scipio's death, she freed the girl and gave her in marriage to one of her own freedmen.[14]

When Quintus Lucretius [Vespillo] was proscribed by the triumvirs, his wife Turia[15] hid him in her bedroom above the rafters. A single maidservant knew the secret. At great risk to herself, she kept him safe from imminent death. So rare was her loyalty that, while the other men who had been proscribed found themselves in foreign, hostile places, barely managing to escape the worst tortures of body and soul, Lucretius was safe in that bedroom in the arms of his wife.[16]

Sulpicia, despite the very close watch her mother Julia was keeping on her so that she would not follow her husband to Sicily (he was Lentulus Cruscellio, proscribed by the triumvirs), nevertheless put on slave's clothing and, taking two maids and the same number of manservants, fled secretly and went to him. She was not afraid to risk proscription herself, and her fidelity to her proscribed spouse was firm.[17]

Invective
'Miserable sorrows for men'

54. *Pandora. Boeotia, early 7th cent. BC (Hesiod, Works and Days 42-105. G)*

In an epic that explains how and why man's life is now so hard, read as a school text throughout antiquity, Hesiod describes how woman was given to man's representative Epimetheus ('Afterthinker') as punishment for his brother Prometheus' ('Forethinker') crimes against Zeus. Later in the poem he offers advice on picking a wife.

For the gods have hidden away and are hiding from men the means of life. If they weren't, you could easily work just for a day to get what would keep you for a year, even if you remained idle – you could put your rudder away over the fireplace, and the work of oxen and of toiling mules would disappear.

But Zeus hid the means of life because he was angry in his heart, because crooked-minded Prometheus deceived him. That is why he devised for men these miserable sorrows. Zeus had hidden fire. But good Prometheus son of Iapetus stole it back for men, away from Zeus the Deviser; he hid it from Thunderer Zeus in a hollow reed.

So Zeus became angry at him and told him: 'Son of Iapetus, since you can devise better than everyone, are you glad that you stole fire and tricked my mind? That theft will be a big pain for you and for men in the future, for I'll give them in return for the fire an evil which they can all enjoy in their hearts while putting their arms round an evil of their very own.' So Zeus spoke, and laughed, father of gods and men.

Zeus ordered famous Hephaestus to mix as fast as he could earth with water, and to put in it a human's voice and strength, and to make its face resemble a deathless goddess's, with the fair form of a virgin. And he ordered Athena to teach her her work, to weave on the intricate loom. And he ordered golden Aphrodite to shed grace on her head and cruel passion and worries that gnaw at the limbs. And he commanded Hermes, slayer of Argos, to put in her a bitch's mind and a thieving heart. So Zeus spoke, and they obeyed Zeus son of Cronus, their lord.

Immediately the famous lame god Hephaestus moulded from earth a thing like a chaste virgin, acting on Zeus' orders. He put life in her and the grey-eyed goddess Athena put clothing on her. Around her, goddesses, the Graces and queenly Persuasion, put golden bands on her skin, and the fair-haired Seasons crowned her with spring flowers. In her breast the Guide Hermes, slayer of Argos, put lies, tricky speeches, and a thieving heart; he did this in accordance with Zeus' plans. Hermes, the gods' herald, put in her a voice, and they named this woman Pandora,[18] because all gods who live on Olympus gave her a gift, a pain to men-who-eat-barley.

And when he had completed this steep trap from which there is no escape, Father Zeus sent famed Hermes, the gods' swift messenger, to Epimetheus, bringing this gift. Nor did Epimetheus think, as Prometheus had told him, not ever to accept a gift from Olympian Zeus but to send it right back again, so that it would not prove an evil for mortals. But he accepted it, and when he had taken the evil he understood what he'd done.

Before that the races of men had lived on the earth without evils and without harsh labour and cruel diseases which give men over to the Fates – for in evil times men grow old quickly. But the woman lifted in her hands the great lid from the jar and scattered these evils about – she devised miserable sorrows for men. Only Hope stayed there inside in her unbroken house beneath the rim of the jar. She did not fly out; before that the woman put back the lid of the jar, according to the plans of Zeus Aegis-holder, gatherer of clouds.

The other thousand miseries fly around among men. The earth is full of evils, and the sea is full of them. Diseases come to men in the day, and at night uninvited, bringing evils for mortals in silence, since Deviser Zeus took away their voices. So there is no way to escape the mind of Zeus.

55. *How to pick a wife. Boeotia, early 7th cent. BC (Hesiod, Works and Days 695-705. G)*

You are at the right age to bring a wife to your house when you are not much less than thirty, and not much more. This is the right time for marriage. Your wife should be four years past puberty and be married to you in the fifth. Marry a virgin, so you can teach her good habits. The best one to marry is the girl who lives near you; look over her in detail, so you don't marry one who'll bring joy to your neighbours.[19] For a man can win nothing better than a good wife, and nothing more painful than a bad one – a dinner-snatcher, who scorches her husband, strong as he may be, without fire, and gives him over to a savage old age.

56. *The nature of women. Boeotia, early 7th cent. BC (Hesiod, Theogony 590-612. G)*

From her is descended a great pain to mortal men, the race of female women, who live with men, and who cannot put up with harsh poverty, but only with plenty. So it is with bees in their roofed hives who feed the drones, those conspirators in evil works. For [the bees] spend the whole day until sunset making white wax, while [the drones] stay within in their roofed cells scraping together the works of others into their stomachs. So high-thundering Zeus made an evil for men, women, conspirators in cruel works. And he gave men another evil to balance a good: the man who escapes marriage and the baneful works of women by preferring not to marry, comes to a deadly old age for want of someone to tend him in old age; while he lives he has plenty to eat, but when he dies distant relatives divide up his livelihood. But for the man who has the lot of marriage, and has a good wife, fitted with intelligence, for him evil balances good in his lifetime; but the man who gets a wife of the wicked sort, lives with undying pain in his heart and his evil is without cure.

57. *The female mind. Amorgos, 6th cent. BC (Semonides, On Women. Tr. H. Lloyd-Jones. G)*

Although the context of this famous poem is lost, its use of animal and inanimate metaphors suggests that it was intended, like Aesop's fables, as social satire.[20] But it is important to note that, as in Hesiod, good behaviour is defined in terms of service to a woman's husband, not by its intrinsic value to the society as a whole, or by a woman's worth to other women or to herself.

In the beginning the god made the female mind separately. One he made from a long-bristled sow. In her house everything lies in disorder, smeared with mud, and rolls about the floor; and she herself unwashed, in clothes unlaundered, sits by the dungheap and grows fat. Another he made from a wicked vixen; a woman who knows everything. No bad thing and no better kind of thing is lost on her; for she often calls a good thing bad and a bad thing good. Her attitude is never the same.

Another he made from a bitch, own daughter of her mother, who wants to hear everything and know everything. She peers everywhere and strays everywhere, always yapping, even if she sees no human being.

A man cannot stop her by threatening, nor by losing his temper and knocking out her teeth with a stone, nor with honeyed words, not even if she is sitting with friends, but ceaselessly she keeps up a barking you can do nothing with.

Another the Olympians moulded out of earth, a stunted creature; you see, a woman like her knows nothing, bad or good. The only work she understands is eating; and not even when the god makes cruel winter weather does she feel the cold and draw a stool near to the fire.

Another he made from the sea; she has two characters. One day she smiles and is happy; a stranger who sees her in the house will praise her, and say, 'There is no woman better than this among all mankind, nor more beautiful.' But on another day she is unbearable to look at or come near to; then she raves so that you can't approach her, like a bitch over her pups, and she shows herself ungentle and contrary to enemies and friends alike. Just so the sea often stands without a tremor, harmless, a great delight to sailors, in the summer season; but often it raves, tossed about by thundering waves. It is the sea that such a woman most resembles in her temper; like the ocean, she has a changeful nature.

Another he made from an ash-grey ass that has suffered many blows; when compelled and scolded she puts up with everything, much against her will, and does her work to satisfaction. But meanwhile she munches in the back room all night and all day, and she munches by the hearth; and likewise when she comes to the act of love, she accepts any partner.

Another he made from a ferret, a miserable, wretched creature; nothing about her is beautiful or desirable, pleasing or lovable. She is mad for the bed of love, but she makes any man she has with her sick. She does great damage to her neighbours by her thieving, and often eats up sacrifices left unburned.

Another was the offspring of a proud mare with a long mane. She pushes servile work and trouble on to others; she would never set her hand to a mill, nor pick up a sieve nor throw the dung out of the house, nor sit over the oven dodging the soot; she makes her husband acquainted with Necessity. She washes the dirt off herself twice, sometimes three times, every day; she rubs herself with scents, and always has her thick hair combed and garlanded with flowers. A woman like her is a fine sight for others, but for the man she belongs to she proves a plague, unless he is some tyrant or king [who takes pride in such objects].

Another is from a monkey; this is the biggest plague of all that Zeus has given to men. Her face is hideous; when a woman like her goes through the town, everyone laughs at her. She is short in the neck; she moves awkwardly; she has no bottom, and is all legs. Hard luck on the poor man who holds such a misery in his arms! She knows every trick and twist, just like a monkey; she does not mind being laughed at, and will do no one a good turn but considers, and spends the whole day planning, how she can do someone the worst possible harm.

Another is from a bee; the man who gets her is fortunate, for on her alone blame does not settle. She causes his property to grow and increase, and she grows old with a husband whom she loves and who loves her, the mother of a handsome and reputable family. She stands out among all women, and a godlike beauty plays about her. She takes no pleasure in sitting among women in places where they tell stories about love. Women like her are the best and most sensible whom Zeus bestows on men.

Zeus has contrived that all these tribes of women are with men and remain with them. Yes, this is the worst plague Zeus has made – women; if they seem to be some use to him who has them, it is to him especially that they prove a plague. The man who lives with a woman never goes through all his day in cheerfulness; he will not be quick to push out of his house Starvation, a housemate who is an enemy, a god who is against us. Just when a man most wishes to enjoy himself at home, through the dispensation of a god or the kindness of a man, she finds a way of finding fault with him and lifts her crest for battle.

Yes, where there is a woman, men cannot even give hearty entertainment to a guest who has come to the house; and the very woman who seems most respectable is the one who turns out guilty of the worst atrocity; because while her husband is not looking ... and the neighbours get pleasure in seeing how he too is mistaken. Each man will take care to praise his own wife and find fault with the other's; we do not realise that the fate of all of us is alike. Yes, this is the greatest plague that Zeus has made, and he has bound us to them with a fetter that cannot be broken. Because of this some have gone to Hades fighting for a woman ...

58. *The best days in a woman's life. Ephesus, 6th cent. BC (Hipponax, Fr. 68 West. G)*

The original context of this famous quotation from the work of a poet famed for his vicious satire is lost.

The two best days in a woman's life are when someone marries her and when he carries her dead body to the grave.[21]

Greek tragedy
'Men ought to beget children somewhere else'

Hesiod implies, in no. 56, that if it were not necessary to have children as companions and support in one's old age, one could simply avoid the problem of living with the 'race of women'; in Euripides' dramas Jason and Hippolytus both propose to do away with women, suggesting that ideally one ought to be able to produce children without resorting to women in the first place.

59. *The uselessness of women. Athens, 467 BC (Aeschylus, Seven Against Thebes 181-202. G)*

King Eteocles reproaches the women who, as the Argive army prepares to attack Thebes, have thrown themselves at the feet of the images of the gods.

I ask you, you intolerable creatures, if you think that your behaviour will be helpful for the state and will bring salvation, or support the army that is besieged, if you fall on the statues of the gods who protect the state, and wail and scream – to the disgust of sensible people?

I would not choose to live with the female sex either in bad times nor during a welcome peace. For if a woman has her way, her boldness is unendurable, and if she is fearful, she is even worse for home and state. And now, by your flight and panic you stir up weak-minded cowardice in our citizens. While affairs outside are going so far as possible in our favour, we are destroyed from within by them – that's what you get from living with a woman.

If there is anyone who does not obey my authority, whether it is a man or a woman or something in between, a sentence of death will be advised against them, so that they cannot avoid a public stoning. The outside is a man's concern – a woman should not consider it; she should stay inside and not cause damage.[22] Have you heard me or not? Or am I talking to a deaf woman?

60. *The unreasonableness of women. Athens, 431 BC (Euripides, Medea 569-75. G)*

Jason objects that Medea refuses to be reasonable about his decision to abandon her and marry the princess of Corinth (cf. no. 28).

You would agree with me, if you weren't annoyed about our marriage, but all you women are alike in this, when your marriage goes well you think you've got everything, but if anything goes wrong in your marriage, you turn what's best into what's most inimical. Men ought to beget children somewhere else, and there should be no female race.

61. *The worthlessness of women. Athens, 428 BC (Euripides, Hippolytus 616-55. G)*

When the old nurse tells Hippolytus that his stepmother Phaedra is passionately in love with him, Hippolytus, who refuses to worship Aphrodite, the goddess of sexual passion, reacts violently to the nurse's message. Although, under the circumstances, Hippolytus might be expected to complain primarily about women's infidelity, instead he first observes that women are an economic liability, and then suggests that they be held in solitary confinement.

(616) Zeus, why have you allowed to dwell in the light of the sun among mankind, an evil counterfeit? If you wanted to sow a mortal race, you did not need to provide it from women, but men could have deposited a sum of bronze or iron or gold in your temples and bought the seed of children, each one contributing according to his worth, and so lived in liberated homes, without women.[23] ... (627) It is clear that a woman is a major evil for this reason: the father who begot her and brought her up pays out a dowry and has her dwell away from home, so that he can be rid of the evil. And the man who brings the tender creature into his house enjoys buying decorations for her adornment and her clothes and with his efforts empties his house of wealth ...

(638) A man is best off with a nonentity – a woman who sits in the house useless in her stupidity. I hate clever women. I don't want a woman in my house thinking more than a woman ought to think, because Aphrodite inspires more mischief in the clever ones, while a helpless woman is freed from folly by the simplicity of her thoughts.[24] (645) Servants ought not to go near women, but they should put voiceless biting beasts into the house with them, so that no one would speak to them and hear what they had to say. But now the evil women sit inside and make evil plans, and the servants carry them outside. That is how you, you evil person, came to arrange a liaison with me and my father's inviolable bed! I will wipe away what you set with streams of running water, purifying my ears. How can I be evil if I feel polluted when I hear what you propose?

Satire and irony
'She may have brought me ten talents, but she has
a nose one cubit long!'

62. *Woman as the equivalent of evil. Athens, 4th cent. BC (Carcinus II, Semele, TGrF Fr. 70 F3. G)*

Lines quoted from a lost play

O Zeus, why need one say evil of women in detail? It would be enough if you say merely woman.

63. *Weighing bad women against good. Athens, 4th cent. BC (Eubulus, a fragment from a lost play, Fr. 77 PCG; Chrysilla, Fr. 115 PCG. G)*

As often, the faults of an individual are attributed to the whole 'race', cf. Euripides, *Hippolytus* 616-68.[25]

I wish the second man who took a wife would die an awful death. I don't blame the first man; he had no experience of that evil. The second man knew what kind of evil a wife was! Oh honoured Zeus, shall I ever say something unkind about women? By Zeus, may I perish then! They are the best possessions one can have. Medea was an evil woman, but Penelope was a good thing; some might criticise Clytemnestra, but I'll set Alcestis against her. Maybe someone else will criticise Phaedra – but, by Zeus, there must be another good wife! Who? Oh, poor me, I've run out of good women, and I still have so many more bad ones to talk about.

64. *The price of a wife. Athens, 4th cent. BC (Alexis, Fr. 150 PCG. G)*

Poor men! We sold away our freedom of speech and our comfort and lead the life of slaves with our wives. We're not free. We can't say we don't pay a price for their dowries: bitterness and women's anger. Compared to that, a man's is honey, for men forgive when someone does them wrong, but women do you wrong and keep on recriminating. They control what doesn't belong to them and neglect what they should control. They break their promises. When there's nothing wrong, they say they're sick every time.[26]

65. *Wives and courtesans compared. Athens, 4th cent. BC (Amphis, Fr. 1 PCG. G)*

An excerpt from a lost comedy.

Besides, isn't a 'companion' (*hetaera*) more well-intentioned than a wedded wife? Yes, far more, and most understandably. For a wife remains at home contemptuous because of the law, but a 'companion' knows that a man must be bought by her attentions or she will need to go and find another.

66. *An overbearing wife. Athens, 4th cent. BC (Menander, Fr. 333 Koerte. G)*

A husband complains that his wife Crobyle, whom he married for her money,[27] has made him get rid of a pretty female slave whom he liked.

Now our beautiful heiress can sleep on both sides. She has accomplished a great and remarkable feat; she has thrown out of the house the girl who was causing her trouble, as she wanted to. So now everyone can look at Crobyle's face and see that she is that famous woman, my wife and ruler. That face she has – 'jackass among apes', as the saying goes. I won't mention the other night that was the beginning of my many problems – poor me, I took Crobyle as wife. She may have brought me ten talents, but she has a nose one cubit long! How can one live with someone so overbearing? By Olympian Zeus and Athena, impossible! The girl is a good servant, and quicker than a word. 'Take her away!' Who can argue with her?[28]

67. *The dangers of literacy. Athens, 4th cent. BC (Menander, Synkrisis I, 209-10 Jäkel = Fr. 702 Kock. G)*

Versions of this statement, originally attributed to the comic poet Menander, were copied out by school children in the the 4th cent. AD.[29]

A man who teaches a woman to write should recognise that he is providing poison to an asp.

68. *The disadvantage of a rich wife. Rome, late 1st cent. AD (Martial, Epigrams 8.12. L)*

A satirist offers his opinion of the husband-wife relationship.

Are you asking why I don't want to take a rich wife? I don't want a husband for a wife. Let the matron, Priscus, stay beneath the husband; otherwise woman and man can't be equals.

69. *Juvenal on women in general. Rome, 2nd cent. AD (Satire 6, exc. L)*

Ancient biographers, characteristically confusing poet and poetry, regarded this famous satire as factual evidence that Juvenal hated women. Stories of the same type were attributed to Lucretius (1st cent. BC), because of his caustic statements about marriage in Book 4 of his *De Rerum Natura*.

Eppia, though the wife of a senator, went off with a gladiator to Pharos and the Nile on the notorious walls of Alexandria (though even Egypt condemns Rome's disgusting morals). Forgetting her home, her husband, and her sister, she showed no concern whatever for her homeland (she *was* shameless) and her children in tears, and (you'll be dumbfounded by this) she left the theatre and Paris the actor behind. Even though when she was a baby she was pillowed in great luxury, in the down of her father's mansion, in a cradle of the finest workmanship, she didn't worry about the dangers of sea travel (she had long since stopped worrying about her reputation, the loss of which among rich ladies' soft cushions does not matter much). Therefore with heart undaunted she braved the waves of the Adriatic and the wide-resounding Ionian Sea (to get to Egypt she had to change seas frequently).

You see, if there's a good reason for undertaking a dangerous voyage, then women are fearful; their cowardly breasts are chilled with icy dread; they cannot stand on their trembling feet. But they show courageous spirit in affairs they're determined to enter illicitly. If it's their *husband* who wants them to go, then it's a problem to get on board ship. They can't stand the bilge-water; the skies spin around them. The woman who goes off with her *lover* of course has no qualms. She eats dinner with the sailors, walks the quarter-deck, and enjoys hauling rough ropes. Meanwhile the first woman gets sick all over her husband.

And yet what was the glamour that set her on fire, what was the prime manhood that captured Eppia's heart? What was it she saw in him, that would compensate for her being called *Gladiatrix*?[30] Note that her lover, dear Sergius, had now started shaving his neck, and was hoping to be released from duty because of a bad wound on his arm. Moreover, his face was deformed in a number of ways: he had a mark where his helmet rubbed him, and a big wart between his nostrils, and a smelly discharge always dripping from his eye. But he was a *gladiator*. That made him look as beautiful as Apollo's friend Hyacinth. This is what she preferred to her children and her homeland, her sister and her husband. It's the *sword* they're in love with: this same Sergius, once released from service, would begin to seem like her husband Veiento.

Do you care about a private citizen's house, about Eppia's doings? Turn your eyes to the gods' rivals. Hear what the Emperor Claudius had to put up with. As soon as his wife thought that he was asleep, this imperial whore[31] put on the hood she wore at night, determined to prefer a cheap pad to the royal bed, and left the house with one female slave only. No, hiding her black hair in a yellow wig she entered the brothel, warm with its old patchwork quilts and her empty cell, her very own. Then she took her stand, naked, her nipples gilded, assuming the name of Lycisca, and displayed the stomach you came from, noble Britannicus. She obligingly received customers and asked for her money, and lay there through the night taking in the thrusts of all comers. Then when the pimp sent the girls home, at last she went away sadly, and (it was all she could do) was the last to close up her cell – she was still burning, her vagina stiff and erected; tired by men, but not yet satisfied, she left, her face dirty and bruised, grimy with lamp smoke, she brought back to her pillow the smell of the brothel.

Isn't there anyone then in such large herds of women that's worth marrying? Let her be beautiful, graceful, rich, fertile, let her place on her porticoes her ancestors' statues; let her be more virginal than the Sabine women (the ones that with their dishevelled hair brought the war with Rome to an end);[32] let her be a phoenix on earth, something like a black swan – but who could stand a wife who has every virtue? I'd rather have (much rather) a girl from Venusia than you, Cornelia, mother of the Gracchi, if along with your great excellence you bring a snob's brow and count your family's triumphs as part of your dowry.[33]

All chance of domestic harmony is lost while your wife's mother is living. She gets her to rejoice in despoiling her husband, stripping him naked. She gets her to write back politely and with sophistication when her seducer sends letters. She tricks your spies or bribes them. Then when your daughter is feeling perfectly well she calls in the doctor Archigenes and says that the blankets are too heavy. Meanwhile, her lover, in hiding shut off from her, impatient at the delay, waits in silence and stretches his foreskin. Maybe you think that her mother will teach her virtuous ways – ones different from her own? It's much more productive for a dirty old lady to bring up a dirty little girl.

There's hardly a case in court where the litigation wasn't begun by a female. If Manilia can't be defendant, she'll be the plaintiff.[34] They'll draw up indictments without assistance, and are ready to tell Celsus the lawyer how to begin his speech and what arguments he should use.

Who doesn't know about the Tyrian wrappers and the ointment for women's athletics? Who hasn't seen the wounds in the dummy, which she drills with continual stabbings and hits with her shield and works through the whole course of exercise – a matron, the sort you'd expect to blow the trumpet at the Floralia[35] – unless in her heart she is plotting something deeper still, and seriously training for the actual games? How can a woman who wears a helmet be chaste? She's denying her sex, and likes a man's strength. But she wouldn't want to turn into a man, since we men get so little pleasure.

Yet what a show there would be, if there were an auction of your wife's stuff – her belt and gauntlets and helmet and half-armour for her left leg. Or she can try the other style of battle – lucky you, when she sells her greaves. Yet these same girls sweat even in muslin, even the thinnest little netting burns their delicacies. Look at the noise she makes when she drives home the blows her trainer showed her, at the weight of her helmet, how solidly she sits on her haunches (like the binding around a thick tree), and laugh when she puts her armour aside to pick up her chamber-pot.

You ask where these monsters come from, the source that they spring from? Poverty made Latin women chaste in the old days, hard work and a short time to sleep and hands calloused and hardened with wool-working, and Hannibal close to the city,[36] and their husbands standing guard at the Colline Gate – that kept their humble homes from being corrupted by vice. But now we are suffering from the evils of a long peace. Luxury, more ruthless than war, broods over Rome and takes revenge for the world she has conquered. No cause for guilt or deed of lust is missing, now that Roman poverty has vanished. Money, nurse of promiscuity, first brought in foreigners' ways, and effete riches weakened the sinews of succeeding generations. What does Venus care when she's drunk? She can't tell head from tail when she eats big oysters at midnight, and when her perfume foams with undiluted wine, when she drinks her conch-shell cup dry, and when in her dizziness the roof turns round and the table rises up to meet two sets of lights.

An even worse pain is the female who, as soon as she sits down to dinner, praises Vergil and excuses Dido's suicide:[37] matches and compares poets, weighing Vergil on one side of the scale and Homer on the other. Schoolmasters yield; professors are vanquished; everyone in the party is silenced. No one can speak, not a lawyer, not an auctioneer, not even another woman. Such an avalanche of words falls, that you'd say it's like pans and bells being beaten. Now no one needs trumpets or bronzes: this woman by herself can come help the Moon when she's suffering from an eclipse.[38] As a philosopher she sets definitions on moral behaviour. Since she wants to seem so learned and eloquent she ought to shorten her tunic up to her knees[39] and bring a pig to Sylvanus[40] and go to the penny bath with the philosophers. Don't let the woman who shares your marriage bed adhere to a set style of speaking or hurl in well-rounded sentences the enthymeme shorn of its premise. Don't let her know all the histories. Let there be something in books she does not understand. I hate the woman who is continually poring over and studying Palaemon's[41] treatise, who never breaks the rules or principles of grammar, and who quotes verses I never heard of, ancient stuff that men ought not to worry about. Let her correct her girlfriend's verses – she ought to allow her husband to commit a solecism.

Pauper women endure the trials of childbirth and endure the burdens of nursing, when fortune demands it. But virtually no gilded bed is laid out for childbirth – so great is her skill, so easily can she produce drugs that make her sterile or induce her to kill human beings in her womb. You fool, enjoy it, and give her the potion to drink, whatever it's going to be, because, if she wants to get bloated and to trouble her womb with a live baby's kicking, you might end up being the father of an Ethiopian – soon a wrong-coloured heir will complete your accounts, a person whom it's bad luck to see first thing in the morning.

70. *Bereavement. Rome, late 1st cent. AD (Martial, Epigram 9.30. L)*

Antistius Rusticus died on the savage shores of Cappadocia. O land guilty of a doleful crime, Nigrina brought back her husband's bones in her arms and complained that the trip was too short; and as she gave the sacred urn to the tomb, which she was jealous of, she saw herself twice bereft of her stolen spouse.

71. *Cicero on Clodia. Rome, 56 BC (Cicero, Pro Caelio 13-16.[42] L)*

Not a comic poet speaking in generalities but a deadly serious advocate in a court of law, Cicero directs his sarcasm and considerable wit against a specific woman. Speaking last in the defence of Marcus Caelius Rufus, a former protégé, Cicero deliberately blurred the formal charges under the law against riot and amused the jury, restive because it had been empanelled on a holiday, with his spicy portrait of the already notorious Clodia, arguing that she had sponsored the prosecution for personal reasons. With what amounted to character assassination, he paid off an old grudge of his own against her brother Clodius (see below, p. 292).

(13) The accusations are two: the gold and the poison. And the same person is on the scene for both. The gold is supposed to have been taken from Clodia[43] and the poison to have been procured to use on her. Everything else is slander, not accusations, better suited to malicious gossip than a court of law. 'Adulterer, lecher, briber' are insults, not accusations. ... I see the author of these two charges, the source, I see a specific person, a mind. 'He needed gold; he took it from Clodia, without witnesses, and kept it for as long as he needed it.' That's the clear proof of an uncommon intimacy. 'Then he decided to kill her, stirred up those he could, got the poison, established the place, and brought it.' Again, this is clear proof of a deep hatred, conceived after having been cruelly jilted.

In this trial, gentlemen of the jury, we are concerned only with Clodia, a noble woman and a notorious one, but I will say no more than is necessary about her to rebut the accusations. However, you, Gnaeus Domitius,[44] smart as you are, understand perfectly that we are concerned only with this woman. If she does not affirm that she lent the gold to Marcus Caelius, if she does not accuse him of having procured the poison for her, our conduct is inappropriate. To use the name of Roman matron when the respect owed to respectable women does not allow it! If, however, this woman were removed from the case, the accusers no longer have a head nor any means to attack Caelius. And surely another thing entirely would be the vigour that I would use were it not for the animosity between me and this woman's husband – excuse me, brother, I always make that mistake. Now, however, I am obliged to proceed with circumspection; and I will not push beyond the limits that my obligations to my client and the case itself demand. And furthermore I never considered it wise to make an enemy of a woman, especially one who is generally considered everybody's friend.

(14) But I would nevertheless begin by asking her whether she wants me to adopt with her a severe, solemn, old-style tone, or whether she prefers something more easy-going and modern. If she prefers the austere style, then I shall have to summon up from the underworld one of those beards – no, not one of the fashionable jobs that she likes so much, but a really serious hairy beard out of the portraits and statues of days gone by – to reprimand her and to speak in my place. Then she can't blame me! Let us imagine, therefore, that there appears a member of her own family: let's conjure up the famous Caecus, the Blind (it will be easier on him, as he can't see her).[45] If he were to rise up right now, he would say something like this:

'Woman, what do you have in common with Caelius? With a youth, a stranger? Why were you so intimate with him as to lend him the gold, or so inimical as to fear poison from him? Did you not see your father as consul? Weren't you told that your uncle, your grandfather, your great-grandfather, your great-great-grandfather, and his father were consuls too? And then, didn't you realise that till just now you were the wife of Quintus Metellus?[46] He, a man of ancient lineage and great energy, a man extraordinarily devoted to his country, had only to step outside his house to overshadow virtually all his fellow citizens in courage, glory, and reputation. Born of a noble house, married into one just as illustrious, how could you get mixed up with someone like Caelius? Is he a relative? a relative by marriage? a friend of your husband? Not at all.This was nothing but sheer, unbridled passion. If the images of your male ancestors don't move you, did not even Quinta Claudia, my illustrious descendant, push you to vie in domestic virtue with the women who brought glory to our house? Not even Claudia, the Vestal Virgin? She who, holding her father close, did not allow his enemy, the tribune of the people, to pull him down from his chariot during his triumph? Why did you let yourself be influenced by the vices of your brother rather than by the qualities of your father and forefathers? And yet these, ever since my day, have been kept going both in the males of the family and, especially, in the females. Did I break the peace with Pyrrhus so that you could make daily treaties with your filthy lovers? Did I built the aqueduct to provide water for your post-incest ablutions? Did I built the road so that you could parade with other women's husbands?'

(15) But why, gentlemen of the jury, did I bring in such a difficult character as old Appius, who might at any moment turn his censorious austerity against Caelius? But I'll get to that later, and in such a way, gentlemen of the jury, that I am sure I will be able to justify the the life of Marcus Caelius even to the severest judges. As for you, woman – that's right, it is I speaking now, for myself – if you intend to justify your actions, your declarations, your calumnies, your machinations, your accusations, then you're going to have to give an accounting, and a clear one, of this great intimacy. The accusers, for their part, speak only of orgies, love affairs, adultery, Baiae,[47] beach parties, banquets, revels, singing, concerts, boat rides; and at the same time they give us to understand that there is nothing they say without your approval. And you, gripped by some sudden madness – were willing to have all this mud dragged into the Forum in front of the jury. So you either have to deny the charges and prove that they are lies or admit that neither your accusation nor your testimony deserve to be believed.

But perhaps you prefer that I behave more like a man of the world. Here's what I'll do with you: I'll pull the gruff, practically rustic old man off the stage and replace him with someone more to your liking, say, your little brother. He's so refined in this sort of thing! and, too, he loves you with all his heart and because of some faintheartedness, I suppose, and fear of the dark, the little brat always slept in your bed. What would he say now: 'Why all this fuss, sister? Why this madness?'

Why, with shout and speech, inflate
A little thing into a great?[48]

You saw a young man, a neighbour. He was tall and handsome, and you liked his face and eyes. You wanted to see him more often. You managed to frequent the same gardens. And now you, a fine lady, want to hold that young man tight with your wealth, given that he is still in the power of a stingy father. But you cannot. He kicks, he spits, he rejects you. He doesn't think your gifts are worth so much. And you turn to another! You have a garden on the Tiber and you were very careful to put it right where the young people go to bathe; there every day you can take all the opportunities you want. Why then pester this one, who doesn't want you?

(16) ... [Caelius'] case is all but won. Against what accusation can he not defend himself? I am not not speaking against that woman, but let us suppose that there is another woman, different from her, who gives herself freely to everybody – I mean everybody – who always has a lover to show off; let us suppose that in her garden, in her house, in her villa at Baiae, she gives complete freedom to the pleasures of all; that she goes so far as to maintain young men and to compensate with her largesse for the stinginess of their fathers; let us suppose that this woman is a widow and lives freely; that she is a hussy and lives brazenly; that she is a wealthy woman and lives extravagantly; that she is a slave to her appetites and lives like a whore. Should I consider a man an adulterer if he takes a little liberty when he meets her?

III. Philosophers on the Role of Women

'The inequality is permanent'

In antiquity the term 'philosopher' described professors of general knowledge, both of how life was and of how life ought to be. Plato's theories of ideal behaviour were later counterbalanced by his student Aristotle's systematic descriptions of observed existence.

72. *The female role. Athens, 4th cent.* BC *(Aristotle, Politics 1254b2-10; 1259a37-b17; 1260a9-24, 29-33; 1262a19-24; 1269b12-70a31; 1277b18-25; 1313b32- 9; 1335a7-17. Tr. B. Jowett. G)*

(1254b2) First then we may observe in living creatures both a despotic and a constitutional rule; for the soul rules the body with a despotic rule, whereas the intellect rules the appetites with a constitutional and royal rule. And it is clear that the rule of the soul over the body, and of the mind and the rational element over the passionate is natural and expedient; whereas the equality of the two or the rule of the inferior is always hurtful. The same holds good of animals as well as of men; for tame animals have a better nature than wild and all tame animals are better off when they are ruled by man; for then they are preserved. Again, the male is by nature superior, and the female inferior; and the one rules, and the other is ruled; this principle, of necessity, extends to all mankind ...

(1259a37) Of household management we have seen that there are three parts: one is the rule of a master over slaves, which has been discussed already, another of a father, and the third of a husband. A husband and father rules over wife and children, both free, but the rule differs, the rule over his children being a royal, over his wife a constitutional rule. For although there may be exceptions to the order of nature, the male is by nature fitter for command than the female, just as the older and full-grown is superior to the younger and more immature. But in most constitutional states the citizens rule and are ruled by turns, for the idea of a constitutional state implies that the natures of the citizens are equal, and do not differ at all. Nevertheless, when one rules and the other is ruled we endeavour to create a difference of outward forms and names and titles of respect ... . The relation of the male to the female is of this kind, but there the inequality is permanent. The rule of a father over his children is royal, for he receives both love and the respect due to age, exercising a kind of royal power. And therefore Homer has appropriately called Zeus 'father of gods and men', because he is the king of them all. For a king is the natural superior of his subjects, but he should be of the same kin or kind with them, and such is the relation of elder and younger, of father and son ...

(1260a9) The freeman rules over the slave after another manner from that in which the male rules over the female, or the man over the child; although the parts of the soul are present in all of them, they are present in different degrees. For the slave has no deliberative faculty at all; the woman has, but it is without authority, and the child has, but it is immature. So it must necessarily be with the moral virtues also; all may be supposed to partake of them, but only in such manner and degree as is required by each for the fulfilment of his duty. Hence the ruler ought to have moral virtue in perfection, for his duty is entirely that of a master artificer, and the master artificer is reason; the subjects, on the other hand, require only that measure of virtue which is proper to each of them. Clearly, then, moral virtue belongs to all of them; but the temperance of a man and of a woman, or the courage and justice of a man and of a woman, are not, as Socrates maintained, the same; the courage of a man is shown in commanding, of a woman in obeying ... (1260a29) All classes must be deemed to have their special attributes; as the poet says of women, 'silence is a woman's glory',[1] but this is not equally the glory of a man. The child is imperfect, and therefore obviously his virtue is not relative to himself alone, but to the perfect man and to his teacher, and in like manner the virtue of the slave is relative to a master ...

(1262a19) They say that in Upper Libya, where the women are common, nevertheless the children who are born are assigned to their respective fathers on the ground of their likeness. And some women, like the females of other animals – for example mares and cows – have a strong tendency to produce offspring resembling their parents, as was the case with the Pharsalian mare called Dicaea [the Just] ...

(1269b12) The licence of the Lacedaemonian women defeats the intention of the Spartan constitution, and is adverse to the good order of the state. For a husband and a wife, being each a part of every family, the state may be considered as about equally divided into men and women; and, therefore, in those states in which the condition of the woman is bad, half the city may be regarded as having no laws. And this is what has actually happened at Sparta; the legislator wanted to make the whole state hardy and temperate, and he has carried out his intention in the case of the men, but he has neglected the women, who live in every sort of intemperance and luxury. The consequence is that in such a state wealth is too highly valued, especially if the citizens fall under the dominion of their wives, after the manner of all warlike races, except the Celts and a few others who openly approve of male loves. The old mythologer would seem to have been right in uniting Ares and Aphrodite, for all warlike races are prone to the love either of men or of women. This was exemplified among the Spartans in the days of their greatness; many things were managed by their women. But what difference does it make whether women rule, or the rulers are ruled by women? The result is the same. Even in regard to courage, which is of no use in daily life, and is needed only in war, the influence of the Lacedaemonian women has been most mischievous. The evil showed itself in the Theban invasion,[2] when, unlike the women in other cities, they were utterly useless and caused more confusion than the enemy. This licence of the Lacedaemonian women existed from the earliest times, and was only what might be expected. For, during the wars of the Lacedaemonians, first against the Argives, and afterwards against the Arcadians and Messenians, the men were long away from home, and, on the return of peace, they gave themselves into the legislator's hand, already prepared by the discipline of a soldier's life (in which there are many elements of virtue), to receive his enactments. But, when Lycurgus, as tradition says, wanted to bring the women under his laws, they resisted, and he gave up the attempt. They, and not he, are to blame for what then happened, and this defect in the constitution is clearly to be attributed to them. We are not, however, considering what is or is not to be excused, but what is right or wrong, and the disorder of the women, as I have already said, not only of itself gives an air of indecorum to the state, but tends in a measure to foster avarice.

(1270a15) The mention of avarice naturally suggests a criticism of the inequality of property. While some of the Spartan citizens have quite small properties, others have very large ones; hence the land has passed into the hands of a few. And here is another fault in their laws; for, although the legislator rightly holds up to shame the sale or purchase of an inheritance, he allows anybody who likes to give and bequeath it. Yet both practices lead to the same result. And nearly two-fifths of the whole country are held by women; this is owing to the number of heiresses and to the large dowries which are customary.[3] It would surely have been better to have given no dowries at all, or, if any, but small or moderate ones. As the law now stands, a man may bestow his heiress on any one whom he pleases, and, if he die intestate, the privilege of giving her away descends to his heir. Hence, although the country is able to maintain 1,500 cavalry and 30,000 hoplites, the whole number of Spartan citizens[4] fell below 1,000 ...

(1277b18) The good man, who is free and also a subject, will not have one virtue only, say justice – but he will have distinct kinds of virtue, the one qualifying him to rule, the other to obey, and differing as the temperance and courage of men and women differ. For a man would be thought a coward if he had no more courage than a courageous woman, and a woman would be thought loquacious if she imposed no more restraints on her conversation than the good man; and indeed their part in the management of the household is different, for the duty of the one is to acquire, and of the other to preserve ...

(1313b32) Again, the evil practices of the last and worst form of democracy are all found in tyrannies. Such are the powers given to women in their families in the hope that they will inform against their husbands, and the licence which is allowed to slaves in order that they may betray their masters; for slaves and women do not conspire against tyrants; and they are of course friendly to tyrannies and also to democracies, since under them they have a good time. For the people too would fain be a monarch ...

(1335a7) Since the time of generation is commonly limited within the age of seventy years in the case of a man, and of fifty in the case of a woman, the commencement of the union should conform to these periods. The union of male and female when too young is bad for the procreation of children; in all other animals the offspring of the young are small and ill-developed, and generally of the female sex, and therefore also in man, as is proved by the fact that in those cities in which men and women are accustomed to marry young, the people are small and weak.

73. *Educating women to make them more like men. Athens, 4th cent.* BC
   (Plato, Republic 5.451c-452d, 454d-e, 455c-456b, 457a-b, 457c-e, 458c-459a, 459d-461e. G)

The *Republic* purports to be Socrates' own account of a discussion in which Socrates presents a sketch of a social system that directly addresses complaints about women's 'different' minds and intractable behaviour, such as those expressed by Jason and Hippolytus (cf. no. 61). Socrates describes an ideal state in which it would be possible for justice to be done to everyone, where only the people most suited to ruling would be allowed to govern. This 'guardian' class, remarkably, would consist of both men and women, but the women would be required to make their behaviour approximate so far as possible to men's (cf. no. 267), rather than vice versa, and distinctive female occupations, such as mothering, are so far as possible eliminated.[5] Before he can proceed with his argument, Socrates insists on securing the assent of his interlocutor, who in the passages cited below is Plato's brother Glaucon.

(451c) As far as our men are concerned, once they have been formed and educated in the way we have been discussing, there is in my opinion only one way for them to possess and use women and children, and that is for them to start as we have made them start. We decided for the purposes of our argument to put these men in the position of guards of a flock.

Let's follow the argument, then, by giving them an analogous birth and upbringing as the guards of a flock, and let's consider whether the analogy is appropriate.

What do you mean? said Glaucon.

As follows: do we think that the females among guard dogs should guard along with the males in everything they undertake to guard, and hunt along with them, and do other things in common, or do the females stay at home inside because they are incapable because of childbearing and -rearing, and the males do the work and have the whole responsibility of guarding the flocks? They do everything in common, except that we will treat the females as weaker, and the males as stronger.

But can you use animals for the same purposes, if you do not provide them with similar upbringing and training?

No, that would be impossible.

Therefore if we use women for the same purposes as men we must teach them the same things.

Yes.

They must be educated in music and in gymnastics.

Yes.

And in addition to those two skills they must be educated in the art of war, and know how to practise it.

That follows from what you are saying.

Perhaps, I said,[6] much of what I have now been saying would, if carried out appear absurd because it is contrary to practice.

It certainly would, said Glaucon.

Which of the ideas do you regard as most absurd? Surely it must be the notion of women exercising naked alongside men in the palaestras,[7] and not just young women, but older women too, like old men in the gymnasia, who like to work out even though they are wrinkled and not attractive to look at.

By Zeus, he said, the notion would appear absurd, according to present-day standards.

But, I said, isn't it true that when we began this discussion we said that we must not be afraid of the type of jokes clever people will make, when they speak against the changes we have proposed in gymnastics and music and not least in the bearing of arms and riding on horseback.

Correct, he said.

(454d) As far as the male and female sexes are concerned, if one appears suited to a particular art or practice, we will say that the other one is inferior to it in that respect. If they appear to be different in just this respect, that the female gives birth, and the male begets, we shall not admit that it has yet been shown that the kind of distinction exists between male and female that we are talking about, but rather will continue to think that the guardians and their wives should have the same responsibilities.

Rightly so, said he.

(455c) Do you know of any human concern in which the male sex is not superior to the female? Or shall we embark on a tedious discussion of weaving or pot-watching or baking, in which the female sex prides itself, and looks most ridiculous in when bested [by men]?

That's true, replied Glaucon, one sex wins out over others in virtually everything, though many women are better in many respects than many men. But on the whole it is as you say.

Therefore, my friend, there are no governmental responsibilities that fall to a female because she is female, or to a male because he is male, but in the same way the natural abilities are divided up in both sexes, and females by nature share all responsibilities, and so do males, except that in all of them a female is a weaker being than a male.

Absolutely.

Should we assign all responsibilities to males, and none to females?

By no means.

But there are, I believe, as we will admit, women who are by nature physicians, and women who are not, and women who are musical, and those who are not?

Of course.

And aren't there women who are athletes, and warlike, and others who are unwarlike and unathletic?

I believe so.

In addition, aren't there women who are eager to learn, and those who hate learning, and women who are courageous, and women who are cowards?

There are.

And there are women who are guardians, and women who are not. And didn't we select the nature of our male guardians in this way?

We did.

Women and men have the same nature as far as the guardianship of the city is concerned, except in those aspects where they are by nature weaker or stronger.

So it seems.

And these special women should be selected to live with the special men and to share the duties of guardianship with them, since they are capable and similar to the men in their nature.

Absolutely.

And shouldn't we give the same responsibilities to the same natures?

Certainly.

We have been brought back again to where we started, and we agree that it is not contrary to their nature to assign gymnastics and music to the wives of the guardians.

Absolutely.

(457a) The wives of the guardians should strip, since they will be clothed in virtue instead of cloaks, and they should share in fighting and the other duties of guardianship of the city, and not do otherwise. But the lighter tasks of guardianship should be given to the women rather than to men because of the female sex's physical weakness. The man who laughs at women exercising, when they are exercising for the noblest reasons, in his laughter 'plucks the fruit of his wisdom before it is ripe',[8] and I think, doesn't know what he is laughing at or what he is doing. For this has been and always will be the best of advice: what is constructive is beautiful, and what is harmful is ugly.[9]

Absolutely right.

(457c) There is a law, I believe, that follows from this and from what we said previously.

What is the law?

That the wives of all these men ought to be shared in common, and that no one woman be married to any one man. And that their children should be shared in common, and no parent should know his own child or child his parent.

This law is much more difficult to accept either as possible or as constructive.

I don't think there is much doubt about its being constructive, since there is no greater good than shared wives and shared children, so far as is possible. But I think that there is the greatest doubt about whether it is possible.

I think that there is considerable doubt about both.

(458c) You now, I said, as the founder of the state, just as you selected the men, will select women for the men as like as possible in nature and give them to them. And the men, since they will have common houses and common meals, with no one having anything special of their own, will be together, and will join together in gymnastics and in the rest of their upbringing, and I believe they will be led by natural inevitability to have sexual relations with one another. Doesn't that seem inevitable to you?

You mean, he said, that sexual rather than logical inevitability is likely to be more effective in persuading and controlling most people.

Certainly, I said. But after that, Glaucon, the rulers will not allow them to have sexual relations in a disorderly manner, or do anything other than what is proper in a city of the blessed. So the law requires. It follows from this that we must make marriages so far as possible sacred. The sacred marriages would be the most beneficial.

Absolutely.

How then can they be made most beneficial? Tell me this, Glaucon, for I see that in your house there are hunting dogs and plenty of aristocratic birds. Is there something, by Zeus, that you have noticed about their marriages and childbearing?

(459a) Like what? he said.

First of all, that although they all are fine animals, aren't there some that are first-rate?

There are.

And do you breed from all in the same way, or do you want particularly to breed from the best?

From the best.[10]

(459d) We agree, then, I said, that among the guardians only the best males must be encouraged to cohabit as often as possible with the best females, and the basest men must be discouraged from cohabiting with the basest women, and the offspring of the best unions raised, and the others not, if we want the flock to be 'tops'.

And all this must take place without the anyone but the rulers themselves knowing, if the flock of guardians is to be as free from conflict as possible.

Absolutely right.

Then we must legislate festival days on which we will bring brides and bridegrooms together, and our poets must write hymns suitable for the marriages that are taking place. We will leave the number of weddings up to the rulers, so that they can keep a limit on the number of men, and take into consideration wars and diseases and other such matters, so that our state will not be too large or too small so far as possible.

Right.

I think we shall have to create some clever lots so that on every occasion the less worthy person will blame his luck and not the rulers.

Certainly, he said.

And prizes must be awarded to those young men who are best in war and otherwise, both the usual prizes and the opportunity for intercourse with women, so that there will be an excuse for having the majority of children begotten by such men.

Correct.

Then officers appointed for the purpose must take the children that are born from such unions – the officers could be male or female or both, for men and women both can hold office –

Yes.

The officers, I think, must take the children of the best men to the pen to particular nurses who live apart from the guardians in another section of the city. As for the children of the inferior men, and the children of other guardians if they are in some way maimed, the nurses must hide them away in a secret and unknown place, as they should.

Yes, if we want the breed of guardians to be pure. The nurses must take care of the children and bring the mothers to the pen when they have milk, and use every means of contriving that no mother knows her own child, and they must provide other women who have milk, if there are not enough guardian mothers, and they must ensure that the mothers nurse for a limited time, and let wet-nurses and nurses take on the lack of sleep and other burdens of child-care.

You are talking, he said, about a much easier process of childbearing for the wives of the guardians.

As it should be, said I. Let's continue to discuss the rest of our programme. We said that children ought to be born to parents in the prime of their lives.

Correct.

Do you agree that for women a reasonable span of time for the prime of life is twenty years, and for men thirty?

Which years in their lives do you mean?

A woman, I said, starting from her twentieth year until her fortieth year should bear children for the state. A man, when he has passed 'the keenest point in the race',[11] from that point until he is fifty-five. (461a)

That is the time, he said, when both male and female will be at their physical and intellectual prime. If someone who is older or younger than this takes part in the public weddings, we must say that such action is unholy and unjust, because he is begetting a child for the state, which, if no one notices it, will be conceived without the sacrifices and prayers which priests and priestesses will offer at every marriage, that from good parents will come better children and from profitable parents more profitable children, but rather this will be the child of darkness and terrible lust.

Correct, he said.

The same law will apply to any male of begetting age who touches a woman in his age-group without the sanction of a ruler. We must say that for the state such a child is a bastard and uncertified and unholy.

Absolutely right, he said.

I think that when men and women pass the time of life for procreation, we should let them be free to marry whomever they wish, except that a man should not marry his daughter or his mother or his daughter's daughters or his mother's mother, and a woman should not marry her son or father and so on in both directions, but when granting all this we must insist that no offspring conceived in such a marriage be allowed to live, and if it forces its way, they must arrange that such a child cannot be raised.

That also, he said, is a reasonable suggestion. But how will the fathers and daughters and all the relations you have mentioned recognise one another?

They cannot know, I said. But reckoning from the day on which he became a bridegroom: he will call children born in the seventh or tenth month from that day[12] his own children, the boys will be his sons, and the girls his daughters, and they will call him father, and he will call their children his grandchildren, and they will call them grandfathers and grandmothers. Everyone who was begotten at the time that their mothers and fathers engendered them will be called sisters and brothers, so that, as we were saying, they won't have sexual relations with one another. But the law will permit brothers and sisters to marry, if the lot so falls and the Delphic oracle approves.

Absolutely right, he said.

That, Glaucon, is the way the guardians of the state will share wives and children in common.

74. *Men and women should be treated alike. Athens, 4th cent. BC (Plato, Laws 6.780e-781d, 7.804e-806c, 8.838a-839b. Tr. T.J. Saunders. G)*

Provisions for women to play a more responsible role in society, no longer attributed directly to Socrates, with more specific commentary than in the *Republic* on the problems inherent in traditional Athenian family structure.

(6.780e) Thanks to some providential necessity, Cleinias and Megillus, you have a splendid and – as I was saying – astonishing institution: communal meals for men. But it is entirely wrong of you to have omitted from your legal code any provision for your women, so that the practice of communal meals for them has never got under way. On the contrary, half the human race – the female sex, the half which in any case is inclined to be secretive and crafty, because of its weakness – has been left to its own devices because of the misguided indulgence of the legislator. Because you neglected this sex, you gradually lost control of a great many things which would be in a far better state today if they had been regulated by law. You see, leaving women to do what they like is not just to lose half the battle (as it may seem): a woman's natural potential for virtue is inferior to a man's, so she's proportionately a greater danger, perhaps even twice as great. So the happiness of the state will be better served if we reconsider the point and put things right, by providing that all our arrangements apply to men and women alike. But at present, unhappily, the human race has not progressed as far as that, and if you're wise you won't breathe a word about such a practice in other parts of the world where states do not recognise communal meals as a public institution at all. So when it comes to the point, how on earth are you going to avoid being laughed to scorn when you try to force women to take their food and drink in public? There's nothing the sex is likely to put up with more reluctantly: women have got used to a life of obscurity and retirement, and any attempt to force them into the open will provoke tremendous resistance from them, and they'll be more than a match for the legislator. Elsewhere, as I said, the very mention of the correct policy will be met with howls of protest. But perhaps this state will be different.

The education of females
(7.804e) Let me stress that this law of mine will apply just as much to girls as to boys. The girls must be trained in precisely the same way, and I'd like to make this proposal without any reservations whatever about horse-riding or athletics being suitable activities for males but not for females. You see, although I was already convinced by some ancient stories I have heard, I now know for sure that there are pretty well

countless numbers of women, generally called Sarmatians, round the Black Sea, who not only ride horses but use the bow and other weapons. There, men and women have an equal duty to cultivate these skills, so cultivate them equally they do. And while we're on the subject, here's another thought for you. I maintain that if these results can be achieved, the state of affairs in our corner of Greece, where men and women do not have a common purpose and do not throw all their energies into the same activities, is absolutely stupid. Almost every state, under present conditions, is only half a state, and develops only half its potentialities, whereas with the same cost and effort, it could double its achievement. Yet what a staggering blunder for a legislator to make!

Cleinias: I dare say. But a lot of these proposals, sir, are incompatible with the average state's social structure. However, you were quite right when you said we should give the argument its head, and only make up our minds when it had run its course. You've made me reproach myself for having spoken. So carry on, and say what you like.

Athenian: The point I'd like to make, Cleinias, is the same one as I made a moment ago, that there might have been something to be said against our proposal, if it had not been proved by the facts to be workable. But as things are, an opponent of this law must try other tactics. We are not going to withdraw our recommendation that so far as possible, in education and everything else, the female sex should be on the same footing as the male. Consequently, we should approach the problem rather like this. Look: if women are not to follow absolutely the same way of life as men, then surely we shall have to work out some other programme for them?

Cleinias: Inevitably.

Athenian: Well, then, if we deny women this position of equality we're now demanding for them, which of the systems actually in force today shall we adopt instead? What about the practice of the Thracians and many other peoples, who make their women work on the land and mind sheep and cattle, so that they turn into serfs indistinguishable from slaves? Or what about the Athenians and all the other states in that part of the world? Well, here's how we Athenians deal with the problem: we 'concentrate our resources', as the expression is, under one roof and let our women take charge of our stores and the spinning and wool-working in general. Or we could adopt the Spartan system, Megillus, which is a compromise. You make your girls take part in athletics and you give them a compulsory education in the arts; when they grow up, though dispensed from working wool, they have to 'weave' themselves a pretty hard-working sort of life which is by no means despicable or useless: they have to be tolerably efficient at running the home and managing the house and bringing up children – but they don't undertake military service. This means that even if some extreme emergency ever led to a battle for their state and the lives of their children, they wouldn't have the expertise to use bows and arrows, like so many Amazons, nor could they join the men in deploying any other missile. They wouldn't be able to take up shield and spear and copy Athena, so as to terrify the enemy (if nothing more) by being seen in some kind of battle-array gallantly resisting the destruction threatening their native land. Living as they do, they'd never be anything like tough enough to imitate the Sarmatian women, who by comparison with such femininity would look like men. Anyone who wants to commend your Spartan legislators for this state of affairs, had better get on with it: I'm not going to change my mind. A legislator should go the whole way and not stick at half-measures; he mustn't just regulate the men and allow the women to live as they like and wallow in expensive luxury. That would be to give the state only half the loaf of prosperity instead of the whole of it.

How to discourage unnatural sexual intercourse
(8.838a) *Athenian*: I want to put the law on this subject on a firm footing, and at the moment I'm thinking of a method which is, in a sense, simplicity itself. But from another point of view, nothing could be harder.

Megillus: What are you getting at?

Athenian: We're aware, of course, that even nowadays most men, in spite of their general disregard for the law, are very effectively prevented from having relations with people they find attractive. And they don't refrain reluctantly, either – they're more than happy to.

Megillus: What circumstances have you in mind?

Athenian: When it's one's brother or sister whom one finds attractive. And the same law, unwritten though it is, is extremely effective in stopping a man sleeping – secretly or otherwise – with his son or daughter, or making any kind of amorous approach to them. Most people feel not the faintest desire for such intercourse.

Megillus: That's perfectly true.

Athenian: So the desire for this sort of pleasure is stifled by a few words?

Megillus: What words do you mean?

Athenian: The doctrine that 'these acts are absolutely unholy, an abomination in the sight of the gods, and at that nothing is more revolting.' We refrain from them because we never hear them spoken of in any other way. From the day of our birth each of us encounters a complete unanimity of opinion wherever we go; we find it not only in comedies but often in the high seriousness of tragedy too, when we see a Thyestes on the stage, or an Oedipus or a Macareus, the clandestine lover of his sister. We watch these characters dying promptly by their own hand as a penalty for their crimes.

Megillus: You're right in this, anyway, that when no one ventures to challenge the law, public opinion works wonders.

Athenian: So we were justified in what we said just now. When the legislator wants to tame one of the desires that dominate mankind so cruelly, it's easy for him to see his method of attack. He must try to make everyone – slave and free, women and children, and the entire state without any exception – believe that this common opinion has the backing of religion. He couldn't put his law on a securer foundation than that.

Megillus: Very true. But how on earth will it ever be possible to produce such spontaneous unanimity?

Athenian: I'm glad you've taken me up on the point. This is just what I was getting at when I said I knew of a way to put into effect this law of ours which permits the sexual act only for its natural purpose, procreation, and forbids not only homosexual relations, in which the human race is deliberately murdered, but also the sowing of seeds on rocks and stones where it will never take root and mature into a new individual and we should also have to keep away from any female 'soil' in which we'd be sorry to have the seed develop. At present however, the law is effective only against intercourse between parent and child, but if it can be put on a permanent footing and made to apply effectively, as it deserves to, in other cases as well, it'll do a power of good. The first point in its favour is that it is a natural law. But it also tends to check the raging fury of the sexual instinct that so often leads to adultery; discourages excesses in food and drink, and inspires men with affection for their own wives. And there are a great many other advantages to be gained, if only one could get this law established.

75. *A Roman philosopher advocates women's education. Rome, 1st cent. AD (Musonius Rufus 3, 4, 13a. G)*

The Stoic philosopher Musonius Rufus (c. AD 30-101) was a Roman of the equestrian order, who like Socrates sought to practise what he taught and who regarded philosophy as a guide to life. A pupil wrote up accounts of his discourses, including views of women that are 'more rational and more humane', and certainly more positive than those of his contemporary St Paul (cf. no. 441). Although most of the same ideas can be found in other pagan writers, they appear to have been expressed by Musonius with great clarity and force.[13]

The study of philosophy
(3) When he was asked whether women ought to study philosophy, he began to answer the question approximately as follows. Women have received from the gods the same ability to reason that men have. We men employ reasoning in our relations with others and so far as possible in everything we do, whether it is good or bad, or noble or shameful. Likewise women have the same senses as men, sight, hearing, smell, and all the rest. Likewise each has the same parts of the body, and neither sex has more than the other. In addition, it is not men alone who possess

eagerness and a natural inclination towards virtue, but women also. Women are pleased no less than men by noble and just deeds, and reject the opposite of such actions. Since that is so, why is it appropriate for men to seek out and examine how they might live well, that is, to practise philosophy, but not women? Is it fitting for men to be good, but not women?

Let us consider in detail the qualities that a woman who seeks to be good must possess, for it will be apparent that she could acquire each of these qualities from the practice of philosophy.

In the first place a woman must run her household and pick out what is beneficial for her home and take charge of the household slaves.

In these activities I claim that philosophy is particularly helpful, since each of these activities is an aspect of life, and philosophy is nothing other than the science of living, and the philosopher, as Socrates says, continually contemplates this, 'what good or evil has been done in his house'.[14] Next, a woman must be chaste, and capable of keeping herself free from illegal love affairs, and pure in respect to the other pleasures of indulgence, and not enjoy quarrels, not be extravagant, or preoccupied with her appearance.[15] Such is the behaviour of a chaste woman. There are still other requirements: she must control anger, and not be overcome by grief, and be stronger than every kind of emotion. That is what the philosopher's rationale entails, and the person who knows it and practises it seems to me to be perfectly controlled, whether it is a man or a woman. So much for the subject of self-control.

Now, wouldn't the woman who practises philosophy be just, and a blameless partner in life, and a good worker in common causes, and devoted in her responsibilities towards her husband and her children, and free in every way from greed or ambition? Who could be like this more than the woman who practises philosophy, so long as she truly is a philosopher, since she must inevitably think that doing wrong is worse than being wronged, because it is more disgraceful to do wrong,[16] and to think that being inferior is preferable to being ambitious, and in addition, to love her children more than her own life? What woman would be more just than someone who behaves like that? Surely it follows that an educated woman would be more courageous than an uneducated woman and a woman who practises philosophy than a woman who is self-taught, since neither fear of death nor any apprehension about suffering would lead her to endure a disgrace, nor would she be afraid of anyone because he was well-born or powerful or rich or indeed because he was – by Zeus – a tyrant. For it is enough that she has practised being high-minded and self-reliant and enduring, since she has nursed her children at her own breast,[17] and helps her husband with her own hands, and does without hesitation what some people would consider slave's work. Wouldn't such a woman be a great help to her husband, and an ornament to her family, and a good example to all who know her?

But, by Zeus, some people say that women who associate with philosophers are inevitably mainly headstrong and bold, if they give up their households and go about with men and practise giving speeches, and argue and attack premises, when they ought to be sitting at home spinning wool.[18] But I would not advise women who practise philosophy or men either to abandon their required work merely to hold discussions, but that they ought to undertake discussions for the sake of the work that they do. For just as there is no need for medical discussion, unless it pertains to human health, similarly there is no need for a philosopher to hold or teach logical argument, unless it pertains to the human soul. Above all we must examine the doctrine that we think women who practise philosophy should follow, to determine if the study that shows restraint to be the greatest good makes them bold, and if the study that leads to the deportment makes them live more carelessly, and if the study that reveals that the worst evil is self-indulgence does not teach self-control, and if the study that establishes household management as a virtue does not encourage them to manage their households. And the study of philosophy encourages women to be happy and to work with their own hands.

Education
(4) When he was asked if sons and daughters should be given the same education, he said that in the case of horses and dogs trainers of horses and of dogs make no distinction between male and female in their training.[19]

Female dogs are trained to hunt just like male dogs, and if you expect female horses to do a horse's job effectively, you must see that they have the same training as the male horses.

In the case of human beings it would seem that males should have something in their education and upbringing distinctive in contrast to the females, as if a man and a woman were not required to have the same virtues, or as if they could aspire to the same virtues through different rather than similar educations.

But it is easy to apprehend that there are not different sets of virtues for men and women. First, men and women both need to be sensible; what need could there be for a foolish man or woman? Second, both need to live just lives. An unjust man could not be a good citizen, and a woman could not run her household well, if she did not run it justly, since if she were unjust she would do wrong to her husband, as they say Eriphyle did to hers.[20] Third, a wife ought to be chaste, and so should a husband, for the laws punish both parties in cases of adultery.[21] Over-indulgence in food and drink and similar problems, excesses that bring disgrace to those who indulge in them, prove that moderation is essential for every human being, whether male or female, for it is only through moderation that we can avoid excess.

You might argue that courage is needed only by men. But that is not true. The best sort of woman must be manly and cleanse herself of cowardice, so that she will not be overcome by suffering or by fear.

If she cannot, how can she be chaste, if someone can compel her to endure disgrace by threatening her or torturing her? Women must be courageous, if (by Zeus) they are not to be inferior to hens and other female birds, who fight beasts much larger than themselves in order to defend their nestlings. How can it be that women do not need courage? That they are capable of taking up weapons, we know from the race of the Amazons who fought many nations in battle. If other women are deficient in this regard, the cause is lack of practice rather than lack of natural inclination ...

Well then, suppose someone says, 'Do you think that men ought to learn spinning like women and that women ought to practise gymnastics like men?' No, that is not what I suggest. I say that because in the case of the human race, the males are naturally stronger, and the women weaker, appropriate work ought to be assigned to each, and the heavier tasks be given to the stronger, and the lighter to the weaker. For this reason, spinning is more appropriate work for women than for men, and household management.

Gymnastics are more appropriate for men than for women, and outdoor work likewise.[22] None the less, some men might appropriately undertake some of the lighter work and work thought more appropriate to women, when the conditions of their body or necessity or time demand it. For all human work is a common responsibility for men and women, and nothing is necessarily prescribed for one sex or the other. Some tasks are more appropriate for one nature, others for the other. For that reason some jobs are called men's work, and others women's. As for matters that pertain to virtue, you would be justified in saying that these are equally the property of both, if we say that both possess no virtues different from the other.

It is reasonable, then, for me to think that women ought to be educated similarly to men in respect of virtue, and they must be taught starting when they are children, that this is good, and that bad, and that they are the same for both, and that this is beneficial and that harmful, and that one must do this, and not that. From these lessons reasoning is developed in both girls and boys, and there is no distinction between them. Then they must be told to avoid all base action. When these qualities have been developed both men and women will inevitably be sensible, and the well-educated person, whether male or female, must be able to endure hardship, accustomed not to fear death, and accustomed not to be humbled by any disaster, for this is how one can become manly.[23] ... If a man knows something about a particular skill, and a woman doesn't, or if the reverse is true, this shows that there is no difference in their education. Only about all the important things do not let one know and the other not, but let them both know the same. If someone asks me, which doctrine requires such an education, I would answer him that without philosophy no man and no woman either can be well educated. I do not mean to say that women need to have clarity with or facility in argument, because they will use philosophy as women use it. But I do not recommend these skills particularly in men. My point is that women ought to be good and noble in their characters, and that philosophy is nothing other than the training for that nobility.

Marriage
(13a) He said that a husband and wife come together in order to lead their lives in common and to produce children, and that they should consider all their property to be common, and nothing private, not even their bodies. For the birth of a human being that such a union produces is a significant event, but it is not sufficient for the husband, because it could have come about without marriage, from some other conjunction, as in the case of animals. In marriage there must be complete companionship and concern for each other on the part of both husband and wife, in health and in sickness and at all times, because they entered upon the marriage for this reason as well as to produce offspring. When such caring for one another is perfect, and the married couple provide it for one another, and each strives to outdo the other, then this is marriage as it ought to be and deserving of emulation, since it is a noble union.[24] But when one partner looks to his own interests alone and neglects the other's, or (by Zeus) the other is so minded that he lives in the same house, but keeps his mind on what is outside it, and does not wish to pull together with his partner or to cooperate, then inevitably the union is destroyed, and although they live together their common interests fare badly, and either they finally get divorced from one another or they continue on in an existence that is worse than loneliness.

IV. Legal Status in the Greek World

'The law expressly forbids children and women ...'

Crete
'She is to keep her property'

76. *Laws relating to women. Gortyn in Crete, c. 450 BC (excerpts from the Gortyn Law Code, Inscr. Creticae 4.72, cols. ii.3-27, ii.45-iv.54, v.1-9. vi.31-46, vi.56-vii.2, vii.15-viii.19, xi.18-19. G)*[1]

The various laws recorded on this long and beautifully incised inscription differ in many respects from Athenian practice (cf. nos. 80 and 81). In Gortyn women appear to have somewhat more independence: instead of a dowry, daughters have a specific portion of the inheritance equal to half of that of a son; under certain (perhaps only remotely possible) circumstances even an heiress might be able to choose her husband; a women can keep her own property (rather than having her dowry returned to her father or *kyrios*) and half of the cloth she has woven during the course of the marriage.

Sexual offences
(ii.3) If a man rapes a free person, male or female, he shall pay 100 staters, and if [the victim] is from the house of an *apetairos*,[2] 10 staters; and if a slave rapes a free person, male or female, he shall pay double. If a free man rapes a serf, male or female, he shall pay 5 drachmas. If a male serf rapes a serf, male or female, he shall pay 5 staters.

If a person deflowers a female household serf, he shall pay 2 staters. If she has already been deflowered, 1 obol if in day-time, 2 obols if at night. The female slave's oath takes precedence.[3]

If anyone makes an attempt to rape a free woman under the guardianship of a relative, he shall pay 10 staters, if a witness testifies.

If someone is taken in adultery with a free woman in her father's house, or her brother's or her husband's, he is to pay 100 staters; if in another man's house, 50 staters; if with the wife of an *apetairos*, 10 staters. But if a slave is taken in adultery with a free woman, he must pay double. If a slave is taken in adultery with a slave, 5 staters.

Disposition of property in divorce
(ii.45) If a husband and wife divorce, she is to keep her property, whatever she brought to the marriage, and one-half the produce (if there is any) from her own property, and half of whatever she has woven within the house; also she is to have 5 staters if her husband is the cause of the divorce. If the husband swears that he is not the cause of the divorce, the judge is to take an oath and decide. If the wife carries away anything else belonging to the husband, she must pay five staters and whatever she carries away from him, and whatever she has stolen she must return to him. About what she denies [having taken], the judge is to order that she must swear by Artemis before the statue of [Artemis] Archeress in the Amyclean temple. If anyone takes anything from her after she has made her denial, he is to pay 5 staters and return the thing itself. If a stranger helps her to carry anything away, he must pay 10 staters and double the amount of whatever the judge swears that he helped her to take away.

Widowhood
(iii.17) If a man dies and leaves children behind, if the wife wishes, she may marry, keeping her own property and whatever her husband gave her according to an agreement written in the presence of three adult free witnesses. If she should take anything away that belongs to her children, that is grounds for a trial. If the husband leaves her without issue, she is to have her own property and half of whatever she has woven within the house, and she is to get her portion of the produce in the house along with the lawful heirs, and whatever her husband may have given her according to written agreement. But if she should take away anything else, it is grounds for a trial.

If a woman dies without issue the husband is to give her property back to her lawful heirs and half of what she has woven within and half of the produce if it comes from her property. If the husband or wife wishes to pay for its transport, it is to be in clothing or twelve staters or something worth 12 staters, but not more.

If a female serf is separated from a male serf while he is alive or if he dies, she is to keep what she has. If she takes anything else away, it is grounds for a trial.

Provisions for children in case of death or divorce
(iii.45) If a wife who is separated from her husband should bear a child, it is to be brought to the husband in his house in the presence of three witnesses. If he does not receive it, it is up to the mother to raise or expose the child. The oath of relatives and witnesses is to have preference, if they brought it.

If a female serf should bear a child while separated [from her husband], she is to bring it to the master of the man who married her, in the presence of two witnesses. If he does not receive the child, it is to belong to the master of the female serf. But if she marries the same man again before the end of the year, the child shall belong to the master of the male serf. The oaths of the person who brought the child and of the witnesses shall have preference.

If a divorced woman should expose her child before presenting it according to the law, she shall pay 50 staters for a free child, and 5 for a slave, if she is convicted. If the man to whom she brings the child has no house, or she does not see him, she shall not pay a penalty if she exposes the child.

If a female serf who is not married conceives and bears a child, the child shall belong to the master of her father. If the father is not alive then to the masters of her brothers.

The father has power over the children and division of property, and the mother over her own possessions. So long as [the father and mother] are alive, the property is not to be divided. But if one of them is fined, the person who is fined shall have his share reduced proportionately according to the law.

If a father dies, the city dwellings and whatever is inside the houses in which a serf who lives in the country does not reside, and the cattle which do not belong to a serf, shall belong to the sons. The other possessions shall be divided fairly, and the sons shall each get two parts, however many they are, and the daughters each get one part, however many they are.

The mother's property shall also be divided if she dies, in the same way as prescribed for the father's. But if there is no property other than the house, the daughters shall receive their share as prescribed. If the father during his lifetime should give to a married daughter, let him give her a share as prescribed, but not more. The daughter to whom he gave or promised her share shall have it, but no additional possessions from her father's property.

(v.1) If any woman does not have property either from a gift by her father or brother or from a pledge or from an inheritance given when the Aithalian clan consisting of Cyllus and his colleagues [were in power], these women are to have a portion, but it will not be lawful to take away gifts given previously.

(vi.31) If a mother dies leaving children, the father has power over the mother's estate, but he should not sell or mortgage it, unless the children are of age and give their consent. If he marries another wife, the children are to have power over their mother's estate.

Determination of social status

(vi.56) If a slave goes to a free woman and marries her, the children shall be free. If a free woman goes to a slave, the children shall be slaves.

Heiresses[4]

(vii.15) The heiress is to marry the oldest of her father's living brothers. If her father has no living brothers but there are sons of the brothers, she is to marry the eldest brother's son. If there are more heiresses and sons of brothers, the [additional heiress] is to marry the next son after the son of the eldest. The groom-elect is to have one heiress, and not more.

If the heiress is too young to marry, she is to have the house, if there is one, and the groom-elect is to have half of the revenue from everything.

If he does not wish to marry her as prescribed by law, the heiress is to take all the property and marry the next one in succession, if there is one. If there is no one, she may marry whomever she wishes of those who ask her from the same phratry.[5] If the heiress is of age and does not wish to marry the intended bridegroom, or the intended groom is too young and the heiress is unwilling to wait, she is to have the house, if there is one in the city, and whatever is in the house, and taking half of the remaining property she is to marry another of those from the phratry who ask her, but she is to give a share of the property to the groom [whom she rejected].

If there are no kinsmen as defined for the heiress, she is to take all the property and marry from the phratry whomever she wishes.

If no one from the phratry wishes to marry her, her relations should announce to the tribe 'Does anyone want to marry her?' If someone wants to, it should be within thirty days of the announcement. If not, she is free to marry another man, whomever she can.

Restrictions concerning adoption

(xi.18) A woman is not to adopt [a child] nor a man under age.

Athens
'He should provide a dowry ...'

77. *Funeral law. Ioulis on Keos, late 5th cent. BC (Ditt. Syll. 1218. G)*

Throughout Greece limits were set by law on the expense, luxury and amount of mourning at funerals. A practical consequence of such legislation is that women's opportunities for gathering and for expressing themselves were restricted. This inscription comes from an island not far from Athens, and is thought to be a copy of an earlier law of the Athenian legislator Solon.[6]

These are the laws concerning the dead: bury the dead person as follows: in three white cloths – a spread, a shroud, and a coverlet – or in fewer, not worth more than 300 drachmas.[7] Carry out [the body] on a wedge-footed bed and do not cover the bier with cloths. Bring not more than 3 choes of wine to the tomb and not more than one chous of olive oil, and bring back the empty jars. Carry the shrouded corpse in silence all the way to the tomb. Perform the preliminary sacrifice according to ancestral customs. Bring the bed and the covers back from the tomb inside the house.

On the next day cleanse the house first with sea water, and then cleanse all the rooms with hyssop. When it has been thoroughly cleansed, the house is to be free from pollution; and sacrifices should be made on the hearth.

The women who come to mourn at the funeral are not to leave the tomb before the men.[8] There is to be no mourning for the dead person on the thirtieth day. Do not put a wine-cup beneath the bed, do not pour out the water, and do not bring the sweepings to the tomb.[9]

In the event that a person dies, when he is carried out, no women should go to the house other than those polluted [by the death]. Those polluted are the mother and wife and sisters and daughters, and in addition to these not more than five women, the daughters' children and cousins; no one else. The polluted when washed with water poured out [from jugs] are free from pollution. (*The next 2 lines are damaged.*)

This law has been ratified by the council and the people. On the third day those who mourn on the anniversary of the death are to be free from pollution, but they are not to enter a temple, and the house is to be free from pollution until they come back from the tomb.

78. *The banker Pasion's will. Athens, 370-60 BC (Apollodorus (= 'Demosthenes'), Against Stephanus 45.29 G)*

Because the terms of the will are so favourable to Pasion's freedman Phormion, who would serve as Archippe's *kyrios* and through her enjoy the income from the substantial property left to her by Pasion, this document was alleged to be a forgery, and subject of a court case. That Pasion married her to Phormion also suggests that she probably was not an Athenian citizen, otherwise an Athenian husband might have been chosen for her. As a resident alien, she was technically Pasion's concubine (*pallake*) rather than his wife.[10]

I, Pasion of Acharnae, have made the following provisions in my will. I leave my wife[11] Archippe to Phormion, and I give Archippe as dowry a talent from my property in Peparethus [off Euboea] and another talent from my property here [in Athens], a tenement house worth 100 minae, the maidservants and gold jewellery, and everything else in the house, all these I leave to Archippe.[12]

79. *Aristotle's will. Athens, 4th cent. BC (Diogenes Laertius 5.11-16, 3rd cent. AD. G)*

This will is recorded by Diogenes along with the wills of several members of his School; the provisions for his substantial estate reflect Aristotle's notions of women's limitations (cf. no. 72), but at the same time show his affection for them and concern for their welfare. In the will Aristotle himself is the speaker; he makes provisions for his concubine Herpyllis and their son Nicomachus, but directs that the bones of his wife Pythias be moved to his grave. In several respects the will seems characteristic of Aristotle's Athenian contemporaries: words for death are avoided, the names of respectable females are avoided, childlessness is regarded as a misfortune, husband and wife are buried together,[13] and due honour is given to the gods.

All will be well. But if something happens, Aristotle has made the following dispositions. Antipater is to be executor in all respects and in general. (12) But until Nicanor [Aristotle's adopted son] takes over, Aristomenes, Timarchus, Hipparchus, Dioteles, and Theophrastus (if he is willing and it is possible for him) are to take care of the children and Herpyllis and their inheritance.

Provisions for his children

When my daughter is grown up, she should be given to Nicanor in marriage. If anything happens to my daughter (may this not happen; it shall not be) before she marries, or after she marries, before she has children, Nicanor is to be *kyrios* for my child and is to see to everything else in a manner worthy both of himself and of us. Nicanor is to care for my daughter and for my son Nicomachus,[14] as he judges best for them, as if he were both their father and their brother. If anything should happen to Nicanor (may it not happen) before he marries my daughter, or before they have children, whatever arrangements he has made shall apply. (13) If [in the case of Nicanor's death] Theophrastus wishes to live with my daughter, the same arrangements shall apply as for Nicanor. If he does not so desire, the executors in consultation with Antipater shall see to the affairs of my daughter and my son as they judge best.

Provisions for his concubine Herpyllis

The executors and Nicander, keeping me in mind and Herpyllis, who has been good to me, should take care also of the other matters [concerning her], and if she wishes to marry, to give her to someone worthy of me. In addition to the other gifts that she has received previously they should give her a talent of silver, from the estate, and three female slaves, if she wishes, and the female slave that she has at present, and the slave Pyrrhaeus. (14) And if she wishes to live in Chalcis, she is to have the guest-cottage by the garden. If she wishes to live at Stagira, she is to have my father's house. Whichever of the two she chooses, the executors are to equip it with furniture that seems to them suitable and that Herpyllis approves.

Provisions for slaves

Nicanor shall see that the slave Myrmex shall be returned to his family in a manner worthy of me with the property that we got from him. Ambracis also is to be freed, and when my daughter marries, she shall be given 500 drachmas and the female slave she has at present. Thale shall receive in addition to the female slave she now has and has bought 2,000 drachmas and a female slave. (15) And for Simo, aside from the money previously given him for another slave, either a slave shall be bought or money given [for the purchase]. When my daughter is married, Tacho shall be freed, and also Philo, and Olympios, and his son. The executors are not to sell any of the slaves who looked after me, but to employ them. When they reach the appropriate age, they should set them free as they deserve.

Provisions for commemorative statues
The executors are to see that the images Gryllion has been commissioned to make are set up when they are finished: these are of Nicanor and of Proxenus, which I had meant to have commissioned, and of Nicanor's mother and the image of Arimnestos that has been completed, as a memorial to him, since he died childless. (16) They should dedicate my mother's statue of Demeter at Nemea, or wherever they think best. Wherever they put my tomb, they should collect and place the bones of Pythias, as she herself requested. Because Nicanor returned safely, he should put up stone statues 4 cubits high in Stagira to Zeus the Preserver and Athena the Preserver, in fulfilment of my vow.

Nos. 80 and 81 are citations of the law that were added in antiquity to the texts of orations by later editors from collections of Athenian laws and decrees. Other such laws are cited in no. 89.[15]

80. *Provisions for female children. Athens, 4th cent. BC ('Demosthenes', Or. 43, Against Macartatus 51, 54. G)*

The dowry system ensured that daughters would inherit some portion of their father's estate, but if there were no sons, laws of succession ensured that so far as possible the money would stay in the father's family through marriage.

Succession
(51) If a man dies intestate and leaves female children, the estate goes with them; if not, his male heirs inherit his property, as follows:[16] if he has brothers from the same father, and if there are legitimate sons of the brothers, they are to inherit the father's share.[17] But if there are no brothers or sons of brothers, their descendants shall inherit as follows. The males shall have precedence and the descendants of the males, if they have any, even though their relationship be more remote. But if there are on the father's side no relations closer than the children of cousins, the male relatives on the mother's side shall inherit according to the same principles. If there are no relatives on either side within those limits, then the next of kin of the father shall inherit. But no illegitimate

son or daughter is to have the right of inheritance either to religious or
civic privileges, since the time of Euclides' archonship [403 BC].

Provisions for dowries
(54) The law about heiresses of the Thetes class:[18] if the next of kin does
not wish to marry her, he should give her in marriage: if he is of the class
of Pentacosiomedimni, he should provide a dowry of 500 drachmas in
addition to what she already has; if he is a Knight, 300 drachmas; if he is
of the class of Zeugitae, 150 drachmas. If there is more than one kinsman
in the same degree of relationship, each should contribute a share to the
heiress. If there is more than one heiress, it is not necessary for any male
relative to provide a dowry for more than one, but the next closest male
relative should provide it, or marry her himself. If the male relative does
not marry her or does not provide a dowry, the archon should compel him
to marry her or to provide a dowry. If the archon cannot get him to
comply, he must consecrate 1,000 drachmas to Hera. Anyone who wishes
to may denounce a man who does not comply [with these regulations] to
the archon.

81. *Married heiresses. Athens, 4th cent. BC (Isaeus 3.64. G)*

The law states that women who have been given in marriage by their
fathers and who have been living with their husbands (and who could
make better provision for them than a father?), that even a woman thus
given in marriage, if her father dies without leaving legitimate sons,
becomes subject to the legal power of their next of kin; and many men
who have already been living with their wives have been deprived of them
[in this manner].[19]

82. *Widow of Diodotus. Athens, c. 400 BC (Lysias, Against Diogeiton 32.11-18. G)*

The widow (whose name is not mentioned) of Diodotus, a rich merchant who
was killed in battle in 409 BC, has studied the accounts of her husband's
estate and accuses her *kyrios* Diogeiton (who was also her father and her
husband's brother) of mishandling the assets and cheating her sons of property that rightfully belonged to them. Her son-in-law represents her in court,
describing how she asked him to summon her male relatives together so she
could confront her brother-in-law in their presence.

Finally the boys' mother begged me to hold a meeting with her father and
her friends. She said that although she had never spoken in the presence
of men before, the severity of her misfortunes compelled her to speak to
us about her troubles in detail ...
At first Diogeiton refused to come, but finally he was compelled to by

his friends. When the meeting was held, the widow asked Diogeiton how he had the heart to have such an attitude towards his brother's children: 'You are their father's brother, and my father, and their uncle and grandfather. Even if you aren't ashamed of what men will think, you ought to fear the gods. When my husband went off to war he gave you a deposit of five talents – I am willing to swear that this is true on the lives of my sons and my younger children in any temple that you select. I am not so pathetic, and I do not think money so important that I would choose to lose my own life after swearing a false oath on my children's lives, nor would I wish unjustly to steal my father's property.'

In addition she proved that he had taken 7 talents and 400 drachmas from marine loans, and produced the records of these transactions. For she showed that when Diogeiton moved away from the house at Collytus to Phaedrus'[20] house her sons had happened upon the accounts which had been mislaid and brought them to her. She revealed that he had taken 100 minae that had been loaned for interest on a mortgage, and that Diogeiton had also taken 2,000 drachmas and valuable furniture, and that grain came to them every year from the Chersonese [from that investment].

'Then you dared to say, even though you had all that money, that their father [Diodotus] had left these children 2,000 drachmas and 30 staters – the sum that was left to me and that I gave you when my husband died. And you thought it acceptable to turn your daughter's sons out of their own house in worn clothes, without shoes, with no attendant, and with no bed-clothes, and without the furniture that their father left them, and without the money he had deposited with you. Meanwhile you are bringing up the children you have had by my step-mother in great luxury. You are justified in doing that, but you have wronged my children, because you threw them out of their house and wanted to make them poor instead of prosperous. And on account of these deeds you are not afraid of the gods, nor are you ashamed that I am aware of what you have done, nor do you honour your brother's memory, but you think us all less important than money.'

Then, gentlemen of the jury, after hearing the many terrible accusations the widow had made, we were struck by what this man had done and by her speech. We saw what her sons had suffered, and we thought of their dead father, and what an unworthy guardian he had left for his estate. We reflected how hard it was to find someone to trust with financial matters. As a result, gentlemen of the jury, none of those present could say a word, but we wept just as much as the widow and her children, and went away in silence.

83. *Property. Athens, 4th cent.* BC *(Isaeus 10.10. G)*

A child is not permitted to make a will. For the law expressly forbids children and women from being able to make a contract [about anything worth] more than a bushel of barley.[21]

84. *Maintenance. Athens, 4th cent.* BC *(Isaeus 3.39. G)*

Even men who give their female relatives as concubines make agreements about what will be given to them as concubines.

85. *Payment of a dowry. Athens, 4th cent.* BC *(IG II².2679. G)*

Renewal of a document in which Pythodorus had assigned a dowry of 4,000 drachmas to his daughter.

In the year Euxenippus was archon;[22] boundary of the lands and houses, securities for the dowry of Xenariste daughter of Pythodorus of Gargettus; this is half, with interest accrued [given to] her, of the 4,000 drachmas[?], until the year Leostratus was archon.[23]

86. *Proof of marriage. Athens, 4th cent.* BC *(Isaeus 8.18- 20. G)*

Proof of legal marriage, offered by the son of the woman who is making claims to her father Ciron's estate. Because she is a respectable woman (unlike Neaera, no. 90), her name is not mentioned.[24]

Therefore it ought to be clear from what I have shown that not only is our mother the legitimate daughter of Ciron, but also it should be clear from this what our father has done for us and the attitude of the wives of his demesmen towards [our mother]. When our father took her in marriage, he held a wedding-feast and summoned three of his friends in addition to his relatives; he also gave a marriage banquet to the phratry according to their established customs. After this the wives of his demesmen also chose our mother to preside at the Thesmophoria[25] along with the wife of Diocles of the deme Pithus and to conduct the ritual together with her. In addition to this, when we were born, our father introduced us to the phratry, and took an oath according to the established customs that he was introducing children born from an Athenian citizen and a lawfully wedded wife. None of the members of the phratry objected or doubted that this was the truth, although there were many of them and they investigated such matters carefully.

Surely you cannot believe that if our mother was the sort of woman that our opponents allege our father would have given a wedding-feast or a marriage banquet; rather, he would have concealed the whole affair, and the wives of other demesmen would not have chosen her to conduct the Thesmophoria with Diocles' wife and put her in charge of the sacred objects. No, they would have turned instead to one of the other wives for these matters, and they would not have admitted us into the phratry; they would have accused our father and refuted his claims, if it had not been completely agreed that our mother was the legitimate daughter of Ciron. But there is no doubt whatever because it was evident and well known by many people. Now summon witnesses that I am telling the truth about this.

87. *A mistress's scheme. Athens, 4th cent. BC (Isaeus 6.17-24. G)*

The sons of Euctemon's mistress, Alce, claim that they were adopted by Euctemon and thus are heirs to his estate. Since his legitimate sons are all dead, his sons-in-law, their successors in the line of inheritance in their capacity as *kyrioi* of Euctemon's daughters, hired Isaeus to protect their interests, alleging that Alce's sons gutted Euctemon's estate.

(17) ... It will perhaps be unpleasant, gentlemen, for [Euctemon's son-in-law] Phanostratus to set forth Euctemon's misfortunes in public; but it will be necessary to say at least something about them, so that you can know the truth and cast your ballot more easily.

(18) Euctemon lived for 96 years, and seemed to be happy for most of that time; he had a considerable estate and children and a wife, and he was reasonably fortunate in other respects as well.[26] But in his old age a considerable misfortune occurred, which wrecked his entire household and destroyed his fortune and brought him into contention with his family.

(19) I shall show as briefly as I can how and why this happened. Euctemon had a freedwoman, gentlemen, who ran a tenement-house for him in the Piraeus and kept prostitutes. One of the prostitutes she acquired was called Alce; I believe many of you know the woman. This Alce, after she had been bought, remained in the house for many years, but when she became old she left the house; (20) while she was living in the house she had relations with a freedman named Dion, who she said is the father of these men [who claim to have been adopted by Euctemon]. Dion raised them as his own children. But some time later Dion incurred a fine and to protect himself withdrew to Sicyon.

This Alce is the person that Euctemon employed to look after his tenement-house in Ceramicus, the one near the postern gate, where wine is sold. (21) While she was living there, gentlemen, she was the cause of many troubles. Euctemon went there to collect the rent and often spent considerable time in the tenement-house, and sometimes had meals with that person, abandoning his wife and children and the house in which he lived. When his wife and sons complained about it, even so he did not stop, but he ended up spending all of his time there, and was so reduced either by drugs or by disease or by some other cause, that he was persuaded by Alce to introduce the elder of her two sons into his phratry under his own name.

(22) When his son Philoctemon did not consent and the phratry did not accept him, and the sacrificial victim was removed from the altar, Euctemon became angry at his son and wishing to insult him announced his engagement to the sister of Democrates of Aphidna, so as to recognise children born to her and bring them into the household, if he did not agree to have Alce's son introduced.

(23) But his relatives realised that he could not have any more children at his age, but that they would be produced by some other means, and that these additional heirs would cause the estate to be divided up even more, and persuaded Philoctemon to let him introduce Alce's son to the phratry on the terms that Euctemon wanted, giving him one farm. (24) And Philoctemon, although ashamed at his father's foolishness, was incapable of dealing with the present problem, and did not oppose it. After these conditions were agreed on, and the child was introduced on these terms, Euctemon broke his engagement to Democrates' sister, and thus showed that he did not intend to marry to have children, but in order to have Alce's son introduced to the phratry.

> In each of the following three cases only one side's argument survives and the verdict is unknown.

88. *A husband's defence. Athens, c. 400 BC (Lysias, On the Murder of Eratosthenes 6-33, 47-50. Tr. K. Freeman. G)*

> Euphiletus, a husband who murdered his wife's lover, Eratosthenes, speaks in his own defence.

(6) Members of the jury, when I decided to marry and had brought a wife home, at first my attitude towards her was this: I did not wish to annoy her, but neither was she to have too much of her own way. I watched her as well as I could, and kept an eye on her as was proper. But later, after my child had been born, I came to trust her, and I handed all my possessions over to her, believing that this was the greatest possible proof of affection.

(7) Well, members of the jury, in the beginning she was the best of women. She was a clever housewife, economical and exact in her management of everything. But then my mother died; and her death has proved to be the source of all my troubles, because it was when my wife went to the funeral that this man Eratosthenes saw her; and as time went on, he was able to seduce her. He kept a look-out for our maid who

goes to market; and approaching her with his suggestions, he succeeded in corrupting her mistress.

(9) Now first of all, gentlemen, I must explain that I have a small house which is divided into two – the men's quarters and the women's – each having the same space, the women upstairs and the men downstairs. After the birth of my child, his mother nursed him; but I did not want her to run the risk of going downstairs every time she had to give him a bath, so I myself took over the upper storey, and let the women have the ground floor. And so it came about that by this time it was quite customary for my wife often to go downstairs and sleep with the child, so that she could give him the breast and stop him from crying.

This went on for a long while, and I had not the slightest suspicion. On the contrary, I was in such a fool's paradise that I believed my wife to be the chastest woman in all the city.

(11) Time passed, gentlemen. One day, when I had come home unexpectedly from the country, after dinner, the child began crying and complaining. Actually it was the maid who was pinching him on purpose to make him behave so because – as I found out later – this man was in the house. Well, I told my wife to go and feed the child, to stop his crying. But at first she refused, pretending that she was glad to see me back after my long absence. At last I began to get annoyed, and I insisted on her going.

'Oh, yes!' she said. 'To leave you alone with the maid up here! You mauled her about before, when you were drunk!'

(13) I laughed. She got up, went out, closed the door – pretending that it was a joke – and locked it. As for me, I thought no harm of all this, and I had not the slightest suspicion. I went to sleep, glad to do so after my journey from the country.

(14) Towards morning, she returned and unlocked the door. I asked her why the doors had been creaking during the night. She explained that the lamp beside the baby had gone out, and that she had then gone to get a light from the neighbours.

I said no more. I thought it really was so. But it did seem to me, members of the jury, that she had done up her face with cosmetics, in spite of the fact that her brother had died only a month before. Still, even so, I said nothing about it. I just went off, without a word.

(15) After this, members of the jury, an interval elapsed, during which my injuries had progressed, leaving me far behind. Then, one day, I was approached by an old hag. She had been sent by a woman – Eratosthenes' previous mistress, as I found out later. This woman, furious because he no longer came to see her as before, had been on the look-out until she had discovered the reason. The old crone, therefore, had come and was lying in wait for me near my house.

'Euphiletus,' she said, 'please don't think that my approaching you is in any way due to a wish to interfere. The fact is, the man who is wronging you and your wife is an enemy of ours. Now if you catch the woman who does your shopping and works for you, and put her through an examination, you will discover all. The culprit,' she added, 'is Eratosthenes from Oea. Your wife is not the only one he has seduced – there are plenty of others. It's his profession.'

With these words, members of the jury, she went off. At once I was overwhelmed. Everything rushed into my mind, and I was filled with suspicion. I reflected how I had been locked into the bedroom. I remembered how on that night the middle and outer doors had creaked, a thing that had never happened before; and how I had had the idea that my wife's face was rouged. All these things rushed into my mind, and I was filled with suspicion.

(18) I went back home, and told the servant to come with me to market. I took her instead to the house of one of my friends; and there I informed her that I had discovered all that was going on in my house.

'As for you,' I said, 'two courses are open to you: either to be flogged and sent to the tread-mill, and never be released from a life of utter misery; or to confess the whole truth and suffer no punishment, but win pardon from me for your wrongdoing. Tell me no lies. Speak the whole truth.'

(19) At first she tried denial, and told me that I could do as I pleased – she knew nothing. But when I named Eratosthenes to her face, and said that he was the man who had been visiting my wife, she was dumbfounded, thinking that I had found out everything exactly. And then at last, falling at my feet and exacting a promise from me that no harm should be done to her, she denounced the villain. She described how he had first approached her after the funeral, and then how in the end she had passed the message on, and in course of time my wife had been overpersuaded. She explained the way in which he had contrived to get into the house, and how when I was in the country my wife had gone to a religious service with this man's mother, and everything else that had happened. She recounted it all exactly.

(21) When she had told all, I said: 'See to it that nobody gets to know of this; otherwise the promise I made you will not hold good. And furthermore, I expect you to show me this actually happening. I have no use for words. I want the fact to be exhibited, if it really is so.'

She agreed to do this.

Four or five days then elapsed, as I shall prove to you by important evidence. But before I do so, I wish to narrate the events of the last day.

(23) I had a friend and relative named Sostratus. He was coming home from the country after sunset when I met him. I knew that as he had got back so late, he would not find any of his own people at home; so I asked him to dine with me. We went home to my place, and going upstairs to the upper storey, we had dinner there. When he felt restored, he went off; and I went to bed.

Then, members of the jury, Eratosthenes made his entry; and the maid wakened me and told me that he was in the house.

I told her to watch the door; and going downstairs, I slipped out noiselessly.

I went to the houses of one man after another. Some I found at home; others, I was told, were out of town. So collecting as many as I could of those who were there, I went back. We procured torches from the shop near by, and entered my house. The door had been left open by arrangement with the maid.

We forced the bedroom door. The first of us to enter saw him still lying beside my wife. Those who followed saw him standing naked on the bed. I knocked him down, members of the jury, with one blow. I then twisted his hands behind his back and tied them. And then I asked him why he was committing this crime against me, of breaking into my house.

He answered that he admitted his guilt; but he begged and besought me not to kill him – to accept a money-payment instead. But I replied: 'It is not I who shall be killing you, but the law of the state, which you, in transgressing, have valued less highly than your own pleasure. You have preferred to commit this great crime against my wife and my children, rather than to obey the law and be of decent behaviour.'

(27) Thus, members of the jury, this man met the fate which the laws prescribe for wrongdoers of his kind.[27]

Eratosthenes was not seized in the street and carried off, nor had he taken refuge at the altar, as the prosecution alleges. The facts do not admit of it: he was struck in the bedroom, he fell at once, and I bound his hands behind his back. There were so many present that he could not possibly escape through their midst, since he had neither steel nor wood nor any other weapon with which he could have defended himself against all those who had entered the room.

(28) No, members of the jury: you know as well as I do how wrongdoers will not admit that their adversaries are speaking the truth, and attempt by lies and trickery of other kinds to excite the anger of the hearers against those whose acts are in accordance with Justice.

To the Clerk of the Court: Read the law.

The Law of Solon is read, that an adulterer may be put to death by the man who catches him.

(29) He made no denial, members of the jury. He admitted his guilt, and begged and implored that he should not be put to death, offering to pay compensation. But I would not accept his estimate. I preferred to accord a higher authority to the law of the state, and I took that satisfaction which you, because you thought it the most just, have decreed for those who commit such offences. Witnesses to the preceding, kindly step up.

The witnesses come to the front of the court, and the Clerk reads their depositions. When the Clerk has finished reading, and the witnesses have agreed that the depositions are correct, the defendant again addresses the Clerk:

Now please read this further law from the pillar of the Court of the Areopagus.

The Clerk reads another version of Solon's law, as recorded on the pillar of the Areopagus Court.

You hear, members of the jury, how it is expressly decreed by the Court of the Areopagus itself, which both traditionally and in your own day has been granted the right to try cases of murder, that no person shall be found guilty of murder who catches an adulterer with his wife and inflicts this punishment. (31) The law-giver was so strongly convinced of the justice of these provisions in the case of married women that he applied them also to concubines, who are of less importance. Yet obviously, if he had known of any greater punishment than this for cases where married women are concerned, he would have provided it. But in fact, as it was impossible for him to invent any more severe penalty for corruption of wives, he decided to provide the same punishment as in the case of concubines.

To the Clerk of the Court: Please read me this law also.

The Clerk reads out further clauses from Solon's laws on rape.

(32) You hear, members of the jury, how the law-giver ordains that if anyone debauch by force a free man or boy, the fine shall be double that decreed in the case of a slave. If anyone debauch a woman – in which case it is *permitted* to kill him – he shall be liable to the same fine. Thus, members of the jury, the law-giver considered violators deserving of a lesser penalty than seducers: for the latter he provided the death penalty; for the former, the doubled fine. His idea was that those who use force are loathed by the persons violated, whereas those who have got their way by persuasion corrupt women's minds, in such a way as to make other men's wives more attached to themselves than to their husbands, so that the whole house is in their power, and it is uncertain who is the children's father, the husband or the lover ...

(47) It is my belief, members of the jury, that this punishment was inflicted not in my own interests, but in those of the whole community. Such villains, seeing the rewards which await their crimes, will be less ready to commit offences against others if they see that you too hold the same opinion of them. (48) Otherwise it would be far better to wipe out the existing laws and make different ones, which will penalise those who keep guard over their own wives, and grant full immunity to those who criminally pursue them. (49) This would be a far more just procedure than to set a trap for citizens by means of the laws, which urge the man who catches an adulterer to do with him whatever he will, and yet allow the injured party to undergo a trial far more perilous than that which faces the law-breaker who seduces other men's wives. (50) Of this, I am an example – I, who now stand in danger of losing life, property, everything, because I have obeyed the laws of the state.

89. *The case for the prosecution in a poisoning trial. Athens, c. 420 BC
(Antiphon, Prosecution of a Stepmother, 1-4, 14-20, 25-7. Tr. K.
Freeman. G)*

The prosecutor is the deceased's son by his first marriage; the defendant is
the deceased's second wife, represented by her sons, the prosecutor's
half-brothers.

(1) Members of the jury:

Young as I am, and still without experience of litigation, I am placed by
this event in a position of terrible difficulty. Either I have to disobey the
injunction laid on me by my father, that I should seek vengeance on his
murderers; or if I do seek vengeance, I am driven into a feud with those
with whom it is least desirable – my half-brothers and their mother. (2)
Events, and my half-brothers themselves, have driven me into bringing
this suit against them. They are the very men who ought naturally to
have come forward as avengers of the deceased, and allies of the avenger.
But in fact, the precise opposite has come about: they have taken their
stand here as my adversaries, on the side of murder as I and my
indictment declare.

(3) My plea to you, gentlemen, is this: if I prove that their mother did by
intention and forethought cause the death of our father, and that she had
been caught before, not once but several times, in the very act of plotting
his murder, inflict punishment – avenge, in the first instance your laws,
which you have received as an inheritance from heaven and your
ancestors, and by which you must be guided when considering
condemnation as judges in this court; avenge, in the second instance him
who is dead and gone, and with him me also, who, alone and deserted, am
left to take his part! (4) You, gentlemen, stand to me now in the place of
my family, because those who should have been his avengers and my
allies have come forward as the dead man's murderers and my opponents.
To whom, then, can anyone turn to for help, or where can he go to seek
sanctuary, except to you and to Justice? ...

(14) There was in our house an upper room, which Philoneus used to
occupy whenever he had business in town. This Philoneus was an honest,
respectable man, a friend of my father's. He had a concubine, whom he
was intending to dispose of to a brothel. My stepmother, having heard of
this, made a friend of this woman; and when she got to know of the injury
Philoneus was proposing to do her, she sent for her. When the woman
came, my stepmother told her that she herself also was being wrongly
treated, by my father; and that if the woman would do as she said, she
was clever enough to restore the love of Philoneus for the concubine, and
my father's love for herself. As she expressed it, hers was the creative
part, the other woman's part was that of obeying orders. (16) She asked
her therefore if she was willing to act as her assistant; and the woman

promised to do so – very readily, I imagine. Later, it happened that Philoneus had to go down to the Piraeus in connection with a religious ceremony to Zeus, Guardian of Property; and at the same time my father was preparing for a voyage to Naxos. It seemed to Philoneus an excellent idea, therefore, that he should make the same trip serve a double purpose: that he should accompany my father, his friend, down to the harbour, and at the same time perform his religious duty and entertain him at a feast. (17) Philoneus' concubine went with them, to help them with the sacrifice and the banquet. When they arrived at the port, they of course performed the sacrifice. When the religious ceremony was over, the woman began to deliberate with herself as to how and when she should administer the drug, whether before dinner or after dinner. The result of her deliberation was that she decided to do so after dinner, thus carrying out the instructions of this Clytemnestra, my stepmother.

(18) The whole story of the dinner would be too long for me to tell or you to hear; but I shall try to narrate the rest to you in the fewest possible words, that is, how the actual administration of the poison was accomplished. When they had finished dinner, they naturally – as one of them was sacrificing to Zeus and entertaining a guest, and the other was about to set off on a voyage and was dining with his friend – they naturally were proceeding to pour libations, and accompany them with an offering of incense. (19) Philoneus' concubine, as she was serving them with the wine for the libation – a libation that was to accompany prayers destined, alas! gentlemen, not to be fulfilled – poured in the poison. And in the belief that she was doing something clever, she gave the bigger dose to Philoneus, thinking that perhaps the more she gave him, the more he would love her. She still did not know that she had been deceived by my stepmother, and did not find out until she was already involved in disaster. She poured in a smaller dose for my father. (20) The two men poured out their libation; and then, taking in hand that which was their own destroyer, they drained their last draught.

Philoneus dropped dead instantly. My father was seized with an illness from which he died in three weeks. For this, the woman who had acted under orders has paid the penalty for her offence, in which she was an innocent accomplice: she was handed over to the public executioner after being broken on the wheel. But the woman who was the real cause, who thought out and engineered the deed – she will pay the penalty now, if you and heaven so decree ...

(25) Which is more just – that the murderer should pay the penalty, or not? Which is more just – to pity rather the dead man, or the woman who killed him? The dead man, I would say. That would be the far more just and more righteous course for you in the eyes of god and man. And so at this point I demand that as she destroyed him without pity and without mercy, so she too shall be destroyed by you and by Justice. (26) She acted of her own free will and compassed his death with guile; he died by force,

an unwilling victim. Can it be denied, gentlemen, that he died by force – a man who was intending to set out on a voyage from this country, and who was dining with his friend? She it was who sent the poison, who gave the order that it should be given him to drink, and so killed my father. What claim has she to be pitied or to win consideration from you or anyone else? She did not see fit to have pity on her husband – no, but she wickedly and shamefully destroyed him.

(27) Pity, as you know, is more properly bestowed in cases of involuntary suffering than of crime and offences committed voluntarily and with malice aforethought. Even as she, fearing neither gods nor heroes nor her fellow-men, destroyed the dead man, so let her in turn be destroyed by you and by Justice! Let her win neither consideration nor pity nor any sort of compunction from you, and thus meet with the punishment she has so justly earned!

90. *The past activities of a courtesan. Athens, 4th cent. BC (Apollodorus (= 'Demosthenes'), Against Neaera, 59. 18-42, 45-60, 72- 3, 78-9, 85-7, 110-14, 122. Tr. K. Freeman. G)*

This case, spitefully brought against the courtesan Neaera's pimp-lover Stephanus years after the facts described, when Neaera was in her seventies, concentrates not only on the legal issue of Neaera's citizenship, but on her past sexual activities.

(18) [Neaera] was one of seven little girls bought when small children by Nicarete, a freedwoman who had been the slave of Charisius of Elis, and the wife of Charisius' cook Hippias. Nicarete was a clever judge of beauty in little girls, and moreover she understood the art of rearing and training them skilfully, having made this her profession from which she drew her livelihood. (19) She used to address them as daughters, so that she might exact the largest fee from those who wished to have dealings with them, on the ground that they were freeborn girls; but after she had reaped her profit from the youth of each of them, one by one, she then sold the whole lot of them together, seven in all: Anteia, Stratola, Aristocleia, Metaneira, Phila, Isthmias, and the defendant Neaera.

(20) Now who were their respective purchasers, and how they were set free by those who bought them from Nicarete, I will explain in the course of my speech, if you wish to hear, and if I have enough time. But the fact that the defendant Neaera did belong to Nicarete and worked as a prostitute open to all comers – this is the point to which I wish to return.

(21) Lysias the professor of rhetoric was the lover of Metaneira. He decided that in addition to the other expenses he had incurred for her, he would like to get her initiated. He thought that the rest of his expenditure went to her owner, but whatever he spent on her over the festival and initiation ceremony would be a present for the girl herself. He therefore

asked Nicarete to come to the Mysteries and bring Metaneira so that she could be initiated and he promised to instruct her himself in the Mysteries.

(22) When they arrived, Lysias did not admit them to his house, out of respect for his wife, who was the daughter of Brachyllus and his own niece, and for his mother, who was somewhat advanced in years and lived in the same house. Instead, he lodged them – that is, Metaneira and Nicarete – with Philostratus of Colonus, who was still a bachelor and also a friend of his. The women were accompanied by the defendant Neaera, who was already working as a prostitute, though she was not yet of the proper age.

(23) As witness to the truth of my statements, namely that she was the slave of Nicarete and used to accompany her and was hired out to anyone willing to pay, I now call upon Philostratus himself.

Philostratus testifies.

(24) On a later occasion, gentlemen, Simos the Thessalian brought Neaera here to the Great Panathenaic Festival. Nicarete also accompanied them, and they put up at the house of Ctesippus son of Glauconidas. The defendant Neaera drank and dined with them in the presence of a large company, as a courtesan would do.

(25) I now call witnesses to the truth of these statements. Please call Euphiletus son of Simon, and Aristomachus son of Critodemus.

They testify.

(26) After that, she worked openly at Corinth as a prostitute, and became famous. Among her lovers were Xenoclides the poet and Hipparchus the actor, who had her on hire. For the truth of these statements, I am unable to put before you the deposition of Xenoclides, because he is debarred by law from giving evidence ... (28) But I now call Hipparchus himself, and I shall compel him to give evidence or else take the oath disclaiming knowledge of the facts, according to the law; otherwise I will subpoena him.

He testifies.

(29) After that, she acquired two lovers, Timanoridas of Corinth and Eucrates of Leucas. These men found Nicarete's charges excessive, as she expected them to pay all the daily expenses of her household; so they paid down to Nicarete 30 minas as the purchase-price of Neaera, and bought her outright from her mistress, according to the law of that city, to be their slave. (30) They kept her and made use of her for as long as they wished. Then, being about to get married, they informed her that they did not wish to see the woman who had been their own mistress plying her trade in Corinth nor kept in a brothel: they would be glad to receive less money for her than they had paid, and to see her also reaping some benefit. They therefore offered to allow her, towards the price of her freedom, 1,000 drachmas, that is, 500 each; as for the 20 minas remaining, they told her to find this sum herself and repay it to them.

Neaera, on hearing these propositions from Timanoridas and Eucrates, sent messages to a number of her former lovers, asking them to come to Corinth. Among these was Phrynion, an Athenian from Paeania, the son of Demon, and the brother of Demochares, a man who was living a dissolute and extravagant life, as the older of you remember. (31) When Phrynion arrived, she told him of the proposition made to her by Eucrates and Timanoridas, and handed him the money which she had collected from her other lovers as a contribution towards the purchase of her freedom, together with her own savings, asking him to make up the amount to the 20 minas, and pay it to Eucrates and Timanoridas, so that she should be free.

(32) Phrynion was delighted to hear this proposition of hers. He took the money which had been contributed by her other lovers, made up the deficit himself, and paid the 20 minas to Eucrates and Timanoridas as the price of her freedom and on condition that she would not practise her profession in Corinth. As a proof of these statements, I will call the man who then witnessed the transaction. Please call Philagrus of the suburb of Melite.

He testifies.

(33) When they arrived here at Athens, he kept her and lived with her in a most dissolute and reckless way. He took her out to dinner with him wherever he went, where there was drinking; and whenever he made an after-dinner excursion, she always went too. He made love to her openly, anywhere and everywhere he chose, to excite the jealousy of the onlookers at his privilege. Among the many houses to which he took her on an after-dinner call was that of Chabrias of the suburb Alexone, when the latter had won the victory at Delphi with a four-horse chariot team which he had bought from the sons of Mitys the Argive, and on his return from Delphi was celebrating victory down at Colias. On that occasion, many men made love to Neaera when she was drunk and Phrynion was asleep, including even some of Chabrias' servants. (34) In proof of this I shall produce before you the actual eye-witnesses.

Please call Chionides and Euthetion.

They testify.

(35) However, finding herself treated with the most outrageous brutality by Phrynion, instead of being loved as she had expected, or having attention paid to her wishes, she packed up the goods in his house, including all the clothes and jewellery which he had provided for her personal adornment, and taking with her two servants, Thratta and Coccalina, ran away to Megara.

(36) This happened when Asteius was Chief Magistrate at Athens[28] during your second war against Sparta. Neaera spent two years in Megara; but her profession did not produce sufficient income to run her house, as she was extravagant, and the Megarians are mean and stingy, and there was no great foreign colony there because it was war-time, and

the Megarians favoured the Spartan side, but you were in command of the seas. She could not go back to Corinth because the terms of her release by Eucrates and Timanoridas were that she should not practise her profession there.

However, peace came.[29] It was then that our opponent Stephanus visited Megara. He put up at her house, as that of a prostitute, and became her lover. She told him her whole life-story and of her ill-treatment at the hands of Phrynion. She longed to live in Athens, but was afraid of Phrynion, because she had done him wrong and he was furious with her. She knew the violence and arrogance of his character. She therefore made the defendant Stephanus her protector, and while they were still in Megara, he talked encouragingly and filled her with hope, saying that Phrynion would be sorry for it if he laid hands on her, as he himself would take her as his wife, and would introduce the sons she already had to his phratrymen as being his own, and would make citizens of them. No one on earth, he said, should do her any harm. And so he arrived here at Athens from Megara with her and her three children, Proxenus, Ariston and a daughter, who now bears the name of Phano. (39) He took her and the children to the little house which he owned, alongside the Whispering Hermes, between the house of Dorotheus the Eleusinian and the house of Cleinomachus, which now Spintharus has bought from him for 7 minas. Thus, the place was the whole of Stephanus' property at that time – he had nothing else.

He had two reasons for bringing her here: first, that he would have a handsome mistress without expense; secondly, that her profession would provide him with the necessaries of life and keep the household, for he had no other source of income, except what he picked up by occasional blackmail.

(40) When Phrynion heard that she was in Athens and living with the defendant, he took some young men with him and went to Stephanus' house to get her. Stephanus asserted her freedom, according to law, and Phrynion thereupon summoned her before the Polemarch, under surety.[30] In proof of this, I will bring before you the Polemarch of that year ...

Please call Aietes.

He testifies.

(41) When she had thus been bailed out by Stephanus and was living with him, she carried on the same profession no less than before, but she exacted a larger fee from those who wished to consort with her, as having now a certain position to keep up and as being a married woman. Stephanus helped her by blackmail; if he caught any rich unknown stranger making love to her, he used to lock him up in the house as an adulterer caught with his wife, and extract a large sum of money from him (42) – naturally, because neither Stephanus nor Neaera had anything, not even enough to meet their daily expenses, but their

establishment was large. There were himself and herself to keep, and three small children – the ones she brought with her to him – and two maids and a man-servant; and above all, she had acquired the habit of good living, as formerly it had been others who had provided her with all necessaries ...

(45) To continue: Phrynion began his law-suit against Stephanus, on the grounds that Stephanus had robbed him of the defendant Neaera and made a free woman of her, and that Stephanus had received the goods of which Neaera had robbed him when she left. However, their friends brought them together and persuaded them to submit the dispute to arbitration. The arbitrator who sat on Phrynion's behalf was Satyrus of Alopece, the brother of Lacedaemonius, and on Stephanus' behalf, Saurias of Lamptrae; they chose as umpire Diogeiton of Acharnae. (46) These three met in the temple, and after hearing the facts from both the litigants and also from the woman herself, they gave their judgment, which was accepted by the litigants: namely, that the woman should be free and her own mistress, but that the goods which Neaera had taken from Phrynion when she left should all be returned to Phrynion, except the clothes and jewellery and maid-servants which had been bought for Neaera herself; further, that she should spend the same number of days with each of them; but that if they agreed to any other arrangement, this same arrangement should hold good; that the woman's upkeep should be provided by the person with whom she was living at the time; and that for the future the litigants should be friends and should bear no malice. (47) Such was the settlement brought about by the decision of arbitrators in the case of Phrynion and Stephanus, concerning the defendant Neaera. In proof of this, the Clerk will read you the deposition.

Please call Satyrus of Alopece, Saurias of Lamptrae, and Diogeiton of Acharnae.

They testify.

The following were the terms of settlement between Phrynion and Stephanus: that each shall keep at his house and have the enjoyment of Neaera for an equal number of days per month, unless they come to some different agreement.

(48) When the business was over, the friends of each party, those who had assisted them at the arbitration and the rest, did as I believe is usual in such cases, especially when a mistress is in dispute: they went to dine with each of them at the times when he had Neaera with him, and she dined and drank with them as mistresses do ...

(49) I have now outlined the facts about Neaera, and have supported my statements with evidence: that she was originally a slave, was twice sold, and practised the profession of a prostitute; that she ran away from Phrynion to Megara, and on her return to Athens was summoned before the Polemarch under surety. I now desire to prove to you that Stephanus himself has given evidence against her, showing that she is an alien.

(50) The daughter of the defendant Neaera, whom she had brought as a little girl to Stephanus' house, was in those days called Strybele, but now has the name Phano. Stephanus gave this girl in marriage, as being his own daughter, to an Athenian citizen, Phrastor, together with a dowry of 30 minas. When she went to live with Phrastor, who was a hardworking man and who had got together his means by careful living, she was unable to accommodate herself to his ways, but hankered after her mother's habits and the dissolute ways of that household, being, I suppose, brought up to a similar licence. (51) Phrastor observed that she was not well-behaved nor willing to be guided by him, and at the same time he found out for certain that she was not the daughter of Stephanus, but only of Neaera, so that he had been deceived on the first occasion when he was betrothed to her. He had understood that she was the daughter of Stephanus and not Neaera, the child of Stephanus' marriage with a freeborn Athenian lady before he began to live with Neaera. Phrastor was most indignant at all this, and considering himself to have been outrageously treated and swindled, he turned the young woman out of his house after having lived with her for a year and when she was pregnant; and he refused to return the dowry.

(52) Stephanus began a suit against him for alimony, lodged at the Odeon, according to the law enacting that if a man divorce his wife, he shall pay back the dowry, or else be liable to pay interest on it at the rate of 18 per cent per annum; and that her legal guardian is entitled to bring a law-suit for alimony at the Odeon, on the wife's behalf. Phrastor also brought an indictment against Stephanus before the Thesmothetae,[31] that Stephanus had betrothed to him, an Athenian citizen, the daughter of an alien woman, pretending that the girl was his own daughter, contrary to the following law. *To the Clerk*: Please read it.

The Clerk of the Court reads out the following law:

If any person give in marriage an alien woman to an Athenian citizen, pretending that she is related to him, he shall be deprived of his citizen status, and his property shall be confiscated, the third part to go to the person securing the conviction. The indictment shall be brought before the Thesmothetae, by any person so entitled, as in the case of usurpations of citizenship.

(53) The Clerk has read out to you the law followed by the Phrastor when he laid an indictment against Stephanus before the Thesmothetae. Stephanus, realising that if convicted of having sponsored the betrothal of an alien woman he ran the risk of incurring the severest penalties, came to terms with Phrastor, giving up the claim to the dowry and withdrawing the suit for alimony; and Phrastor likewise withdrew his indictment before the Thesmothetae. In proof of this I shall call Phrastor before you, and shall compel him to give evidence according to the law.

(55) Now let me put before you another piece of evidence, derived from Phrastor and the members of his phratry and family, to prove that

Neaera, the defendant, is a foreigner. Not long after Phrastor had repudiated Neaera's daughter, he fell ill. His condition became serious, and his life was in grave danger. He had for a long time been at variance with his relatives, and he regarded them with resentment and dislike. Besides, he was childless. Thus he was seduced during his illness by the attentions of Neaera and her daughter, (56) who went to him while he was ill and had no one to nurse him, bringing all the things necessary for his complaint and looking after him; and you know yourselves, of course, the value of a woman's presence during illness, as nurse to a sick man. And so he was persuaded to take back the child which Neaera's daughter had borne after being turned out of Phrastor's house during her pregnancy – which happened when he found out that she was the daughter, not of Stephanus, but of Neaera, because of his resentment at the deception – to take it back and to accept it as his legitimate son. (57) His reasoning was human and natural; he was ill and had no hope of recovery, and so in order to prevent his relatives from getting his property, and himself from dying childless, he adopted the child as his legitimate son and took him into his house. He would never have done this if he had been well, as I shall show you by a weighty and undeniable piece of evidence.

(58) As soon as Phrastor got up after this illness, and recovered his health and strength, he took as wife an Athenian woman according to law, namely the legitimate daughter of Satyrus of Melite, the sister of Diphilus. This, then, is a proof for you that his acceptance of the child was not voluntary but the result of pressure; his illness, his childlessness, their nursing and this enmity towards his relatives, whom he did not wish to be his heirs if anything happened to him. But this will be shown more clearly by what happened next.

(59) When Phrastor during his illness presented the child, his son by Neaera's daughter, to his phratry and to the Brytidae, to which family Phrastor belongs, the members of his family, knowing, doubtless, who the woman was whom Phrastor had originally taken to wife, namely Neaera's daughter, and knowing of her divorce by him, and also that it was his illness which was the cause of his consenting to take back the child, voted against the child's acceptance and refused to register him as one of themselves. (60) Phrastor began a lawsuit against them for refusing to register his son. The members of his family then challenged him before an arbitrator to swear by the sacred victims that he did verily and truly believe the child to be his son by a free Athenian woman, legally married to him. On the issue of this challenge to Phrastor by the members of his family before the arbitrator, Phrastor defaulted and did not take the required oath ...

(72) Yet the defendants Stephanus and Neaera had reached such a pitch of impudence that they were not content with merely declaring [Phano] to be a free-born Athenian woman. They noticed that Theogenes

of Cothocidae had been chosen by the lot as King-Archon, a man of good family, but poor and without business experience; so Stephanus supported him at his examination, and helped him out with his expenses. When he entered upon office, Stephanus wormed his way in, and having bought from him the office of assessor, he gave him this woman, Neaera's daughter, as wife, guaranteeing her to be his own daughter: such was his contempt for you and for the laws! (73) So this woman Phano performed for you the secret sacrifice for the safety of the state; she looked upon mysteries which she, as an alien, had no right to behold. This was the sort of woman who entered into the holy place where no other of all the great Athenian people can enter – only the wife of the King-Archon. She administered the oath to the reverend priestesses who officiate at the sacrifices; she went through the ceremony of the Bride of Dionysus, and carried out the ancestral religious duties of the state, fulfilling numerous sacred and mysterious functions. How can it be in accord with piety that things which the rest of the community are not allowed even to hear spoken of should actually be done by any woman chosen by chance, especially such a woman as this, and one who is guilty of such actions? ...

(78) I should like to call before you the sacred Herald, who attends upon the wife of the King-Archon when she administers the oath to the reverend priestesses when they are carrying their baskets at the altar, before they touch their sacred victims. This is in order that you may hear the oath and the words spoken in so far as it is permitted to hear these, and may know how holy and ancient is the customary rite.

The sacred herald comes forward and reads the oath administered to the priestesses by the wife of the King-Archon before they are permitted to officiate at the sacrifices.

Oath of the reverend priestess: 'I practise chastity, and am pure and undefiled of all things which bring impurity, including intercourse with men; I perform the sacrament of the wine-festival and the holy Bacchic rites according to the ancestral usage and at the appointed times.'

(79) You have now heard the oath and the ancestral usage, in so far as it is permitted to hear them; and how the woman whom Stephanus betrothed to Theogenes the King-Archon as his own daughter performed these sacrifices and administered the oath to the reverend priestesses, when it is forbidden even to the women who look on at them to repeat these mysteries to any other person.

The Magistrates investigate the identity of Theogenes' wife, and Theogenes divorces her.

(85) *To the jury*: You will see from this that it was proper for her [Phano] as a woman of such a character and such activities, not only to keep away from all these rites, from seeing, from sacrificing, from performing any of the ceremonies laid down by ancestral usage for the safety of the state: she should have been debarred from all public occasions at Athens. The law decrees that where a woman is found with

an adulterer, she is forbidden to attend any of the public sacrifices, even those which the laws permit an alien woman or slave to attend for the purpose of worship and prayer.

(86) The only class of woman forbidden by law to attend the public sacrifices is the woman caught in adultery; if she attends and breaks the law, the law allows any person who wishes to inflict upon her with impunity any punishment short of death, the right of punishment being legally granted to any chance person. The reason why the law permitted the infliction with impunity of any ill-treatment upon her except death, was to avoid any pollution or sacrilege in the temple; it holds out for women a threat terrifying enough to deter them from unrestraint or any sort of misbehaviour, and compel them to carry out their duties at home, teaching them that if anyone misbehaves in this fashion, she will be banished not only from her husband's house but from the public places of worship. (87) That this is so will be clear to you when you hear the law itself read out ...

Law on adultery: If the husband catches the adulterer in the act, he (the husband) shall not be permitted to continue cohabitation with the wife. If he continues cohabitation, he shall be disfranchised. It shall not be lawful for the woman to be admitted to the public sacrifices, if she has been caught with an adulterer. If she gains entrance, she shall be liable to suffer any ill-treatment whatsoever, short of death, and impunity ...

From the summation of the argument: (110) What would any one of you say if, having acquitted Neaera, you went home to your wife, or daughter, or mother, and she asked you, 'Where have you been' – you would answer, 'We have been trying a case.' She will then ask, 'Whose?' and you will of course answer, 'Neaera's. She was accused of living with an Athenian citizen as his wife, although she herself is an alien, and this is illegal; she was also accused of giving her daughter, a prostitute, in marriage to Theogenes the King-Archon, so that this girl performed the secret sacrifices for the safety of the state and went though the ceremony of being given as bride to Dionysus'; and you will enumerate the rest of the charges against Neaera, saying how well, accurately, and carefully they were stated by the prosecution. (111) You womenfolk, hearing this, will say, 'Well, what did you do?' and you will reply, 'We acquitted her.' Then will not the indignation of all the most decent women be excited against you, because you have judged Neaera no less deserving than themselves of a share in public life and public worship? And the foolish women will have received a clear mandate from you to do as they like, since you and the laws have granted them impunity; for you will have shown by your lax and easygoing attitude that you yourselves are in sympathy with this woman's way of life.

(112) It would be much better that this trial had never been held than that you should vote for acquittal, for there will then be complete liberty to prostitutes to live as wives with whom they please, and to claim as the

father of their children the man they happen to be with. Your laws will lose their force and the ways of harlots will be supreme. You should therefore also look to the interests of the women of this city, and see to it that the daughters of the poor are not deprived of the chance to marry. (113) At present, even if a man is in straitened circumstances, the law decrees a suitable dowry for his daughter, if nature has given her looks which are at all tolerable. But if this law is trampled upon by your acquittal of this woman, and its force is annulled, then the profession of the prostitutes will spread to all daughters of citizens whose poverty prevents their being given in marriage; and the prestige of freeborn women will pass to the prostitutes, if they are granted impunity and licence to produce children as they please, and to take part in religious worship and the rites and privileges of the State.

(114) Each one of you must believe, therefore, that he is giving his vote in defence of his wife, or his daughter, or his mother, or on behalf of the state, the laws and religion – to prevent respectable women from acquiring the same standing as the prostitute, and to protect those who have been reared by their families in every propriety and with every care, and given in marriage according to law, from having no better position than this woman, who with every sort of licentious behaviour surrendered herself dozens of times a day to dozens of men, whenever anyone asked her.

(122) This is matrimony: when a man begets children and presents his sons to his phratry and deme, and gives his daughters, as being his own, in marriage to their husbands. *Hetaerae* we keep for pleasure, concubines (*pallakai*) for daily attendance upon our person, but wives for the procreation of legitimate children and to be the faithful guardians of our households. So that if he had formerly married an Athenian woman, and these children are hers and not Neaera's, he could have proved it by the most accurate testimony, that of the female slaves handed over for examination by torture.

Amorgos[32]
'With the agreement of the woman and her guardian'

Athenian women are mentioned only in transactions about their dowries; outside Athens women apparently had more control over their property.

91. *A mortgage. Amorgos, 3rd cent. BC (Finley 9. G)*

Boundary of the household and garden which Antenor son of Cledicus mortgaged to Pasariste daughter of Evagoras with Samon as guardian, for 90 drachmas of silver, according to agreements deposited with Evaces son of Critolaus.

92. *Security for a dowry. Amorgos, c. 300 BC (Finley 155. G)*

Boundary of the houses and gardens adjoining the houses put up as security to Nicesarete for her dowry, consecrated and dedicated to Aphrodite Urania in Aspis by Nicesarete, wife of Naucrates, and her guardian Naucrates, and according to the wills deposited in the temple of Aphrodite and with Eunomides the archon and with the official Ctesiphon.

93. *Transactions with a society. Amorgos, 3rd cent. BC (Finley 8. G)*

Boundary of the lands in ... and of the house and gardens of Xenocles located in Phylincheia and of the recorded pledges mortgaged, with the agreement of the woman Eratocrate and her guardian Brychion to the society and to Aristocritus chief of the society and to his wife Echenice, for the surety which he had put Xenocles down for on behalf of the society, which Aristagoras had collected according to the law of the society members.

94. *Leased property. Amorgos, late 4th cent. BC (Finley 130. G)*

The estate of orphans during their minority ordinarily was transferred from their guardians to lessees, but in Athens girls were never named as beneficiaries of a will.

Boundary of the leased property of Simone and Demodice, daughters of Simon, in the [properties] of Dexibius. Lessee Dexibius. Aristotimus son of Xanthides set the evaluation at one third; he was sent by the archons Xanthippides son of Xanthippides, Praxiteles son of Theognotus ...

Sparta
'Virtue is the same for men and for women'

The constitution of the Spartan (Lacedaemonian) state was unique in ancient Greece. Its social institutions and its famous discipline were designed for a single purpose: to protect the state by maintaining the best fighting force in the world, and both its male and female citizens were involved in achieving this aim. The distinctive laws of Sparta were attributed by writers in the fifth century and after to a legendary lawgiver, Lycurgus. After Sparta defeated Athens in the Peloponnesian war, much credit was given by Athenians to the special character of the Spartan constitution. Lycurgus' reforms, as described by writers like Xenophon, bear so striking a resemblance to the legislation for the ideal state proposed by Socrates in Plato's *Republic* (no. 73), that one may have influenced the other.[33]

95. *Opinions attributed to the sophist Gorgias, 5th cent. BC (Fr. 82 B 19 D-K = Plato, Meno 71e. G)*

If you want a definition of virtue for a man, it is easy to give: virtue for a man is to be able to conduct affairs of state and to help one's friends and harm one's enemies, and to take care that he avoids being harmed himself. If you want a definition of female virtue, it is not difficult to provide: it is that she must run the household well, preserve what it contains and what belongs to her husband.

96. *A saying attributed to the philosopher Antisthenes, 4th cent. BC (Fr. 72 Decleva Caizzi = Diogenes Laertius 6.42. G)*

Virtue (*arete*) is the same for men and for women.[34]

97. *The education of Spartan mothers (Xenophon, Constitution of the Lacedaemonians 1.2-9. 4th cent. BC. G)*

It was not by imitating the customs of other states, but by knowingly doing the opposite to most of them, that Lycurgus made his fatherland pre-eminently successful.

(1.3) To begin at the beginning, here is his legislation about the procreation of children. Other people raise the girls who will bear the children and who are supposed to have a good upbringing with the most limited portions of food and the smallest possible amount of delicacies. They make sure they abstain from wine completely or give it to them mixed with water.

The other Greeks think that girls ought to sit in isolation doing wool work, leading a sedentary existence like many craftsmen. How could they expect that girls raised in this way could produce significant offspring? (1.4) By contrast, Lycurgus thought that slave women could make a sufficient quantity of clothing.

But as far as free women were concerned, because he thought childbearing was their most important function, he decreed that the female sex ought to take bodily exercise no less than the male. He established competitions of running and of strength for women with one another, just as he did for the men, because he thought that stronger offspring would be born if both parents were strong.

(1.5) As for a wife's sexual relations with her husband, Lycurgus saw that men in other cultures during the first part of the time had unlimited intercourse with their wives, but he knew that the opposite was right. He made it a disgrace for the husband to be seen approaching or leaving his wife. As a result it was inevitable that their desire for intercourse increased, and that as a result the offspring (if there were any) that were born were stronger than if the couple were tired of each other.

(1.6) In addition, he stopped men from taking a wife whenever they chose and decreed that they marry when they were in their prime, because he thought that this was better for their offspring. (1.7) He saw that in cases where it happened that an old man had a young wife, the men were particularly protective of their wives, and he knew that the opposite was right. He required that the older man bring in a man whose body and mind he admired and have him beget the children. (1.8) But in case a man did not want to cohabit with his wife, but wanted worthy children, he made a law that he could beget children from a woman who was noble and had borne good children, if he could persuade her husband.[35] (1.9) He agreed to allow many such arrangements, for the wives who wanted to have two households and husbands who wanted to acquire brothers for their children, who had blood and powers in common, but did not inherit their property.[36]

Thus Lycurgus had different ideas about the begetting of children, and anyone who wishes to may judge whether or not he succeeded in producing in Sparta men who were superior in height and strength from the men in other states!

98. *The advantages of Spartan education and marriage customs (Plutarch, Life of Lycurgus 14-16, excerpts, 2nd cent. AD. G)*

(14.1) As for education, he considered it to be a lawgiver's most significant and noblest work. For that reason he began first off by considering legislation about marriage and childbirth. For Aristotle is wrong when he says that it was because he tried and failed to make the women chaste that he gave up the idea of controlling the freedom and dominance the women had acquired because they were compelled to be in charge when their husbands left them behind [while they were on campaign] and so were more considerate of them than was appropriate, and addressed them as ladies.[37]

Rather it was that Lycurgus took particular care about the women as well as the men. (14.2) He made the young women exercise their bodies by running[38] and wrestling and throwing the discus and the javelin, so that their offspring would have a sound start by taking root in sound bodies and grow stronger, and the women themselves would be able to use their strength to withstand childbearing and wrestle with labour pains. He freed them from softness and sitting in the shade and all female habits, and made it customary for girls no less than boys to go naked in processions and to dance naked at certain festivals and to sing naked while young men were present and looking on.[39]

(14.3) On occasion the girls made good-natured jokes about young men who had done something wrong, and again sang encomia set to music to the young men who deserved them, so as to inspire in the young men a desire for glory and emulation of their deeds. The man who was praised for his courage and was celebrated by the girls went away proud because of their praise.[40] But the sting of their jokes and mockery was as sharp as serious admonition, because along with the other citizens the kings and the senators attended the spectacle. (14.4) There was nothing shameful in the girls' nakedness, because it was accompanied by modesty and self-control. It produced in them simple habits and an intense desire for good health, and gave the female sex a taste for noble sentiments, since they shared with the males virtue and desire for glory. As a result they tended to speak and think the kind of thing that Gorgo, the wife of King Leonidas, is reported to have said. When (as it seems) a foreigner said to her, 'You Spartans are the only women who rule over their men', she replied, 'Because only we are the mothers of men.'[41]

(15.1) These customs also provided an incentive for marriage. I mean the naked processions of maidens and competitions in full view of the young men, who were attracted to them (as Plato says) 'by sexual if not by logical inevitability'.[42] In addition, Lycurgus attached disgrace to bachelorhood; bachelors were forbidden to watch the naked processions. (15.3) Men married the girls by kidnapping them, not when they were small and immature, but when they had reached their full prime. Once the girl had been kidnapped a so-called bridesmaid cropped her hair close to her head, clothed her in a man's cloak and sandals, and left her lying on a pallet in the dark. The bridegroom, not drunk or debauched, but sober, and after having dined as usual at the common table, came in and undid her belt[43] and carried her off to the marriage bed.

(15.4) After spending a short time with his wife he went off in a dignified way to his usual quarters, in order to sleep with the other young men. He went on acting like this from then on: he would spend his days and sleep at night with his comrades, go to his wife secretly and cautiously, because he was ashamed and afraid that someone would discover him in her room, and meanwhile his wife was devising and planning with him how they might make opportunities for secret meetings. (15.5) They carried on like this for some time, so long that some of them had children before they saw their wives in the daylight.

Such interviews not only provided opportunity to practise self-control and moderation, but kept their bodies fertile and always fresh for loving and eager for intercourse, because they were not satisfied and worn out by continual intercourse, but had always some remnant of an incentive for their mutual passion and pleasure.

(15.6) By endowing marriage with such restraint and order, he was equally able to dispel empty and womanish jealousy, by ensuring that although they removed unworthy offences from marriage, they could share the begetting of children with their fellows, and they made fun of anyone who turned to murder or war on the grounds that they could not share or participate in such practices. It was possible for an older man with a younger wife, if he was pleased with and thought highly of one of the virtuous young men, to bring him to his wife and having filled her with noble seed, to adopt the child as his own. Similarly it was possible for a good man, who admired the chaste wife of another man, to persuade her husband to let him sleep with her, so that he could plant his seed in a good garden plot and beget good children, to be brothers and kin to the best families ... (15.9) His physical and political programme at that time was very far from the laxity among the women that was said to have developed later, and there was no thought of adultery among them.

(16.1) Fathers did not have authority over raising their offspring.

Instead, the father took his child and brought it to a place called Lesche,[44] where sat the elders of the tribe. They examined the child, and if it was well-formed and strong, ordered it to be raised, and gave it one of the nine thousand lots.

But if the child was ill-born and maimed, they discarded it in the so-called Apothetae, a kind of pit near Mount Taygetus,[45] (16.2) on the grounds that it was not profitable for it to live, either for itself or for the state, if it were not well-framed and strong right from the start. This is why [Spartan] women washed infants not in water but in wine, in order to test their strength. For it is said that undiluted wine causes convulsions in babies who are epileptic or weak, and that healthy babies are tempered by it and their frames strengthened.

(16.3) Their nurses took special care in their craft, so that they were able to raise infants without swaddling cloths around their limbs, and left their figures free, and the babies were contented with their regime, and not fussy about food, and not scared of the dark or afraid to be left alone, and free of ignoble irritability and whining. For this reason certain foreigners purchased Spartan nurses for their children. They say that Amycla, the nurse of the Athenian Alcibiades,[46] was a Spartan.

99. *Anecdotes. Sparta, 5th cent. BC? (Plutarch, Sayings of Spartan Women = Moralia 240c-242d, excerpts, 2nd cent. AD. G)*

Spartan women were renowned for their courage and their determination to enforce a strict code of honour on their menfolk.

Anecdotes about Gorgo, daughter of Cleomenes, king of Sparta (cf. no. 160), and wife of another king, Leonidas.

5. When Gorgo was asked by a woman from Attica, 'Why are you Spartan women the only ones who rule over their husbands?' she answered, 'Because only we are the mothers of men.'[47]

6. When her husband Leonidas was about to go off to Thermopylae, in order to encourage him to be worthy of Sparta, she asked what she should do,[48] he said, 'Marry a good husband and bear good children.'

Anecdotes about other women.

8. Another woman was burying her son, when an ordinary old woman came up to her and said: 'Poor woman, what a misfortune.' The first woman said, 'No, what good fortune, by the twin gods, for this is why I bore him, so that he might die for Sparta, and now that is what has come to pass.'

9. When an Ionian woman prided herself on something she had woven, a Spartan woman boasted of her four beautiful sons, saying, 'Such should be the works of a fine woman and this is what she should be proud of and boast about.'

16. When another Spartan woman handed her son his shield, she exhorted him, 'Son, come back either with this or on it.'

26. When a young woman who had had a secret love affair aborted her baby, she endured bravely and never uttered a sound, so that her father and the other people nearby did not know that she had been in labour. Bearing her suffering with propriety cancelled out her impropriety.

27. When a Spartan woman was sold as a slave and asked what she knew how to do, she said, 'To be faithful.'

28. Another, when taken as a captive and asked the same question, answered, 'To run a household well.'

29. When someone asked another woman if she would be good, if he bought her, she said that she would, 'and also if you do not buy me.'

30. When another was being sold as a slave, and asked by the auctioneer what she knew how to do, she replied, 'To be free.' When the man who bought her ordered her to do things that were not appropriate for a free woman, she said, 'You will regret that you have deprived yourself of such a possession', and committed suicide.

100. *A Greek historian's account of the behaviour of Etruscan women. Chios, 4th cent. BC (Theopompus, Histories 115, FGrHist F204 = Athenaeus 517d-518a. G)*

Several features of the libertine conduct attributed by Theopompus to the Etruscans occur also in Plato's ideal State (no. 73) and in Xenophon's description of Sparta (no. 97). However inaccurate this account may be of Etruscan behaviour, it provides (by inversion) a guide to what a fourth-century Greek considered normal in his own culture.[49]

Sharing wives is an established Etruscan custom. Etruscan women take particular care of their bodies and exercise often, sometimes along with the men, and sometimes by themselves. It is not a disgrace for them to be seen naked. They do not share their couches with their husbands but with the other men who happen to be present, and they propose toasts to anyone they choose. They are expert drinkers and very attractive.

The Etruscans raise all the children that are born, without knowing who their fathers are. The children live the way their parents live, often attending drinking parties and having sexual relations with all the women. It is no disgrace for them to do anything in the open, or to be seen having it done to them, for they consider it a native custom. So far from thinking it disgraceful, they say when someone asks to see the master of the house, and he is making love, that he is doing so-and-so, calling the indecent action by its name.

When they are having sexual relations either with courtesans or within their family, they do as follows: after they have stopped drinking and are about to go to bed, while the lamps are still lit, servants bring in courtesans, or boys, or sometimes even their wives. And when they have enjoyed these they bring in boys, and make love to them. They sometimes make love and have intercourse while people are watching them, but most of the time they put screens woven of sticks around the beds, and throw cloths on top of them.

They are keen on making love to women, but they particularly enjoy boys and youths. The youths in Etruria are very good-looking, because they live in luxury and keep their bodies smooth. In fact all the barbarians in the West use pitch to pull out and shave off the hair on their bodies.

Egypt
'Possessing with him the property that they have in common'

The papyrus, a plant which grew abundantly in the Nile, was used by the Egyptians to produce a writing material which they exported throughout the Mediterranean. While the damp weather of other countries caused the papyrus sheets to disintegrate, Egypt's climate preserved them. As a result, the majority of the hundreds of thousands of papyri which survive today come from Egypt, and most were discovered in rubbish-piles and town dumps. Papyri written in Greek, the language of Egypt after its occupation by Alexander the Great, survive from the late fourth century BC to the end of the ancient world.

While many fragments have provided literary texts, we are concerned here with the category known as 'documentary papyri', which includes private letters (often dictated to professional scribes by illiterate correspondents), public documents, and records of financial transactions, both public and private. Like inscriptions, papyri can tell us about the ordinary people whom historians have ignored, but they go further than the stone remains in giving us priceless, often touching glimpses into the daily life of the lower classes.

101. *A marriage contract. Tebtunis, 92 BC (Tebtunis papyrus I 104. G)*

This contract not only specifies the financial obligations of both parties, but explains what constitutes unacceptable behaviour. Both husband and wife are required to be chaste within the context of the household, but although nothing prevents the husband from having relations with other women or men outside the home, the wife cannot leave the house for longer than a few hours without the husband's permission.

(1) In the year 22, Mecheir 11, an agreement between Philiscus son of Apollonius, a Persian of the Epigone[50] and Apollonia also called[51] Kellauthis daughter of Heraclides, a Persian, with her brother Apollonius acting as guardian. Philiscus acknowledges that he has received from her in copper money the sum of two talents and four thousand drachmas, as the dowry that had been agreed upon for the same Apollonia ... (*some words missing*) ... Dionysius is the keeper of the contract. (2) In the twenty-second year of the reign of king Ptolemy also called Alexander, who is the god Philometor, in the time of the priest of Alexander and of the others as recorded in Alexandria, in the month Xandikos 11, Mecheir 11, at Kerkeosiris of the Polemon division of the Arsinoe nome. Philiscus son of Apollonius, a Persian of the military settlement acknowledges to Apollonia also called Kellauthis, daughter of Heraclides, a Persian with her brother Apollonius acting as guardian that he has received from her in copper money the sum of two talents and four thousand drachmas as the dowry that had been agreed upon on behalf of the same Apollonia.

Apollonia agrees to live with Philiscus in obedience to him, as is appropriate for a wife to her husband, possessing with him the property that they have in common. Philiscus, when he is at home and when he is away from home, is to provide her with every necessity and a cloak and other possessions customary for a wife at a level appropriate to their means, and Philiscus is not permitted to bring into the household another wife in addition to Apollonia or a concubine or a catamite nor is he permitted to beget children with another woman so long as Apollonia is alive, nor to set up another household unless Apollonia is in charge of it, and he promises not to throw her out or insult or mistreat her and not to alienate any of their joint property in a way that would be injurious to Apollonia. If Philiscus is shown to have done any of these things or if he has not provided her with the necessities or the cloak or the other possessions as specified, Philiscus must immediately return the dowry of two talents and four thousand drachmas of copper money.

Similarly, Apollonia is not to stay away for a night or a day from Philiscus' household without Philiscus' knowledge, nor is she to live with another man or to cause ruin to the common household or to bring disgrace on Philiscus in whatever brings disgrace to a husband. If Apollonia voluntarily wants a separation from Philiscus, Philiscus is to return her dowry intact within ten days from the time when she asks for it. If he does not return the dowry as specified, he must pay her the original sum plus one half. Witnesses are Dionysius son of Patron, Dionysius son of Dionysius, Heracles son of Diocles, all six Macedonians of the military settlement. Dionysius is keeper of the contract.

(3) I, Philiscus son of Apollonius, a Persian of the military settlement,

agree that I have received a dowry of two talents, four thousand drachmas in copper money as specified, and have deposited the agreement, which is valid, with Dionysius. The said Dionysius son of Hermaiscus has written this on his behalf because Philiscus does not know letters. (4) I, Dionysius, have received the contract, which is valid.

Placed in the registry in the year 22, Mecheir 11. (*On the reverse*) An agreement between Apollonia and Philiscus ... marriage ... (*names of principals and witnesses appended*)

102. *Annulment of a marriage contract. Alexandria, 1st cent. BC (Berlin papyrus 1104. G)*

To Protarchus, from Dionysarion, daughter of Protarchus, with her brother Protarchus as guardian, and from Hermione, daughter of Hermias, a citizen, on the authority of her brother's son, Hermias, son of ... Dionysarion agrees that the contract is invalidated which the son of Hermione, Hermias, made with her, with Hermione serving as bondsman ... It is agreed, on behalf of her deceased husband, that Dionysarion take from Hermione's house by hand the dowry which she brought to Hermias, with Hermione serving as bondsman: a dowry of clothes to the value of 240 silver pieces, earrings, and a ring ... The contract is invalidated with all documents sealed by her. Dionysarion is not to enter suit against Hermione, nor is any man acting on her behalf, not for any of the deceased Hermias' possessions nor concerning the dowry or support nor about any other written or unwritten agreement made in the past up to the present day. Since Dionysarion has become pregnant, she is not to sue her for childbirth, because she is more persuasive on that account; she is permitted to expose her baby and to join herself in marriage to another husband. She agrees that if she breaks this authorised agreement she is subject to damages and the established fine ...

103. *Agreement to transfer a concubine. Egypt, 284/3 BC (Elephantine papyrus 3.25. G)*

Elaphion of Syria, with Pantarces as her guardian, herewith pays Antipatrus of Arcadia a fee of 300 drachmas for having maintained her. Antipatrus is hereby forbidden to sue her, to demand that he is supporting her or to reduce her to slavery on any condition, and so is anyone acting on his behalf. If he violates this agreement, his action is invalid and his agent and Antipatrus must pay a fine of 3,000 drachmas to Elaphion or to the men currently maintaining her. This writ shall be in effect from the time Elaphion or someone acting on her behalf serves it on Antipatrus, as Elaphion has written it. Witnesses. Signed Pancrates of Arcadia, Caphisias of Phocis, Diphilus of Phocis, Epinicus of Chalcis, Athenagoras of Alexandria, Xenocles of Rhodes.

104. *Problems over a dowry. Oxyrhyncha, early 2nd cent.* BC *(Tebtunis papyrus 776. G)*

To Ptolemaeus, state official, from Senesis daughter of Menelaus, one of the women living in Oxyrhyncha in the Polemon area. I lived with Didymus son of Peteimouthes from the said village, on the terms of an Egyptian alimentary silver contract for [?] gold pieces in accordance with the laws of the country, and for this money and my maintenance he had pledged all his property, including a house in the aforesaid village. But the accused wished to deprive me of this and went round to one person after another in the said village and wanted to alienate the house from me. But they did not go along with him because I would not give my consent. After that he tried to give it as collateral to the treasury for Heraclides the tax farmer, and accordingly thinks he can exclude me from my rights.

On account of this I beg and beseech you; do not allow me, a defenceless woman,[52] to be deprived of the property pledged for my dowry because of the irresponsibility of the accused, but if you will, order that a letter be written to Ptolemaeus the treasurer asking him not to accept the house from Didymus as collateral. If this is done, I shall have your assistance. Farewell.

105. *A petition from a wife requesting restitution of a dowry. Oxyrhynchus, 1st cent.* AD *(Oxyrhynchus papyrus 281. G)*

To Heraclides priest and chief justice, also in charge of the circuit judges and the other courts, from Syra, daughter of Theon. I married Sarapion, having brought him a dowry valued at 200 drachmas, according to agreement. By taking him into my parents' house because he was completely destitute, I conducted myself blamelessly in every respect. But Sarapion, after he squandered all my dowry as he liked, rendered no account of it, and disgraced me and insulted me and laid hands on me and deprived me of the necessities of life, and later deserted me when I had become destitute. For this reason I ask you to order him to appear before you so that he will be compelled to return the dowry with 50 per cent interest. Without prejudice to any other charges that I have or will make against him.

106. *A petition from a husband complaining that his wife stole his property. Oxyrhynchus, 1st cent.* AD *(Oxyrhynchus papyrus 282. G)*

To the governor Alexandrus from Tryphon son of Dionysius of the city of Oxyrhynchus. I married Demetrous the daughter of Heraclides and I supported her in a manner that exceeded my resources. She became dissatisfied with our marriage and eventually went off and they[53] took off property belonging to me, a list of which is appended. Accordingly I ask that she be brought before you so that she can get the punishment she deserves and return my property to me. Without prejudice to any other charges that I have made or will make against her. The articles she carried off ... are worth 40 drachmas.

V. Legal Status in the Roman World

'If the woman is in her own power ...'

Early Rome
'Romulus compelled the citizens'

107. *The laws of the kings. Rome, 8th/7th cent. BC (FIRA², vol. 1, p. 3. Tr. ARS, rev. L)*

Although the history of Rome's regal period is based in large part on legend, and was so in antiquity, tradition was strong, and many of Rome's laws and customs, committed to writing much later, have their roots in the distant past. The laws attributed to the kings of Rome and the Twelve Tables, which follow, have been reconstructed by modern editors from these later citations.

Laws attributed to Romulus, the founder; traditional dates, 753-716 BC

4. Romulus compelled the citizens to rear every male child and the first-born of the females, and he forbade them to put to death any child under three years of age, unless it was a cripple or a monster from birth. He did not prevent the parents from exposing such children, provided that they had displayed them first to the five nearest neighbours and had secured their approval. For those who disobeyed the law he prescribed the confiscation of half of their property as well as other penalties.

6. By the enactment of a single ... law ... Romulus brought the women to great prudence and orderly conduct ... The law was as follows: A woman united with her husband by a sacred marriage[1] shall share in all his possessions and in his sacred rites.

7. The cognates sitting in judgment with the husband ... were given power to pass sentence in cases of adultery and ... if any wife was found drinking wine Romulus allowed the death penalty for both crimes.

9. He also made certain laws, one of which is severe, namely that which does not permit a wife to divorce her husband, but gives him power to divorce her for the use of drugs or magic on account of children[2] or for counterfeiting the keys or for adultery. The law ordered that if he should divorce her for any other cause, part of his estate should go to the wife and that part should be dedicated to Ceres. Anyone who sold his wife was

sacrificed to the gods of the underworld.

10. It is strange ... when he established no penalty against patricides, that he called all homicide patricide.

11. If a daughter-in-law strikes her father-in-law she shall be dedicated as a sacrifice to his ancestral deities.

Laws attributed to Numa Pompilius; traditional dates, 716-673 BC

9. On the Vestal Virgins he conferred high honours, among which was the right of making a will while their fathers lived and of doing all other juristic acts without a guardian.

12. A royal law forbids the burial of a pregnant woman before the child is extracted from the womb. Whoever violates this law is deemed to have destroyed the child's expectancy of life along with the mother.

13. A concubine shall not touch the altar of Juno. If she touches it, she shall sacrifice, with her hair unbound, a ewe lamb to Juno.

108. *The Twelve Tables (excerpts). Rome, 450 BC (traditional date) (FIRA², vol. 1, p. 23. Tr. ARS. L)*

These laws, the basis of Roman civil law, have their origins in what the Romans called *mos maiorum*, the tradition of their ancestors. The codification and publication of the ancestral laws on twelve bronze tablets in the Roman Forum represented a victory for the plebeian class, which hitherto had been subject to prejudiced legal interpretations by the patricians. Though some of the laws became outdated, the code was never abolished.

Table IV. Paternal power

1. A notably deformed child shall be killed immediately.

3. To repudiate his wife, her husband shall order her ... to have her own property for herself, shall take the keys, shall expel her.[3]

4. A child born within ten months of the father's death shall enter into the inheritance ...

Table V. Inheritance and guardianship

1. ... Women, even though they are of full age, because of their levity of mind shall be under guardianship ... except Vestal Virgins, who ... shall be free from guardianship.[4]

2. The conveyable possessions of a woman under guardianship of male agnates[5] shall not be acquired by prescriptive right unless they are transferred by the woman herself with the authorisation of her guardian ...

4. If anyone who has no direct heir dies intestate, the nearest male agnate shall have the estate.

5. If there is not a male agnate, the male clansmen shall have the estate.

6. The agnatic relatives are guardians of those who are not given a guardian by will.[6]

Table VI. Ownership and possession
5. ... If any woman is unwilling to be subjected in this manner to her husband's marital control, she shall absent herself for three successive nights in every year and by this means shall interrupt his prescriptive right of each year.[7]

Table X. Sacred law
4. Women shall not tear their cheeks or shall not make a sorrowful outcry on account of a funeral.

109. *Husbands' punishment of wives in early Rome (Valerius Maximus, Memorable Deeds and Sayings 6.3.9-12, 1st cent. AD. L)*

Egnatius Metellus[8] ... took a cudgel and beat his wife to death because she had drunk some wine. Not only did no one charge him with a crime, but no one even blamed him. Everyone considered this an excellent example of one who had justly paid the penalty for violating the laws of sobriety. Indeed, any woman who immoderately seeks the use of wine closes the door on all virtues and opens it to vices.

There was also the harsh marital severity of Gaius Sulpicius Gallus.[9] He divorced his wife because he had caught her outdoors with her head uncovered: a stiff penalty, but not without a certain logic. 'The law,' he said, 'prescribes for you my eyes alone to which you may prove your beauty. For these eyes you should provide the ornaments of beauty, for these be lovely: entrust yourself to their more certain knowledge. If you, with needless provocation, invite the look of anyone else, you must be suspected of wrongdoing.'

Quintus Antistius Vetus felt no differently when he divorced his wife because he had seen her in public having a private conversation with a common freedwoman. For, moved not by an actual crime but, so to speak, by the birth and nourishment of one, he punished her before the crime could be committed, so that he might prevent the deed's being done at all, rather than punish it afterwards.

To these we should add the case of Publius Sempronius Sophus[10] who disgraced his wife with divorce merely because she dared attend the games without his knowledge. And so, long ago, when the misdeeds of women were thus forestalled, their minds stayed far from wrongdoing.

110. *The first divorce for sterility. Rome, 235 BC (Aulus Gellius, Attic Nights 17.21.44, 2nd cent. AD. L)*

In the 519th year after the founding of Rome,[11] Spurius Carvilius Ruga –

on the advice of his friends – became the first Roman to divorce his wife for sterility. He swore an oath before the censors that he had taken a wife in order to have children.

111. *Punishment for adultery. Rome, 2nd cent. BC (Aulus Gellius, Attic Nights 10.23, 2nd cent. AD L)*

An excerpt from a speech of Marcus Cato[12] on the life and customs of women of long ago and on the right of the husband to kill a wife caught committing adultery.

Those who have written about the life and culture of the Roman people say that women in Rome and Latium 'lived an abstemious life', which is to say that they abstained altogether from wine, called *temetum* in the early language, and that it was the custom for them to kiss their relatives so they could tell by the smell whether they had been drinking.[13] Women, however, are said to have drunk the wine of the second press, raisin wine, myrrh-flavoured wine and that sort of sweet drink. These things are found in these books, as I said, but Marcus Cato reports that women were not only judged but also punished by a judge as severely for drinking wine as for committing adultery.

I have copied Cato's words from a speech called *On the Dowry*, in which it is stated that husbands who caught their wives in adultery could kill them: 'The husband,' he says, 'who divorces his wife is her judge, as though he were a censor;[14] he has power if she has done something perverse and awful; if she has drunk wine she is punished; if she has done wrong with another man, she is condemned to death.' It is also written, regarding the right to kill: 'If you catch your wife in adultery, you can kill her with impunity; she, however, cannot dare to lay a finger on you if you commit adultery, nor is it the law.'

The Roman jurists[15]
'This woman does not seem to have a just defence'

The following texts derive from the writings of the Roman jurists, the legal specialists who emerged as the primary architects and interpreters of Roman private law during its classical period (50 BC-AD 250). The term 'Roman law' is used to refer to a system of legal norms which evolved from many different sources, including statutes (*leges*), such as the Twelve Tables (above, no. 108), edicts of magistrates, decrees of the senate, and pronouncements of the emperor. The most abundant and influential source for Roman law, however, is the body of jurisprudence developed in the writings of the Roman jurists.

The jurists have no counterparts in the Anglo-American system of law. They constituted an élite of legal professionals whose primary work was construing and refining the law Romans used in bringing lawsuits (*actiones*) against each other.

The legal literature produced by the jurists does not constitute 'the law' in the sense of statute or legislation. Nor do their writings record judgments or opinions delivered in the courts to decide cases. Rather, the jurists functioned in an advisory capacity, consulting with those using and administering the legal system. Their opinions were applied directly to cases heard in the Roman courts. They drew upon both factual situations and hypothetical cases to discuss and develop points of law. Consequently, much of the interest of these texts is in the details of the situations presented. As the imperial bureaucracy grew, the jurists increasingly served the emperors as legal experts.

The jurists produced an enormous body of legal literature primarily intended to be read and studied by other jurists. The selections below draw from a number of different types of juristic works. The *Institutes* of Gaius (nos. 112, 113, 132) was a textbook in four books aimed at legal instruction. The *Rules* (*Regulae*) of Ulpian (nos. 117, 133, 137, 141) and the *Opinions* (*Sententiae*) of Paul (nos. 188, 135, 123, 146) are later epitomes, or collections, attributed to the works of these jurists. The remaining material excerpted here is from the *Corpus Iuris Civilis*, the compilation of Roman law ordered by the Emperor Justinian shortly after his accession at Constantinople in AD 527. This work consists of several parts, of which the *Digest* is the single largest surviving source for Roman private law (it is about one and a half times the length of the Bible). Promulgated late in AD 533, the *Digest* consists of excerpts from juristic literature, reorganised into 432 titles in fifty books. Each individual excerpt is cited by reference to book number, title number, and then the individual *lex* or opinion, including the name of the jurist and the particular legal work from which it is drawn (for example, no. 116, *Digest* 23.2.36, Paul, *Questions*, book 5). The other parts of the *Corpus* are the *Institutes*, a textbook modelled on that of Gaius, and the *Codex*, a compilation of imperial responses (*constitutiones*) to legal petitions, some from as early as the second century AD. Another portion of the *Corpus*, the *Novels* (*Novellae*), preserves later pronouncements of Justinian and is not relevant here, but see no. 291.[16]

On women's status within the family
'The daughter still continues in guardianship'

112. *On guardianship (Gaius, Institutes 1.144-5, 190-1. Tr. Gordon and Robinson. L)*

The jurist Gaius (his family name and origin are unknown) was active as a teacher of law in the second century AD (150-180). Although he was apparently not one of the influential jurists of his own day, his work as a teacher and writer was much valued in the post-classical period. His *Institutes* is especially important since it has survived more or less in its original form and, as the basis for Justinian's *Institutes*, exerted a tremendous influence on later legal education in Europe.

By the time Gaius was writing, guardianship of women was a mere form, and by the reign of Constantine (306-337), it had vanished altogether.

(144) Where the head of a family has children in his power he is allowed to appoint guardians for them by will. That is, for males while under

puberty but for females however old they are, even when they are married. For it was the wish of the old lawyers that women, even those of full age, should be in guardianship as being scatterbrained.[17] (145) And so if someone appoints a guardian in his will for his son and his daughter and both of them reach puberty, the son ceases to have a guardian but the daughter still continues in guardianship. It is only under the Julian and Papian-Poppaean Acts that women are released from guardianship by the privilege of children. We speak, however, with the exception of the Vestal Virgins, whom even the old lawyers wished to be free of restraint in recognition of their priesthood; this is also provided in the Twelve Tables.

(190) There seems, on the other hand, to have been no very worthwhile reason why women who have reached the age of maturity should be in guardianship; for the argument which is commonly believed, that because they are scatterbrained they are frequently subject to deception and that it was proper for them to be under guardians' authority, seems to be specious rather than true. For women of full age deal with their own affairs for themselves, and while in certain instances that guardian interposes his authorisation for form's sake, he is often compelled by the praetor to give authorisation, even against his wishes. (191) For this reason, a woman is not granted any action against her guardian on account of the guardianship; but where guardians are dealing with the affairs of male or female children, when the wards grow up the action on guardianship calls the guardians to account.

113. *Patria potestas and adoption (Gaius, Institutes 1.97-8, 100-1, 103-4. Tr. Gordon and Robinson. L)*

The jurist Gaius gives later interpretations of the concept of *patria potestas*, the power of the father over his own family, which was a fundamental principle of Roman law. Compare the laws given in the Twelve Tables (above no. 108), some of which, since the original text is lost, have been reconstructed from Gaius' paraphrase.

(97) We have just set out the rules under which our real children fall into our power.[18] This also happens with those whom we adopt. (98) Adoptions can be done in two ways, either by authority of the people or through the jurisdiction of a magistrate, for instance a praetor. ... (100) That form of adoption effected by the people takes place nowhere except Rome; but the latter form commonly takes place in the provinces before the provincial governors. (101) Women are not adopted by the authority of the people; this is the received opinion. On the other hand, women too are commonly adopted before the praetor or, in the provinces, before the proconsul or legate. ... (103) Another feature common to both kinds of adoption is that people unable to have children, eunuchs, can adopt. (104) But women

cannot adopt by any method, because they do not have power even over their real children.

114. *Patria potestas (Justinian, Institutes 1.9 pr.-3; 1.11 pr., 10. L)*

(1.9 pr.) Our children, the issue of a valid Roman marriage, are in our power. (1) Marriage or matrimony is the union of male and female, involving shared life together. (2) The power which we have over our children is a right peculiar to Roman citizens, for there are no other men who have such control over their children as we have. (3) Therefore whoever is born of you and your wife is in your power, just as he who is born of your son and his wife, that is to say, your grandson and granddaughter, are equally in your power, and your great-grandson and great-granddaughter, and so forth. But the child born of your daughter is not in your power, but in that of its own father.

(1.11 pr.) Not only are our natural children under our authority as we have already stated, but those whom we adopt as well ... (10) Women also cannot adopt because they have not even power over their own children, but by the indulgence of the emperor they can do so by way of consolation for the children they have lost.

115. *Guardianship (Justinian, Codex 9.10.1. L)*

This text records a pronouncement of the Emperor Constantine in AD 326.

When a guardian violates the chastity of his female ward, he shall be sentenced to deportation, and all his property shall be confiscated to the treasury, though he deserves to have suffered the penalty which the law imposes on rapists.

116. *Guardianship (Digest 23.2.36; 48.5.7. L)*

(23.2.36) (Paul,[19] *Questions*, book 5) A guardian or a curator cannot marry an adult[20] who is committed to his care, unless she has been betrothed to, or intended for him by her father, or where the marriage takes place to comply with a condition in his will.

(48.5.7) (Marcianus,[21] *Institutes*, book 10) A guardian who takes his female ward as a wife in violation of the decree of the senate is not legally married to her; and a guardian or curator can be prosecuted for adultery if he marries a ward under twenty-six years of age who has not been betrothed to him or intended for him, or named for this purpose in her father's will.

117. *Guardianship (Ulpian, Rules 11.1. L)*

The jurist Domitius Ulpianus, or Ulpian, was a native of Tyre but a Roman citizen. Together with Paul (see no. 118), he served as clerk at the court of Papinian[22] while the latter was praetorian prefect (AD 205-211). The last of his several posts was that of praetorian praefect, which he held from 222 until his assassination by the praetorian guard in 223. Ulpian was an enormously prolific writer, whose works account for forty per cent of the *Digest*. The *Rules (Regulae)* are a post-classical epitome of his work.

Guardians are appointed for males as well as for females, but only for males under puberty, on account of their infirmity of age; for females, however, both under and over puberty, on account of the weakness of their sex as well as their ignorance of legal matters.

118. *Pregnancy, status and paternity (Paul, Opinions 2.24.1-9. L)*

The jurist Julius Paulus, or Paul, was, along with his younger contemporary Ulpian, an extraordinarily prolific jurist of the late classical period. He served as a clerk to the praetorian prefect Papinian and on the imperial council of Septimius Severus (AD 193-211). It is possible that he also became praetorian prefect during the reign of Alexander Severus (AD 222-235). Although his exact dates are unknown, most of his writings date from the reign of Commodus (AD 180-192) to that of Alexander Severus. He wrote more than eighty-five works in more than three hundred books, perhaps the most important of which was the commentary on the Edict of the Urban Praetor, in 80 books. The *Opinions (Sententiae)* was an anthology of selections from the works of Paul (and possibly of other jurists) compiled towards the end of the third century AD. It would have served as a concise summary of the principles of law and is valuable for preserving many juristic texts in a pre-Justinianic form.

(1) If a female slave conceives, and has a child after she has been manumitted, the child will be free.

(2) If a free woman conceives and has a child after having become a slave, the child will be free; for this is demanded by the favour conceded to freedom.

(3) If a female slave conceives, and in the meantime is manumitted, but, having subsequently again become a slave, has a child, it will be free; for the intermediate time can benefit but not injure freedom.

(4) A child born to a woman who should have been manumitted under the terms of a trust is born free, if it comes into the world after the grant of freedom is in default.

(5) If, after a divorce has taken place, a woman finds herself to be pregnant, she should within thirty days notify either her husband or his father to send witnesses for the purpose of making an examination of her condition: and if this is not done, they shall in any event be compelled to recognise the child of the woman.

(6) If the woman does not announce that she is pregnant, or does not admit witnesses sent to make an examination of her, neither the father

nor the grandfather will be compelled to support the child, but the neglect of the mother will not offer any impediment to the child's being considered the proper heir of his father.

(7) Where a woman denies that she is pregnant by her husband, the latter is permitted to make an examination of her, and appoint persons to watch her.

(8) The physical examination of the woman is made by five midwives, and the decision of the majority shall be held to be true.

(9) It has been decided that a midwife who introduces the child of another in order that it may be substituted shall be punished with death.

119. *Children of slaves (Digest 5.3.27 pr.-1. L)*

(Ulpian, *Edict*, book 15) (pr.) The children of female slaves and their children are not considered to be profits,[23] because it is not customary for female slaves to be acquired for breeding purposes; their offspring are, nevertheless, an increase of the estate; and since all these form part of the estate, there is no doubt that the possessor ... should hand them over to the heir. (1) Moreover, rents which have been collected from leasing of urban property are included in the action; even though they may have been collected from a brothel, for brothels are kept on the premises of many respectable persons.

On the Julian marriage laws
'We must plan for our lasting preservation'

In 18 BC, the Emperor Augustus turned his attention to social problems at Rome. Extravagance and adultery were widespread. Among the upper classes, marriage was increasingly infrequent, and many couples who did marry failed to produce offspring. Augustus, who hoped thereby to elevate both the morals and the numbers of the upper classes in Rome, and to increase the population of native Italians in Italy, enacted laws to encourage marriage and having children (*lex Julia de maritandis ordinibus*), including provisions establishing adultery as a crime.

The law against adultery made the offence a crime punishable by exile and confiscation of property. Fathers were permitted to kill daughters and their partners in adultery. Husbands could kill the partners under certain circumstances and were required to divorce adulterous wives. Augustus himself was obliged to invoke the law against his own daughter, Julia, and relegated her to the island of Pandateria.[24]

The Augustan social laws were badly received and were modified in AD 9 by the *lex Papia Poppaea*, named after the two bachelor consuls of that year. The earlier and later laws are often referred to in juristic sources as the *lex Julia et Papia*.

In part as a result of Christian opposition to such policies, the laws were eventually nearly all repealed or fell into disuse under Constantine and later emperors, including the emperor Justinian. Only the prohibitions against intermarriage, as that between senators and actresses, remained.

The first three of the texts that follow do not come from the Roman jurists but give background for the passing of the laws. The remaining texts in this section are from legal works interpreting the provisions of this legislation by a number of jurists. The juristic sources are also our best source for the actual provisions of the laws.

120. *Men must marry. Rome, 131 BC (Fr. 6 Malcovati. L)*

Speech of the censor Quintus Caecilius Metellus Macedonicus[25] about the law requiring men to marry in order to produce children. According to Livy (*Per.* 59), in 17 BC Augustus read out this speech, which seemed 'written for the hour', in the senate in support of his own legislation encouraging marriage and childbearing (see no. 121).

If we could survive without a wife, citizens of Rome, all of us would do without that nuisance; but since nature has so decreed that we cannot manage comfortably with them, nor live in any way without them,[26] we must plan for our lasting preservation rather than for our temporary pleasure.

121. *Prizes for marriage and having children. Rome, 1st cent. AD (Dio Cassius, History of Rome 54.16.1-2, early 3rd cent. AD. G)*

[Augustus] assessed heavier taxes on unmarried men and women without husbands, and by contrast offered awards for marriage and childbearing. And since there were more males than females among the nobility, he permitted anyone who wished (except for senators) to marry freedwomen, and decreed that children of such marriages be legitimate.

122. *Augustus' law. Rome, 18 BC (Suetonius, Life of Augustus 34. L)*

He reformed the laws and completely overhauled some of them, such as the sumptuary law, that on adultery and chastity, that on bribery, and marriage of the various classes.

Having shown greater severity in the emendation of this last than the others, as a result of the agitation of its opponents he was unable to get it approved except by abolishing or mitigating part of the penalty, conceding a three-year grace-period (before remarriage) and increasing the rewards (for having children).

Nevertheless, when, during a public show the order of knights asked him with insistence to revoke it, he summoned the children of Germanicus,[27] holding some of them near him and setting others on their father's knee; and in so doing he gave the demonstrators to understand through his affectionate gestures and expressions that they should not object to imitating that young man's example.

Moreover, when he found out that the law was being sidestepped through engagements to young girls[28] and frequent divorces, he put a time limit on engagement and clamped down on divorce.

123. *The consequences of adultery (Paul, Opinions 2.26.1-8, 10-12, 14-17. L)*

(1) In the second chapter of the *lex Julia* concerning adultery, either an adoptive or a natural father is permitted to kill with his own hands an adulterer caught in the act with his daughter in his own house or in that of his son-in-law, no matter what his rank may be.

(2) If a son under paternal power, who is the father, should surprise his daughter in the act of adultery, while it is inferred from the words of the law that he cannot kill her, still, he ought to be permitted to do so.

(3) Again, it is provided in the fifth chapter of the *lex Julia* that it is permitted to detain an adulterer who has been caught in the act for twenty hours, calling neighbours to witness.

(4) A husband cannot kill anyone taken in adultery except persons who are infamous, and those who sell their bodies for gain, as well as slaves. His wife, however, is excepted, and he is forbidden to kill her.

(5) It has been decided that a husband who kills his wife when caught with an adulterer should be punished more leniently, for the reason that he committed the act through impatience caused by just suffering.

(6) After having killed the adulterer, the husband should at once dismiss his wife, and publicly declare within the next three days with what adulterer and in what place he found his wife.

(7) A husband who surprises his wife in adultery can only kill the adulterer when he catches him in his own house.

(8) It has been decided that a husband who does not at once dismiss his wife whom he has taken in adultery can be prosecuted as a pimp.

(10) It should be noted that two adulterers can be accused at the same time with the wife, but more than that number cannot be.

(11) It has been decided that adultery cannot be committed with women who have charge of any business or shop.[29]

(12) Anyone who has sexual relations with a free male without his consent shall be punished with death.

(14) It has been held that women convicted of adultery shall be punished with the loss of half of their dowry and a third of their goods, and by relegation to an island. The adulterer, however, shall be deprived of half his property, and shall also be punished by relegation to an island; provided the parties are exiled to different islands.

(15) It has been decided that the penalty for incest, which in the case of a man is deportation to an island, shall not be inflicted upon the woman; that is to say when she has not been convicted under the *lex Julia* concerning adultery.

(16) Sexual intercourse with female slaves, unless they have deteri-

orated in value or an attempt is made against their mistress through them, is not considered an injury.

(17) In a case of adultery a postponement cannot be granted.

124. *Petitions to the emperor (Justinian, Codex 9.9.1, 8, 11, 17 pr.-1. L)*

A reply from the year AD 197 to a petition brought by a woman, Cassia, to the emperors Severus and Caracalla. What is interesting is not that it was denied but that Cassia evidently thought she had a fighting chance of winning.

(1) The *lex Julia* declares that wives have no right to bring criminal accusations for adultery, even as regards their own marriage, for while the law grants this privilege to men it does not concede it to women ...

A reply from the Emperor Alexander Severus in AD 224.

(8) The *lex Julia* relating to chastity forbids the two parties guilty of adultery, that is to say, the man and the woman, from being defendants on a charge of adultery at the same time, and in the same case, but they can both be prosecuted in succession.

A reply from Alexander Severus in AD 226.

(11) No one doubts that a husband cannot accuse his wife of adultery if he continues to retain her in marriage.

A reply from the emperors Valerianus and Gallienus, AD 257.

(17 pr.) You can resume marital relations with your wife without fear of being liable to the penalty prescribed by the *lex Julia* for the suppression of adultery, as you did nothing more than file the written accusation, for the reason that you assert that you afterwards ascertained that you were impelled by groundless indignation to accuse her; (1) for he alone will be liable to the penalty specifically mentioned by the law who is aware that his wife has been publicly convicted of adultery, or that she is an adulteress, as he cannot pretend ignorance of the fact, and yet retain her as his wife.

125. *Adultery (Digest 48.5.1; 48.5.2.2, 8; 48.5.9; 48.5.11 pr.-2; 48.5.12.8-9, 12-13; 48.5.20.3. L)*

(48.5.1) (Ulpian, *On Adultery*, book 1) The Julian law on adultery was introduced by the divine Augustus ...

(48.5.2) (Ulpian, *Disputations*, book 8) (2) The crime of pimping is included in the Julian law of adultery, as a penalty has been preserved against a husband who profits pecuniarily by the adultery of his wife, as well as against one who retains his wife after she has been taken in adultery.

(8) If the husband and the father of the woman appear at the same time for the purpose of accusing her, the question arises, which of them should be given the preference? The better opinion is that the husband should be entitled to the preference, for it may well be believed that he will prosecute the accusation with greater anger and vexation ...

(48.5.9) (Papinian[30]) Anyone who knowingly lends his house to enable unlawful sexual intercourse or adultery to be committed there with a matron who is not his wife, or with a male, or who pecuniarily profits by the adultery of his wife, no matter what may be his status, is punished as an adulterer ...

(48.5.11) (Papinian, *On Adultery*, book 2) (pr.) A matron[31] means not only a married woman but also a widow. (1) Women who lend their houses, or have received any compensation for (revealing) unlawful intercourse which they know, are also liable under this section of the law. (2) A woman who gratuitously acts as a procuress for the purpose of avoiding the penalty for adultery, or hires her services to appear in the theatre, can be accused and convicted of adultery under the decree of the senate.

(48.5.12) (Papinian, *Adultery*, sole book) (8) A woman, prosecuted for adultery after the death of her husband, (9) asks for delay on account of the youth of her son. I answered: This woman does not seem to have a just defence who offers the age of her son as a pretext for evading a legal accusation. For the charge of adultery brought against her does not necessarily prejudice the child, since she herself may be an adulteress, and the child still have the deceased for his father.

(12) A woman, having heard that her absent husband was dead, married another, and her first husband afterwards returned. I ask, what should be decided with reference to this woman? The answer was that the question is one of both law and of fact; for if a long time had elapsed without any proof of unlawful sexual intercourse having been made, and the woman, having been induced by false rumours, and, as it were, released from her former tie, married a second time in accordance with law, as it is probable that she was deceived, she can be held to have done nothing deserving of punishment. If, however, it is established that the supposed death of her husband furnished an inducement for her marrying a second time, as her chastity is affected by this fact, she should be punished in proportion to the character of the offence.

(13) I married a woman accused of adultery, and, as soon as she was convicted, I repudiated her. I ask whether I should be considered to have furnished the cause of the rupture. The answer was that, since by the Julian law you are prohibited from keeping a wife of this kind, it is clear

that you should not be considered to have furnished the cause for the divorce. Therefore, the law will be applied just as if a divorce had taken place through the fault of the woman.

(48.5.20) (Ulpian, *Lex Julia on Adultery*, book 2) (3) If the adulterer should be acquitted, a married woman cannot be accused, either by the person who prosecuted the adulterer and was defeated, or even by another. So also if the accuser agrees with the adulterer through collusion and the adulterer is acquitted, he has given to the married woman immunity against all other accusers. She can be accused if she should cease to be married, for the law only protects a woman as long as she is married.

126. *Concubinage (Digest 25.7.1.2; 25.7.4; 32.49.4; 48.5.35(34) pr. Tr. T.A.J. McGinn; 48.5.14 pr., 3, 8. L)*[32]

(25.7.1.2) (Ulpian, *On the Lex Julia et Papia*, book 2) I do not think that a man who keeps as a concubine a woman convicted of adultery is liable under the *lex Julia* on adultery, although he would be if he married her.

(25.7.4) (Paul, *Responsa*, book 19) A woman must be considered to be a concubine on the basis of intention alone.

(32.49.4) (Ulpian, *To Sabinus*, book 22) It makes little difference if it is to a wife or to a concubine that someone makes a legacy of things bought and acquired for her. The only real difference between them is that of social status.

(48.5.14) (Ulpian, *On Adultery*, book 2) (pr.) Where the woman who commits adultery is not a wife but a concubine, the partner cannot accuse her as a husband, because she is not his wife; still, he is not prohibited by law from bringing an accusation as a third party,[33] provided that she, in giving herself as a concubine, did not forfeit the name of a matron, for instance because she was the concubine of the patron. (3) The Divine Severus and Antoninus stated in a rescript that this offence could even be prosecuted in the case of a woman who was betrothed, because she is not permitted to violate any marriage whatever, nor even the expectation of matrimony.

(8) Where a girl less than twelve years old is taken into the house of a man, commits adultery, and afterwards remains with him until she has passed that age, and begins to be his wife, she cannot be accused of adultery by her husband, for the reason that she committed it before reaching the marriageable age; but, according to a rescript of the Divine Severus, which is mentioned above, she can be accused because she was betrothed at the time.[34]

(48.5.35(34) pr.) (Modestinus, *Rules*, book 1) He who keeps a free woman for the sake of a sexual relationship, and not for marriage, commits unlawful intercourse,[35] unless to be sure, she is a concubine.

127. *The right of life and death (Digest 48.5.21; 48.5.22; 48.5.23 pr.-2,*
4; 48.5.24 pr.-4; 48.5.25 pr.-3; 48.5.26 pr.; 48.5.27 pr.-1. L)

(48.5.21) (Papinian, *On Adultery*, book 1) The right is granted to the
father to kill an adulterer with a daughter while she is under his power.
Therefore no other relative can legally do this, nor can a son in paternal
power, who is a father.

(48.5.22) (Ulpian, *On Adultery*, book 1) (pr.) Hence it can happen that
neither the father nor the grandfather can kill the adulterer. This is not
unreasonable, for he cannot be considered to have anyone in his power
who is not subject to his power.

(48.5.23) (Papinian, *On Adultery*, book 1) (pr.) In this law, the natural
father is not distinguished from the adoptive father. (1) In the accusation
of his daughter, who is a widow, the father is not entitled to the
preference. (2) The right to kill the adulterer is granted to the father in
his own house, even though his daughter does not live there, or in the
house of his son-in-law ... (4) Hence the father, and not the husband, has
the right to kill the woman and any adulterer; for the reason that, in
general, paternal affection is solicitous for the interests of the children,
but the heat and impetuosity of the husband, who decides too quickly,
had to be restrained.

(48.5.24) (Ulpian, *On Adultery*, book 1) (pr.) What the law says, that is,
'if he finds the adulterer in his daughter', does not seem to be superfluous;
for it signifies that the father shall have this power only if he surprises
his daughter in the very act of adultery. Labeo also adopts this opinion;
and Pomponius[36] says that the man is killed when caught in the very
performance of the sexual act. This is what Solon and Dracho mean by 'in
the act' (*en ergôi*).

(1) It is sufficient for the father for his daughter to be subject to his
power at the time when he kills her, although she may not have been at
the time when he gave her in marriage; for suppose that she had
afterwards come under his power.

(2) Therefore the father shall not be permitted to kill the parties
wherever he surprises them, but only in his own house, or in that of his
son-in-law. The reason for this is, that the legislator thought that the
injury was greater where the daughter caused the adulterer to be
introduced into the house of her father or her husband.

(3) If, however, her father lives elsewhere, and has another house in
which he does not reside, and his daughter is caught there, he cannot kill
her.

(4) Where the law says, 'He may kill his daughter at once,' this must be
understood to mean that having today killed the adulterer he cannot
reserve his daughter to be killed some days later; and vice versa; for he
should kill both of them with one blow and one attack, being inflamed by
the same resentment against both. But if, without any connivance on his

part, his daughter should take to flight, while he is killing the adulterer, and she should be caught and put to death some hours afterwards by her father, who pursued her, he will be considered to have killed her immediately.

(48.5.25) (Macer,[37] *Criminal Proceedings*, book 1) (pr.) A husband is also permitted to kill a man who commits adultery with his wife, but not everyone without distinction, as the father is; for it is provided by this law that the husband can kill the adulterer if he surprises him in his own house (but not in the house of his father-in-law), or if the adulterer was formerly a pimp; or formerly exercised the profession of an actor or appeared on the stage to dance or sing; or had been convicted in a criminal prosecution and not been restored to his civil rights; or if he is the freedman of the husband or the wife, or of the father or mother, or of the son or the daughter of either of them (nor does it make any difference whether he belonged exclusively to one of the persons above mentioned, or was held in common with another), or if he is a slave.

(1) It is also provided that a husband who has killed any one of these must dismiss his wife without delay.

(2) It is held by many authorities to make no difference whether the husband is his own master, or a son in paternal power.

(3) With reference to both parties, the question arises, in accordance with the spirit of the law, whether the father can kill a magistrate, and also where his daughter is of bad reputation, or a wife has been illegally married, whether the father or the husband will still retain his right; and what should be done if the father or husband is a pimp, or is branded with ignominy for some reason or other. It may properly be held that those have a right to kill who can bring an accusation as a father or a husband.

(48.5.26) (Ulpian, *Lex Julia on Adultery*, book 2) (pr.) It is provided as follows in the fifth section of the Julian law: 'That where a husband has caught an adulterer in the act of sexual intercourse with his wife, and is either unwilling or not allowed to kill him, he can hold him lawfully and without deceit for not more than twenty consecutive hours of the day and night, in order to obtain evidence of the crime.'

(48.5.27) (Ulpian, *Disputations*, book 3) (pr.) A woman cannot be accused of adultery during marriage by anyone who, in addition to the husband, is permitted to bring the accusation; for a third party should not annoy a wife who is approved by her husband, and disturb a quiet marriage, unless he has previously accused the husband of pimping (for his wife). (1) When, however, the charge has been abandoned by the husband, it is proper for it to be prosecuted by another.

128. *Social status and marriage (Digest 23.2.44 pr.-1, 6-8; 25.7.1 pr.-1, 4; 25.7.2. L)*

(23.2.44) (Paul, *Lex Julia et Papia*, book 1) (pr.) It is provided by the *lex*

Julia that: 'A senator, or his son, or his grandson or great-grandson by his son shall not knowingly or in bad faith become betrothed to or marry a freedwoman, or a woman who is or has been an actress or whose father or mother practises, or has practised the profession of an actor. Nor shall the daughter of a senator, or a granddaughter by his son, or a great-granddaughter by this grandson marry a freedman, or a man whose father or mother practises, or has practised the profession of an actor, whether they do so knowingly, or in bad faith. Nor can any one of these parties knowingly, or in bad faith become betrothed to or marry a woman of this type.'

(1) Under this head a senator is forbidden to marry a freedwoman, or a woman whose father or mother has exercised the profession of an actor. A freedman is also forbidden to marry the daughter of a senator.

(6) If the father or mother of a freeborn woman, after the marriage of the latter should begin to exercise the profession of the stage, it would be most unjust for the husband to have to repudiate her, as the marriage was honourably contracted, and children may already have been born. (7) It is evident that if the woman herself goes on the stage, she should be repudiated by her husband. (8) Senators cannot marry women whom other freeborn men are forbidden to take as wives.

(25.7.1) (Ulpian, *Lex Julia et Papia*, book 2) (pr.) Where a freedwoman is living in concubinage with her patron, can she leave him without his consent, and either marry someone else or become his concubine? I think that a concubine should not have the right to marry if she leaves her patron without his consent, since it is more respectable for a patron to have his freedwoman as a concubine than as a wife.[38]

(1) I agree with Atilicinus,[39] that only those women with whom intercourse is not unlawful can be kept in concubinage without the fear of committing a crime ... (4) It is clear that anyone can keep a concubine of any age unless she is less than twelve years old.

(25.7.2) (Paul, *Lex Julia et Papia*, book 2) Where a patron, who has a freedwoman as his concubine, becomes insane, it is more humane to hold that she remains in concubinage.

129. *Social status (Digest 23.2.34.3; 23.2.42 pr.-1. L)*

(23.2.34) (Papinian, *Replies*, book 4) (3) Where the daughter of a senator marries a freedman, her father's lapse does not make her a lawful wife, for children should not be deprived of their rank on account of an offence of their parent.

(23.2.42) (Modestinus, *Formation of Marriage*, sole book) (pr.) In unions of the sexes, it should always be considered not only what is legal, but also what is decent. (1) If the daughter, granddaughter, or great-granddaughter of a senator should marry a freedman, or a man who practises the profession of an actor, or whose father or mother did so, the marriage will be void.

On marriage
'The union of male and female'

130. *Consent as the basis of marriage*[40] *(Digest 23.2.1; 23.2.24; 23.1.11; 23.2.22; 23.1.12 pr.-1; 23.1.7.1; 23.2.2. Tr. T. Honoré. L)*

(23.2.1) (Modestinus,[41] *Rules*, book 1). Marriage is the union of male and female and the sharing of life together, involving both divine and human law.

(23.2.24) (Modestinus, *Rules*, book 1). Cohabitation with a free woman is to be considered marriage not concubinage, unless she is a prostitute.

(23.1.11) (Julianus,[42] *Digest*, book 16). Engagement like marriage comes about by the consent of the parties, and so a daughter-in-power's consent is needed for an engagement as it is for a marriage.

(23.2.22) (Celsus,[43] *Digest*, book 15). If under pressure from his father a man takes a wife, whom he would not have married if he had followed his own inclination, still, though there is no marriage without consent, he contracted a marriage; he is regarded as having preferred to do so.

(23.1.12) (Ulpian, *On Betrothal*, sole book) (pr.) A daughter who does not oppose her father's will [as regards her engagement] is taken to agree. (1) She is free to disagree[44] only if her father chooses her a fiancé who is unworthy or of bad character.

(23.1.7.1) (Paul, *Edict*, book 35) For an engagement the same people have to agree as for a marriage. Nevertheless, Julian writes that the father of a daughter-in-power is understood to consent unless he explicitly disagrees.

(23.2.2) (Paul, *Edict*, book 35) A marriage can only exist if all agree, that is the parties and those in whose power they are.

131. *Consent as the basis of marriage (Justinian, Codex 5.1.1, 5.4.14, 8.38.2. Tr. T. Honoré. L)*

Pronouncement *(constitutio)* of the emperors Diocletian and Maximian in the year AD 293.

(5.1.1) A fiancée is not forbidden to break off the engagement and marry another.

Pronouncement of the emperors Diocletian and Maximian (AD 284-291).

(5.4.14) No one can be compelled to marry in the first place or to be reconciled after parting. So you understand that freedom to contract and dissolve a marriage should not be converted into compulsion.[45]

Pronouncement of the Emperor Alexander Severus in the year AD 223.

(8.38.2) It was decided of old that marriages should be free. Hence it is settled that an agreement not to divorce is not valid and neither is a promise to pay a penalty on divorce.

132. *Marital subordination (Gaius, Institutes 1.108-18, 136-37a. Tr. Gordon and Robinson. L)*

(108) Now let us examine persons who are subordinate to us in marriage.[46] This is also a right peculiar to Roman citizens. (109) While it is customary for both men and women to be in power, only women fall into marital subordination. (110) Formerly there used to be three methods by which they fell into subordination: by usage, by sharing of bread, and by contrived sale.[47] (111) A woman used to fall into marital subordination by usage if she remained in the married state for a continuous period of one year: for she was, as it were, usucapted by a year's possession, and would pass into her husband's kin in the relationship of a daughter. The Twelve Tables therefore provided that if any woman did not wish to become subordinate to her husband in this way, she should each year absent herself for a period of three nights, and in this way interrupt the usage of each year.[48] But this whole legal state was in part repealed by statute, in part blotted out by simple disuse.

(112) Women fall into marital subordination through a certain kind of sacrifice made to Jupiter of the Grain,[49] in which bread of coarse grain[50] is employed, for which reason it is also called the sharing of bread. Many other things, furthermore, have to be done and carried out to create this right, together with the saying of specific and solemn words in the presence of ten witnesses. This legal state is still found in our own times; for the higher priests, that is the priests of Jupiter, of Mars, and of Quirinus, as also the Sacred Kings,[51] are chosen only if they have been born in marriage made by the sharing of bread, and they themselves cannot hold priestly office without being married by the sharing of bread.

(113) Women fall into marital subordination through contrived sale, on the other hand, by means of mancipation, that is by a sort of imaginary sale; for in the presence of not less than five adult Roman citizens as witnesses, and also a scale-holder, the man to whom the woman becomes subordinate 'buys' her. (114) A woman, however, can make a contrived sale not only with her husband, but also with a third party. A contrived sale is indeed said to be made either for the purpose of marriage or of a formal trust. For when she makes a contrived sale with her husband, so as to take the status of a daughter, she is said to have made a contrived sale for the purpose of marriage. On the other hand, the woman who makes a contrived sale for some other purpose, whether with her husband or with a third party – for instance, for the purpose of evading a

guardianship – is said to have made a contrived sale for a fiduciary purpose. (115) This last is as follows: if a woman wishes to set aside the guardians she has and to get another, she makes a contrived sale of herself with their authorisation; then she is remancipated by the other party to the contrived sale to the person whom she wishes, and, when she has been formally manumitted by him, she comes to have this man as guardian. He is called the 'fiduciary guardian' as will appear below. (115a) Formerly a contrived sale used also to take place for the purpose of making a will; for at one time women, with certain exceptions, had no right to make a will unless they had made a contrived sale and been remancipated and manumitted. But, on the proposal of the late emperor Hadrian, the senate remitted this requirement of making a contrived sale. [A woman who makes a fiduciary contrived sale with an outsider does not stand as a daughter to him, but (115b) she who] makes a contrived sale with her husband for a fiduciary purpose nevertheless comes to stand as a daughter. For if for any reason at all a wife should become subordinate to her husband, the received opinion is that she acquires the rights of a daughter.

(116) It remains for us to describe what persons are in bondage.[52] (117) All children, whether male or female, who are in the power of their father can be mancipated by him in the same way as slaves can. (118) The same rule applies to persons in marital subordination; for women can be mancipated by the other parties to the contrived sale in the same way as children by their father. This is so to the extent that, although she stands as a daughter to the other party only in that she is married to him, yet when she is not married and therefore does not stand as a daughter to the other party, she can nevertheless be mancipated by him. ...

(136) [Moreover, women who fall into marital subordination cease to be in the power of their father. But for those married by sharing of bread as the wife of a priest of Jupiter,] it is provided [by a resolution of the senate moved by] Maximus and Tubero that such a woman is regarded as being in marital subordination only so far as religious observances are concerned; in other matters, on the other hand, she is viewed just as if she had not fallen into marital subordination. However, women who have fallen into subordination by a contrived sale are freed from their parent's power; nor does it matter if they are subordinate to their husband or to some other person, although only those women who are subordinate to a husband are viewed as standing to him as a daughter.

(137) [Women cease to be in marital subordination in the same ways as daughters are freed from paternal power. Just as daughters emerge from power by one mancipation so, by one mancipation, do women] cease to be subordinate; if such women should be manumitted after that mancipation they are made independent.[53] (137a) [The difference between a woman who has made a contrived sale with a third party and her who has made one with her husband is that the former can compel

the other party to remancipate her to whomever she wishes, but] the latter can no more compel [her husband] [to do this] than can a daughter her father. A daughter certainly cannot in any matter compel her father, even if she is an adoptive daughter; but once a woman has sent notice of divorce, she can compel her husband just as if she had never been married to him.

133. *Social status and citizenship of children (Ulpian, Rules 5.8-10. L)*

(8) When legal marriage takes place, the children always follow the father, but if it does not take place, they follow the condition of the mother; except where a child is born of an alien father, and a mother who is a Roman citizen, as the *lex Minicia* directs that where a child is born of parents one of whom is an alien, it shall follow the condition of the inferior parent.

(9) A child born of a father who is a Roman citizen and a Latin mother is a Latin; one born of a free man and a female slave is a slave; since the child follows the mother as in cases where there is no legal marriage.

(10) In the case of children who are the issue of a legally contracted marriage, the time of conception is considered; in the case of those who were not legitimately conceived, the time of their birth is considered; for instance, if a female slave conceives and brings forth a child after having been manumitted, the child will be free; for while she did not lawfully conceive, as she was free at the time the child was born, the latter will also be free.

134. *Marriage after adultery (Digest 23.2.34.1. L)*

(Papinian, *Replies*, book 1) (1) Where a man has accused his wife of adultery in accordance with his right as a husband, he is not forbidden, after the annulment of the marriage, to marry her again, but even if he accused her when he was not her husband, the marriage which they later contract will be valid.

135. *Eligibility for marriage (Paul, Opinions 2.19.1-2, 6-9; 2.20.1; 4.10.1-2. L)*

2.19(1) Betrothal can take place between persons over or under the age of puberty. (2) Marriage cannot legally be contracted by persons who are subject to the power of their father, without his consent; such agreements, however, are not dissolved, for the consideration of the public welfare is preferred to the convenience of private individuals. (6) Marriage cannot be contracted, but cohabitation[54] can exist between slaves and persons who are free. (7) An insane person of either sex cannot contract marriage, but a valid marriage is not dissolved by madness. (8)

An absent man can marry a wife; an absent woman, however, cannot marry. (9) It has been decided that a freedman who claims to marry his patroness, or the wife and the daughter of his patron, shall be sentenced to the mines, or to labour on the public works, according to the dignity of the person in question.

2.20(1) A man cannot keep a concubine at the same time that he has a wife. Hence a concubine differs from a wife only in the regard in which she is held.[55]

Property within marriage
4.10(1) Illegitimate children are not prevented from claiming the legal heirship of their mother, because, as their estates ought to pass to their mother, so the estate of their mother should pass to them.

(2) The estate of a mother who died intestate cannot pass to a daughter who is either a female slave, or a freedwoman by virtue of the Claudian decree of the senate; because neither slaves nor freedmen are understood to have mothers under the civil law.

136. *Conditions for the dissolution of marriage (Digest 24.2.1, 3. L)*

(Paul, *Edict*, book 35) (1) Marriage is dissolved by divorce, death, captivity, or by any other kind of servitude which may happen to be imposed upon either of the parties.

(3) It is not a true or actual divorce unless there is the intention to establish a perpetual parting of their ways. Therefore, whatever is done or said in the heat of anger is not valid, unless the determination becomes apparent by the parties persevering in their intention, and hence where a message of repudiation is sent in the heat of anger and the wife returns in a short time, she is not held to have divorced her husband.

137. *The dowry (Ulpian, Rules 6.1-2, 4, 6-7, 10, 12-13. L)*

(1) A dowry is either transferred, declared by the giver, or promised by agreement.[56]

(2) A woman who is about to be married can declare her dowry, and her debtor can do so, at her direction; a male ascendant of the woman related to her through the male sex, such as her father or paternal grandfather, can likewise so do. Any person can give or promise a dowry.

(4) When a woman dies during marriage, her dowry given by her father reverts to him, a fifth of the same for each child she leaves being retained by the husband, no matter what the number may be. If her father is not living, the dowry remains in the hands of the husband.

(6) When a divorce takes place, if the woman is in her own power, she herself has the right to sue for the recovery of the dowry. If, however, she is under the power of her father, he having been joined with his daughter,

can bring the action for the recovery of the dowry ...

(7) If the woman dies after the divorce, no right of action will be granted to her heir, unless her husband has been in default in restoring her dowry.

(10) A portion is retained on account of children, when the divorce took place either through the fault of the wife, or her father, if she is in his power; for then a sixth part of the dowry is retained in the name of each child, but not more than three-sixths altogether ...

(12) A sixth of the dowry is also retained on the ground of a flagrant breach of morals; an eighth, where the offence is not so serious. Adultery alone comes under the head of a flagrant breach of morals; all other improper acts are classed as less serious.

(13) The adultery of a husband, if he is of age, is punished by requiring him to return the dowry at once, if it was to have been returned after a certain time; if his offence is less grave, it must be returned within six months ...

On legal powers of women
'The woman has a right of action'

138. *How women could make use of their freedom to contract (Digest 45.1.121.1. Tr. T. Honoré. L)*

(Papinian) To protect herself effectively a woman who was about to marry a man stipulated from him that if he resumed relations with his concubine during the marriage, he would pay her two hundred. I replied that there was no reason why if that happened the woman could not sue on the stipulation, which was in accordance with sound morality.

139. *The wife's property (Justinian, Codex 9.12.1. L)*

A reply from the emperors Severus and Antoninus in the year AD 206.

Those who seize the property of a wife as a pledge on account of a debt of her husband, or because of some public civil liability which he has incurred, are considered to have been guilty of violence.

140. *Division of property between husband and wife (Digest 24.1.31 pr.-1; 12.4.9 pr. L)*

(24.1.31) (Pomponius, *On Sabinus*, book 4) (pr.) Where a husband makes clothing for his wife out of his own wool, although this is done for his wife and through solicitude for her, the clothing, nevertheless, will belong to the husband; nor does it make any difference whether the wife assisted in preparing the wool, and attended to the matter for her husband.

(1) Where a wife uses her own wool, but makes women's clothes for herself with the aid of female slaves belonging to her husband, the garments will be hers, and she will owe her husband nothing for the labour of his slaves; but where the clothing is made for her husband, it will belong to him, if he paid his wife the value of the wool. ...

(12.4.9) (Paul, *On Plautius*, book 17) (pr.) If I intend to give money to a woman, and pay it to her betrothed as dowry by her direction but the marriage does not take place, the woman has a right of action for its recovery ...

141. *The husband's liability (Ulpian, Rules 7.2. L)*

If a husband in anticipation of divorce abstracts anything belonging to his wife, he will be liable to an action for the removal of property.

On sexual mores
'The law brands with infamy ...'

142. *Adultery defined (Justinian, Codex 9.9.22, 23 pr., 24, 26, 28. L)*

The emperors Diocletian and Maximian
(22) If a woman whom you have carnally known indiscriminately sold herself for money, and prostituted herself everywhere as a harlot, you did not commit the crime of adultery with her. [AD 290]

(23 pr.) Slaves cannot make accusations of adultery for violation of cohabitation.[57] [AD 290]

(24) Although it is clear from the trial record that you are consumed with the lust of immoderate desire, still, as it has been ascertained that you had intercourse with a female slave, not a free woman, it is clear that by a sentence of this kind your reputation suffers, rather than that you become infamous. [AD 291]

(26) Adultery committed with a man whom a woman afterwards married is not extinguished by the fact of the marriage. [AD 294]

Constantius, AD 326
(28) It should be ascertained whether the woman who committed adultery was the owner of the inn, or only a servant; and if, by employing herself in servile duties (which frequently happens), she gave occasion for intemperance, since if she were the mistress of the inn, she would not be exempt from liability under the law. Where, however, she served liquor to the men who were drinking, she would not be liable to accusation as having committed the offence, on account of her inferior rank, and any freemen who have been accused shall be discharged, since chastity is expected only of those women who are in a lawful relationship and count

as matrons, while the rest are immune from the severity of the law, since their lowly way of life does not call for them to observe these requirements of the law. ...

143. *Prostitution (Digest 23.2.43 pr.-6; 23.2.41 pr.-1. L)*

(23.2.43) (Ulpian, *Lex Julia et Papia*, book 1) (pr.) We hold that a woman openly practises prostitution, not only where she does so in a brothel, but also if she is accustomed to do this in a tavern or inn or anywhere else where she manifests no regard for her modesty.

(1) We understand the word 'openly' to mean indiscriminately, that is to say, without choice, and not if she commits adultery or unlawful intercourse, but where she sustains the role of a prostitute. (2) Moreover, where a woman, having accepted money, has intercourse in return for payment with only one or two persons, she is not considered to have openly prostituted herself. (3) Octavenus,[58] however, says very properly that where a woman publicly prostitutes herself without doing so for money, she should be included in this category. (4) The law brands with infamy not only a woman who practises prostitution, but also one who has formerly done so, even though she has ceased to act in this manner; for the disgrace is not removed even if the practice is subsequently discontinued. (5) A woman is not to be excused who leads a shameful life under the pretext of poverty. (6) The occupation of a pimp is not less disgraceful than the practice of prostitution.

(23.2.41) (Marcellus,[59] *Formation of Marriage*, sole book) (pr.) It is understood that disgrace attaches to those women who live unchastely, and earn money by prostitution, even if they do not do so openly.

(1) If a woman became the concubine of someone other than her patron, I say that she does not preserve the honourable status of a matron.[60]

144. *Punishments. AD 326 (Justinian, Codex 9.11.1 pr. L)*

An example of the exceptionally severe punishments for which the emperor Constantine is known.

When a woman is convicted of having secretly had sexual intercourse with her slave, she shall be sentenced to death, and the rascally slave shall perish by fire.

145. *Marriage with a freedman (Digest 23.2.13. L)*

(Ulpian, *On Sabinus*, book 34) Where a patroness is so degraded that she even thinks that marriage with her freedman is honourable, it should not be prohibited by a judge to whom application is made to prevent it.

146. *How a woman loses her social status (Paul, Opinions 2.21A.1-4. L)*

(1) If a freeborn woman, who is also a Roman citizen or a Latin, forms a union with the slave belonging to another, and continues to cohabit with him against the consent and protest of the owner of the slave, she becomes a female slave.

(2) If a freeborn woman forms a union with the slave of a ward, she becomes a female slave by the denunciation of the guardian.

(3) Although a woman cannot permit her freedwoman to cohabit with the slave of another without the permission of her guardian, still, by denouncing her who has formed such a union with her slave, she will acquire the woman as her slave.

(4) A general agent, a son under paternal power, and a slave, who denounces her by order of his father, master or principal, makes a woman a female slave under such circumstances ...

147. *Rape (Justinian, Codex 9.9.20. L)*

The laws punish the detestable wickedness of women who prostitute their chastity to the lusts of others, but do not hold those liable who are violated by force and against their will. And, moreover, it has very properly been decided that their reputations are not lost, and that their marriage with others should not be prohibited on this account.

Roman Egypt
'It is not permitted to Romans to marry their sisters or their aunts'

148. *Marriage and inheritance. Alexandria, 2nd cent.* AD *(Berlin papyrus 1210. Tr. J.G. Winter. G)*

The *idiologus*, the chief financial officer of Roman Egypt, administered the imperial account, which consisted of funds acquired from means other than taxation (fines and confiscations, for example). The papyrus from which these extracts are taken contains a summary of the rules by which the idiologus carried out his duties. This document reveals fiscal oppressions not only of women but of an entire province.

6. An Alexandrian, having no children by his wife, may not bequeath to her more than one quarter of his estate; if he does have children by her, her share may not exceed those of each son.

23. It is not permitted to Romans to marry their sisters or their aunts; it is permitted in the case of the daughter of brothers. [The *idiologus*] Pardalas, however, confiscated the property when brothers and sisters married.

24. After death, the *fiscus*[61] takes the dowry given by a Roman woman over 50 to a Roman man under 60.

26. And when a *Latina*[62] over 50 gives something to one over 60 it is likewise confiscated.

27. What is inherited by a Roman of 60 years, who was neither child nor wife, is confiscated. If he has a wife but no children and registers himself, the half is conceded to him.

28. If a woman is 50 years old, she does not inherit; if she is younger and has three children, she inherits;[63] but if she is a freedwoman, she inherits if she has four children.

29. A freeborn Roman woman who has an estate of 20,000 sesterces, so long as she is unmarried, pays a hundredth part annually; and a freedwoman who has an estate of 20,000 sesterces pays the same until she marries.

30. The inheritances left to Roman women possessing 50,000 sesterces, who are unmarried and childless, are confiscated.

31. It is permitted a Roman woman to leave her husband a tenth of her property; if she leaves more, it is confiscated.

32. Romans who have more than 100,000 sesterces, and are unmarried and childless, do not inherit; those who have less, do.

33. It is not permitted to a Roman woman to dispose of her property by will without a stipulated clause of the so-called *coemptio fiduciaria*.[64] A legacy by a Roman woman to a Roman woman who is a minor is confiscated.

38. The children of a woman who is a citizen of Alexandria and an Egyptian man remain Egyptians, but inherit from both parents.

39. When a Roman man or a Roman woman marries a citizen of Alexandria or an Egyptian, without knowledge (of the true status), the children follow the lower class.

46. To Roman men and citizens of Alexandria who married Egyptian women without knowledge (of their true status) it was granted, in addition to freedom from responsibility, also that the children follow the father's station.

52. It is permitted for Roman men to marry Egyptian women.

53. Egyptian women married to ex-soldiers come under the clause of misrepresentation if they characterise themselves in business transactions as Roman women.

54. Ursus[65] did not allow an ex-soldier's daughter who had become a Roman citizen to inherit from her mother if the latter was an Egyptian.

149. *A final dowry payment. Egypt, AD 122 (Tebtunis Family papyrus 21. G)*

Affidavits about the receipt of a final dowry payment, made fifteen years after a first instalment of 500 drachmas. The text of the actual agreement[66] specifies that the woman is now 48, her cousin 52, her brothers 44 and 38, and her mother 75.

I, Didymarion, daughter of Heraclides, with my cousin Cronion son of
Lusanius as guardian, agree that I have received from my brothers
Valerius and Lysimachus 600 silver drachmas described under the terms
of an agreement my father (made with them on my behalf), under the
terms of which (a) I shall not bring suit against them for any transaction
whatever made before the present day; (b) I have received the set of
earrings (gold with genuine pearls weighing four quarters) and the cloak
as specified. I, Cronion have written this on her behalf since she does not
know letters.

I, Lysimachus son of Heraclides, and my mother Didyme daughter of
Lysimachus on my authority testify that a receipt has been made out to
me, Lysimachus, and to Valerius for 600 drachmas, and that my mother
Didyme has made a present to her daughter Didymarion of earrings and
a purple cloak, and that she guarantees that she will keep unassigned
and unencumbered the half share of the house and courtyard in Tebtunis
which she turned over to her. I, Lysimachus, have written this for her
since she does not know letters.

150. *Dowry payment through a bank. Egypt, AD 143 (Michigan papyrus 6551. G)*

The receipt of the dowry became the most important aspect of the marriage
contract; hence the conclusion of the present agreement through the bank.[67]
See plate 14b.

Copy of a draft of the (bank at ...). Year 7 of Imperator Caesar Titus
Aelius Hadrianus Antoninus Augustus Pius, Hathyr 8, Chaeremonis
daughter of N.N. granddaughter of Socrates with as guardian her relative
Sarapion son of Seuthes to Pasion son of N.N.: (it is acknowledged) that
he has received from Chaeremonis a dowry upon herself of 40 silver
drachmas and 20 drachmas of a white chiton. And they will live together
with each other, Pasion supplying her with all that is necessary and with
clothing as befits a married woman in proportion to his means; and when
a separation takes place, Pasion will return to Chaeremonis the
aforementioned dowry and the chiton in the same valuation.

151. *Legitimacy. Alexandria, 2nd cent. AD (Cattaoui papyrus 3, 4. G)*

When Crotis argued through her lawyer Philoxenus that she was a
citizen when she was living with Isidorus (who was a citizen) and that
afterwards, when he had gone off to his regiment on campaign, she had
by him a son Theodorus, who is the subject of her petition, that she
neglected to file a birth certificate but that it was clear that the son was
his because of his testament that he wrote down in which he made him
heir of his estate. After the will of Julius Martial,[68] a soldier in the first
Theban unit, was read, the judge Lupus conferred with his colleagues and

stated: 'It is impossible for Martial to have a legitimate son while he was a soldier on campaign, but he was within the law when he made him an heir in his will.'

When Octavius Valens and Cassia Secunda came before the court in regard to one of the cases that had been postponed, the prefect Eudaemon, conferring with his court, stated: 'Yesterday also, the moment the transcript of the honourable Heliodorus was read and the reason why the case had been postponed had been explained, it was evident that the mother of this child was pleading about a forbidden matter, and today also I declare that I have reviewed the facts bearing on this issue and confirm what I maintained yesterday.

'When a man has entered the army, whether in a regiment or a tactical unit or in a company, a son born to him cannot be legitimate. Since he is not the lawful son of his father, who is an Alexandrian, he cannot be an Alexandrian. This child was born to Valens when he was on campaign with his unit. He is his bastard son. He cannot be enrolled in the citizenry of Alexandria.'

And he added: 'Yesterday you said that you had other children. How old are they? When were they born?' Octavius Valens answered: 'One was just born, the other is older.'

Eudaemon said: 'The older one was born some time while you were in the army?'

Valens answered: 'While I was with my regiment and so also was the younger child'.

Eudaemon said: 'Realise that these children are in the same condition as your other son. Some things cannot be changed.'

Valens said: 'But if it were necessary for me to be out of town on business, you yourself would order that I would receive justice through a trustee. How have these children behaved unjustly?'

Eudaemon said: 'It was foolish of me to explain at length what I could have said briefly. Since you are attempting the impossible, neither this boy nor your other sons can be citizens of Alexandria.'

152. *A mother's last will and testament. Oxyrhynchus, AD 133 (SB X.10756, excerpts. G)*

This is the will of Taarpaesis, being of sound mind, also called Isidora, daughter of Apollonius (son of Apollonius) and of Tsenamounis from the city of Oxyrhynchus, with her half-brother Apollon, son of Apollonius and Diogenis from the same city as guardian,[69] a public document ... I, Taarpaesis, also called Isidora, daughter of Apollonius, make my will as follows and leave after my death my children as executors, Ptolemaeus, Berenice, and Isidora (also called Apollonarion).

To Ptolemaeus: from my property in the city of Oxyrhynchus in the south Colonnade district, the house, atrium, courtyard, furnishings, entrances and exits; in the village of Phoboou, the walled lands in the sections from the west to the north, a fourth share of the garden, with the palm trees therein and plants and the well built of baked brick, with its furnishings and everything that belongs to it, and entrances and exits; and in the middle sections of that village my father's walled land, where there is a house and a hall, with entrances and exits, and near the same village.

(*Here follow details of parcels of land, one of which she had inherited from her mother.*) To Berenice and Isidora (also called Apollonarion), because of the agreement each of them has with her husband under the terms of which each keeps her own possessions; also under my will, share and share alike, from my property in front of Herais Teos and other places in the city of Oxyrhynchus in the same south Colonnade district, and half the village of Phoboou in the east section of my father's property, a half share of the house and hall, with entrances and exits.

I leave to the son of my aforesaid first daughter Berenice, Eision son of Heraclides, one field, the property that I own near Ophis ...

All other property that I leave, furniture, equipment, household goods, accounts receivable, etc., go to Psenesis[70] who is also called Eision Ptolemaeus, if he survives me; if he does not, then to my aforesaid son Ptolemaeus. This aforesaid Psenesis (also called Eision) will have from the time that I die as long as he lives the income from and habitation of all property remaining to me after taxes, and when Psenesis (also called Eision) dies, my daughter Berenice will have the income after taxes and the assignment of the one field to her son Eision. If Ptolemaeus and Isidora die without issue, it is my wish that whatever they leave of my possessions in Ptolemaeus' estate go to my two daughters Berenice and Isidora (also called Apollonarion) equally, and what is left in Isidora's (also called Apollonarion) estate go to Berenice if she survives, who should allow Psenesis (also called Eision) as long as he lives the income, habitation rights and furnishings previously assigned to him. I am satisfied with the preceding terms.

I am 59 years of age, with a scar on the instep of my right foot, and my seal is Aphrodite's. I, Apollon, son of Apollonius and Diogenis, her half-brother, authorise my signature to the aforewritten ... I, Onnophrius son of Thonis, have written out the will on their behalf, since they do not know letters; I am about 53 years of age with a scar on my left foot. (*Witnesses.*)

153. *Calpurnia Heraclea, a woman landowner. Oxyrhynchus, Egypt, AD 246 (Oxyrhynchus papyrus 3048. G)*

An official proclamation requiring the registration of private stocks during a grain shortage, with the official response made by the owner, from the copy used by her estate agents. An inventory preserved on another papyrus

(Oxyrhynchus papyrus 3047) shows that Calpurnia's holdings were extensive.

On the authority of his excellency the *iuridicus* Aurelius Tiberius: all who have grain in the city or in the nome are required to register [it], in order that the city may have provisions and public needs may be filled, tomorrow, which is the 22nd day of Phamenoth, without any loss themselves, for he shall receive the price of six denarii set by our most illustrious leader,[71] in the knowledge that if anyone is found not to have registered [his grain], not only the grain but the household in which it is discovered shall be forfeited to the sacred treasury. Year 3, Phamenoth 21. A copy of the reply. To his excellency the *iuridicus* Aurelius Tiberius from Calpurnia Heraclea (also known as Eudamia) daughter of Theon, fellow of the Museum, etc., acting through her guardians Aurelius Pecyllus (also known as Theon) the gymnasiarch, prytanis and councillor of the city of Oxyrhynchus and Chaeremon (also known as Demetrius), etc.,[72] I register according to your instructions the grain that I am in possession of through my agents in my property near Souis, 3,020 artabas; in Dosithe 245 artabas ... in Iseum Tryphonis 220 artabas; in Thmnoenepsobthis 460 artabas; in Lile 280 artabas; in Satyru 820 artabas... From the above-mentioned properties monthly allowances are given to the agents and stewards and farmers and boys and monthly workers. And in Satyru ... 287 artabas has been pledged (?) already from the preceding month Mecheir to Copres and ... pos, cooks in the city, because the oil had become old and rancid. Year three, Phamenoth 22.

154. *A woman's petition to act without a kyrios. Oxyrhynchus, Egypt, AD 263 (Oxyrhynchus papyrus 1467. G)*

Legislation (cf. 148, section 28) enabled women with three or more children (the *ius trium liberorum*) to serve as their own *kyrios*.[73]

Petition addressed to the most eminent prefect from Aurelia Thaisus also called Lolliane. [Laws exist] that grant authority to women who are honoured with the right of three children and that enable them to transact business without a *kyrios* in all household business they transact, and in particular women who are literate. Therefore, since I have been blessed with the honour of children, being literate and able to write with proficiency, in full confidence I petition your eminence with this application for the right to transact business without hindrance in all household affairs.[74] I beg you to retain this application, without prejudice to my rights, in your eminence's office, and offer my eternal gratitude to you for your assistance. Farewell. Aurelia Thaisus also known as Lolliane has sent this petition for presentation. In the year 10 (*emperor's name omitted*), Epeiph 21. (*added*) Your application shall be kept in the office.

155. *A prostitute and her mother. Hermoupolis, Egypt, 4th-5th cent.* AD *(Berlin papyrus 1024.6-8, excerpts G)*

A transcript of a legal protocol recording the judge's decision in a murder case. Although the defendant was a senator, the judge recognises the rights of his female victims.

Case against a certain senator, Diodemus of Alexandria, who was in love with a public prostitute. He was dining with the prostitute at evening time. Diodemus killed the prostitute, and when Zephyrus learned about it, he ordered Diodemus to be put into prison ... (*The other senators ask that he be released, but Zephyrus insists that he must remain in prison.*)

(7) Diodemus admits that he killed the prostitute. A certain Theodora, a old woman and a pauper, asks that Diodemus be compelled for her support to provide some small consolation for her daughter's life. For she said, 'This is why I gave my daughter to the pimp, so that I might have a means of support. Now that my daughter is dead I am deprived of my support, and on this account I ask that some small amount, appropriate for a woman, be given for my support.'

The prefect's decision: You killed this woman, Diodemus, in a disgraceful way, a woman who gives a bad impression of human fortune, because she spent her life in an unholy manner and in the end sold (*some letters missing*). And indeed I pity the poor creature, who when she was alive was laid out for those who wanted her, like a dead body. The poverty of her lot was so insistent that she sold her body and brought dishonour upon her name and reputation and took on a prostitute's life with its many hardships ... (8). I order that because you have destroyed the honour of the city council with the sword that you be banished as a murderer. Theodora, the poor old mother of the dead woman, who because of her own poverty deprived her daughter of her chastity, and so also caused her death, is to receive as her share one tenth of Diodemus' property; this is what is required by law, with humanitarian considerations supporting the law's authority.

156. *A husband's complaint about a drunken assault on his wife. Oxyrhynchus, Egypt,* AD *110-112 (Oxyrhynchus papyrus 2758. G)*

To the governor Archias from Herclas the son of Pausirion from the city of Oxyrhynchus. On the past fifth day in the evening Apollos the son of Heraclides from the same city, a native of the same district approached my wife Taamois when she was standing in front of the door. He was drunk and insulted her and pulled up her skirts, in the presence of many men whose names I will report on the day set for the hearing. Accordingly I submit my petition, and ask for retribution so that my family and I may be protected from injury by him in the future. In the 12th (?) year of the reign of the Emperor Caesar Nerva Trajan Augustus Germanicus Dacicus ...

157. *A woman greengrocer brings a charge of assault and battery against another woman and her husband. Bacchias, Egypt,* AD *114 (Berlin papyrus 22. G)*

To Sarapion the *strategus* in the division of Heraclides of the Arsinoite nome from Tarmuthis the daughter of Phimon, greengrocer from the village of Bacchias, at the present time without a guardian. On the 4th of the present month Parmouthi, although she had absolutely no grievance against me, Taorsenophis, the wife of Ammonius also called Phimon, elder of the village of Bacchias, entered my house and started an unreasonable disagreement with me; she tore my dress and my cloak, and in the course of the disagreement she took away the money that I had in the house for the price of the vegetables that I sold, namely 15 drachmas. And on the 5th day of the same month her husband Ammonius (also called Phimon) came on the pretext of looking in my house for my husband. He picked up my lamp, and went through my house and carried off with him a pair of bracelets that I had of unstamped silver weighing 40 drachmas, while my husband was out of town.[75] Accordingly I ask that the accused be brought before you for the punishment that they deserve. Farewell. Tarmouthis is about 30 years old, with a mark on her right foot. In the 17th year of the Emperor Caesar Nerva Trajan Augustus Germanicus Dacicus. Pharmouthi 6.

158. *A violent quarrel. Oxyrhynchus, Egypt, 3rd cent.* AD *(Oxyrhynchus papyrus 3644. G)*

This letter from a son to his father written in phonetic (rather than orthodox) spelling gives an account of a fight between two women over possessions.

Heras to his father Popontos, greetings. I have sent our Harpochras to you in order to get the letters of credit from my brother ... because I was detained by my friend Ceras and he used force to compel me to swear to him that they would be delivered to him within 20 days. I found that Sabina had injured Syra and I heard from her how she had been injured and I learned from everyone that because Syra would not release to her what she had in her possession, Sabina hit her with the key to the out-building[76] that she had in her hand and Syra has stayed in bed until today. No one has been able to find Sabina for ten days and I hear that she is in the Heracleopolite nome. Harpochras will tell you what he heard she did in the city. I pray for your good health. Paophi 14. (*Note added in margin*:) Be sure not to detain Harpochras, because there is a hurry for the credits.

159. *A wife's complaint against an abusive husband. Oxyrhynchus, Egypt, 4th cent.* AD *(Oxyrhynchus papyrus 903. G)*

Although the names of the addressee and parties involved are missing, this sensational account appears to be taken from a petition to a court complaining of the misconduct of a husband in his role as *kyrios* (cf. no. 82).

Now concerning the insulting allegations he made about me: he shut up his own daughters and mine, along with my foster-daughters and his agent and his son for seven whole days in his cellars, and treated his slaves and my slave Zoe violently, [virtually] killing them with blows. He stripped my foster-daughters naked and set fire to them, in complete violation of the law. And he said to the foster-daughters, 'Give me everything that belongs to her', and they said that they had nothing that belonged to me. To the slaves as they were being beaten he said, 'What did she take from my house?' Under torture they said, 'She has taken nothing that belongs to you; all your property is safe.' Zoilus accused him because he had locked up his foster-son. He said to Zoilus: 'Have you come on account of your foster-son or to speak on behalf of a certain woman?'[77]

He swore in the presence of the bishops and his own brothers, 'From now on I shall not hide all my keys from her and I shall not attack her and insult her from now on. (*Added above the line*:) He trusted his slaves but not me. He made a marriage agreement, and after his contract and his oaths he hid the keys from me again. When I went to the church in Sambatho, he also shut the outside doors and said about me 'Why did you go to church?' He made many abusive comments to my face, and further insulted me by speaking through his nose.

Of the public grain in my name valued at 100 drachmas he did not pay one artaba. He locked up the accounts after he got hold of them and said, 'Put down the price of the grain as 100 artabas', but he paid nothing, as I said. He told his slaves, 'Bring reinforcements so they can lock her up.'

Choous his assistant was sent to prison and Euthalmus posted bail for him, but ran short of money. I took a little extra and gave it to Choous. When he met me in Antinoöpolis when I had my bathing bag containing my ornaments, he also said to me, 'If you have some money with you, I shall take it because of what you gave to Choous as bail for his imprisonment.' All this is verified by his mother's testimony.

Also he kept on tormenting my soul about his slave-girl Anilla, both in Antinoöpolis and here. He said: 'Throw out this slave since she knows what she has taken', perhaps because he wished to implicate me and use it as an excuse to take all my possessions. I did not put up with her being sent away. And he kept on saying that 'a month from now I'm going to take a mistress[78] for myself.' God knows that this is true.

VI. Public Life

'A woman who had risen high'

Women's bravery in legend and history
'An impulsive courage, divinely inspired'

Legend
'Do you see how well Artemisia is fighting?'

160. *The courage of the poet Telesilla. Argos, 5th cent. BC (Plutarch, On the Bravery of Women 4, Moralia 245c-f, 2nd cent. AD. G)*

No action taken by women for the common good is more famous than the conflict against Cleomenes[1] by the Argive women, which they fought at the instigation of the poetess Telesilla. They say that she was the daughter of a distinguished family but, because she was sickly in body, inquired about her health at Delphi; the oracle said to cultivate the Muses. In obedience to the god she applied herself to song and harmony and was quickly cured of her suffering and admired by the women for her poetry.

But when Cleomenes king of Sparta had killed many Argives (but not, as some have imagined, 7,777) and marched against the city, an impulsive courage, divinely inspired, impelled the younger women to defend their country against the enemy. With Telesilla as general, they took up arms and made their defence by manning the walls around the city, and the enemy was amazed. They drove Cleomenes off after inflicting many losses. They also repulsed the other Spartan king, Demaratus, who (according to Socrates)[2] managed to get inside and seize the Pamphylacium. After the city was saved, they buried the women who had fallen in battle by the Argive road, and as a memorial to the achievements of the women who were spared they dedicated a temple to Ares Enyalius ... Up to the present day they celebrate the Festival of Impudence (Hybristika) on the anniversary [of the battle], putting the women into men's tunics and cloaks and the men in women's dresses and head-coverings.[3]

To restore the balance of the sexes in the city, they did not (despite

Herodotus) marry the women to slaves, but to the best men in the surrounding towns, whom they made citizens of Argos. The women appeared not to show respect for their husbands and despised them when they slept with them as if they were inferior, so they made a law that says that women who have beards may spend the night with their husbands.

161. *Marpessa and the defence of Tegea. Arcadia, 7th cent.* BC *(Pausanias, Guide to Greece 8.48.4-5, 2nd cent.* AD. *G)*

A similar story is given as the explanation or *aition* of a festival in Tegea.[4]

In the agora of Tegea there is an image of Ares. It is carved on a stele, and the Tegeans give him the title Feaster of Women (*gynaikothoinas*). In the war with Sparta, when king Charillus[5] made the first invasion, the women took up arms and lay in ambush under the hill that is now called Guard Hill (*phylaktris*). When the two armies met and the men on both sides were carrying out many notable actions, they say that the women appeared among them and were the ones who routed the Spartans. Marpessa, who had the additional name Choire,[6] surpassed the other women in courage, and Charillus himself was among the Spartan prisoners. He was set free without ransom, and swore that the Spartans would never attack Tegea again, and then broke the oath. The women offered a sacrifice to Ares for their own victory without the men, and gave the men no share in the meat of the sacrificial victim. That is how Ares got his title Feaster of Women.

162. *A memorial to Telesilla. Argos, 2nd cent.* AD *(Pausanias, Guide to Greece 2.20.8. G)*

Above the theatre is a temple of Aphrodite, and in front of the seated statue [of the goddess] there is a stele with a relief of Telesilla, who wrote poems.[7] Her books have been thrown down at her feet, and she is looking at a helmet that she holds in her hand and is about to put onto her head.

163. *Thargalia. Miletus, early 5th cent.* BC *(Anon., Tract. de Mulieribus 11. G)*

It is said that at the time that Antiochus was king of Thessaly, Thargalia came to marry Antiochus. After he died she ruled Thessaly for 20 years, and when the king of Persia invaded Greece she entertained him and sent him on his way without any loss to her country.

164. *Artemisia, the sea-captain. Salamis, 480* BC *(Herodotus, Histories 8.87-8. G)*

A local legend from Halicarnassus, a city in Asia Minor and Herodotus'

home. Halicarnassus was an ally of Persia in the second war with Greece, at
the battle of Salamis in 480.

I cannot offer a precise account of how anyone else fought, either on the
Greek or the Persian side, but as far as Artemisia is concerned, this is
what happened, and as a result of it she rose in King Xerxes' estimation.

The king's forces had been thrown into great confusion, and at this
point Artemisia's ship was being chased by an Athenian ship. She wasn't
able to get away (three friendly ships were in her way, and her own ship
happened to be closest to the enemy). So she decided to act as follows, and
the plan worked out well for her.

As she was being pursued by the Athenian ship, she attacked at full
speed a friendly ship, manned by Calyndians and the king of Calynda
himself, Damasithymus. Whether she had been involved in a dispute
with him while they were at the Hellespont, I can't say; nor whether her
action was premeditated or whether the Calyndian ship had the bad luck
to get in her way. In any case, she attacked it and sank it, and used her
good luck to get herself a double advantage. When the captain of the
Athenian ship saw that she was attacking a Persian ship, he thought that
Artemisia's ship either was Greek or had defected from the Persians and
was fighting on the Athenian side, so he turned away and took off after
other ships.

That was the first benefit, to be able to get away and not be killed. The
second was that by doing damage she rose higher as a result in Xerxes'
estimation. The story goes that when the king was watching the battle
and saw her ship making its attack, one of the bystanders said: 'Master,
do you see how well Artemisia is fighting and that she has sunk an enemy
ship?' The king asked if this were truly Artemisia's achievement, and
they confirmed that it was, because they recognised her ship's insignia;
they believed that the ship she had destroyed was the enemy's. In
addition to everything else, she had the good luck that there were no
survivors from the Calyndian ship to accuse her. Xerxes is said to have
remarked on what he had been told: 'My men have turned into women,
and my women into men.'

165. *Cloelia the hostage. Traditionally, Rome, 506 BC (Livy, History of
Rome 2.13.6-11. Late 1st cent. BC-early 1st cent. AD. L)*

The Romans made a treaty with the Etruscan Lars Porsenna, king of
Clusium, and sent ten boys and ten girls as hostages. In his account of the
legendary events of the period, Livy places the episode of Cloelia, a story of
the physical prowess and daring of an adolescent, near the spectacular acts
of bravery and self-sacrifice of Mucius Scaevola and Horatius at the bridge.
In later accounts of women's physical and moral courage, such as those told

by Appian (no. 167), the heroines are almost invariably married women
defending their husbands.

Seeing that the Romans so respected courage, women too were inspired to
carry out acts of heroism, and Cloelia, one of the girls given as hostages,
since the Etruscan camp was situated not far from the bank of the Tiber,
eluded the guards, and swam the Tiber amidst a rain of enemy spears at
the head of a group of other girls. They all reached Rome safely and she
restored them to their families. When the king found out, he was furious
at first and sent emissaries to Rome to ask that Cloelia be given back; he
did not care about the other girls. But his anger turned to admiration and
he said that her undertaking had been greater than that of a Cocles or a
Mucius, and gave it to understand that, although he would consider the
non-restoration of the hostage equivalent to breaking the treaty, he
would none the less return her unharmed. Each side trusted the other:
the Romans, according to the treaty, returned the pledge of peace, and the
Etruscan king not merely respected her courage but honoured it; he
praised the girl and said that he would give her half the hostages: she
should herself choose the ones she wanted. They were brought before her
and it is said she picked the boys, the appropriate choice for her young
age, and by agreement of the hostages themselves it was the right thing,
as they preferred to have released the persons at the greatest risk of
harm by the enemy. Peace was re-established, and the Romans rewarded
this act of courage – new in a woman – with a new kind of honour, an
equestrian statue. At the top of the Via Sacra a statue of the girl on
horseback was set up.[8]

166. *The rape of Lucretia. Traditionally, Ardea, near Rome, c. 510 BC
(Livy, History of Rome 1.57.6-58. Late 1st cent. BC-early 1st cent.
AD. L)*

While they were drinking at Sextus Tarquinius' house, where Tarquinius
Collatinus, son of Egerius, was also dining, the conversation happened to
turn to their wives. Each one praised his own, and the discussion heated
up. Collatinus said there was no need for all the talk as only a few hours
were needed to prove beyond a doubt that his wife was the most virtuous.

'We are young and strong. Why don't we get on our horses and make a
surprise visit. Then we'll see with our own eyes how our wives behave
when we're not around.' The wine had got them fired up.

'Let's go!' they cried and flew off towards Rome, which they reached as
twilight was falling. There they found the daughters-in-law of the king
banqueting with their friends. They continued on to Collatia to check on
Lucretia, whom they found, not at dinner like the others, but in the
atrium of the house, with only her maidservants, working at her wool by
lamplight.

There was no question who won the contest. She greeted her husband and the Tarquins, and the victorious husband graciously invited the others to dine. That was when Sextus Tarquinius became inflamed by lust and became possessed by the idea of raping Lucretia.

A few days later, unbeknown to Collatinus, Sextus Tarquinius returned to Collatia with a single companion. The household received him warmly, as no one realised why he had come, and after dinner he was shown to the guestroom already seething with passion.

When he was sure everyone in the house was asleep, he went, with his sword drawn, to Lucretia's room, where she was asleep. With his left hand he pinned her to the bed and said, 'Not a sound, Lucretia. It is I, Sextus Tarquinius. I've got a sword in my hand. One sound and you will die.' The terrified woman, awakened like that, was sure she was going to die. Tarquinius confessed his love and tried to persuade her with a combination of entreaties and threats. But when he saw that the fear of death was having no effect, he tried that of dishonour.

He said that next to her dead body he would place the corpse of a slave with his throat cut. That way it would seem that she had been killed in the act of adultery. With such terror his lust triumphed over her tenacious chastity, and then he went away, proud of having blotted the woman's honour.

Lucretia, overwrought by her ordeal, send a messenger to her father in Rome and her husband in Ardea for them to come to her each with one trusted friend and that they should hurry as something terrible had happened. Spurius Lucretius came with Publius Valerius, son of Volesus, while her husband brought Lucius Junius Brutus, with whom he happened to be returning to Rome when he met his wife's messenger.

They found Lucretia weeping in her room. 'Are you all right?' asked her husband. 'No', she replied, 'how can anything be all right if a woman has lost her honour? In your bed, Collatinus, you'll find the sign of another man. But only my body was violated, my mind is innocent, as my death shall attest. Promise me that the adulterer will be punished. He is Sextus Tarquinius. Last night he came, an enemy masquerading as a guest and by force of arms took his pleasure. But that pleasure, if you are men, will be death for him as well as for me.'

They all promised and reassured her that she, who had been forced, was not guilty, that only the author of the crime was. 'You'll see,' she said, 'what punishment he deserves. As for me, although I absolve myself of guilt, I do not release myself from paying the penalty. From now on, no woman can use the example of Lucretia to live unchaste.' With that she took the dagger she had hidden in her clothes, plunged in into her heart, and fell forward dead. Her husband and father cried out.

History
'Paetus, it doesn't hurt'

167. *Women who risked their lives to save their husbands. Rome, 43 BC*
(Appian, Civil War 4.39-40, 2nd cent AD. G)

According to the historian Appian, writing in Greek in the second century
AD, the proscriptions following the assassination of Julius Caesar (cf. no.
174) elicited remarkable examples of wives' devotion to their husbands.

Acilius managed to escape from the city without being detected, but when
a slave told the soldiers where he was, he persuaded them by a promise of
greater financial reward to send some of their number to his wife with a
special token that he gave them. When they came she gave them all her
jewellery so that they would do what they promised, without knowing
whether they would, but she was not disappointed in their loyalty. The
soldiers hired a ship for Acilius and sent him to Sicily.

Lentulus' wife asked him if she could accompany him in his escape and
kept an eye on him for this purpose, but he did not wish her to share the
danger with him; he managed to escape to Sicily without her noticing.
When Pompey appointed him praetor there he let her know that he was
safe and serving as praetor. When his wife knew where in the world he
was, she got away from her mother (who she knew was watching her) and
escaped with two slaves. She travelled with the slaves in difficult and
rough conditions, like a fellow-slave, until she sailed from Rhegium[9] to
Messina, landing in the evening. She discovered without difficulty where
the praetor's tent was, and found Lentulus living not as a praetor should,
but on a pallet and with dishevelled hair and wretched food because he
was longing for his wife.

(40) Apuleius' wife threatened to inform on him if he escaped without
her. So he unwillingly took her along, and successfully avoided suspicion
in his escape because he was travelling openly with his wife and male and
female slaves.

Antius' wife wrapped him in a bag of bed coverings and gave the bag to
hired porters, and he managed to get from his house to the sea, from
where he escaped to Sicily.

Rheginus' wife hid him in a sewer at night, which the soldiers had not
been prepared to enter by day because of the stench, and the next night
she disguised him as a charcoal-seller and had him drive a donkey
carrying the charcoal. She herself went on a short distance ahead, being
carried in a litter. When a soldier at the city-gates became suspicious of
the litter and searched it, Rheginus became apprehensive and ran up and
like a wayfarer told the soldier not to harass women. After the soldier had
addressed him angrily, as if he were a charcoal-seller, he recognised
Rheginus (he had been with him on campaign in Syria) and said, 'Please
go ahead, general, for that is the title that I still ought to use for you.'

Coponius' wife asked Antony for her husband's freedom; she had been chaste before that, and now cured one misfortune by another.

168. *A funeral eulogy. Rome, 1st cent.* BC *(ILS 8393. Tr. E. Wistrand. L)*

The following unusually long funerary inscription is traditionally known as the 'Laudatio Turiae', as attempts have been made to identify the deceased woman with the Turia described by Valerius Maximus (see no. 53). Its form resembles that of the customary eulogy read aloud at the funeral. The speaker is the woman's husband.[10]

(*heading*) ... of my wife

Left-hand column (line 1) ... through the honesty of your character ...

(2) ... you remained ...

(3) You became an orphan suddenly before the day of our wedding, when both your parents were murdered together in the solitude of the countryside. It was mainly due to your efforts that the death of your parents was not left unavenged. For I had left for Macedonia, and your sister's husband Cluvius had gone to the Province of Africa.[11]

(7) So strenuously did you perform your filial duty by your insistent demands and your pursuit of justice that we could not have done more if we had been present. But these merits you have in common with that most virtuous lady your sister.

(10) While you were engaged in these things, having secured the punishment of the guilty, you immediately left your own house in order to guard your modesty and you came to my mother's house, where you awaited my return. (13) Then pressure was brought to bear on you and your sister to accept the view that your father's will, by which you and I were heirs, had been invalidated by his having contracted a *coemptio*[12] with his wife. If that was the case, then you together with all your father's property would necessarily come under the guardianship of those who pursued the matter; your sister would be left without any share at all of that inheritance, since she had been transferred to the *potestas*[13] of Cluvius. How you reacted to this, with what presence of mind you offered resistance, I know full well, although I was absent.

(18) You defended our common cause by asserting the truth, namely, that the will had not in fact been broken, so that we should both keep the property, instead of your getting all of it alone. It was your firm decision that you would defend your father's written word; you would do this anyhow, you declared, by sharing your inheritance with your sister, if you were unable to uphold the validity of the will. And you maintained that you would not come under the state of legal guardianship, since there was no such right against you in law, for there was no proof that your father belonged to any gens that could by law compel you to do this. For even assuming that your father's will had become void, those who prosecuted had no such right since they did not belong to the same *gens*.

(25) They gave way before your firm resolution and did not pursue the matter any further. Thus you on your own brought to a successful conclusion the defence you took up of your duty to your father, your devotion to your sister, and your faithfulness towards me.

(27) Marriages as long as ours are rare, marriages that are ended by death and not broken by divorce. For we were fortunate enough to see our marriage last without disharmony for fully 40 years. I wish that our long union had come to its final end through something that had befallen me instead of you; it would have been more just if I as the older partner had had to yield to fate through such an event.

(30) Why should I mention your domestic virtues: your loyalty, obedience, affability, reasonableness, industry in working wool, religion without superstition, sobriety of attire, modesty of appearance? Why dwell on your love for your relatives, your devotion to your family? You have shown the same attention to my mother as you did to your own parents, and have taken care to secure an equally peaceful life for her as you did for your own people, and you have innumerable other merits in common with all married women who care for their good name. It is your very own virtues that I am asserting, and very few women have encountered comparable circumstances to make them endure such sufferings and perform such deeds. Providentially Fate has made such hard tests rare for women.

We have preserved all the property you inherited from your parents under common custody, for you were not concerned to make your own what you had given to me without any restriction. We divided our duties in such a way that I had the guardianship of your property and you had the care of mine. Concerning this side of our relationship I pass over much, in case I should take a share myself in what is properly yours. May it be enough for me to have said this much to indicate how you felt and thought.

(42) Your generosity you have manifested to many friends and particularly to your beloved relatives. On this point someone might mention with praise other women, but the only equal you have had has been your sister. For you brought up your female relations who deserved such kindness in your own houses with us. You also prepared marriage-portions for them so that they could obtain marriages worthy of your family. The dowries you had decided upon Cluvius and I by common accord took upon ourselves to pay, and since we approved of your generosity we did not wish that you should let your own patrimony suffer diminution but substituted our own money and gave our own estates as dowries. I have mentioned this not from a wish to commend ourselves but to make clear that it was a point of honour for us to execute with our means what you had conceived in a spirit of generous family affection.

(52) A number of other benefits of yours I have preferred to to mention ... (*several lines missing*)

Right-hand column (2a) You provided abundantly for my needs during my flight and gave me the means for a dignified manner of living, when you took all the gold and jewellery from your own body and sent it to me and over and over again enriched me in my absence with servants, money and provisions, showing great ingenuity in deceiving the guards posted by our adversaries.

(6a) You begged for my life when I was abroad[14] – it was your courage that urged you to this step – and because of your entreaties I was shielded by the clemency of those against whom you marshalled your words. But whatever you said was always said with undaunted courage.

(9a) Meanwhile when a troop of men collected by Milo, whose house I had acquired through purchase when he was in exile, tried to profit by the opportunities provided by the civil war and break into our house to plunder, you beat them back successfully and were able to defend our home. (*About 12 lines missing*)

(0) ... exist ... that I was brought back to my country by him (Caesar Augustus), for if you had not, by taking care for my safety, provided what he could save, he would have promised his support in vain. Thus I owe my life no less to your devotion than to Caesar.

(4) Why should I now hold up to view our intimate and secret plans and private conversations: how I was saved by your good advice when I was roused by startling reports to meet sudden and imminent dangers; how you did not allow me imprudently to tempt providence by an overbold step but prepared a safe hiding-place for me, when I had given up my ambitious designs, choosing as partners in your plans to save me your sister and her husband Cluvius, all of you taking the same risk? There would be no end, if I tried to go into all this. It is enough for me and for you that I was hidden and my life was saved.

(11) But I must say that the bitterest thing that happened to me in my life befell me though what happened to you. When thanks to the kindness and judgment of the absent Caesar Augustus I had been restored to my country as a citizen, Marcus Lepidus, his colleague, who was present, was confronted with your request concerning my recall, and you lay prostrate at his feet, and you were not only not raised up but were dragged away and carried off brutally like a slave. But although your body was full of bruises, your spirit was unbroken and you kept reminding him of Caesar's edict with its expression of pleasure at my reinstatement, and although you had to listen to insulting words and suffer cruel wounds, you pronounced the words of the edict in a loud voice, so that it should be known who was the cause of my deadly perils. This matter was soon to prove harmful for him.

(19) What could have been more effective than the virtue you displayed? You managed to give Caesar an opportunity to display his clemency and not only to preserve my life but also to brand Lepidus' insolent cruelty by your admirable endurance.

(22) But why go on? Let me cut my speech short. My words should and can be brief, lest by dwelling on your great deeds I treat them unworthily. In gratitude for your great services towards me let me display before the eyes of all men my public acknowledgment that you saved my life.

(25) When peace had been restored throughout the world and the lawful political order re-established, we began to enjoy quiet and happy times. It is true that we did wish to have children, who had for a long time been denied to us by an envious fate. If it had pleased Fortune to continue to be favourable to us as she was wont to be, what would have been lacking for either of us? But Fortune took a different course, and our hopes were sinking. The courses you considered and the steps you attempted to take because of this would perhaps be remarkable and praiseworthy in some other women, but in you they are nothing to wonder at when compared to your other great qualities and I will not go into them.

(31) When you despaired of your ability to bear children and grieved over my childlessness, you became anxious lest by retaining you in marriage I might lose all hope of having children and be distressed for that reason. So you proposed a divorce outright and offered to yield our house free to another woman's fertility. Your intention was in fact that you yourself, relying on our well-known conformity of sentiment, would search out and provide for me a wife who was worthy and suitable for me, and you declared that you would regard future children as joint and as though your own, and that you would not effect a separation of our property which had hitherto been held in common, but that it would still be under my control and, if I wished so, under your administration: nothing would be kept apart by you, nothing separate, and you would thereafter take upon yourself the duties and the loyalty of a sister and a mother-in-law.

(40) I must admit that I flared up so that I almost lost control of myself; so horrified was I by what you tried to do that I found it difficult to retrieve my composure. To think that separation should be considered between us before fate had so ordained, to think that you had been able to conceive in your mind the idea that you might cease to be my wife while I was still alive, although you had been utterly faithful to me when I was exiled and practically dead!

(44) What desire, what need to have children could I have had that was so great that I should have broken faith for that reason and changed certainty for uncertainty? But no more about this! You remained with me as my wife, for I could not have given in to you without disgrace for me and unhappiness for both of us.

(48) But on your part, what could have been more worthy of commemoration and praise than your efforts in devotion to my interests: when I could not have children from yourself, you wanted me to have them through your good offices, and since you despaired of bearing

children, to provide me with offspring by my marriage to another woman.

(51) Would that the life-span of each of us had allowed our marriage to continue until I, as the older partner, had been borne to the grave – that would have been more just – and you had performed for me the last rites, and that I had died leaving you still alive and that I had had you as a daughter to myself in place of my childlessness.

(54) Fate decreed that you should precede me. You bequeathed me sorrow through my longing for you and left me a miserable man without children to comfort me. I on my part will, however, bend my way of thinking and feeling to your judgments and be guided by your admonitions.

(56) But all your opinions and instructions should give precedence to the praise you have won so that this praise will be a consolation for me and I will not feel too much the loss of what I have consecrated to immortality to be remembered for ever.

(58) What you have achieved in your life will not be lost to me. The thought of your fame gives me strength of mind and from your actions I draw instruction so that I shall be able to resist Fortune. Fortune did not rob me of everything since it permitted your memory to be glorified by praise. But along with you I have lost the tranquillity of my existence. When I recall how you used to foresee and ward off the dangers that threatened me, I break down under my calamity and cannot hold steadfastly by my promise.

(63) Natural sorrow wrests away my power of self-control and I am overwhelmed by sorrow. I am tormented by two emotions: grief and fear – and I do not stand firm against either. When I go back in thought to my previous misfortunes and when I envisage what the future may have in store for me, fixing my eyes on your glory does not give me strength to bear my sorrow with patience. Rather I seem to be destined to long mourning.

(67) The conclusions of my speech will be that you deserved everything but that it did not fall to my lot to give you everything as I ought; your last wishes I have regarded as law; whatever it will be in my power to do in addition, I shall do.

(69) I pray that your Di Manes will grant you rest and protection.

169. *Pythias, a courageous slave-woman. Rome,* AD *63 (Dio Cassius, History of Rome 62.13.4. Early 3rd cent.* AD. *G)*

All the other members of Octavia's entourage except for Pythias sided with Sabina in her attacks on Octavia.[15] They despised Octavia because she had fallen out of favour, and played up to Sabina because she had power. Pythias alone refused to tell lies about Octavia, although she was cruelly tortured. Finally, when Tigellinus[16] threatened her, she spat in his face and said, 'My queen's private parts are purer than your mouth.'

170. *On Arria. Rome, 1st cent.* AD *(Pliny the Younger, Letters 3.16.* AD *97/107. L)*

Fannia was the granddaughter of the famous Arria the Elder, a Stoic, who committed suicide when her husband, Caecina Paetus, was condemned to death in AD 42 by the emperor Tiberius. Her daughter, Arria the Younger, Fannia's mother, stopped from doing as her mother had when her own husband, P. Clodius Thrasea Paetus, was condemned in 66, under Nero. She was later banished by Domitian, but returned after his death and became a friend of Pliny. In this letter, Pliny is writing about events that happened more than half a century earlier.

Arria was by no means a political innocent and would certainly have shared the blame for her husband's role in the conspiracy. Her choice of a glorious death over living in widowhood in greatly reduced circumstances (her husband's property would have been confiscated), or possibly even exile, quickly earned her a place in the pantheon of Roman matrons.

To Nepos.

I think I have noticed that the most celebrated words and deeds of the most illustrious men and women are not always the greatest. This opinion was confirmed yesterday when I spoke with Fannia. She is the granddaughter of the Arria who gave her husband not just consolation at his death but also an example. Fannia told me many things about her grandmother not so well known as that story but no less significant. I think you will be as impressed to read about them as I was when I heard them.

Caecina Paetus, Arria's husband, and her son were mortally ill at the same time. The son died. He was a youth of great beauty and modest, and was dear to his parents not just because his was their son. Arria took care of the funeral without her husband's even knowing of the death. But that's not all. Whenever she entered his room, she pretended that their son was alive and improving. If he asked about the son's health, she answered that he had rested well or that he had a good appetite. Then, when her tears were about to overflow, she would leave, and give herself to sorrow. Then she would pull herself together and go back in with a calm expression on her face, as if she had left her mourning outside the door. It was noble indeed when she took the dagger, plunged it into her breast, withdrew it, and uttered those famous words, 'Paetus, it doesn't hurt.' But when she did that, immortality was before her eyes. How much nobler it was, without the prospect of glory and fame, to hide her grief and act like a mother after her son had died.

Paetus was a partisan of Scribonianus in Illyria in the rising against Claudius; he was brought as a prisoner to Rome when Scribonianus was killed. When he was about to embark on the ship, Arria begged the soldier: 'You will certainly allow a man of consular rank to have a few slaves to look after his food and clothing. Let me come along and I'll do their jobs myself.' But they refused. So she followed behind the huge ship in a tiny fishing boat.

When at the imperial palace she met the wife of Scribonianus offering evidence to the prosecution, she said, 'Am I to listen to you who could go on living after Scribonianus died in your arms?' From that it is clear that her decision to die a noble death was not taken on the spur of the moment.

Then, too, when her son-in-law Thrasea was trying to dissuade her from her intent to die, he said, among other things, 'Would you want your daughter to die with me if I were to die?' She replied, 'I would, if she lived as long and as happily with you as I have with Paetus.' That made everyone all the more anxious for her and she was carefully watched. But she realised it and said, 'You're wasting your time. You can make me die painfully but you cannot stop me from dying.' Having said which, she jumped up from her chair and ran to the wall, upon which she banged her head and fell down unconscious. When she came to she said, 'I told you I would do it the hard way if you stopped me from doing it the easy way.'

Don't you think that these words are greater than the famous 'Paetus, it doesn't hurt' to which they led? But that's what everyone remembers, while no one mentions the other. Whence we can infer, as I said at the beginning of this letter, that the most famous acts are not necessarily the most noble. Farewell.

171. *Arria's death, AD 42. (Martial, Epigrams 1.13. late 1st cent AD. L)*

The poet Martial, too, records Arria's famous words.

When chaste Arria handed to Paetus the sword she had drawn from her own breast, she said, 'If you believe me, the wound I made does not hurt, but the one you are going to make, that one, Paetus, hurts me.'

172. *On Fannia. Rome, AD 107 (Pliny the Younger, Letters 7.19. L)*

From Pliny to Priscus.

I am most concerned about Fannia's health. She contracted this illness while she was taking care of Junia, a Vestal Virgin, first on her own initiative (as Junia was a relative) and subsequently by order of the priests. For virgins, while obliged by serious illness to leave the atrium of Vesta, are given into the care of some matron. Fannia was diligently performing this duty when she fell ill. She has constant fever and a cough that is getting worse; she is emaciated and generally in decline. Only her spirit is vigorous, worthy of her husband Helvidius and father Thrasea. but everything else is going down, and I am not merely afraid but deeply saddened. It pains me that so great a woman will be snatched from the eyes of her people, and who knows when her like will be seen again.

What chastity, what sanctity, what dignity, what constancy! Twice she followed her husband into exile, and the third time she herself was exiled on his account. For when Senecio, on trial for writing the life of Helvidius, said in his own defence that Fannia had asked him to write it, Mettius Carus asked threateningly whether she had. 'I did ask him,' she replied; and to whether she had given him her husband's diaries – 'I did give them.' And to whether her mother knew about this, 'She does not.' In other words, she did not utter a single word to reduce the danger to herself. She even took into her exile its very cause – those books which the senate had through the compulsion and fear of the times ordered suppressed – for she had managed to save them when her goods were confiscated.

How pleasant she is, how kind, how respectable and amiable at once – two qualities rarely found in the same person. Indeed, she will be a woman whom later we can show our wives, from whose fortitude men too can draw an example, whom now while we can still see and hear her we admire as much as those women whom we read about. To me her very house seems to totter on the brink of collapse, shaken at its foundations, even though she leaves descendants. How great must be their virtues and their accomplishments for her not to die the last of her line!

My anguish is even greater because I feel I am reliving the death of her mother, that – I can find no higher praise – great mother of a great woman, who, as she is given back to us in her daughter, so will be taken from us yet again, and I must suffer the old wound reopened as well as the new one. I honoured and loved both – I do not know which the more, nor did they want me to decide. My services were theirs in good times and bad; I comforted them in exile and avenged them when they returned. But that was not enough to repay my debt to them, and I am all the more eager that she be saved, so that I will have time to do so. There are my worries as I write to you; if some god turns them into joy, I won't complain about my present fears.

Farewell.

Political life
'Statia asks you to vote for ...'

173. *Women demonstrate and obtain repeal of the Oppian law. Rome, 195 BC (Livy, History of Rome 34.1, excerpts. Late 1st cent. BC–early 1st cent. AD. L)*

In 215 BC, after its disastrous defeat by Hannibal at Cannae, Rome passed the Oppian law, an emergency measure which limited women's use of expensive goods. Twenty years later, the crisis having long since passed, the law was repealed against the objections of many conservatives, here represented by the consul and champion of traditional values, Marcus Porcius Cato. Livy's reconstruction of the debate over the law's repeal devotes considerable space to ethical issues raised in legislation initiated in his own time by the emperor Augustus (see p. 103).

Among the troubles of great wars, either scarcely over or yet to come, something intervened which, while it can be told briefly, stirred up enough excitement to become a great battle. Marcus Fundanius and Lucius Valerius, the tribunes of the people, brought a motion to repeal the Oppian law before the people. Gaius Oppius had carried this law as tribune at the height of the Punic War, during the consulship of Quintus Fabius and Tiberius Sempronius. The law said that no woman might own more than half an ounce of gold nor wear a multicoloured[17] dress nor ride in a carriage in the city or in a town within a mile of it, unless there was a religious festival. The tribunes, Marcus and Publius Junius Brutus, were in favour of the Oppian law and said that they would not allow its repeal. Many noble men came forward hoping to persuade or dissuade them; a crowd of men, both supporters and opponents, filled the Capitoline Hill. The matrons, whom neither counsel nor shame nor their husbands' orders could keep at home, blockaded every street in the city and every entrance to the Forum. As the men came down to the Forum, the matrons besought them to let them, too, have back the luxuries they had enjoyed before, giving as their reason that the republic was thriving and that everyone's private wealth was increasing with every day. This crowd of women was growing daily, for now they were even gathering from the towns and villages. Before long they dared go up and solicit the consuls, praetors, and other magistrates; but one of the consuls could not be moved in the least, Marcus Porcius Cato,[18] who spoke in favour of the law:

'If each man of us, fellow citizens, had established that the right and authority of the husband should be held over the mother of his own family, we should have less difficulty with women in general; now, at home our freedom is conquered by female fury, here in the Forum it is bruised and trampled upon, and, because we have not contained the individuals, we fear the lot ...

'Indeed, I blushed when, a short while ago, I walked through the midst of a band of women. Had not respect for the dignity and modesty of certain ones (not them all!) restrained me (so they would not be seen being scolded by a consul), I should have said, "What kind of behaviour is this? Running around in public, blocking streets, and speaking to other women's husbands! Could you not have asked your own husbands the same thing at home? Are you more charming in public with others' husbands than at home with your own? And yet, it is not fitting even at home (if modesty were to keep married women within the bounds of their rights) for you to concern yourselves with what laws are passed or repealed here." Our ancestors did not want women to conduct any – not even private – business without a guardian; they wanted them to be under the authority of parents, brothers, or husbands; we (the gods help us!) even now let them snatch at the government and meddle in the Forum and our assemblies. What are they doing now on the streets and crossroads, if they are not persuading the tribunes to vote for repeal? Give the reins to their unbridled nature and this unmastered creature, and hope that they will put limits on their own freedom; unless you do something yourselves, this is the least of the things imposed upon them either by custom or by law which they endure with hurt feelings. They want freedom, nay licence (if we are to speak the truth), in all things.

'If they are victorious now, what will they not attempt? ... As soon as they begin to be your equals, they will have become your superiors ...

'What honest excuse is offered, pray, for this womanish rebellion? "That we might shine with gold and purple," says one of them, "that we might ride through the city in coaches on holidays and working-days, as though triumphant over the conquered law and the votes which we captured by tearing them from you; that there should be no limit to our expenses and our luxury." ...

'The woman who can spend her own money will do so; the one who cannot will ask her husband. Pity that husband – the one who gives in and the one who stands firm! What he refuses, he will see given by another man. Now they publicly solicit other women's husbands, and, what is worse, they ask for a law and votes, and certain men give them what they want. You there, you, are easily moved about things which concern yourself, your estate, and your children; once the law no longer limits your wife's spending, you will never do it by yourself. Fellow citizens, do not imagine that the state which existed before the law was passed will return. A dishonest man is safer never accused than acquitted, and luxury, left alone, would have been more acceptable than it will be now, as when wild animals are first chafed by their chains and then released. I vote that the Oppian law should not, in the smallest measure, be repealed; whatever course you take, may all the gods make you happy with it.'

After this, when the tribunes of the people, who had declared that they would oppose the motion to repeal, had added a few remarks along the same lines, Lucius Valerius spoke on behalf of the motion which he himself had brought:

'[Cato] used up more words castigating the women than he did opposing the motion, and he left in some uncertainty whether the women had done the deeds which he reproached on their own or at our instigation. I shall defend the motion, not ourselves, against whom the consul has hurled this charge, more for the words than for the reality of the accusation. He has called this assemblage "secession" and sometimes "womanish rebellion", because the matrons have publicly asked you, in

peacetime when the state is happy and prosperous, to repeal a law passed
against them during the straits of war ...

'What, may I ask, are the women doing that is new, having gathered
and come forth publicly in a case which concerns them directly? Have
they never appeared in public before this? Allow me to unroll your own
Origines[19] before you. Listen to how often they have done so – always for
the public good. From the very beginning – the reign of Romulus – when
the Capitoline had been taken by the Sabines and there was fighting in
the middle of the Forum, was not the battle halted by the women's
intervention between the two lines? How about this? After the kings had
been expelled, when the Volscian legions and their general, Marcius
Coriolanus, had pitched camp at the fifth milestone, did not the matrons
turn away the forces which would have buried the city? When Rome was
in the hands of the Gauls, who ransomed it? Indeed the matrons agreed
unanimously to turn their gold over to the public need. Not to go too far
back in history, in the most recent war, when we needed funds, did not
the widows' money assist the treasury? And when new gods were
summoned to bring their power to our difficulties, was it not all the
matrons who went to the sea to meet the Idaean Mother? You say these
cases are different. I am not here to say they are the same; it is enough to
prove that nothing new has been done. Indeed, as no one is amazed that
they acted in situations affecting men and women alike, why should we
wonder that they have taken action in a case which concerns themselves?
What, after all, have they done? We have proud ears indeed, if, while
masters do not scorn the appeals of slaves, we are angry when honourable
women ask something of us ...

'Who then does not know that this is a recent law, passed twenty years
ago? Since our matrons lived for so long by the highest standards of
behaviour without any law, what risk is there that, once it is repealed,
they will yield to luxury? For if the law were an old one, or if it had been
passed to restrain feminine licence, there might be reason to fear that
repeal would incite them. The times themselves will show you why the
law was passed. Hannibal was in Italy, victorious at Cannae. Already he
held Tarentum, Arpi and Capua. He seemed on the verge of moving
against Rome. Our allies had gone over to him. We had no reserve troops,
no allies at sea to protect the fleet, no funds in the treasury. Slaves were
being bought and armed, on condition that the price be paid their owners
when the war was over. The contractors had declared that they would
provide, on that same day of payment (after the war), the grain and other
supplies the needs of war demanded. We were giving our slaves as rowers
at our own expense, in proportion to our property rating. We were giving
all our gold and silver for public use, as the senators had done first.
Widows and children were donating their funds to the treasury. We were
ordered to keep at home no more than a certain amount of wrought and
stamped gold and silver. At a time like that were the matrons so taken up

with luxury and fancy trappings that the Oppian law was needed to restrain them, when, since the rites of Ceres had been suspended because all the women were in mourning, the senate ordered mourning limited to thirty days? To whom is it not clear that poverty and misfortune were the authors of that law of yours, since all private wealth had to be turned over to public use, and that it was to remain in effect only as long as the reason for its writing did? ...

'Shall it be our wives alone to whom the fruits of peace and tranquillity of the state do not come? ... Shall we forbid only women to wear purple? When you, a man, may use purple on your clothes, will you not allow the mother of your family to have a purple cloak, and will your horse be more beautifully saddled than your wife is garbed? ...

'[Cato] has said that, if none of them had anything, there would be no rivalry among individual women. By Hercules! All are unhappy and indignant when they see the finery denied them permitted to the wives of the Latin allies, when they see them adorned with gold and purple, when those other women ride through the city and they follow on foot, as though the power belonged to the other women's cities, not to their own. This could wound the spirits of men; what do you think it could do the spirits of women, whom even little things disturb? They cannot partake of magistracies, priesthoods, triumphs, badges of office, gifts, or spoils of war; elegance, finery and beautiful clothes are women's badges, in these they find joy and take pride, this our forebears called the women's world. When they are in mourning, what, other than purple and gold, do they take off? What do they put on again when they have completed the period of mourning? What do they add for public prayer and thanksgiving other than still greater ornament? Of course, if you repeal the Oppian law, you will not have the power to prohibit that which the law now forbids; daughters, wives, even some men's sisters will be less under your authority – never, while her men are well, is a woman's slavery cast off; and even they hate the freedom created by widowhood and orphanage. They prefer their adornment to be subject to your judgment, not the law's; and you ought to hold them in marital power and guardianship, not slavery; you should prefer to be called fathers and husbands to masters. The consul just now used odious terms when he said "womanish rebellion" and "secession". For there is danger – he would have us believe – that they will seize the Sacred Hill as once the angry plebeians did, or the Aventine. It is for the weaker sex to submit to whatever you advise. The more power you possess, all the more moderately should you exercise your authority.'

When these speeches for and against the law had been made, a considerably larger crowd of women poured forth in public the next day; as a single body they besieged the doors of the Brutuses, who were vetoing their colleagues' motion, and they did not stop until the tribunes took back their veto. After that there was no doubt but that all the tribes would repeal the law. Twenty years after it was passed, the law was repealed.

174. *Sempronia, a revolutionary. Rome, 1st cent. BC (Sallust, Conspiracy of Catiline 24.3-25. L)*

The historian Sallust regarded the conspiracy led by Catiline in 62 BC as a result of moral decline; in his account, Catiline's supporter Sempronia egregiously lacks the qualities for which virtuous Roman matrons are celebrated, but possesses others.

(24.3) At that time Catiline is said to have attracted many people of every sort, including some women. These had first sold their bodies to finance their luxuries, but later, when age set a limit to this activity – but not to their tastes – fell heavily into debt. Catiline believed he could use these women to win over the urban slaves, set fire to the city, and either enlist or kill their husbands.

(25) One of these women was Sempronia, whose masculine boldness had already led her to commit many crimes. This woman was favoured by fortune in birth and beauty as well as in her husband and children. She was well read in Greek and Latin literature; she played the lyre and danced with greater skill than propriety warrants; and she had a number of other accomplishments, all of the sort that promote dissipation. But to her nothing was more worthless than modesty and chastity. It is not easy to say which she threw away more wantonly, her money or her reputation. She was so oversexed that it was more often she who went after men than the other way around. She had often broken promises, disavowed her debts, and been an accessory to murder. Love of luxury combined with poverty had driven her headlong. And yet, she had real talents. She could write verse, make jokes, and converse with modesty, tenderness or wantonness. She was a woman of considerable wit and charm.

175. *A portrait of Cleopatra. Egypt, 1st cent. BC (Plutarch, Life of Mark Antony 25.5-28.1, 29. 2nd cent. AD. G)*

'For Rome, who had never condescended to fear any nation or people, did in her time fear two human beings; one was Hannibal, and the other was a woman.'[20] In Roman literature during her lifetime and just after her death[21] (e.g. Vergil's characterisation of Dido in the *Aeneid*; Horace, *Odes* 1.37), Cleopatra represented the dangerous appeal of decadence and corruption. A highly educated Greek, with the wealth of Egypt at her disposal, she was mistress first of Julius Caesar and then of Mark Antony. In Plutarch's account traditional anecdotes are related with considerable sympathy and admiration.

[Caesar and Pompey knew Cleopatra when she was] still a girl, and ignorant of the world,[22] but it was a different matter in the case of Antony, because she was ready to meet him when she had reached the time of life when women are most beautiful and have full understanding. So she prepared for him many gifts and money and adornment, of a magnitude appropriate to her great wealth and prosperous kingdom, but she put most of her hopes in her own personal magical arts and charms.

(26) Although she had received many letters from Antony and his friends asking her to come to meet him [in Cilicia], she took his summons so lightly and laughed at it, that she sailed up the Cydnus river in a barge with a gilded stern, with purple sails outstretched, pulled by silver oars in time to piping accompanied by fifes and lyres. She herself lay under a gold-embroidered awning, got up like Aphrodite in a painting, with slaves dressed as Erotes fanning her on either side. Likewise the prettiest slave-women, dressed like Nereids and Graces, were at the tillers and the ropes. Remarkable perfumes from many censers surrounded them. People followed after Cleopatra on both sides of the river, and others came downstream from the city to see the sight. When finally the entire crowd in the marketplace had disappeared, Antony was left sitting on the tribunal by himself, and word got round that Aphrodite was leading a festival procession to Dionysus for the benefit of Asia.

Antony sent messengers inviting her to dinner. She insisted instead that he come to her. Because he wished to show his readiness to accept her invitation and his friendship, he obeyed her summons and came. The preparations she had made for him were indescribable, and he was particularly struck by the number of lights. Many are said to have been lowered and lit up at the same time, ordered and arranged in such intricate relationships with one another, and patterns, some in squares, some in circles, so that it was a sight among the most noteworthy and beautiful.[23]

(27) The next day he invited her in return, and he considered it a matter of honour to exceed the magnificence and care of her entertainment, but when he was outdone and vanquished by her in both respects, he was the first to make fun of himself for his bombast and rusticity. Cleopatra saw the soldierly and common nature of Antony's jokes, and she used the same soldier's humour towards him in a relaxed and confident manner. For (as they say) it was not because her beauty in itself was so striking that it stunned the onlooker, but the inescapable impression produced by daily contact with her: the attractiveness in the persuasiveness of her talk, and the character that surrounded her conversation was stimulating. It was a pleasure to hear the sound of her voice, and she tuned her tongue like a many-stringed instrument expertly to whatever language she chose, and only used interpreters to talk to a few foreigners; usually she gave responses by herself, as in the case of Ethiopians, Troglodytes, Hebrews, Arabs, Syrians, Medes, Parthians, and she is said to have learned the languages of many other peoples,

although her predecessors on the throne did not bother to learn Egyptian, and some had even forgotten how to speak the Macedonian dialect.[24]

(28) She took such hold over Antony, that while his wife Fulvia was carrying on the war in Rome against Octavian on his behalf, and the Parthian army had been gathered in Mesopotamia (the general of that Army, Labienus was now being addressed by the generals of the King of Persia as Commander of the Parthians) and was about to invade Syria, Antony was carried off by Cleopatra to Alexandria, and amused himself there with the pastimes of a boy on holiday and games, and spent and luxuriated away that (as Antiphon says) most precious of commodities, time ...

(29) Cleopatra used not (as Plato says) the four kinds of flattery,[25] but many, and whether Antony was in a serious or playful mood she could always produce some new pleasure or charm, and she kept watch over him and neither by day or night let him out of her sight. She played dice with him and hunted with him and watched him exercising with his weapons, and she roamed around and wandered about with him at night when he stood at people's doors and windows and made fun of the people inside, dressed in a slave-woman's outfit; for he also attempted to dress up like a slave.

He returned from these expeditions having been mocked in return, and often beaten, although most people suspected who he was. But the Alexandrians got pleasure from his irreverence and accompanied it with good timing and good taste, enjoying his humour and saying that he showed his tragic face to the Romans and his comic one to them.

Although it would be a waste of time to catalogue all of his amusements, one time he went fishing and had the misfortune not to catch anything while Cleopatra was present. So he ordered the fisherman secretly to dive underneath and attach fish that had already been caught to his hooks, but Cleopatra was not fooled after she saw him pull up two or three. She pretended to be amazed and told her friends and invited them to come as observers on the next day. After a large audience had gathered on the fishing boats and Antony had lowered his line, Cleopatra told one of her slaves to get in ahead of the others and attach a salted fish from the Black Sea to his hook. When Antony thought he had caught something he pulled it up, and when (as might be expected) loud laughter followed, she said, 'General, leave the fishing rod to us, the rulers of the Pharos and Canopus; your game is cities and kingdoms and countries.'

176. *Hortensia's speech. Rome, 42 BC (Appian, Civil Wars 4.32-4, 2nd cent. AD. G)*

Since Appian wrote in Greek during the second century AD, what follows is his own version of what Hortensia said, though it is known (cf. no. 213) that her speech was preserved and read many years after it was delivered. When the triumvirs Octavian, Antony and Lepidus were unable to raise enough money by selling the property of the people they had proscribed (or condemned to death by judicial process for political revenge or financial expediency), they decided to pass an edict demanding evaluations of the property of the 1,400 wealthiest women, in order to collect money from them. The speech had an effect: the next day the triumvirs reduced considerably the number of women to be taxed, and instead decreed that men worth 100,000 sesterces or more were required to make substantial contributions.

[These] women decided to ask the wives of the triumvirs for help.[26] They were not disappointed by Octavian's sister or by Antony's mother, but when Antony's wife Fulvia threw them out of the house, they did not put up with the insult and pushed their way into the forum onto the tribunal of the triumvirs, while the people and the guards stood aside for them. This is what they said, through Hortensia who was selected as their spokesman:

'As was appropriate for women like ourselves when addressing a petition to you, we rushed to your womenfolk. But we did not get the treatment we were entitled to from Fulvia, and have been driven by her into the Forum. You have already stolen from us our fathers and sons and husbands and brothers by your proscriptions, on the grounds that they had wronged you. But if you also steal from us our property, you will set us into a state unworthy of our family and manners and our female sex. If you claim that you have in any way been wronged by us, as you were by our husbands, proscribe us as you did them. But if we women have not voted any of you public enemies, if we did not demolish your houses or destroy your army or lead another army against you; if we have not kept you from public office or honour, why should we share the penalties if we have no part in the wrongdoing?

Why should we pay taxes when we have no part in public office or honours or commands or government in general, an evil you have fought over with such disastrous results? Because, you say, this is a time of war? And when have there not been wars? And when have women paid taxes? By nature of their sex women are absolved from paying taxes among all mankind. Our mothers on one occasion long ago were superior to their sex and paid taxes, when your whole government was threatened and the city itself, when the Carthaginians were pressuring you. They gave willingly, not from their land or their fields or their dowry or their households, without which life would be unlivable for free women, but only from their own jewellery, and not with a fixed price set on it, nor under threat of informers and accusers or by force, but they gave as much as they themselves chose.[27] Why are you now so anxious about the government or the country? But if there should be a war against the Celts or Parthians, we will not be less eager for our country's welfare than our mothers. But we will never pay taxes for civil wars, and we will not cooperate with you against each other. We did not pay taxes to Caesar or to Pompey, nor did Marius ask us for contributions, nor Cinna nor Sulla, even though he was a tyrant over this country. And you say that you are re-establishing the Republic!'

After Hortensia made this speech, the triumvirs were angry that women had the nerve to hold a public meeting while the men were silent, and that women demanded an accounting from the triumvirs, and that they would not supply the money while the men were serving in the army. They ordered the lictors to drive them away from the tribunal, until the lictors were stopped by the shouts of the crowd outside and the triumvirs postponed the proceedings till the next day.

177. *Caenis, concubine of the Emperor Vespasian. Rome, AD 71-5 (Dio Cassius, History of Rome 65.14.1-5. G)*

Many appeals to emperors were made through their women, in this case through a concubine rather than a wife.[28]

At this time also Vespasian's concubine Caenis[29] passed away. I mention her because she was extraordinarily faithful and because she had an excellent memory. Once, when Claudius' mother Antonia ordered her to write a secret letter to Tiberius about Sejanus, and then to erase it immediately, so that no trace of it remained,[30] Caenis replied, 'Mistress, your orders are meaningless. For I carry everything that you have written, and anything else you tell me in my mind and no one can ever erase them.' I think that she was remarkable for this response, and also because Vespasian got so much pleasure from her company; because of this she became very powerful, and acquired untold capital, so that the emperor was thought to have made money because of her efforts. For she received large sums from many sources, selling government offices to some, and to others procuratorships, generalships and priesthoods, and sometimes even imperial decisions. Vespasian never executed anyone for money, but he granted pardons to many who paid for them. And it was Caenis who took the money, though it was suspected that Vespasian was happy to delegate to her the job of taking money from the others.

178. *Women advocates. Rome (Valerius Maximus, Memorable Deeds and Sayings 8.3. 1st cent. AD. L)*

We must be silent no longer about those women whom neither the condition of their nature nor the cloak of modesty could keep silent in the Forum or the courts.

Amasia Sentia, a defendant, pleaded her case before a great crowd of people and Lucius Titius, the praetor who presided over the court.[31] She pursued every aspect of her defence diligently and boldly and was acquitted, almost unanimously, in a single hearing. Because she bore a man's spirit under the appearance of a woman, they called her Androgyne.

Gaia Afrania,[32] the wife of the senator Licinius Buccio, a woman disposed to bring suits, always represented herself before the praetor: not because she had no advocates, but because her impudence was abundant. And so, by constantly plaguing the tribunals with such barking as the Forum had seldom heard, she became the best-known example of women's litigiousness. As a result, to charge a woman with low morals, it is enough to call her 'Gaia Afrania'. She prolonged her life until Caesar's second consulship[33] with Publius Servius as his colleague; for it is better to record when such a monster died than when it was born.

Hortensia, the daughter of Quintus Hortensius,[34] when the triumvirs burdened the matrons with a heavy tribute[35] and no man dared take their defence, pleaded the case before the triumvirs, both firmly and successfully. For by bringing back her father's eloquence, she brought about the remission of the greater part of the tax. Quintus Hortensius lived again in the female line and breathed through his daughter's words. If any of her male descendants had wished to follow her strength, the great heritage of Hortensian eloquence would not have ended with a woman's action.

179. *Electioneering. Pompeii, 1st cent.* AD *(CIL IV.207, 171 [= ILS 6431a], 913, 3291 [= ILS 6415], 1083, 6610, 3678 [= ILS 6414], 3684, 3527 [= ILS 6408a]. Tr. J.C. Fant. L)*

Although women could not vote, the frequency with which their names appear in the electoral graffiti of Pompeii indicates that they took a lively interest in local politics, endorsing candidates publicly with or without husbands or male associates.

(207) Nymphodotus, along with Caprasia, asks you to vote for Marcus Cerrinius Vatia for the aedileship.

(171) Caprasia along with Nymphius – her neighbours too – ask you to vote for Aulus Vettius Firmus for the aedileship; he is worthy of the office.

Caprasia was probably the proprietor of the wine shop on which the second *programma* was painted. Nymphodotus was most likely a retainer of the Helvian family, on whose house the first notice appeared.

(913) Amandio, along with his wife, asks you to vote for Gnaeus Helvius Sabinus for aedile; he is worthy of public office.

(3291) Pyramus, Olympionica and Calvus ask your support for Marcus Casellius Marcellus.

A notice put up by Pyramus for the same candidate has been found in another part of the city. Were these three partisans campaign workers, or did they just work at the same bakery around the corner?

(1083) Recepta, not without Thalamus, asks that you make Gnaeus Helvius Sabinus aedile and Lucius Ceius Secundus duovir.

(6610) Epidia, not without Cosmus, asks you to vote for Marcus Samellius for aedile.

(3678) Statia and Petronia ask you to vote for Marcus Casellius and Lucius Alfucius for aediles. May our colony always have such citizens!

(3684) Statia asks you to vote for Herennius and Suettius for the aedileship.

We cannot know whether the Statias are one and the same woman.

(3527) Appuleia and Narcissus, along with their neighbour Mustius, ask you to vote for Pupius for the aedileship.

180. *The family of Julia Domna. Rome, 3rd cent. AD (Dio Cassius, History of Rome, 78.2, 18; 79.23, excerpts. Early 3rd cent. AD. G)*

Julia Domna, born in Syria, was the wife of the emperor Septimius Severus (193-211) and mother of his successor, Caracalla (Antoninus, 211-217). She was known for her love of learning and her wit. After her husband's death, she supported her younger son, Geta, in his unsuccessful claim to the throne against Caracalla.

(78.2) Antoninus had planned to murder his brother Geta at the Saturnalia, but he was unable to, because his evil intentions were so well known as to make concealment impossible. From this point on there was constant conflict between them, with each planning against them other, and many, counterplots. Since many soldiers and athletes were guarding Geta, both at home and abroad, by day and by night, Antoninus persuaded his mother to summon both of them to her room, on the pretext that he wanted a reconciliation. Since Geta trusted her, Antoninus went in with him, and when they were inside, a group of centurions who had been assembled by Antoninus, rushed out and struck Geta, who had run to his mother as soon as he saw them and put his arms round her neck and held himself to her bosom, weeping and crying out, 'Mother, mother, who bore me, who bore me, help, I am being murdered.'

And because she had been deceived in this way, she saw her son murdered most impiously and dying in her lap. In a manner of speaking, she received his death into the same womb from which he had been born; she was completely covered with blood, so that she did not take any account of the wound inflicted on her own hand. But Antoninus did not allow her to weep or to lament her son, even though she had seen him die so piteously (for he was twenty-two years and nine months old), but she was forced to rejoice and be cheerful as if she had been very fortunate, so closely watched were all her words and gestures and expressions. Thus it was only she, the wife of the emperor and the mother of emperors, who could not weep even in private over so great a misfortune.

(78.18) (*During the year 214-215*) [Antoninus continued] to pollute himself and break the law and squander money. Neither in these matters nor in any others did he pay attention to his mother, although she gave him much excellent advice. And yet he assigned to her the supervision of petitions and correspondence in both languages, except for very urgent cases, and included her name along with his own and that of the legions in correspondence with the Senate, stating that she was well, and with expressions of high praise. Need I mention that she held public receptions for all the most prominent men, as did the emperor himself? But while she involved herself in philosophical discussions still more intensely with these men, he said that he himself needed nothing but the essentials, and in addition stated pompously that he could live on the simplest fare, while in fact there was nothing from the earth, sea or air that we did not provide for him at both public and private expense.

(79.23) (*At the time of Caracalla's assassination in AD 217*) Julia, Tarautas' (Caracalla's) mother, happened to be in Antioch, and at the news of his death, she was so shocked that she struck herself violently and tried to starve herself. She had hated him while he was alive, but now that he was dead she missed him, not because she wished that he was alive, but because she hated to return to private life. For this reason she complained bitterly about [his assassin and successor] Macrinus. Then, when he did not make any changes in her royal retinue or in her cohort of the Praetorian guards, and sent her friendly greetings, although he had heard what she had said about him, she was encouraged, and put aside her desire for death. She did not make any reply to his message, but [began to plot] with her soldiers ... so that she might become sole ruler like Semiramis or Nitocris, since she was in a manner of speaking from the same part of the world.[36] ... (*Some lines are missing, in which her plot was discovered.*)

When Macrinus ordered her to leave Antioch as soon as she could and go wherever she wished, and she had heard what was being said in Rome about Caracalla, she no longer wanted to live, and although she was already dying of cancer (she had had for some time a dormant cancer of the breast, which she had inflamed by the blow that she gave herself on the chest at the time of her son's death, she brought on her death by starving herself.

And so a woman who had risen high from a common origin, who during her husband's reign had led a miserable existence because of Plautianus,[37] and who had seen the younger of her two sons slaughtered on her own bosom, and who had always hated her older son and had learned of his death in such a violent manner, fell from power while she was alive and killed herself ... This is what happened to Julia, and her body was brought to Rome and placed in the tomb of Gaius and Lucius.[38] Later, however, her bones, along with her son Geta's, were moved by her sister Maesa to the precinct of Caracalla.

Women's organisations
'They elected from among themselves ...'

181. *A trade union? Rome, late 3rd-early 2nd cent.* BC *(Plautus, Cistellaria 22-41. L)*

Prostitutes, pimps and their customers are the mainstays of the comedies of Plautus and Terence, which should be enjoyed in their entirety. In this brief extract, the character Syra, a madam, suggests that what the prostitutes need is a little organisation, as the *matronae* have already learned.

It certainly seems right to me, Selenium dear, that our class should be kind to each other and stick together, when you see those highborn women, those top matrons, how they cultivate their friendship and how tight they are with one another. If we were to do the same thing, if we imitate them, even then we can hardly live, they hate us so much. They want us poor women to need their wealth. They want for us to be able to do nothing on our own but to have to ask them all the time for favours. If you go to them, you prefer to leave than go inside, the way they publicly flatter women of our rank, but in private, if they get the chance they pour cold water on us – they're so crafty. They claim we always go with their men, they say we are their concubines, and try to squelch us. Because we are freedwomen, both your mother and I became prostitutes. She brought you up, and I brought up this one [Gymnasium], your fathers being from various quarters. I didn't make my girl become a prostitute because of pride but so that I shouldn't starve.

Allusions in inscriptions to groups of women are a bit mysterious. In some cases they seem to indicate women's burial societies or perhaps a sort of unofficial ladies' auxiliary for the purpose of keeping feast days and honouring the dead. Not all the contexts, however, are funerary. At the least, the texts show that women organised outside the home for some social or religious purpose. If Elagabalus' *senaculum* did exist, it would have been at far too exalted a level to bear any resemblance to the organisations referred to in the inscriptions, with one perplexing exception, which in any case antedates his reign.

182. *A women's club. Alexandria, 1st cent.* AD *(JEA 4 (1917) 253 f. G)*

The many analogous extant inscriptions are for men's clubs.

... for the women's [club] from the common treasury ... the president and Titiris the ... have [dedicated a statue] of ... aris the high priestess.

183. *The curia of women.*[39] *Lanuvium, 2nd cent.* AD *(CIL XIV.2120 = ILS 6199. L)*

To Gaius Sulpicius Victor, father of Roman knights, a most blameless man, patron of the city, the senate and people of Lanuvium, on account of his incomparable service and immense generosity towards them, voted that an equestrian statue should be erected and dedicated it. On account of this dedication, he distributed to each man of the decurions, Augustales and *curiae* 24 sesterces, and to the *curia* of women he gave a double banquet.

184. *The women's collegium. Rome, 1st/2nd cent.* AD *(CIL VI.10423. L)*

To well-deserving Ti...[40] The women's *collegium* [put this up].

185. *A grant for funeral rites.*[41] *Feltria, 2nd cent.* AD *(CIL V.2072. L)*

To the gods of the dead. To Lucius Veturius Nepos, who, in order that they might carry out his funeral rites, gave the Ciarnenses 1,600 sesterces, and the women 400 sesterces, so that the Ciarnenses might celebrate his birthday with incense, sausage and wine, the Herclanenses the *parentalia*, and the women the roses.[42] He did this while he was still alive.

186. *The matrons. Trajan's Forum, Rome, 3rd cent.* AD *(CIL VI. 997 = ILS 324. L)*

Julia Augusta,[43] mother of emperors and camps, restored this for the matrons. Sabina Augusta[44] [put this up] for the matrons.

187. *Raising money. Rome, 3rd cent.* BC *(Livy, History of Rome 27.37.8-9. Late 1st cent.* BC*-early 1st cent.* AD. *L)*

In 206 BC the temple of Juno on the Aventine Hill was struck by lightning.

When the soothsayers said that the omen had to do with the matrons and that the goddess must be appeased with a gift, those matrons who lived in the city or within the tenth milestone were called together on the Capitoline Hill by an edict of the curule aedile, and they elected from among themselves twenty-five to whom they would bring a sum of money from their dowries. From that the gift of a golden bowl was made and

VI. Public Life

157

carried to the Aventine and was purely and chastely dedicated by the
matrons.

188. *A meeting of married women. Rome, 1st cent. AD (Suetonius, Life
of Galba 5.1. L)*

Although a formally constituted body of women cannot be inferred from the
following text, the *conventus* referred to may be more than a casual
gathering in someone's drawing room.

[The Emperor Galba] did his duty by matrimony, but when he lost his
wife Lepida and his two sons by her, he remained celibate and could no
more be tempted by any prospect, not even Agrippina [the Younger], who,
widowed by the death of Domitius, had gone after the still-married Galba
with every means to such a degree that in a meeting of married women[45]
Lepida's mother chastised her and even slapped her.

189. *A women's 'senate'. 3rd cent. AD (Hist. Aug. Elag. 4.3-4, 4th cent.
AD. L)*

That the Emperor Elagabalus (AD 218-222) instituted a senate of women for
the extremely frivolous purposes described below is unlikely. The text, from
an often imaginative collection of imperial biographies, is worth noting,
however, for its allusion to an earlier organisation.[46]

He established a *senaculum*,[47] a senate for women, on the Quirinal Hill.
Earlier there had been a matrons' assembly[48] there but only for special
festivals or when a matron was given the insignia of 'consular marriage',
which the early emperors gave their female relatives, especially those
whose husbands were not nobles so that their marriage would not make
them lose their own noble rank.

Now, however, under the influence of Symiamira,[49] the *senaculum*
passed all sorts of ridiculous laws for matrons, like what sort of clothes
they could wear in public, who had precedence over whom, who was to
kiss first, who could ride in a chariot, or on a horse, or on a beast of
burden, or on a donkey, or who could ride in a mule-drawn carriage or a
litter, and what the litter could be made of – leather or bone – and
whether it could be decorated with ivory or silver, and who could have
gold and silver ornaments on her shoes.

190. *A plan to restore the 'senate'. Rome, AD 270-5 (Hist. Aug. Aurel.
49.6, 4th cent. AD. L)*

The same source credits the Emperor Aurelian (AD 270-275) with
remembering Elagabalus' brainchild (if it existed).

He had wanted to restore to the matrons their senate, or rather
senaculum, with the proviso that those women who had earned
priesthoods with the senate's approval should occupy the highest
positions.

Honorific inscriptions
'She has been honoured by the people'

191. *The chaste Asë. Lycia, AD 100 (Pleket 15. G)*

Timarchus of Arneae son of Diotimus, to Asë (who was also called
Dimanthis), his daughter and daughter also of Pinnarma, daughter of
Diodotus, in loving remembrance. She has also been honoured by the
people: the people of Arneae and the entire vicinity honoured with a gold
wreath and a bronze statue Asë (who was also called Dimanthis,
daughter of Timarchus of Arneae son of Diotimus), a woman who was
chaste and cultivated, and who glorifies both her city and her family with
praise won for her conduct, in recognition of her virtue and the
incomparable and enviable manner in which she exemplifies every
admirable quality of womanhood.

192. *Aufria, woman of letters. Delphi, 2nd cent. AD (Fouilles de Delphes
4, 79. G)*

Aufria, who came to Delphi from another city (in Bithynia? the inscription is
damaged) received public honours for her series of talks at the Pythian
games, apparently in the form of commemorative statues.

With good fortune. The city of Delphi has decreed that Aufria of ... is a
citizen of Delphi, since she was present at the festival of the god, and
demonstrated the entire range of her education, and delivered many
excellent and enjoyable lectures at the assembly of Greeks at the Pythian
games ...

193. *Lalla of Arneae (gymnasiarch). Lycia, c. AD 100 (Pleket 14. G)*

To Lalla of Arneae, daughter of Timarchus son of Diotimus, Masas,
because she had set him free, in accordance with her will.

194. *A benefactress. Priene, 1st cent. BC (Pleket 5. G)*

Phile, daughter of Apollonius wife of Thessalus son of Polydeuces; as the
first woman *stephanephorus*[50] she dedicated at her own expense a cistern
and the water pipes in the city.

195. *Food for children. Tarracina, 2nd cent.* AD *(CIL X.6328 = ILS 6278. Tr. J.C. Fant. L)*

Caelia Macrina left money for the construction of the building to which this inscription was originally attached, and at the same time endowed an alimentary fund (i.e. to provide cash grants for food) for 200 children of her city. Alimentary grants could be either private or governmental, and were customarily larger for boys than for girls.[51] Caelia follows this pattern but is slightly more generous to girls than was usual. The shorter period allowed for girls to receive support reflects their younger age at marriage (often 13 or 14 years old).

Caelia Macrina, daughter of Gaius, by her will ordered 300,000 sesterces to be used [for the construction of this building]. She left ... sesterces for its decoration and maintenance. To the people of Tarracina, in memory of her son Macer, she left 1,000,000 sesterces, so that the income from the money might be given to 100 boys [and to 100 girls] under the title of 'alimenta'; 5 denarii [= 20 sesterces] each month to each citizen boy up to the age of 16, and 4 denarii [= 16 sesterces] each month to each citizen girl up to the age of 14, so that 100 boys and 100 girls might always be receiving [the grant] in succession.

196. *Eumachia. Pompeii, 1st cent.* AD *(CIL X. 810 = ILS 3785; CIL X. 813 = ILS 6368; Maiuri, 1965, 83. L)*

Eumachia was priestess and prominent citizen of the city of Pompeii. She was patroness of the guild of fullers (cleaners, dyers and clothing makers), one of the most influential trade-guilds of the city because of the importance of the wool industry in Pompeii's economy. Although her ancestry was humble, the fortune she inherited from her father, a brick manufacturer, enabled her to marry into one of Pompeii's older families. She provided the fullers with a large and beautiful building which was probably used as the guild's headquarters.

Over each of the two entrances to the Building of Eumachia in the Civil Forum (the dedication refers to the Emperor Tiberius and his mother, Livia, whose statue was found inside the building):

Eumachia, daughter of Lucius (Eumachius), public priestess, in her own name and that of her son, Marcus Numistrius Fronto, built with her own funds the porch, covered passage, and colonnade and dedicated them to Concordia Augusta and to Pietas.

On the base of a statue (now in the Museo Archeologico Nazionale, Naples) of Eumachia, with her head veiled as a priestess:

To Eumachia, daughter of Lucius, public priestess, the fullers [dedicated this statue].

On her tomb in the cemetery outside the Porta Nuceria:

Eumachia, daughter of Lucius, [built this] for herself and for her household.

197. *Junia Theodora. Corinth, c. AD 43 (Pleket 8, excerpts. G)*

The people of Patara[52] have decreed: Whereas Junia Theodora, a Roman resident in Corinth, a woman held in highest honour ... who copiously supplied from her own means many of our citizens with generosity, and received them in her home and in particular never ceased acting on behalf of our citizens in regard to any favour asked – the majority of citizens have gathered in assembly to offer testimony on her behalf. Our people in gratitude agreed to vote: to commend Junia and to offer testimony of her generosity to our native city and of her good will, and declares that it urges her to increase her generosity towards the city in the knowledge that our people also would not cease in their good will and gratitude to her and would do everything for the excellence and the glory that she deserved. For this reason (with good fortune), it was decreed to commend her for all that she had done.

198. *Flavia Publicia Nicomachis. Phocaea, Asia Minor, 2nd cent. AD (Pleket 19. G)*

The council and the people, to Flavia Publicia Nicomachis, daughter of Dinomachus and Procle ... their benefactor, and benefactor through her ancestors, founder of our city, president for life, in recognition of her complete virtue.

199. *Modia Quintia. Africa Proconsularis, 2nd/3rd cent. AD (CIL VIII.23888. L)*

The town council decreed a statue of Modia Quintia, daughter of Quintus Modius Felix, perpetual priestess, who, on account of the honour of the priesthood, adorned the portico with marble paving, coffered ceilings and columns, exceeding in cost her original estimate with an additional contribution and quite apart from the statutory entry fee [for the priesthood] and also [built] an aqueduct. By decree of the town council, [erected] with public funds.

200. *Aurelia Leite. Paros, c. AD 300 (Pleket 31. G)*

A monument set up by the husband of a benefactress to record the honours given her by her city.

To the most renowned and in all respects excellent Aurelia Leite, daughter of Theodotus, wife of the foremost man in the city, Marcus Aurelius Faustus, hereditary high priest for life of the cult of Diocletian and his co-rulers, priest of Demeter and gymnasiarch. She was gymnasiarch[53] of the gymnasium which she repaired and renewed when it had been dilapidated for many years. The glorious city of the Parians, her native city, in return for her many great benefactions, receiving honour rather than giving it, in accordance with many decrees, has set up a marble statue of her. She loved wisdom, her husband, her children, her native city: (*in verse*) this woman, with her wisdom, best of mothers, his wife Leite, renowned Faustus glorifies.

201. *Scholasticia. Ephesus, Christian period (JÖAI 43 [1956] 22-3. G)*

Epigram for the statue of a woman who restored two public baths.[54]

You see here, stranger, the statue of a woman who was pious and very wise, Scholasticia. She provided the great sum of gold for constructing the part of the [buildings] here that had fallen down.

Victors
'With my swift-running horses'

Women victors in athletic contests all appear to have been sponsored by men and to have had professional charioteers.

202. *A royal victor. Sparta, early 4th cent. BC (AP XIII.16. G)*

My father and brothers were kings of Sparta. I, Cynisca, won a victory with my swift-running horses[55] and set up this statue. I claim that I am the only woman from all Greece to have won this crown.

203. *Winner of a four-horse chariot race. Oxyrhynchus, 268/7 BC (FGrHist 257aF6 = Oxyrhynchus papyrus 2082. G)*

Bilistiche[56] of Magnesia's four-colt chariot. She was the *hetaera* of Ptolemy Philadelphus.

204. *Winner of a two-horse chariot race. Larisa, early 2nd cent. BC (IG IX.ii.526.19-20. G)*

From a list of victors in various competitions from all over the Greek world.

Aristoclea from Larisa, daughter of Megacles, in the two-horse chariot race.

205. *From the Panathenaic victor lists.*[57] *Athens, 2nd cent.* BC *(IG II².2313.9-15; 2313.60; 2314.50- 1. G)*

(2313.9-15) (194/3 BC) Zeuxo of Argos, daughter of Polycrates,[58] in the horse race ... Encrateia of Argos, daughter of Polycrates, in the four-horse chariot race; Hermione of Argos, daughter of Polycrates ...

(2313.60) (190/89 BC) Zeuxo of Cyrene, daughter of Ariston, in the four-horse chariot race ...

2314.50-1) (182 BC) Zeuxo of Argos from Achaea, daughter of Polycrates, in the four-horse chariot race ...

206. *Women victors. Delphi, c.* AD *45 (Pleket 9. G)*

Hermesianax, son of Dionysius, of Caesaria in Tralles (also from Corinth), for his daughters, who themselves have the same citizenships.

(1) Tryphosa, at the Pythian Games with Antigonus and Cleomachis as judges, and at the Isthmian Games, with Juventius Proclus as president, each time placed first in the girls' single-course race.

(2) Hedea, at the Isthmian Games with Cornelius Pulcher as judge, won the race in armour, and the chariot race; at the Nemean Games she won the single-course race with Antigonus as president and also in Sicyon with Menoites as president. She also won the children's lyre contest at the Augustan Games in Athens with Nuvius son of Philinus as president. She was first in her age group ... citizen ... a girl.

(3) Dionysia won at ... with Antigonus as president, the single-course race at the Asclepian Games at the sanctuary of Epidaurus with Nicoteles as president.

To Pythian Apollo.

Not all memorable victories were athletic.

207. *Melosa. Athens, 5th cent.* BC *(FH 177m. G)*

An inscription on a black-figure vase.

I am Melosa's prize. She won a victory in the girls' carding contest.

VII. Private Life

'She will share her secrets'

Correct behaviour
'A woman's greatest virtue is chastity'

208. *Chastity. Italy, 3rd/2nd cent. BC (Thesleff, pp. 151-4. G)*

A treatise attributed to Phintys, a female member of the Pythagorean community in southern Italy.[1] Works said to be written by Pythagoras' wife or daughter Theano, and his daughter Myia (no. 250), survive, along with letters and treatises attributed to other women.[2] These writings are probably not original or even written by women, but rather consist of rhetorical exercises and treatises composed by men at different times and places. Certainly the content of what they wrote deals with topics particularly dear to the hearts of men: women's duties,[3] women's chastity, how to behave when your husband acquires a mistress (put up with it cheerfully).[4]

In general a woman must be good and orderly – and this no one can become without virtue ... A woman's greatest virtue is chastity. Because of this quality she is able to honour and to cherish her own particular husband.

Now some people think that it is not appropriate for a woman to be a philosopher, just as a woman should not be a cavalry officer or a politician ... I agree that men should be generals and city officials and politicians, and women should keep house and stay inside and receive and take care of their husbands. But I believe that courage, justice and intelligence are qualities that men and women have in common ... Courage and intelligence are more appropriately male qualities because of the strength of men's bodies and the power of their minds. Chastity is more appropriately female.

Accordingly a woman must learn about chastity and realise what she must do quantitatively and qualitatively to be able to obtain this womanly virtue. I believe that there are five qualifications: (1) the sanctity of her marriage bed, (2) the cleanliness of her body, (3) the manner in which she chooses to leave her house, (4) her refusal to

163

participate in secret cults or Cybeline ritual, (5) her readiness and moderation in sacrificing to the gods.

Of these the most important quality for chastity is to be pure in respect to her marriage bed, and for her not to have affairs with men from other households. If she breaks the law in this way she wrongs the gods of her family and provides her family and home not with its own offspring but with bastards. She wrongs the true gods, the gods to whom she swore to join with her own ancestors and her relatives in the sharing of life and the begetting of children according to law. She wrongs her own fatherland, because she does not abide by its established rules ... She should also consider the following: that there is no means of atoning for this sin; no way she can approach the shrines or the altars of the gods as a pure woman, beloved of god ... The greatest glory a free-born woman can have – her foremost honour – is the witness her own children will give to her chastity towards her husband, the stamp of likeness they bear to the father whose seed produced them ...[5]

As far as adornment of her body is concerned, the same arguments apply. She should be dressed in white, natural, plain. Her clothes should not be transparent or ornate. She should not put on silken material, but moderate, white-coloured clothes. In this way she will avoid being over-dressed or luxurious or made-up, and not give other women cause to be uncomfortably envious. She should not wear gold or emeralds at all; these are expensive and arrogant towards other women in the village.[6] She should not apply imported or artificial colouring to her face – with her own natural colouring, by washing only with water, she can ornament herself with modesty ...

Women of importance leave the house to sacrifice to the leading divinity of the community on behalf of themselves and their husbands and their households. They do not leave home at night nor in the evening, but at midday, to attend a religious festival or to make some purchase, accompanied by a single female servant or decorously escorted by two servants at most.[7] They make modest sacrifices to the gods also, according to their means. They keep away from secret cults and Cybeline orgies in their homes. For public law prevents women from participating in these rites, particularly because these forms of worship encourage drunkenness and ecstasy.[8] The mistress of the house and head of the household should be chaste and untouched in all respects.

209. *Greek and Roman customs compared. Rome, 1st cent.* BC
   (Cornelius Nepos, Lives, praef. 6. L)

They consider that many of the customs we think are appropriate are in bad taste. No Roman would hesitate to take his wife to a dinner party, or to allow the mother of his family to occupy the first rooms in his house and to walk about in public. The custom in Greece is completely different:

a woman cannot appear at a party unless it is among her relatives; she can only sit in the interior of the house, which is called the women's quarters (*gynaeceum*); this no male can enter unless he is a close relation.

210. *Imperial upbringing. Rome, 1st cent.* AD *(Suetonius, Life of Augustus 64.4-5. L)*

He brought up his daughters and granddaughters so that they even became accustomed to weaving and spinning[9] and forbade them to speak or do anything except publicly and that was not fit to be entered in the imperial diary. He kept them from contact with strangers, to the point that he wrote to Lucius Vinicius, a noble and distinguished young man, that he had 'behaved badly when he went to visit my daughter at Baiae'.[10]

211. *Seating for gladiatorial shows. Rome 27 BC-AD 14 (Suetonius, Life of Augustus 44.5-7. L)*

While formerly women had been used to attend gladiatorial shows together with men, [the emperor Augustus] ordered that they could attend only if they were accompanied and if they sat in the highest rows.

To the Vestal Virgins he assigned a reserved seat in the theatre facing the tribunal of the praetor. He kept women away from athletic displays. Indeed, during the Pontifical Games[11] he postponed till the following morning a boxing match that had been called for, and issued an edict to the effect that women should not come to the theatre before the fifth hour.[12]

212. *The household of P. Larcius Nicia. Campania, 1st century* BC *(ILLRP 977 = CLE 56 = CIL I². 1570 = CIL X.6009. L)*

Publius Larcius Nicia, freedman of Publius; Saufeia Thalea, freedwoman of Aulus; Lucius Larcius Rufus, son of Publius; Publius Larcius Brocchus, son of Publius; Larcia Horaea, freedwoman of Publius [and Saufeia].[13]

I was respected by good people and was envied by no woman of character. I was obedient to my old master and mistress, and to this man, my husband, I was dutiful. They honoured me with my freedom, he with a [matron's] robe. I kept the house for twenty years, beginning as a little girl. My last day made its judgment; death snatched away my soul but did not take my life's honour.

Lucius Eprius Chilo, messenger of the tribune of the people, Epria Cri... (*The rest is lost.*)

Education of females
'She worked hard to learn letters'

213. *The education of Eurydice, Philip of Macedon's mother. Aegae, 3rd*
    cent. BC (Pseudo-Plutarch, Moralia 14b-c. 2nd cent. AD. G)

We ought therefore to try every appropriate means of disciplining our
children, following the example of Eurydice. She was an Illyrian and a
complete barbarian, but late in life she became involved in education
because of her children's studies. The epigram she set up to the Muses
provides adequate documentation of her love for her children: 'Eurydice
of Hierapolis set up this tablet, when she had satisfied her desire to
become learned; for she worked hard to learn letters, the repository of
speech, because she was a mother of growing sons.'

214. *The need for educated parents. Rome, 1st cent. AD (Quintilian,*
    Institutes of Oratory 1.1.6. L)

As for parents, I should like them to be as well educated as possible, and I
am not speaking just of fathers. We know that Cornelia, the mother of the
Gracchi, contributed greatly to their eloquence, for the erudition of her
speech has been handed down even to the present day in her letters.
Laelia, too, daughter of Gaius [Laelius],[14] is said to have brought back the
elegance of her father's speech in her own; and the oration which
Hortensia, Quintus' daughter, made before the triumvirs is read not
merely as an honour to her sex.[15]

215. *Heraidous, a girl who is learning to read. Egypt, 2nd cent. AD*
    (Giessen papyrus 80, 95. G)

Fragment of a letter; the names of the writer and addressee(s) are lost.

(80) Heraidous sends greetings ... so do Helen and Tinoutis and her
father and everyone in the household and the mother of dearest
Heraidous. Send the pigeons and small fowl, which I am not accustomed
to eat, to Heraidous' teacher. Helen, Apollonius' mother, asks you to keep
her son Hermaeus in hand. Whatever I did not eat send as a gift to my
daughter's teacher, so that he may take trouble over her. My best wishes
to you. Choiak 17.

(95) Please see that I have the necessary equipment for school, such as a
book for Heraidous to read ...

1. Relief in Pentelic marble showing a maenad leaning on her thyrsos. Roman copy of a Greek original, perhaps by Callimachus, c. 420-410 BC. (Metropolitan Museum of Art, Fletcher Fund, 1935, New York)

2. Black-figure hydria showing women standing inside the portico of a fountain house; Athens, c. 520 BC (Museum of Fine Arts, Boston)

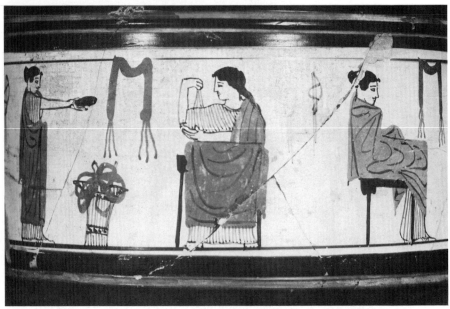

3. White-ground pyxis showing women in a domestic scene (a wool basket is on the floor); Athens, c. 475-440 BC (British Museum, London)

4. Wall painting from Villa at Boscoreale, showing woman playing the cithara;
1st cent. BC. (Metropolitan Museum of Art, Rogers Fund, 1903, New York)

5. Terracotta figurines of two women playing knucklebones, South Italian Greek,
c. 300 BC (British Museum, London)

6. Roman Muse sarcophagus, in marble, showing the deceased woman holding a scroll and surrounded by Minerva and the nine Muses; mid-3rd cent. AD (Nelson-Atkins Museum of Art, Kansas City)

7. Reverse of an *aureus* (gold coin) of Septimius Severus, AD 202, showing Julia Domna with her sons Caracalla and Geta (the emperor is on the obverse). The portrait of Geta is a rarity: when Caracalla killed his brother, he also ordered his name and image to be cancelled. (American Numismatic Society, New York)

8. Terracotta figurine group. Two tambourine players on a camel, Eastern Roman Empire (Emory University Museum of Art and Archaeology, Atlanta)

9. Scenes of women working in wool and weaving, on a black-figure lekythos by the Amasis Painter, from Athens, c. 540 BC. (Metropolitan Museum of Art, Fletcher Fund, 1931, New York)

10. Red-figure medallion in white-ground cup showing a woman and baby; Athens, c. 475-450 BC (Photo ACL, Brussels; Musées royaux d'art et d'histoire, inv. A 890, Brussels)

COMBAT OF WOMEN GLADIATORS.

11. Marble relief from Halicarnassus showing two women, armed with swords and shields, engaged in gladiatorial combat. For the inscription, see no. 295. (British Museum, London)

12. Red-figure kylix (interior) showing two women (or girls) walking. The gesture and difference in dress indicate that the figure on the right is older or of superior status. (Metropolitan Museum of Art, Rogers Fund, 1906)

13. Terracotta relief showing a midwife and her assistant delivering a baby. From a tomb in the necropolis of Isola Sacra (near Ostia), 2nd cent. AD (Museo di Ostia; photo, Fototeca Unione)

14(a). Epitaph of a midwife on marble, 2nd cent. AD (Kelsey Museum of Archaeology, no. KM 869, Ann Arbor)

14(b). Papyrus recording a dowry payment (University of Michigan, Ann Arbor). Examples of the kinds of materials used to reconstruct the history of women in antiquity. For translations of the texts, see nos. 378 and 150 respectively.

15. Mosaic representations of Saints Perpetua *(left)* and Felicitas *(right)*, in the Oratorio di Sant'Andrea, Museo Arcivescovile, Ravenna, early 6th cent. AD (Photo Anderson)

Intellectual life
'An author of books'

216. *Plato's female pupils. Athens, 4th cent. BC (Diogenes Laertius 3.46; Themistius, Orations 295e; Oxyrhynchus papyrus 3656. G)*

Diogenes names seventeen of Plato's many male pupils:

Along with them there were two women, Lasthenia of Mantinea and Axiothea of Phlius; she dressed like a man, according to Dicaearchus.[16]

Themistius uses the case of Axiothea as an illustration of the powerful attractions of Plato's philosophy:

For Axiothea, when she had read some of Plato's *Republic*[17] left her home in Arcadia and went to Athens. She attended Plato's lectures without anyone noticing that she was a woman ...

... after Plato's death [Lasthenia?] also studied with Speusippus, according to Hippobotus, and then with Menedemus the Eretrian.[18] Again Hieronymus of Rhodes writes about her in his treatise on Physics. Aristophanes the Peripatetic similarly tells the story in his treatise on Painlessness that the girl was pretty and full of unaffected charm.

217. *A female philosopher.[19] Athens, 3rd cent. BC (Diogenes Laertius 6.96-8. 3rd cent. AD. G)*

Hipparchia fell in love with both Crates' discourses and his way of life. She paid no attention to any of her suitors, their money, their high birth or their good looks. To her Crates was everything. And in fact she threatened her parents that she would kill herself, if they didn't let her marry him. Her parents begged Crates to dissuade her. He did everything he could, but finally when he couldn't persuade her, he stood up and took off his clothes in front of her and said: 'This is your bridegroom; these are his possessions; plan accordingly!' He didn't think she would be able to be his partner unless she could share in the same pursuits.

But the girl chose him. She adopted the same dress and went about with him; she made love to him in public; she went to dinner parties with him.[20] Once, when she went to a dinner party at Lysimachus' house, she put down Theodorus called the Atheist by using the following trick of logic: if an action could not be called wrong when done by Theodorus it could not be called wrong when done by Hipparchia. Therefore, if Theodorus does nothing wrong when he hits himself, Hipparchia does nothing wrong if she hits Theodorus. He had no defence against her logic, and started to pull off her cloak.[21]

But Hipparchia did not get upset or excited as other women would. Then when he said to her: 'Here I am, Agave, who left behind my shuttles beside my loom.'[22] 'Indeed it is I,' said Hipparchia; 'Theodorus – you don't think that I have arranged my life so badly, do you, if I have used the time I would have wasted on weaving for my education?' These and many other stories are told about the woman philosopher.

218. *Epigram on Hipparchia. 3rd cent.* BC *(Antipater of Thessalonica, AP VII.413, 1st cent.* BC. *G)*

I, Hipparchia, have no use for the works of deep-robed women; I have chosen the Cynics' virile life. I don't need capes with brooches or deep-soled slippers; I don't like glossy nets for my hair. My wallet is my staff's travelling companion, and the double cloak that goes with them, the cover for my bed on the ground. I'm much stronger than Atalanta from Maenalus, because my wisdom is better than racing over the mountain.

219. *A learned woman. 1st cent.* AD *(The Suda.[23] FHG 3.520 ff. G)*

Pamphile was an Epidaurian, a learned woman, the daughter of Soterides, who is also said to have been an author of books,[24] according to Dionysius in the thirteenth book of his *History of Learning*; or, as others have written, it was Socratides her husband. She wrote historical memoirs in 33 books, an epitome of Ctesias' history is three books, many epitomes of histories and other books, about controversies, sex[25] and many other things.

220. *Agrippina's memoirs. Rome, 1st cent.* AD *(Tacitus, Annals 4.53. L)*

Agrippina the Younger, known to history as the murdered mother of the Emperor Nero, wrote the story of her life and her family in sufficient detail for it to have been of use to the historian Tacitus, who cites the work.

But Agrippina [the Elder] was still angry and ill. When Caesar[26] paid her a visit, she wept long and silently, then began to berate him and plead with him by turns. He should help her out of her loneliness and give her a husband. She was still young and healthy and no other comfort was available to honest women. And there were plenty of men in Rome who would consider it an honour to take in the widow and children of Germanicus. But the emperor, who was not blind to the political aspects of her request, gave no outward sign either of displeasure or fear, and left her forthwith, despite her insistence, without a reply.

I read about this incident in the memoirs of Agrippina the Younger, mother of the Emperor Nero, in which she recorded for posterity her own life and her family's travails.

221. *A philosopher. Apollonia, Mysia, 2nd/3rd cent. AD (Pleket 30. G)*

For Magnilla the philosopher, daughter of Magnus the philosopher, wife of Menius the philosopher.

222. *A Roman philosopher. Rome. (CIL VI.33898 = ILS 7783. L)*

Pious Euphrosyne, learned in the nine Muses,[27] philosopher, she lived 20 years.

223. *Women's eloquence. Rome, 46 BC (Cicero, Brutus 58.211. L)*

We have read the letters of Cornelia, mother of the Gracchi; it appears that her sons were brought up not so much at their mother's breast as by her speech. I often heard the speech of Laelia, Gaius' daughter; we saw that she was touched by her father's refinement and so were her two daughters, the Muciae, whose speech is also known to me, and I have heard both her granddaughters, the Liciniae, one of whom, the wife of Scipio, you, Brutus, I believe, have heard speak.

224. *Sulpicia. Rome, late 1st cent. AD (Martial, Epigrams 10.35. Late 1st cent. AD. L)*

The work of the second Roman woman poet named Sulpicia (for the first see nos. 22 and 23), who lived in the Flavian period (AD 69-96), is not preserved. If Martial's praise of her work is any guide, her poems must have lacked the passion and immediacy of those of her earlier namesake.

Let all girls read Sulpicia if they want to please their husbands alone. And let every husband read Sulpicia who wants to please his bride alone. She doesn't write about the Colchian's[28] fury or Thyestes' deadly dinner; she doesn't believe in Scylla and Byblis: but she teaches chaste and honest loves, the games, the delights, the humour of love. He who appreciates her poetry will say that no woman was more mischievous, and no woman more modest. I believe the nymph Egeria exchanged such pleasantries with Numa in his dripping cave. And, Sappho, if she'd been your teacher or classmate, you'd have learned more and kept your chastity intact. But if hard Phaon had seen you and her together at the same time, he'd have loved Sulpicia. In vain: that girl wouldn't live as the wife of Jupiter himself or the lover of Bacchus or Apollo if her Calenus were ever taken from her.[29]

225. *Sayings attributed to Aspasia by Socrates. Athens, 5th cent.* BC *(Xenophon, Memorabilia 2.36; Oeconomicus 3.15. G)*

On occasion, men can be educated by wise women (cf. also no. 424). In Plato's *Symposium* Socrates claims to have learned about passion from Diotima of Mantinea; in the *Menexenus* he says he learned about rhetoric from Aspasia, and there was a considerable literature (now lost) about their relationship.[30]

Advice about matchmaking

Aspasia once told me that good matchmakers whose good reports are true are successful in creating marriages. She did not wish to recommend matchmakers who told lies, because the people they deceive hate each other and the matchmaker as well. I am convinced that she was right, so that I can't give any recommendation about you that I can't give truthfully.

Characterisation of a good wife

I will recommend Aspasia to you, who can explain the whole matter to you better than I can. I believe that a wife who is a good partner plays an equal role with her husband in benefiting the household. Possessions come into the household mainly as a result of the husband's efforts, but most of the outgoings are under the wife's stewardship. If both do their jobs well, the household prospers, but if they do them badly the household is diminished.

Women and women
'Your true and sweet friendship'

226. *Biote. Athens, late 5th cent.* BC *(CEG 97 = IG II².10954. G)*

Because of your true and sweet friendship, your companion[31] Euthylla placed this tablet on your grave, Biote, for she keeps your memory with her tears, and weeps for your lost youth.

227. *Praxidice and Dyseris. Thessaly, early 5th cent.* BC *(FH 152. G)*

A dedicatory epigram for an offering.

Praxidice made this garment, Dyseris designed it: the skill of both is united.

228. *The dildo. Egypt, 3rd cent.* BC? *(Herodas, Mime 6. G)*

A poem representing a discussion between two middle-class women about the virtues of a particular dildo, referred to here not by its generic name *olisbos* ('slipper'), but euphemistically as a 'pacifier' (*baubon*, from *baubao*, 'sleep'), made by a shoemaker named Kerdon, 'Greedy'. The poet manages to imply that the two famous women poets Nossis and Erinna are collaborators in their activities.

Koritto: Metro, sit down. (*To her slave*) Get up and give the lady your chair – I have to tell her to do everything – you couldn't do anything on your own, could you? Bah, she's a stone, sitting in the house, not a slave. But when I measure out your barley ration you count the crumbs, and if even a little bit falls off the top you complain for the entire day – the walls fall in with your shouting. Oh, now you're polishing and making it shine, you pirate, just when we need it. Offer a prayer to my friend, since without her here you'd have had a taste of my hands.

Metro: Dear Koritto, our necks are worn out by the same yoke: I bark like a dog yelling at these unmentionable creatures day and night. But the reason I've come to your house – get the hell out of the way, you smart-arses, all ears and tongues, and days-off the rest of the time – please, don't hold back, dear Koritto, who was the man that made the red Pacifier for you?

Koritto: Metro – you haven't seen it have you?

Metro: Nossis, Erinna's daughter, had it a couple of days ago. Mm, nice gift.

Koritto: Nossis? Where'd she get it?

Metro: Will you tell on me if I tell you?

Koritto: By your sweet eyes, dear Metro, nothing you say will be heard escaping from Koritto's mouth.

Metro: Bitas' wife Euboule gave it to her and told her no one should find out about it.

Koritto: *Women*. That woman will wear me out. She begged me and I took pity on her and gave it to her, Metro, before I could even get to use it myself. And she snatches it away like some hidden treasure and gives it to people who shouldn't get it. A fond farewell to friends like that. She can look for somebody else instead of me to lend my things to Nossis – in case you think that for her (if I'm complaining more than is right, forgive me, Nemesis). If I had a thousand, I wouldn't give her one, not even a rotten one.

Metro: No, Koritto, don't let anger flare in your nostrils, when you hear of some silly story. It's a respectable woman's duty to put up with anything. I'm the one who's responsible, because I chatter so much, and I ought to have my tongue cut out. But what I particularly wanted to find out from you, who made it for you? If you love me, tell me. Why are you looking at me and laughing? Is this the first time you've ever seen me, Metro? Why are you behaving in such an affected way? Please, Koritto, don't hold back, and tell me who made it.

Koritto: Oh, why plead with me? Kerdon made it.

Metro: Who? Tell me! Kerdon? There are two Kerdons. One has grey eyes, Myrtaline's neighbour (Kylaethis' daughter). But he couldn't sew a plectrum for a lyre. The other one lives near Hermodorus' tenement houses, as you go out from Main Street. He was somebody once, but now he's got old. The old lady, Kylaethis, used to use him. (*Piously*) May her friends and family remember her in death.

Koritto: As you say, Metro, it isn't either of *them*. He is – I don't know, either from Chios or Erythrae, bald, a little man. You'd say he was Prexinus – they're as alike as fig and fig, except when he talks, then you know it's Kerdon and not Prexinus. He works at home and sells undercover – every door these days fears the tax collectors. But his workmanship – what workmanship. You'd think Athena's hands, not Kerdon's went into it. I – he came bringing *two* of them, Metro. When I saw them, my eyes swam at the sight – men don't have such firm pricks! Not only that, but its *smoothness* is sleep, and its straps are like wool, not leather. You couldn't find a kinder woman's shoemaker.

Metro: Why did you let the other one go?

Koritto: Metro, what didn't I do to get it? What sort of charm didn't I use to besiege him? I kissed him, and rubbed his bald head, and gave him something sweet to drink, and called him 'Daddy' – the only thing I didn't give him to use was my body.

Metro: Well, you should have given him that if he'd asked for it.

Koritto: Yes, I would have. But it's not a good idea to talk about what's not becoming a lady. Bitas' wife Euboule was there grinding. She has worn down my millstone night and day and turned it into trash, just so she wouldn't need to spend four obols to have her own sharpened.

Metro: How did he manage to come to your house, all this long way, dear Koritto? Don't hold back from me.

Koritto: Artemeis sent him, the wife of Kandas the tanner – she pointed my house out.

Metro: Artemeis always finds out about new discoveries – she can outdrink ... But since you couldn't rescue the two of them you ought to have found out who ordered the other one.

Koritto: I begged him, but he swore that he wouldn't tell me.

Metro: What you're telling me means that I must take a trip. I'm going now, to Artemeis' house, so I can find out who this Kerdon is. Stay well, Koritto dear. (*Ambiguously*) *Someone* is hungry, and it's time for me ...

Koritto: Close the door. You – count the hens, give them some darnel seed. You can be sure bird-snatchers will steal them, unless you hold them in your lap.

---

229. *Going to a festival. Egypt, 3rd cent. BC (Theocritus, Idyll 15, excerpts. G)*

Gorgo, a housewife, visits her friend Praxinoa on the day of the festival of Adonis in Alexandria.

Gorgo: Is Praxinoa in?

Praxinoa: Gorgo dear – how long it's been – yes, I'm in. I'm amazed that you've come at last. See that she has a chair, Eunoa; put a cushion on it.

Gorgo: Thank you.

Praxinoa: Sit down.

Gorgo: I'm so incompetent. I barely got here in one piece, Praxinoa, there was such a crowd, so many chariots, everywhere boots, everywhere men wearing cloaks. And the road is endless. Every time you move further away.

Praxinoa: It's that crazy man. He brings me here to the ends of the earth, and gets me a hovel, not a house, so that we can't be neighbours, out of spite, envious brute; he never changes.

Gorgo: Don't talk about your husband that way, dear, when the little boy is around. You see, Praxinoa, how he's looking at you. Don't worry, Zopyrion, sweet baby – she isn't talking about Daddy.

Praxinoa: The child understands, by the great goddess.

Gorgo: Nice Daddy.

Praxinoa: Daddy (that man) the other day – just the other day I said to him: 'Daddy, go and buy some soap and rouge at the booth,' and he came back with salt, the big ox.

Gorgo: Mine's like that too. He's a spendthrift, Diocleidas. For seven drachmas he bought dog skins, pluckings of old wallets – five fleeces, yesterday, all of it dirt, work and more work. But come on, get your dress and your cloak. Let's go to the house of the king, rich Ptolemy, to see Adonis. I hear the queen has done a beautiful job of decorating it.

Praxinoa: In fine homes everything's fine.

Gorgo: When you've seen it, what won't you be able to say to someone who hasn't? It must be time to go.

Praxinoa: Every day is a holiday if you don't work. Eunoa – you lazy – pick up that spinning and put it back in the centre again. Weasels like to sleep on soft beds. Move, bring me some water, right now. She was supposed to bring water; she brought soap. Give it to me anyway. Not so much, you pirate. Pour on the water. Stupid – why are you getting my cloak wet? Now stop. I've washed as well as the gods permit it. Where is the key to the big chest? Then bring it.

Gorgo: Praxinoa, that pleated dress suits you. Tell me – how much did the cloth cost off the loom?

Praxinoa: Don't remind me, Gorgo. More than two minas of pure silver. I put my heart into the handwork.

Gorgo: Well, it lives up to your expectations. You can say that.

Praxinoa: Bring me my cloak and my hat. Put them on right. I'm not taking you, baby. Mormo Bogy; horse will bite you. Cry as much as you like, I won't let you be lame. Let's go. Phrygia, take the baby and play with him, call the dog inside, and lock the front door.

230. *The go-between. Egypt, 3rd cent.* BC? *(Herodas, Mime 1. G)*

A conversation between a *hetaera*, Metriche, whose man has been away in Egypt, and her old 'nurse' Gyllis (cf. Neaera's household arrangements in Megara, above, no. 90).

Metriche (to her slave Threissa): Someone is making a noise at the door. See which of the farm workers has come in from the fields.

Threissa: Who's at the door?

Gyllis: It's me.

Threissa: Who are you? Are you afraid to come closer?

Gyllis: Look, here I am. I've come closer.

Threissa: Who are you?

Gyllis: Gyllis, Philaenis' mother.[32] Go inside and tell Metriche I'm here.

Threissa (to Metriche): You're being called by ...

Metriche: Who?

Threissa: Gyllis.

Metriche: Old ma Gyllis. Go away for a bit, slave. What Fate sent you to come to us, Gyllis? *(With ironic exaggeration)* Why have you come like a god to mortals, for it's already five months, I think, since anyone has seen you – I swear by the Fates, coming to the door of this house?

Gyllis: I live far off,[33] child, and the mud in the back alleys comes up to my knees. I have only the strength of a fly. My old age drags me down. It stands like a shadow beside me.

Metriche: Quiet! Don't bring false charges against your age. You're still able, Gyllis, to use your arms to throttle your adversaries.

Gyllis: Yes, joke away. Just like women your age. But joking won't keep you warm. Why, dear child, how long have you been a widow, tossing alone on your lonely bed? It has been ten months since Mandris went off to Egypt. He hasn't even sent you a letter. He has forgotten you, and drunk from a new cup. Egypt is the House of Aphrodite. Everything that exists anywhere in the world is in Egypt, money, gymnasia, power, tranquillity, fame, sights, philosophers, gold, young men, the shrine of the Sibling Gods Ptolemy and Arsinoë, a good king, the Museum, wine, all the good things Mandris could want, and women, more of them, I swear by the Maiden who is Hades' wife, than the stars which the heaven boasts that it holds, and their looks – like the goddesses who once set out to be judged for their beauty by Paris (may they not hear what I am saying). Well, poor thing, what are you thinking of, as you warm your chair? You'll find out you have grown old and the ashes will gulp down your life's prime. Look elsewhere and for two or three days, change your mind and be happy and find a new man. A ship isn't safe in port with only one anchor. If Death comes, there will be no one to resurrect us. A cruel winter ... no one knows ... Mortals' life is uncertain. But now no one is standing near us?

Metriche: Not a soul.

Gyllis: Then listen. This is what I wanted to come here to tell you. There is Gryllus,[34] son of Matacine, Pataicius' wife; he has won five prizes in Games: as a boy in Delphi, and twice in Corinth when he was first getting a beard, and then he beat his opponents in boxing twice at Olympia. He's nicely rich; he doesn't stir a straw on the ground; he's an untouched sea as far as sex is concerned. When he saw you at the festival of the Descent of Mise,[35] his passions were inflamed, his heart was stung by desire, and, my child, he won't leave my house by night or by day, but weeps over me and wheedles me and says he is dying of passion. So my dear child Metriche, grant the Goddess this one misdemeanour. Dedicate yourself, before you find that age has looked upon you. You will profit in two ways ... and you will be given more than you imagine. Think it over. Do what I say. I am your friend. I swear by the Fates.

Metriche: Gyllis, your white hair has made your wits dull. I swear by Mandris' safe return home and beloved Demeter I wouldn't have listened calmly to any other woman. I would have taught her to limp to her lame song and to have considered my door's threshold an enemy. My friend, don't you come ever again to my house with one more message like this, but bring me the kind of message that ought to be brought to young girls by old women. You let Pytheas' daughter Metriche warm her chair. No one laughs at Mandris. But those aren't the words Gyllis needs to hear, as the saying goes. Threissa, wipe out the cup and pour her three sixth-parts of straight wine, drop some water into it and give it to her to drink.

Gyllis: No, thank you.

Metriche: Here, Gyllis, drink it.

Gyllis: No thank you. I didn't come here to lead you astray, but because of the Holy Rites.

Metriche: On account of them, Gyllis.

Gyllis (*she takes the wine*): ... Well, my child, it is sweet. I swear by Demeter, Gyllis has never drunk sweeter wine than this. Good luck to you, child, take care of yourself. May my Myrtale and Sime stay young,[36] while Gyllis is still alive and breathing.

231. *Lesbians as a bad omen. Daldis, Lydia, late 2nd cent.* AD *(Artemidorus, On the Interpretation of Dreams 1.80. G)*

From a a list of predictions based on dreams about 'unnatural sexual intercourse'.

If [in a dream] a woman penetrates another woman, she will share her secrets with the woman she has penetrated. If she does not know the woman she has penetrated, she will attempt futile actions. If a woman is penetrated by another woman, she will be divorced from her husband or become a widow. None the less she will learn the secrets of the woman with whom she had sexual intercourse.

232. *A letter from a soldier's wife complaining about the behaviour of another soldier's daughters. Egypt, 4th cent. AD (Grenfell papyrus I.53. G)*

The abrupt style and eccentric spelling of these letters convey an unusual sense of spontaneity. The addresses of neither husband nor wife are specified, and the precise nature of the problem described is not entirely clear: presumably some male member of Artemis' household has become the lover of one of Sarapion's daughters.

Artemis to Theodorus her own husband. Above all I pray to the dear Lord that we have found you well. I have sent this letter and maforte[37] with your fellow soldier Apion. Your children send their love and Allous often complains of you, for although you have written frequently and sent love to everyone to her alone you have not sent your love! Ara sends her love.

(*The enclosed letter*) Artemis to Sarapion also known as Isidorus. The soldier Phanes writes and you are continuing in your folly. May the prefect swiftly suppress your folly. He writes me that you are amazed at me, and say that the prefect does not want home-wreckers. If you want to condone the prostitution of your daughters, do not criticise me but blame the elders of the church [if I tell you] how these daughters of yours have made their escape by saying 'we want husbands' and how Lucra was caught in the act with her lover, after she made herself a neighbourhood nuisance;[38] as a result of this they hate me because for your sake we have described their actions. If you know who the man is, put up with it; we are the first to reveal that he is of better birth than someone; and I myself am hardly the daughter of a slave!

I am writing this to you, Theodorus, so that [Sarapion] will make every effort because of the situation and it is essential that you show him the letter. Give this to Theodorus the soldier from his son [*sic*].

Women and men
'It is incredible how much I miss you'

233. *The rape of the Sabine women. Rome, traditionally 8th cent. BC (Livy, History of Rome 1.9. Late 1st cent. BC-early 1st cent. AD. L)*

The historian Livy retells the legend of the Sabine women: how they were snatched from their families at a religious festival to populate Rome and how their hearts and minds were won over by violence followed by sweet words and childbearing.

The Roman state had become strong enough to hold its own in war with all the peoples along its borders, but a shortage of women meant that its greatness was fated to last for a single generation, since there was no prospect of offspring at home nor any prospect of marriage with their neighbours. Then, in accordance with the decision of the senate, Romulus sent messengers to the neighbouring peoples to ask for alliance and the right of marriage for the new people: cities, like everything else, start small but later, if their own excellence and the gods assist them, they grow in strength and in fame. It was certain that at the beginning of Rome the gods had been propitiated and that it would not lack in valour. Therefore, men should not disdain to join blood and family ties with other men.

But nowhere were the emissaries given a fair hearing. Some scorned, others feared the great power growing in their midst, both for themselves and for their descendants. In more than one place the emissaries were asked, even as they were being sent packing, why they hadn't offered asylum to women (criminals) too: that way they'd have had their marriage and with others of their own rank! The youth of Rome took this insult badly and began to think seriously about the use of force. Romulus, to gain time till he found the right occasion, hid his concern and prepared to celebrate the Consualia, the solemn games in honour of equestrian Neptune. He then ordered that the spectacle be announced to the neighbouring peoples. He gave the event great publicity by the most lavish means possible in those days. Many people came, some simply out of curiosity to see the new city, and especially the nearest neighbours, from Caenina, Crustuminum and Antemnae; the entire Sabine population came, wives and children included. Received with hospitality in the houses, after having seen the position of the city, its walls, and the large number of buildings, they marvelled that Rome had grown so fast. When it was time for the show, and everybody was concentrating on this, a prearranged signal was given and all the Roman youths began to grab the women. Many just snatched the nearest woman to hand, but the most beautiful had already been reserved for the senators and these were escorted to the senators' houses by plebeians who had been given this assignment. The story goes that one woman, far and away the most beautiful, was carried off by the gang of a certain Thalassius, and because many wanted to know where they were taking her, they repeatedly shouted that they were taking her to Thalassius, and that is how the nuptial cry came to be.[39]

The party was over, and the grieving parents of the girls ran away, accusing the Romans of having violated the laws of hospitality and invoking the god who was supposed to have been honoured at that day's festival. Nor did the girls themselves hold much hope. But Romulus went among them in person to assure them that none of this would have happened if their fathers hadn't been so inflexible in not letting them marry their neighbours. But now they would have the status of wives with all the material rewards and civil rights of citizenship and they would have children, than which nothing is dearer. They should cool their anger and give their hearts to the men who had already taken their bodies. A good relationship often begins with an offence, he said. And their husbands would treat them with extra kindness in hope of making up for the parents and country they so missed. The men added their blandishments, saying that they'd been motivated by love and passion, entreaties which are very effective with women.

234. *'Birth control'. Paros, 7th cent. BC (Archilochus, Fr. 196a West. G)*

A poem representing conversation between a girl and a young man who wants to make love to her. She suggests he ask another girl. He promises instead not to get her pregnant.

'But if you are in a hurry and desire drives you on, there is in our house a girl who is eager ... young and delicate. I think she has a perfect figure. You ... her.'

So she spoke, and I answered: 'Daughter of Amphimedo (she was a good woman, though now she lies beneath the broad earth), there are many other pleasures for young men besides the Sacred Act. One of those will do. The rest you and I will discuss at leisure when ... I'll follow your orders: beneath the lintel and below the gate – don't begrudge me, dear; I'll put ashore at your garden's grass.[40] But realise this: another man can have Neobule.[41] Alas, she's overripe; her girlhood's flower has fallen, and the charm she had before; [she can't get] enough – a mad-woman who shows no measure ... she can go to hell ... If I had such a wife I'd give my neighbours pleasure.[42] I much prefer you. You aren't faithless or two-faced; she's more bitter and takes on too many. I'm afraid that in my haste I'd hurry to produce blind and premature offspring, like a bitch.'

Those were my words. I took the girl and laid her down among the flowers. I covered her with my soft cloak and held my arm around her neck. She stopped trembling like a fawn; I touched her breasts gently with my hand; she revealed her new young skin. I touched her fair body everywhere and sent my white force aside, touching her blonde hair.

235. *The courtesan Aspasia, mistress of Pericles. Athens, 5th cent. BC (Plutarch, Life of Pericles 24.1-6, 32.1-2. 2nd cent. AD. G)*

(24.1) This may be the right place to discuss Aspasia, and to ask what techniques or powers gave her such great control of the principal politicians and caused the philosophers to make her an important subject of discourse.[43] (24.2) My sources agree that her family was from Miletus, and that she was the daughter of Axiochus. They say that she was following the example of a certain Thargelia, an Ionian woman of the past, when she set her sights on men of power. This Thargelia was a particularly beautiful woman and was endowed with charm as well as wit. She lived with many Greek men, and she won all of her consorts over to the king of Persia, and through them sowed the seeds of sympathy for the Persian cause in the most influential and important men.

(24.3) They say that Pericles had high regard for Aspasia as a philosopher and politician. Socrates, in fact, came to see her with his disciples, and his friends brought their wives to hear her, although she ran a disreputable and improper business, because she trained young *hetaerae*. (24.4) According to Aeschines,[44] Lysicles the sheep-seller, a man of no family and humble birth, became the most important man in Athens because he lived with Aspasia after Pericles' death. In the *Menexenus* of Plato (the first part of which is a parody, but it contains at least some historical truth), it is said that the woman had the reputation of associating with many Athenians as a teacher of rhetoric.[45]

(24.5) But Pericles' affection for Aspasia appears rather to have been erotic [rather than as pupil to teacher]. His own wife was a close relation of his, and had been married first to Hipponicus, by whom she had Callias the Rich. Then by Pericles she had Xanthippus and Paralus. Then, because their marriage was unsatisfactory, he gave her over to another husband and took Aspasia and loved her very much. It is said that he greeted her with a kiss both when he went off to the Agora and when he came home.

(32.1) About this time [c. 430 BC] Aspasia was a defendant in a trial for impiety. Hermippus the comic poet was the prosecutor, and accused her of bringing freeborn women to a house for Pericles.[46] ... But Pericles begged Aspasia off, by weeping floods of tears for her at the trial, as Aeschines says, and by imploring the jurors [to spare her].[47]

236. *Disadvantages of a liberal education. Athens, 4th cent. BC (Xenophon, Memorabilia 2.7. G)*

Xenophon, a pupil of Socrates, applied his teacher's philosophy to every aspect of life. Here he portrays Socrates using deductive reasoning on a practical problem: his friend Aristarchus finds himself with a household of female relatives to maintain; Socrates offers the revolutionary advice that they should be put to work making cloth, likes slaves, so that they can pay for their upkeep.

'Yes, Socrates, indeed I don't know where to turn. After the civil war began,[48] many people fled to the Piraeus. My female relatives were left behind and all collected at my house – sisters and nieces and cousins, so that there are fourteen freeborn persons in the household. Now we can get no food or income from our land because the enemy has control of it, and we get no rents from the houses we own because of the depopulation in Athens. No one is buying our furniture and one can't borrow money anywhere – a man could find more money looking in the street than he could trying to raise a loan. It's hard, Socrates, to look on and see my relatives dying, but it is impossible to support them in hard times like these.'

After Socrates heard this he asked, 'How is it that Ceramon manages to provide for so many people, not just for himself and his family, but to save enough in addition that he is able to be a rich man? Meanwhile you with your many people to take care of are afraid that all of you will die from want of the necessities of life.'

Aristarchus replied, 'The reason is, by Zeus, that he has slaves to provide for, while my people are freeborn.'

'Which do you think are better, your freeborn people or Ceramon's slaves?' 'I think the freeborn people at my house!'

'But,' said Socrates, 'isn't it shocking that Ceramon should live well off the work of people of a lower order, while you who have far better people are in want?'

'Indeed,' said Aristarchus, 'he is supporting technicians but mine have been educated like free persons.'

237. *Melite. Athens, 365-340 BC (CEG 530 = IG II².12067. G)*

An inscription on a tablet that shows a woman holding out her hand to her husband. The verses awkwardly represent a dialogue between husband and wife.

'Farewell, tomb of Melite; a good woman lies here. You loved your husband Onesimus; he loved you in return. You were the best, and so he laments your death, for you were a good woman.'

'And to you farewell, dearest of men; love my children.'[49]

238. *Betrayal. Athens, 4th cent. BC (Menander, Fr. 15, Antinoöpolis papyrus. G)*

In this fragment of a lost comedy, a young husband complains that the wife he loves has betrayed him.

Who in this city has suffered more dreadfully than I? By Demeter and Heaven! I have been married for five months, and since the night I was married – queen Night, I call you as witness to the truth of what I say – I haven't been away from bed a single night, away from my wife. ... I wanted her, honestly ... I was tied to her by her noble character and her unaffected way of life; she loved me and I loved her.[50]

239. *A butcher and his wife. Rome, 1st cent. BC (ILLRP 793 = CIL*
I².1221 = CIL VI.9499 = ILS 7472 = CLE 959. L)

A man and a woman, hands joined, are shown in relief on this travertine
tombstone now in the British Museum.

(*On the left*) Lucius Aurelius Hermia, freedman of Lucius, a butcher from
the Viminal Hill.

My wife, who died before me, chaste in body, my one and only – a loving
woman who possessed my heart, she lived as a faithful wife to a faithful
husband with affection equal to my own, since she never let avarice keep
her from her duty. Aurelia Philematio, freedwoman of Lucius.

(*On the right*) Aurelia Philematio, freedwoman of Lucius.

When I was alive I was called Aurelia Philematium. I was chaste and
modest; I did not know the crowd; I was faithful to my husband. He
whom, alas, I have lost was my fellow freedman and was truly more than
a father to me. When I was seven years old, he took me to his bosom; now
at 40, I am possessed by violent death. He, through my diligent
performance of duty, flourished at all [times ...]. (*The rest is lost.*)

240. *Graffito on a tomb. Porta Nuceria cemetery, Pompeii, 1st cent. AD*
(CIL IV.10231. L)

Atimetus got me pregnant.[51]

241. *Women unfavourably compared with boy lovers. Egypt, 2nd cent.*
AD (Achilles Tatius, Leucippe and Clitophon 2.37.5-9, 38.1-3. G)

From a debate between defenders of heterosexual and homosexual
intercourse in one of the most popular ancient Greek novels.

(37.5) '... I am just a beginner in dealings with women, and have only had
intercourse with women who sell sex. A man who has been further
initiated into the mysteries could probably tell you more. Still, I'll speak
in defence of women, even though I have limited experience. (37.6) A
woman's body is moist in the clinch, and her lips are soft in response to
kisses. On account of this she holds the man's body in her arms, with it
completely joined to her flesh, and he is surrounded with pleasure when
he has intercourse with her. (37.7) She stamps her kisses on his lips like
seals on wax, and when she has experience she can make her kisses
sweeter, by not only wishing to use her lips, but also her teeth, grazing
round her lover's mouth and biting his kisses. And her breast when it is
caressed provides its own particular pleasure. (37.8) At the height of
orgasm she goes mad with pleasure, and opens her mouth in passion. At
this time tongues keep company with each other, and so far as possible

they also make love to one another; you can make your pleasure greater by opening your mouth to her kisses. (37.9) Towards the end of the orgasm the woman begins to pant with hot pleasure ...'

(38.1) 'To me you sound less like a beginner in sex than an old pro, surrounding us with all these female complications. Now listen to what I have to say in defence of boys. (38.2) Everything women do is false, both words and actions. Even if a woman appears to be beautiful, it is the laborious contrivance of make-up. Her beauty is all perfume, or hair dye, or potions. And if you strip her of all these devices, she'll look like the jackdaw in the fable, stripped of all his feathers.[52] (38.3) A boy's beauty isn't fostered by the scent of myrrh or by other false odours; a boy's sweat smells sweeter than all women's perfumes ...'

242. *Advice on marriage. Boeotia, 2nd cent.* AD *(Plutarch, Moralia 138a-146a, excerpts. 2nd cent.* AD. *Tr. R. Warner. G)*

Suggestions to a young friend and his wife; the husband is urged to be understanding and faithful, but it is expected that most adjustments will be made by the wife.

Now you two have been brought up together in philosophy, and so, by way of a wedding present for you both, I have made and am sending you a summary of what you have often heard. I have put things down briefly and side by side, to make them easier to remember. I pray that the Muses may stand by Aphrodite and help her! For they know that it is no more important for a lyre or a lute to be properly tuned than it is for the proper care of marriage and family life to be set to harmony by reason, mutual adjustment, and philosophy. Indeed, the ancients gave Hermes a place at the side of Aphrodite, indicating that in the pleasures of love reason is especially valuable; and they also gave a place to Persuasion and to the Graces, so that married people should have what they want from each other through persuasion and not by quarrelling and fighting with each other.

1. Solon advised the bride to eat a quince before getting into bed with her husband, and by this, I think, he meant that from the very beginning the pleasures coming from the lips and the voice should be harmonious and delightful.

2. In Boeotia after they have veiled the bride they put a garland of asparagus on her head, this being a plant with very rough spines and yet with an extremely pleasant taste. So the bride will make gentle and sweet her partnership with her husband if he does not shrink from her and get angry with her when in the early stages she is difficult and disagreeable. The people who cannot put up with girlish tantrums at the beginning are just like those who because unripe grapes are sour leave the bunches of ripe grapes for others to eat. Many newly married women, too, who get

angry with their husbands in the first days find themselves in the position of people who put up with being stung by the bees, but never reach out for the honeycomb.

9. When the moon is a long way from the sun, she looks large and bright to us; but when she comes near she fades away and hides. With a good wife it is just the opposite; she ought to be most conspicuous when she is with her husband, and to stay at home and hide herself when he is not there.

11. When music is played in two parts, it is the bass part which carries the melody. So in a good and wise household, while every activity is carried on by husband and wife in agreement with each other, it will still be evident that it is the husband who leads and makes the final choice.

18. A young Spartan girl was once asked whether she had yet started making advances to her husband. She replied: 'I don't to him; he does to me.' This, I think, is how a married woman ought to behave – not to shrink away or object when her husband starts to make love, but not herself to be the one to start either. In the one case she is being over-eager like a prostitute, in the other she is being cold and lacking in affection.

19. A wife ought not to make friends of her own, but to enjoy her husband's friends together with him. And the first and best friends are the gods in whom her husband believes and to shut her door to all magic ceremonies and foreign superstitions. For no god can be pleased by stealthy and surreptitious rites performed by a woman.

20. Man and woman are joined together physically so that the woman may take and blend together elements derived from each and so give birth to a child which is common to them both, so that neither of the two can tell or distinguish what in particular is his or hers. It is very right too that married people should have the same kind of partnership in property. They should put everything they have into a common fund; neither of the two should think of one part as belonging to him and the other as not belonging; instead each should think of it all as his own, and none of it as not belonging to him.

27. The economical woman ought not to neglect cleanliness and the wife who is devoted to her husband should also show a cheerful disposition; for economy ceases to please when it is combined with dirt, as does the most proper behaviour in a wife when combined with an austere manner.

34. It should be the same with married people – a mutual blending of bodies, property, friends and relations. Indeed what the Roman lawgiver had in mind, when he prohibited an exchange of gifts between man and wife, was not to deprive them of anything, but to make them feel that everything belonged to both of them together.

35. In the African city of Leptis there is an old custom that on the day after her marriage the bride sends to her husband's mother and asks her for a pot. She does not give it and says that she hasn't got one, the idea

being that the bride should recognise from the beginning a step-motherly attitude in her mother-in-law and, if something worse happens later on, should not be angry or resentful. A wife ought to realise what the position is and try to do her best about it. Her mother-in-law is jealous of her because her son loves her. And the only way of dealing with this is for her to win her husband's affection for herself and at the same time not to detract from or lessen his affection for his mother.

39. At all times and in all places wives and husbands should try to avoid quarrelling with each other, but they ought to be especially careful of this when they are together in bed. There was a woman in labour who, when the pains were on her, kept saying to those who were trying to get her to bed, 'What's the good of going to bed? It was by going to bed that I got this.' But it is not easy to escape the disagreements, harsh words and anger that may arise in bed except just then and there.

48. But it is a finer thing still for a man to hear his wife say, 'My dear husband, "but to me you are"[53] guide, philosopher and teacher in all that is most beautiful and most divine.' In the first place these studies will take away a woman's appetite for stupid and irrational pursuits. A woman who is studying geometry will be ashamed to go dancing and one who is charmed by the words of Plato or Xenophon is not going to pay any attention to magic incantations. For if they do not receive the seed of a good education and do not develop this education in company with their husbands they will, left to themselves, conceive a lot of ridiculous ideas and unworthy aims and emotions.

Pliny the Younger's third wife, Calpurnia, was an orphan and several years his junior. She was a native of Pliny's home town, Comum (Como), in northern Italy. His letters to her and about her (nos. 243-7) should be read not as private correspondence but as representations of his beliefs and attitudes intended for publication.

243. *To Calpurnia Hispulla. Rome, AD 104-108 (Pliny the Younger, Letters 4.19. L)*

This letter is addressed to his wife's aunt and nearest living female relative.

Since you are a model of devotion and you loved your dear, wonderful brother with a tenderness he reciprocated, and you love his daughter as if she were your own, and now that you have taken his place you are more than an aunt to her, I am sure you will be happy to hear that she is proving worthy of her father, her grandfather, and you. She is highly intelligent, and extremely frugal; she loves me, which is a sign of chastity. Her love for me has made her take up books. She reads and rereads my writings and even memorises them. She is solicitous for me when I am starting a new case and happy with me when it is over. When I am in court, she has messengers tell her how the case is going. When I read my own work aloud, she sits discreetly behind a curtain and soaks up the praise. She accompanies herself on the lyre as she sings my verses, with no instructor but love, the best teacher of all.

I take this as evidence that the harmony between us will continue to grow stronger for the rest of our lives. For it's not my youth or body she loves – they are gradually declining – but my glory. But that is because she was brought up and taught by you. With you she saw only what was moral and honest, and she learned to love me thanks to your encouragement. For while you honoured my mother in place of your own, you have helped form me since I was a child, so that I should become what my wife now sees me as. Therefore, we both thank you, for what you have given each of us, as if we were chosen one for the other. Farewell.

244. *To his wife Calpurnia. Rome,* AD *104-108 (Pliny the Younger, Letters 6.4. L)*

I never complained more about my duties than when they kept me from accompanying you to Campania, when you had to go there for your health, and even from following you there immediately. Now especially I would like to see with my own eyes whether you are getting stronger and putting on some weight, and whether you are enjoying the pleasures of your retreat and the luxuries of the region without ill effect. Indeed, I would still worry about you when you were away even if you were not ill; there is an anxious suspense in not knowing about someone you love dearly. Now uncertainty about your illness and your absence frightens me along with various other worries. I fear and imagine everything, and – typical of frightened people – I see with my mind's eye exactly what it is I wish least to happen. Please, then, ease my anxiety and write to me once a day, or even twice. I'll feel more secure – but then will start worrying again as soon as I've finished the letters. Farewell.

245. *To Calpurnia. Rome,* AD *104-108 (Pliny the Younger, Letters 6.7. L)*

You write that you are not a little affected by my absence and that your only solace is to hold my books and sometimes put them by you in my place. It is gratifying for me to think you long for me like this and take comfort in these consolations. For my part, I read and reread your letters and pick them up again and again as though I had just received them; but that only makes my longing for you worse. For, if your letters contain so much sweetness, your conversation contains even more. Nevertheless, keep writing, although the pleasure is tinged with pain. Farewell.

246. *To Calpurnia. Rome,* AD *104-108 (Pliny the Younger, Letters 7.5. L)*

It is incredible how much I miss you – first of all, because I love you, but then because we are not used to being apart. I stay awake at night conjuring up your image, and during the day at the times when I usually visit you, my feet literally carry me to your rooms. But when I do not find you there, I retreat, lovesick, like a lover locked out. My only relief I find in court, trying my friends' cases. You can judge for yourself what a life this is: my rest I take in work, my solace in care.

247. *To Calpurnius Fabatus, his wife's grandfather. Rome,* AD *104-108 (Pliny the Younger, Letters 8.10. L)*

Your wish that we give you a great-grandchild cannot be greater than your sorrow will be to hear that your granddaughter has had a miscarriage. She is young and inexperienced and did not realise she was pregnant, so did not take proper care of herself and even did some things she should not have done at all. She has learned a severe lesson and nearly paid for her mistake with her life. Therefore, though it is unfortunate at your age to be deprived of seeing your posterity, you should thank the gods, though they denied you your great-grandchild this time, that they preserved your granddaughter. They will surely grant your wish in future: we at least now know that she is capable of conceiving a child.

I am giving you the same advice and encouragement as I give myself. You cannot want great-grandchildren more than I want children. Descent from your side and mine will give them an easy path to office and a well-known name and an established family tree. Let them now be born and turn our sorrow into joy. Farewell.

248. *From a husband who misses his wife and wants her to come back. Oxyrhynchus, Egypt, 2nd cent.* AD *(Oxyrhynchus papyrus 528. G)*

This letter is written in an awkward style, with poor spelling.

Serenus to his sister and wife Isidora, very many greetings. Above all I pray that you are well and make an act of veneration to Thoeris who loves you. I want you to know that since you left me I have been weeping at night and grieving by day. Not since we bathed together on the 12th Phaophi did I bathe or anoint myself until the 12th Athur. You sent me letters that could have shaken a stone, so much did your words move me. I wrote you back immediately and on the 12th sent sealed letters along with your letters. Aside from your saying and writing 'Colobus has made me a prostitute', Colobus says that 'your wife sent me a message to say that you (Serenus) sold the chain and himself put me in the boat.' You say this so that I will no longer be believed about my embarkation. See how often I have sent messages to you. Tell me whether or not you are coming. (*On the back*) Give this to Isidora from Serenus.

Babies
'If it is a female, expose it'

249. *Exposure of a female child. Oxyrhynchus, Egypt, 1 BC (Oxyrhynchus papyrus 744. G)*

A letter from a husband to his wife directing her not to raise her baby if it is female. Exposed children were left to be raised by others or to die.[54]

Hilarion to Alis his sister,[55] heartiest greetings, and to my dear Berous and Apollonarion. Know that we are still even now in Alexandria. Do not worry if when all the others return I remain in Alexandria. I beg and beseech of you to take care of the little child, and as soon as we receive wages I will send them to you. If – good luck to you! – you bear offspring, if it is a male, let it live; if it is a female, expose it. You told Aphrodisias, 'Do not forget me.' How can I forget you? I beg you therefore not to worry.
The 29th year of Caesar, Pauni 23.

The following texts are about nurses, mothers and the nursing of babies. For texts on wet-nursing as employment, see nos. 329, 332, 334, and for the medical aspects of nursing, nos. 379-82.

250. *Hiring a wet-nurse. Italy, 3rd/2nd cent. BC (Thesleff, pp. 123-4. G)*

A letter on how to hire a wet-nurse, with a characteristically Pythagorean emphasis on measure and balance in all things.

Myia to Phyllis, greetings. Here is my advice to you now that you have become a mother. Choose a proper and clean wet-nurse, a modest woman who is inclined neither to drowsiness nor to drunkenness. Such a woman can make the best judgments about how to care for children appropriately, particularly if she has milk to nourish them and is not easily persuaded to sleep with her husband, for it is in this that she has an important part, foremost and prefatory to the whole of the child's life, in her nursing, as concerns his being raised well, for he will do everything well, at the proper time. The nurse will give him the nipple and breast not at his whim, but after due consideration. In this way she will encourage the baby's health. She will not succumb to sleep when she is tired, but when the newborn wants to rest. She will offer the child no small relief.

The wet-nurse should not be temperamental or talkative or uncontrolled in her appetite for food, but orderly and temperate, practical, not a foreigner, but a Greek.[56] It is best if the baby is put down to sleep when it is well filled with milk. Such rest is sweet for little ones and such feeding most effective. If other food is given, it should be as simple as possible. One should stay away from wine completely because it has such a powerful effect or mix it sparingly with its evening meal of milk. She should not give him continual baths; it is better to have occasional temperate ones. Along the same lines, the atmosphere around the baby should have an even balance of hot and cold, and his housing should be neither too airy nor too close. Moreover, his water should not be too hard nor too soft, nor his bed too rough, rather, it should fall comfortably on his skin. In each of these areas Nature desires what is rightfully hers, not luxuries.

This much then I think it is useful to write at present – my hopes based on Nursing according to Plan. With the god's help, I shall in the future provide the possible and appropriate reminders about the child's upbringing.

251. *Graxia who nursed her own children. Rome, 2nd-3rd cent.* AD *(CIL VI.19128. L)*

Inscription on a marble sarcophagus

Of Graxia Alexandria, distinguished for her virtue and fidelity. She nursed her children with her own breasts. Her husband Pudens the emperor's freedman [dedicated this monument] as a reward to her. She lived 24 years, 3 months, 16 days.

252. *A letter from a parent offering to pay for a wet-nurse. Egypt, second half of 3rd cent.* AD *(London papyrus 951 verso. G)*

... I hear that you have forced her to breast-feed. If you wish, let the baby have a wet-nurse. I do not want my daughter to breast-feed. Many affectionate greetings to my dearest daughter Apollonia and to Euphrosyne. Greetings to Pinna. Your brother Besas sends affectionate greetings and to Syros and his wife. Do everything you can so that she comes after the Calends as has been specified.

253. *The philosopher Favorinus on breast-feeding (Aulus Gellius, Attic Nights 12.1, excerpts. 2nd cent.* AD. *L)*

Conservative reaction against women's wish to rebel against biologically determined roles.[57] Favorinus also condemns abortion at 12.1.8.[58]

A discourse of the philosopher Favorinus, in which he persuades a noble lady to nurse her children herself, with her own milk, and not with that of other nurses.

It was once announced in my presence to Favorinus the philosopher that the wife of an auditor and disciple of his had just given birth and the family been increased by a newborn son. 'Let us go', he said, 'to see the boy and congratulate the father.'

The man was of senatorial rank and a noble family. All of us with Favorinus at the time went along. As soon as he entered the house, Favorinus embraced the father, congratulated him, and sat down. He proceeded to ask how long the labour had lasted and how difficult it had been, and was told that the girl, exhausted by the labour and long time without sleep, was taking a nap. At last he began to speak at some length. 'I have no doubt', he said, 'that she will nurse the baby with her own milk.' But when the girl's mother said that her daughter should be spared this and nurses provided – so as not to add the burdensome and difficult task of nursing to the pains of childbirth', he said, 'I pray you, woman, let her be completely the mother of her own child. What sort of half-baked, unnatural kind of mother bears a child and then sends it away? To have nourished in her womb with her own blood something she could not see, and now that she can see it not to feed it with her own milk, now that it's alive and human, crying for its mother's attentions? Or do you think', he said, 'that women have nipples for decoration and not for feeding their babies? ...

' "But it's not important", I hear said, "as long as the baby is alive and well-fed whose milk it drinks." Why then does not the same person, if he understands so little of nature, not also think that it doesn't matter in whose body a human being is formed? ...

'Why in heaven's name corrupt that nobility of body and mind of the newborn human being, which was off to a fine start, with the alien and degraded food of the milk of a stranger? Especially if the person you use to supply milk is, as is often the case, from a foreign and barbarian nation, or if she is dishonest, or ugly, or immodest, or unchaste, or a drinker; usually the only qualification for the post is that of having milk. ...

'The disposition of the nurse and the quality of the milk play a great role in character development; the milk is, from the beginning, tinged with the father's seed, and affects the baby from the mother's mind and body as well.

'And furthermore who could forget or belittle that those who desert their newborn and send them away to be fed by others cut or at least loosen the bond and that joining of mind and love by which nature links parents to their children ...'[59]

Parents and children
'These are my jewels'

254. *Posilla Senenia. Monteleone Sabino, 1st cent.* BC *(ILLRP 971. L)*

Posilla Senenia, daughter of Quartus and Quarta Senenia, freedwoman of Gaius.

Stranger, stop and, while you are here, read what is written: that a mother was not permitted to enjoy her only daughter, whose life, I believe, was envied by some god.

Since her mother was not allowed to adorn her while she was alive, she does so just the same after death; at the end of her time, [her mother] with this monument honours her whom she loved.

255. *A mother's request. Henchir Thina, Algeria, Imperial period (CIL VIII.9491 = CLE 151. L)*

My son, your mother asks you to take her with you.

256. *A mother's last wish. Philippeville, Algeria (CIL VIII.8123 = CLE 1287. L)*

Here lies Pompeia Chia, who lived 25 years.

I hope that my daughter will live chastely and learn by my example to love her husband.

257. *A mother's instructions about her son's education. 2nd/3rd cent.* AD *(Oxyrhynchus papyrus 930. G)*

(*The beginning of the letter is lost*) ... hurry and write to me about what you may need. I was sad to learn from the daughter of our teacher Diogenes that he had gone down the river. I never had to worry about him because I knew that he would take the best care of you that he could. I took care to write and to ask about your health and to find out what you were reading. He said it was the sixth book [of the *Iliad*] and supplied me with full information about your attendant. So now, my son, you and your attendant must take care to engage a proper teacher for you. Your sisters send many greetings; so do the children (avert the evil eye!) of Theonis and all of our friends by name. My greetings to your esteemed attendant Eros. (*Addressed*) To her son Ptolemaeus.

258. *The good old days. Rome, late 1st cent.* AD *(Tacitus, Dialogue 28, excerpts. L)*

The historian Tacitus looks back on the time when mothers played a role in their sons' education and thus, directly or indirectly, had a share in Rome's greatness.

In the old days, every child born to a respectable mother was brought up not in the room of a bought nurse but at his mother's knee. It was her particular honour to care for the home and serve her children. An older female relative, of tested character, was picked to be in charge of all the children in the house. And no one dared do or say anything improper in front of her. She supervised not only the boys' studies but also their recreation and games with piety and modesty. Thus, tradition has it, Cornelia, mother of the Gracchi, Aurelia, mother of Julius Caesar, and Atia, mother of Augustus, brought up their sons and produced princes.

259. *Cornelia's children. Rome, 2nd cent. BC (Valerius Maximus, Memorable Deeds and Sayings 4.4 pr., 1st cent. AD. L)*

This familiar anecdote illustrates the perfection to which a Roman mother might aspire.

A Campanian matron who was staying with Cornelia, mother of the Gracchi, was showing off her jewels, the most beautiful of that period. Cornelia managed to prolong the conversation until her children got home from school. Then she said, 'These are *my* jewels.'

260. *A letter from Cornelia to Gaius Gracchus. 2nd cent. BC (Cornelius Nepos, Fr. 2 Winstedt. Tr. A. Gratwick. L)*

A letter from Cornelia to her son Gaius Gracchus, urging him not to seek the Tribunate, purportedly written from Misenum in 131 BC, where she had retired after the assassination of her other Tribune son, Tiberius Gracchus.[60] He did not, however, listen to his mother, and was killed in a riot in 121 BC.

I would take a solemn oath, that apart from those who killed Tiberius Gracchus, no one has given me so much pain as you in this matter, who ought to undertake the part of all the children I have ever had, and to make sure that I should have as little worry as possible in my old age, and that, whatever your schemes might be, you should wish them to be agreeable to me, and that you should count it a sin to take any major step against my wishes, especially considering that I have only a little part of life left.

Is it quite impossible to cooperate for even that short space of time without your opposing me and ruining our country? Where will it all end? Will our family ever cease from madness? Can a bound ever be put to it? Shall we ever cease to dwell on affronts, both causing and suffering them? Shall we ever begin to feel true shame for confounding and destroying the constitution? But if that is quite impossible, when I am dead, then seek the Tribunate.

Do what you like so far as I am concerned, when I am not there to know it. When I am dead, will you sacrifice to me and invoke me as your hallowed parent. At that time will you not be ashamed to seek the intercession of those hallowed ones whom alive and present you treated with such abandonment and desertion? May Jove above not let you persist in this nor let such lunacy enter your mind! But if you do persist, I fear that through your own fault you will encounter so much trouble throughout your whole life that at no time will you be able to rest content.

261. *Seneca to his mother. Corsica, AD 41/9. (Seneca, On Consolation 16. L)*

Lucius Annaeus Seneca, Stoic philosopher, politician and tutor to the young Nero, spent eight years (AD 41-9) in Corsica, exiled because the empress Messalina had accused him of adultery with Julia Livilla, Caligula's sister. During this period he wrote the long essay *To Helvia on Consolation*, from which this extract is taken, to comfort his mother, Helvia. He urges her to limit her grief on grounds that excessive grieving would be like a woman, and she is better than that.

Do not use the excuse that you are a woman, who has the right to weep immoderately, but not without limit; and if our ancestors gave widows by law up to ten months for mourning, it was in reaction to the tenacity of women's grief. They did not forbid mourning; they limited it; for to suffer for the rest of one's life for the loss of a loved one is as inhuman as showing no grief at all. The best compromise between devotion and reason is to feel the grief and to suppress it. Do not look at certain women whose period of bereavement ends only with their own death (you know some who lost their children and put on mourning and never took it off). From you, life, harder from the very beginning, requires more. A woman who never had women's defects cannot now plead womanhood as an excuse.

You – unlike so many – never succumbed to immorality, the worst evil of the century; jewels and pearls did not bend you; you never thought wealth was the greatest gift to the human race; the bad example of lesser women – dangerous even for the virtuous – did not lead you to stray from the old-fashioned, strict upbringing you received at home. You never were ashamed of your fertility, as though the number of children you had mocked your age. You never tried to hide your pregnancy as though it were indecent, like other women who seek to please only with their beauty. Nor did you ever extinguish the hope of children already conceived whom you were carrying. You never polluted yourself with make-up, and you never wore a dress that covered about as much on as it did off. Your only ornament, the kind of beauty that time does not tarnish, is the great honour of modesty.

So you cannot use your sex to justify your sorrow when with your virtue you have transcended it. Keep as far away from women's tears as from their faults. But not even women will let you nurse your wound till it eats you up. Once you have got over the first wave of sorrow, they will invite you to pick yourself up, at least if you look at the examples of women who deserve to be ranked with great men. Fortune took all but two of Cornelia's twelve children. If you count the numbers, she lost ten; if you consider the value, she lost the Gracchi.[61] But when those around her wept and cursed her fate, she forbade them to blame Fortune, which had given her the Gracchi as her sons. The man who said in public, 'You would speak ill of my mother, who brought me into the world?' should have had her as his mother. How much prouder the remark of the mother: for the son what counted was the birth of the Gracchi, for the mother their death as well.

Rutilia followed her son Cotta[62] into exile and was so attached to him that she preferred exile to separation and would not return until he did. But when, after he returned and his career was flourishing, he died, she bore the loss with no less courage than that she had needed to follow him, and no one saw her crying after the funeral. She showed strength of spirit towards her son in exile, and wisdom when she lost him. For nothing could deter her from her maternal devotion, and nothing could detain her in useless and foolish sorrow.

I want you to be one of those women. You have always emulated their life; you will do well to follow their example in suppressing your grief.

262. *The death of the Helvidiae.* AD 104/5 *(Pliny the Younger, Letters 4.21. L)*

How awful what happened to the sisters Helvidiae![63] They both died giving birth to daughters. My grief is acute, but no worse than what is right under the circumstances. It is sad indeed to see two such fine girls in the bloom of youth felled by their own fertility. I am very sorry too for their infants, orphans at birth, and for their fine husbands, and even for myself. I continue to be devoted to their late father, as my writings and actions attest. Now only one of his three children survives, all that remains of a family so recently supported by so many members.

It will go a long way towards assuaging my grief if Fortune keeps that one safe and makes him as good as his father and grandfather. I am the more anxious for his health and character now that he is all that remains of the family. You know how soft I go, how frightened I get when someone I love is concerned; so you won't be surprised that where I am very afraid, I am also full of high hopes. Farewell.

263. *The death of Minicia Marcella. Rome,* AD *105/6 (Pliny the Younger, Letters 5.16. L)*

To Aefulanus Marcellinus.

I could not be more sad as I write to you that our friend Fundanus has lost his younger daughter. I've never seen anyone more cheerful or agreeable or worthy of a long life – even immortality – than that girl. She was just under fourteen but was as wise as an old woman and as sedate as a matron without losing her girlish sweet and virginal modesty. How she would throw her arms around her father's neck! How she loved her nurses and pedagogues and teachers for the services they provided her! How studiously and intelligently she read, and how sparingly she played! She suffered her last illness with such sobriety, patience and constancy. She did as she was told by the doctors, and she cheered up her sister and her father. When her body could no longer support her, her spirit went on till the last, broken neither by the illness itself nor fear of death – all the more reason why her loss is so great.

Her death is all the more bitter for its timing. She was engaged to marry an excellent young man. The date was set and we were all invited. But our joy was changed to sorrow. I cannot find the words to describe my grief when I heard Fundanus himself (so grief multiplies itself) ordering that the money that had been delegated to clothes, pearls and gems for the wedding be spent on incense, ointments and spices for the funeral. He is indeed a wise and scholarly man, having dedicated himself since he was young to the nobler subjects and arts; but now he rejects all he used to hear and often said, and his devotion has supplanted every other virtue. But if you consider what he has lost, you will forgive, or even praise, him. He has lost a daughter who was as like him in manner as in physical appearance and who copied her father in everything with a marvellous similarity.

Then, if you write to him during his justifiable grief, remember not to use conventional expressions of consolation that he might construe as reproof but to be soft and sympathetic. He will accept consolation more easily with time. Just as a fresh wound recoils from the healing hand but later receives, even seeks, it, so a mind when its grief is fresh rejects consolation, soon desires it and calmly accepts what is offered. Farewell.

264. *Epitaph of Minicia Marcella.* AD *105 (CIL VI.16631 = ILS 1030. L)*

Minicia Marcella's epitaph was found in the family tomb outside Rome. It is inscribed in fine lettering on a large funerary altar decorated with an eagle, which can be seen next to that of her mother in the courtyard of the Terme Museum in Rome.

To the gods of the dead. The tomb of Minicia Marcella, daughter of Fundanus. She lived 12 years, 11 months, 7 days.

One of the unhappiest father-daughter relationships of antiquity (that we know about) was that of the Emperor Augustus and his daughter Julia.

265. *Julia, daughter of Augustus. Rome, 1st cent.* AD *(Seneca, On Benefits 6.32.1. L)*

The divine Augustus relegated his daughter, who was shameless beyond any taunt of shamelessness, and published the sins of the imperial house: that she had admitted flocks of lovers, that she had wandered through the city in nocturnal revels; that the very forum and rostra from which her father had made known his law on adultery[64] suited the daughter for fornication; that she ran daily to the statue of Marsyas, since she switched from adulteress to working girl and sought the right to every sort of liberty with an unknown lover.

266. *Julia's wit. Rome, 1st cent.* BC *(Macrobius, Saturnalia 2.5.1-10. c.* AD *400. Tr. H. Lloyd- Jones. L)*

Avienus, the narrator of this section, has just told a number of Augustus' jokes.

'Should you like us to recall also some of the sayings of his daughter Julia? If you will not think I talk too much, I shall first say a few words about her character, unless any of you has anything serious and worth learning to bring forward.' Everyone urged him to go ahead with what he had begun, so he began talking about Julia, saying something like this: (2) 'She was in her thirty-eighth year, a time of life when if she had behaved reasonably she would have been almost elderly; but she abused the indulgence of fortune no less than that of her father. Of course her love of literature and considerable culture, a thing easy to come by in that household, and also her kindness and gentleness and utter freedom from vindictiveness had won her immense popularity, and people who knew about her faults were amazed that she combined them with qualities so much their opposite.

(3) 'Her father had more than once, speaking in a manner indulgent but serious, advised her to moderate her luxurious mode of life and her choice of conspicuous associates. But when he considered the number of his grandchildren and their likeness to Agrippa, he was ashamed to entertain doubts about his daughter's chastity. (4) So Augustus persuaded himself that his daughter was light-hearted almost to the point of indiscretion, but above reproach, and was encouraged to believe that his ancestress Claudia had also been such a person. He used to tell his friends that he had two somewhat wayward daughters whom he had to put up with, the Roman republic and Julia.[65]

(5) 'One day she came into his presence in a somewhat risqué costume,

and though he said nothing, he was offended. The next day she changed her style and embraced her father, who was delighted by the respectability which she was affecting. Augustus, who the day before had concealed his distress, was now unable to conceal his pleasure. "How much more suitable", he remarked, "for a daughter of Augustus is this costume!" Julia did not fail to stand up for herself. "Today", she said, "I dressed to be looked at by my father, yesterday to be looked at by my husband."

(6) 'Here is another well-known story. At a gladiatorial show Livia[66] and Julia drew the attention of the people by the dissimilarity of their companions; Livia was surrounded by respectable men, Julia by men who were not only youthful but extravagant. Her father wrote that she ought to notice the difference between the two princesses, but Julia wittily wrote back, "These men will be old when I am old."

(7) 'Julia's hair began early to go grey, and she used to pluck out hairs in private; one day her father came in suddenly and surprised her beauty specialists at their work. Augustus noticed the grey hairs on their clothing. In another conversation some time later he raised the question of age, and asked his daughter whether as time went on she would rather be grey-haired or bald, and when she replied that she would rather be grey-haired, he contradicted her by saying, "So why are those women in such a hurry to make you bald?"

(8) 'After listening to a serious friend who tried to persuade her that she would do better if she copied her father's frugal habits, Julia said, "He forgets that he is Caesar, but I remember that I am Caesar's daughter."

(9) 'When people who knew about her shocking behaviour said they were surprised that she who distributed her favours so widely gave birth to sons who were so like Agrippa, she said, "I never take on a passenger unless the ship is full." '

The home
'The god arranged that the work and supervision
indoors are a woman's task'

267. *How to train a wife. Athens, 4th cent.* BC *(Xenophon, On Household Management [Oeconomicus] 6.17-10.13 excerpts. G)*

In Plato's dialogues Socrates often seeks out and examines people who claim to be experts in a topic and usually manages to show that they have only a confused understanding of their subjects. In Xenophon's dialogue Socrates describes a conversation he had with Ischomachus, in which he tried to learn from Ischomachus how he managed to have such leisure from managing his estate. Ischomachus explains that he leaves the management up to his wife, and describes to Socrates how he trained her. By using simple analogies and creating polarities, Ischomachus explained to his wife that the role assigned to women by society is natural, since it was ordained by the gods, and that it works to the advantage of both sexes.

Although in this dialogue Ischomachus claims that he has trained his wife to run the household effectively, it seems likely that he was deceived about the extent of his wife's innocence and malleability.[67] In the course of her education, Ischomachus has not allowed his wife to assume any unusual authority; she runs the house, but remains accountable to him. It is important to remember that in training her his purpose is to serve his own convenience, not hers; Ischomachus is not concerned with his wife's particular needs as a female, but rather wants her to behave as little like a conventional woman as possible.[68]

(6.17) Since I had heard everyone – men, women, foreigners and Athenians – call him an excellent person, I thought I ought to try to get to know him. (7.1) One day I saw him sitting in the stoa of Zeus Eleutherios, and since I thought I had the time, I went up to him and sat down next to him and asked, 'Why is it that you are sitting here at leisure, contrary to your usual behaviour? Usually you are busy doing many things, or at least something, and have no time to waste in the Agora.'

(7.2) Ischomachus replied, 'You wouldn't see me here now, Socrates, if I weren't waiting for some foreigners.'

'But when you're not waiting for someone', I said, 'by the gods, how do you spend your time and what do you do? I want to learn from you what you do in order to be known as an excellent person, since you don't spend your time indoors, nor does your physique look as if you do.'

(7.3) Ischomachus laughed at my question about what he did in order to be known as an excellent person, and he seemed happy to reply as follows: 'I don't know whether some people talk with you about me and call me by that name. No one calls me "excellent person" when they're looking for a contribution for fitting out a trireme or supporting a chorus; they ask for me plainly by own name, Ischomachus son of my father.[69] But now, Socrates, as to your question why I don't spend time indoors any more, that is because my wife is completely capable of running my household affairs.'

(7.4) 'Ischomachus', I said, 'this in fact is what I'd like to learn from you – did you teach your wife yourself what she needed to know or did you take her from her father and mother knowing everything she was supposed to do?'

(7.5) Ischomachus replied, 'What could she have known when I married her, since she wasn't fifteen years old when she came to me, and in the time before that she had lived such a protected life that she saw and heard as little as possible, and asked the fewest questions?'

(7.6) 'Aren't you satisfied that she came knowing only how to take the wool and produce clothes, and seeing how the spinning was distributed to the women slaves?'[70]

'She came to me, Socrates, quite knowledgeable about food, a matter that seems to me important for both men and women to know about.'

(7.7) I then asked, 'But what about other matters, Ischomachus? Did you teach your wife yourself to do what she needed to do?'

'No indeed, Socrates', Ischomachus said, (7.8) 'not before I offered a sacrifice and prayed that I could teach and she could learn what was best for us both.'

I asked: 'Did your wife join you in offering sacrifice and making the prayer?'

'Yes, indeed', he said, 'she offered to fulfil many vows to the gods if all went as it should, and it was clear that she would be attentive to what she was taught.'

(7.9) 'By the gods, Ischomachus', I said, 'explain to me, what did you start to teach her first? It would give me more pleasure to hear you recount that than a success in games or with horses.'

(7.10) And Ischomachus answered: 'What did I do, Socrates? Since she was already manageable and domesticated enough to participate in a discussion, I asked her something like this: "Tell me, my dear, do you know why I married you and your parents gave you to me in marriage? (7.11) I know and it is obvious to you too that it would have been possible to sleep beside someone else. But I took counsel on my own behalf and your parents on yours how we might best share a home and children, if I chose you, and your parents chose me, as they apparently did, from the other possible candidates. (7.12) If the god allows it, children will be born, and then we will consult together how we will best educate them. This will be an advantage that we can share, to obtain the best allies and supporters in our old age.[71]

(7.13) ' "But now there is the home we share, as follows. I shall share with you all my property, and you have shared with me everything you brought with you. We do not need to make an accounting of which of us contributed the larger amount, but you should realise that whichever of us is the better partner will make the most worthy contribution."

(7.14) 'Then, Socrates, my wife answered me: "But what can I contribute? What potential do I have? The only accomplishment I learned from my mother is to behave properly."

(7.15) ' "Yes, by Zeus, my dear, that's what my father taught me also. But it is the task of a proper husband and wife to keep their property as well as possible and see that so far as possible other property accrues from their just and good behaviour."

(7.16) ' "What is it that I can do", asked my wife, "that might cause the household to prosper?"

' "By Zeus", I said, "you can try to do what the gods made you able to do and custom advises."

(7.17) ' "And what is that?" she asked.

' "I think", I said, "that it is a most important responsibility, unless you think that the work the leader bee supervises in her hive is unimportant." '

(7.18) ' "For it seems to me, my dear", Ischomachus told me he said, "that the gods took considerable care to establish this yoke as it is called, male and female, so that it might be most effective in partnership. (7.19) First of all this yoke exists so that the race of living things will be continued by the begetting of children, and then human beings provide themselves with care in their old age by means of this yoke. Furthermore, humans do not live their lives in the open air, as animals do, but it's evident that they require roofs over their heads. (7.20) But it is important for humans to conserve what they are going to bring into their homes from the work they do outside in the open air – for ploughing and sowing and growing and herding are all of them outdoor work, which provide our provisions.

(7.21) ' "It is important then, when the provisions are brought into the home, for someone to keep them safe and to do the work of the household. A home is required for the rearing of infant children, and a home is required for making food out of the harvest. Similarly a home is required for the making of clothing from wool. (7.22) Since both indoor and outdoor matters require work and supervision", I said, "I believe that the god arranged that the work and supervision indoors are a woman's task, and the outdoors are the man's. (7.23) For the god made a man's body and soul better able to endure the cold and heat of travel and military service, so that he assigned to him the outdoor work. But the god endowed the woman with a body less able to endure these hardships and so", Ischomachus told me he said, "I believe that he assigned the indoor work to her. (7.24) With this in mind the god made the nursing of young children instinctive for woman and gave her this task, and he allotted more affection for infants to her than to a man.

(7.25) ' "The god designated that the woman should guard what is brought into the household, because he knew that a fearful soul is better at guarding. He also gave a greater share of fearfulness to the woman than to the man. Because he knew that it would be necessary for the one who did the outdoor work to defend the household, if someone tried to hurt it, he allotted to him a greater share of courage. (7.26) But because it was necessary for both to give and take, he divided the shares of memory and concern equally between them, so that it is impossible to decide whether the female or the male excels in this respect. (7.27) And self-control where needed he divided equally, and the god allowed whichever of the two was better, whether it was the man or the woman, to get more advantage from this benefit. (7.28) Because the natures of the two sexes are not equally well equipped in all the same respects, for that reason they have greater need of one another and the yoke is mutually beneficial, because what one lacks the other has.

(7.29) ' "Now, my dear", I said, "since we both understand what has been assigned to us by the god, each of us must try to accomplish the work appropriate to us. (7.30) This is what the law intends", Ischomachus told me he said, "when it yokes man and wife. Since the god made them partners in their children, so the law makes them partners in their household. And the law shows that the arrangement of the god made each more competent in certain respects. For it is better for a woman to remain indoors than to go outside, and it is more disgraceful for a man to remain inside than to take care of the work outside. (7.31) If anyone does something contrary to the nature the god gave him, it is quite possible that his disorderliness will not escape the notice of the gods and that he will pay the penalty for ignoring his proper work or doing a woman's work.

(7.32) ' "I believe", I said, "that the leader bee has the same kind of work assigned to her by the god."

' "And what sort of work is it", said my wife, "that the leader bee does that resembles the kind of work I ought to do?"

(7.33) ' "It is", said I, "that the leader bee, although she stays within the hive, does not allow the bees to be lazy, but she sends outside those bees who ought to work outside, and she knows what each of them brings into the house and receives it, and she keeps it until it is needed. When the time comes to use it, she sees that each bee gets her just share. (7.34) And she supervises those who weave the wax inside, and sees that they weave well and efficiently, and she looks after the young that are being born and sees that they are cared for. And when the little bees are grown and are ready to go to work, she sends them out with the leader of the new hive."

(7.35) ' "Will it then be my job", asked my wife, "to do this?"

' "It will be your job", I said, "to remain indoors and to send out those members of the household who must work outdoors, (7.36) and to supervise those who must work indoors, and to receive what is brought in and to allocate what each must spend, and you must decide what surplus needs to remain, and watch that the expenditure set aside for a year is not used up in a month. When fleeces are brought to you, you must take care that they become cloaks for those who need them. And you must take care that the grain that is stored remains edible. (7.37) One of your duties, however", I said, "you may find unwelcome, which is, if one of the household slaves is ill, you must see to it that he is looked after."

' "By Zeus", said my wife, "that would be a welcome task, because the slaves who are cared for would be grateful and better inclined towards me than before."

(7.38) 'And I', Ischomachus said, 'was pleased with her answer and replied, "Isn't it because of this sort of concern also on the part of the leader bee that the bees are so dependent on her, that when she leaves, none of the bees thinks of being left behind, but they all follow her?"

(7.39) 'And my wife replied: "I would be surprised if the work of the leader bee didn't apply to you more than to me. (7.40) For my keeping watch over and managing what is inside would seem to be inconsequential, if you didn't supervise how whatever is outside was brought in."

' "But my bringing it in would be inconsequential", I said, "if there were no one to keep it safe once it got there. Don't you see", I said, "how people pity the people in the proverb who draw water in a broken jug, because they toil in vain."[72]

' "By Zeus", said my wife, "indeed they are to be pitied if that is what they do."

(7.41) ' "Other pleasant responsibilities", I said, "remain for you, such as when by taking a woman who is ignorant of wool-working you make her into a skilled worker and she becomes twice as valuable to you, and when by taking someone who is ignorant of housekeeping and serving and make her into a skilful and faithful servant you have someone completely worthwhile, and when you have the power to favour the proper and helpful members of your household, and it is possible for you to punish anyone who proves to be useless. (7.42) And the greatest pleasure of all will be if you prove to be better than me, and make me your slave, and you won't need to fear that with advancing age you will have a lower standing in the household, but you will be confident that as you grow older you will become a better partner for me and guardian of the house for our children and have a proportionately higher standing in the household.[73] (7.44) For personal excellence", I said, "does not come from beauty, but increases in human life on account of virtue." It is something like that, Socrates, that I seem to remember telling her in our first discussion.'

(8.1) 'And, Ischomachus', I said, 'did you discover that as a result of your discussion she became more inclined to take over?'

'Yes, by Zeus,' said Ischomachus, 'in fact I know that she was upset and very embarrassed when I asked for something that had been brought in from outside and she couldn't provide it. (8.2) But when I saw that she was troubled I said to her, "Don't be discouraged, my dear, that you can't give me what I happen to ask for ... No", I said, "you are not to blame for this, but I am, because I turned things over to you without putting them in order and arranging everything so that you would know where to store everything and from where to retrieve it" ' ...

(8.3-9.14) Ischomachus then discusses the importance of order in human life, the best example being the arrangement of a ship, and describes his plans for the arrangement of his household.

(9.15) 'Then I directed my wife to make regulations, and to supervise their enforcement within the household, and whenever she thought fit to demand an accounting of its inventory, in the way a captain of the watch might demand an accounting from his guards and inquire if everything is in good order, as the council investigates the cavalry, and like a queen[74] to praise and honour the deserving members of the force, and to criticise and punish the deficient members ...'

(9.18) 'Well then, Ischomachus', I said, 'when your wife heard this did she manage to comply?'

'Yes indeed, Socrates', he said, 'she told me that I was mistaken if I thought my directions about looking after everything involved difficulties. It would be more difficult, she said, if I had directed her not to look after her own work rather than to insist that she cared about the welfare of the household. (9.19) For a proper woman was created in order to care for her children and not to neglect them, and so she said that a proper woman would prefer to care for the welfare of her own possessions rather than to neglect them.'

(10.1) When I heard that his wife gave him that answer, I said, 'By Hera, Ischomachus, your wife has a man's intelligence.'[75]

'I can give you other illustrations of her great intelligence, to show that once she heard me she quickly obeyed.'

'Give me some examples', I said, 'because I enjoy hearing about the excellence of a living female more than I would if [the famous painter] Zeuxis showed me a drawing that he had made of a beautiful woman.'

(10.2) Ischomachus then said, 'One time, Socrates, I saw that she had covered her face with white lead, so that she would seem to have a paler complexion than she really had, and put on thick rouge, so that her cheeks would seem redder than in reality, and high boots, so that she would seem taller than she naturally was.[76]

(10.3) So I said, "Tell me, my dear, would you consider me more worthy of your love as a partner in our shared wealth, if I told you what I was worth, and didn't boast that I had more than I actually had, and didn't hide anything from you, or if I tried to deceive you by saying that I had more than I in fact had, and showed you counterfeit money and necklaces of gold plate and said that they were real?" (10.4)

'She interrupted me at that point and said, "Don't say such things; don't become that sort of man, because if you did, I couldn't love you from my heart." I replied: "Haven't we come together, my dear, as partners in each other's bodies?" She replied: "At least so people say." (10.5) "Then tell me", I said, "if I would seem to you to be a more worthy bodily partner, if I cared for myself and tried to make myself more healthy and strong, and because of that were in reality healthy-looking, or if I smeared myself with vermilion and and put flesh colour on my eyes[77] and presented myself to you and made love to you deceiving you and presenting you with vermilion to see and touch rather than my own skin." (10.6) "I would not", she said, "enjoy touching vermilion as much as your own skin and I do not enjoy looking at flesh colour as much as your own and I would not enjoy seeing your eyes covered with make-up as in good health."

(10.7) "Don't think then, my dear", Ischomachus told me he said, "that I enjoy the colour of white lead more than the colour of your own skin, but just as the gods made horses prefer horses and cattle prefer cattle, and sheep sheep, so human beings prefer the natural human body. (10.8) You might successfully fool someone outside the household by this kind of deception, but insiders always get caught when they try to deceive one another. For they can be found out when they get up in the morning before they have time to prepare or they are caught out by sweat or put to the test by tears and exposed completely by washing."

(10.9) 'What, by the gods', I asked, 'was her response to that?' 'What else than that', he said, 'she never put on make-up again, but tried to present herself with a clean face and suitably dressed. And she asked me if I could advise her how she might look beautiful in reality, and not just appear to be beautiful. (10.10) And I advised her, Socrates', he said, 'not always to sit about like a slave, but with the help of the gods to try to stand over the loom like a master and to teach what she understood better than another, and to learn what she knew less well, and to keep an eye on the baker, and to stand near the housekeeper when she was doling out portions, and to go around making sure that each thing was in its proper place. For these tasks seemed to me to provide both supervision and exercise.[78] (10.11) For I said it would be good exercise to moisten and knead the bread and to shake out and fold cloaks and coverlets. I said that if she had taken exercise in this matter she would both eat better and be more healthy and in truth have a healthier colour. (10.12) Her looks, when she is competing with a slave girl, because she is appropriately cleaner and better dressed, are more sexually stimulating, especially since the wife gratifies her husband voluntarily, but the slave girl is forced to acquiesce. (10.13) Women who sit around pretentiously ask to be categorised with the women who use make-up and deceit. And now, Socrates', he said, 'you understand that my wife, after she received this training, conducts her life in the way that I taught her and as I have just explained to you.'

268. *Letter from a woman about domestic matters. Oxyrhynchus, Egypt. 3rd cent. AD (Italian Society papyrus 1080. G)*

Diogenis to her brother Alexander, greetings. As you told Taamois about a house where we could move into, we found a house where we will go before we move to Agathinus. The house is near the Isaeum, near Claudianus' house … we are moving in Phamenoth. I want you to know that we have recovered 120 drachmas from Bottus. I sent you … of purple dye by Sarapicus. I gave Bolphius the letters which you sent me to give him. Many greetings to little Theon. Eight toys have been brought for him by the woman you told me to greet and these I have sent to you. To Aurelius Alexander.

269. *Letter from a woman managing an estate. Oxyrhynchus, 2nd cent. AD (Hamburg papyrus 86. G)*

Ptolema to her brother Antas, greetings. You write to Longinus to await the prefect's arrival; but look, the prefect has already started on his journey. If you can disentangle yourself safely, get here soon, before the prefect, so that we can have the little one evaluated.[79] All the fields are in good condition. The southern irrigated field of the 17 *arurae* has been sold for grazing of cattle. Your cattle have eaten an *arura* and have gone to Pansoue. All the land there is being used for grazing. The west side of the vegetable garden is being used for grass-cutting. We have sold the grass in our allotments for 112 drachmas, except for the 6 eastern irrigated fields. Grass is selling very cheap. Through Vetrianus three *arurae* were sold at 130 drachmas for grass, and also through him three at 68 drachmas for grazing sheep. Longinus and Sarapion and everyone at home sends greetings. Vibius has gone to Psenuris to sell the grain. All your family is well. Farewell. Mecheir 30.

Celebrations
'Maidens are sad when they marry, but widows are happy'

270. *Attempts to explain Roman marriage customs. 2nd cent.* AD *(Plutarch, Roman Questions 50, 105 = Moralia 276d-e, 289a-b. G)*

(50) Why does the Priest of Zeus (Flamen Dialis) resign his office when his wife dies, as Ateius relates[80]?

Is it because the man who has married a wife and lost her is more unfortunate than one who has never married? For the household of a man who is married is complete, and the one who has married but lost his wife is not only incomplete but also impaired.

Or does the wife assist her husband in the performance of rituals, so that he cannot perform many of the rites without his wife's being present, and it is not only impossible for him to marry another after he has lost his first wife, but also unseemly? For this reason it was not possible in former times for him to divorce his wife and it is still, it seems, not possible at present, though in my time [the Emperor] Domitian granted a petition [to do so]. The priests were present at the dissolution of the marriage, and performed many terrifying and strange and gloomy rites.

(105) What is the explanation of the custom that it is not possible for maidens to marry during public holidays, but widows can marry?

Is it, as Varro observed, because maidens are sad when they marry, but widows are happy, and during a festival one must not be forced to do anything sad? Or is it rather that it is good for maidens to be married in a large company, and disgraceful for widows? A first marriage is an object of admiration, and the second deprecated, because women are ashamed if they remarry when their first husbands are alive, and sad when they die? Therefore widows prefer a quiet ceremony to commotions and processions. Festivals distract many people, so that they have no time for weddings.

Or is it because the Romans seized the maiden daughters of the Sabines during a festival and started a war, and so they consider it a bad omen to marry during religious holidays?

271. *A wedding invitation. Oxyrhynchus, Egypt 3rd cent.* AD *(Oxyrhynchus papyrus 111. G)*

Herais requests your company at dinner in celebration of the marriage of her children at her house tomorrow, the fifth, at nine o'clock.

272. *A birthday party. Vindolanda, England, 2nd cent.* AD *(Tab. Vindol. Inv. No. 85/87. L)*

An invitation contained in a letter on a folded tablet. Wives of officers were permitted to accompany their husbands on active service, and presumably both Severa and her friend Lepidina lived in houses near the Roman Camp near Hadrian's Wall. The greeting added, almost certainly by Severa in her own hand, is the earliest known example of Latin handwriting by a woman.[81]

(*Address on the back of the tablet*) To Sulpicia Lepidina, wife of Flavius Cerialis, from Severa.

(*In a scribe's hand*) Claudia Severa to her friend Lepidina, greetings. On the third day before the Ides of September, sister, I cordially invite you to be sure to come to us for the day of the celebration of my birthday; if you came the day would bring me greater pleasure because of your presence.

Please give my greetings to your [husband] Cerialis. My [husband] Aelius and my little son send greetings. (*Added in her own hand*) I shall expect you, sister; farewell, sister, my dearest soul, as I hope to keep well; and hail.

Epitaphs
'I lie here, a marble statue, instead of a woman'

Epitaphs preserve ideals more faithfully than historical fact, but as such constitute a record of models of approved public and private behaviour in women's lives.

273. *Phrasicleia. Athens, c. 540 BC (CEG 2. G)*

The tomb of Phrasicleia: I shall be called a maiden always. This is the name the gods gave me in place of 'wife'.

274. *Bitte. Amorgos, 450 BC (CEG 153. G)*

I lie here, a marble statue, instead of a woman, a memorial to Bitte, and of her mother's sad grief.[82]

275. *Xenoclea. Piraeus, 360? BC (CEG 526 = IG II².12335. G)*

Leaving two young girls, Xenoclea, daughter of Nicarchus, lies here dead; she mourned the sad end of her son, Phoenix, who died out at sea when he was eight years old.

There is no one so ignorant of grief, Xenoclea, that he doesn't pity your fate. You left behind two young girls and died of grief for your son, who has a pitiless tomb where he lies in the dark sea.

276. *From a husband (CIL VI.29149. Tr. R. Lattimore. L)*

To my dear wife, with whom I lived 2 years, 6 months, 3 days, 10 hours. On the day of her death I gave thanks to god and man.

277. *A widower. Pisa, Imperial period (CIL XI.1491 = ILS 8461. L)*

To the gods of the underworld.

To Scribonia Hedone, with whom I lived 18 years without a quarrel. At her wish, I swore that after her I would not have another wife.

278. *Epitaph with curse. Lambaesis, Algeria (CIL VIII.2756. L)*

What were the proofs of an existence now ended, these final writings declare, consolations for death on the spot where the eternal memory of name or of race is preserved.

Here lies Ennia Fructuosa, dearest wife, whose modesty was proved and whose obedience praised.

At the age of 15 she became a matron and accepted the name of spouse: in which she was not able to live more than 13 years. Who thus bore the lot of death she did not deserve. Struck down by a spell, she lay dumb for a period, so that her spirit was torn out by force rather than rendered up to nature. The gods above and the gods below will be the avengers of this certain crime.

Aelius Proculinus her husband, tribune of the legion III Augusta, put up this (stone).

279. *A devoted couple. Africa, Imperial period (ILA, p. 54, no. 175. L)*

Sacred to the spirits of the dead of Vibia, wife of Caelius. She lived 40 years. Here she lies.

Sacred to the spirits of the dead of Claudius Januarianus. He lived 75 years. Bonosa put up (this stone) for her husband.

I competed with you, wife, in devotion, virtue, frugality and love, but I lost. May everybody have the same fate.

Januarianus put this up for his wife.

280. *From the second husband. Monferrato, Imperial period (CIL V.7453 = CLE 1578. L)*

To the gods of the dead and to the memory – Simplicius, farewell – of Statilia Tigris. She lived 36 years.

O too beautiful and always modest with your husbands, you lay in two marriage beds, where two children were born of love. If the first one could have beaten fate, he would have put up this inscription of praise. But I, unfortunate man who have now lost a woman like you, am doing it instead after enjoying 16 years of your chaste love.

Publius Vibius Verissius, while he was still alive, put this up for himself and for his incomparable wife. Euphilus to Simplicius.

Two funerary altars dedicated by grieving parents now in the Terme Museum, Rome.

281. *From a father. Rome, 1st cent. AD (CIL VI.22560. L)*

The altar is decorated with the bust of a girl.

To the gods of the dead.

(The altar of) Minucia Suavis, wife of Publius Sextilis Campanus. She lived 14 years, 8 months, 23 days. Her father Tiberius Claudius Suavis (put this up).

282. *From a mother. Rome, Imperial period (CIL VI.38605. L)*

To the gods of the dead.

(The altar of) Marcia Doris, daughter of Quintus. She lived 28 years, 8 months, 6 days. Marcia Doris, her most unhappy mother, put up (this monument) to her best and most devoted daughter, and for herself, and for her descendants.

VIII. Occupations

'I worked with my hands'

Apprenticeship
'To learn the weaver's trade'

283. *An apprenticeship agreement. Oxyrhynchus, 2nd cent. AD (Oxyrhynchus papyrus 1647. G)*

An agreement between Platonis, also called Ophelia, daughter of Horion, of the city of Oxyrhynchus, with her full brother Plato as guardian, and Lucius son of Ision and Tisasis, of Aphrodisium in the Small Oasis: Platonis, also called Ophelia, has apprenticed to Lucius her slave Thermuthion, who is under age, to learn the weaver's trade, for four years starting at the beginning of the coming month Tubi of the present year, during which time she is to feed and clothe the girl and bring her to her instructor every day from sunrise to sunset so that the girl can perform all the duties assigned to her by him that are relevant to the aforesaid trade; her pay for the first year to be 8 drachmas a month, for the second similarly 12, for the third 16, for the fourth 20. The girl is to have each year 18 days off for festivals, but if she does no work or is sick for some days, she is to remain with her instructor for an equal number of days at the end of her time of service. The instructor is to pay for trade taxes and expenses.

Self-employment
'Owner of a farm'

284. *An incentive to female enterprise, 1st cent. AD (Suetonius, Life of Claudius 19. L)*

In an all-out effort to increase grain imports, the Emperor Claudius offered incentives to potential outfitters of ships, including women. A relief of a ship decorating the grandiose tomb of a wealthy freedwoman at Pompeii may be explained by this passage.[1]

To citizens he offered exemption from the *lex Papia Poppaea*, to holders of

Latin rights, he offered full citizenship, and to women the right of four children,[2] rules which are still in effect today.

285. *Valeria Maxima, owner of a farm. Cantalupo di Bardello (near Tibur), 1st cent. BC (CIL VI.3482 = ILS 7459. L)*

Valeria Maxima, mother, owner of a farm, dearest daughter of Valeria, who lived 36 years, 2 months, 12 days, on her farm in the district of Mandela in the precinct of Hercules, rests in peace.

Prostitution[3]
'They care about making money'

286. *Nemeas the aulos player, 4th cent. BC (Athenaeus, 13.587C. G)*

Hyperideas mentions Nemeas the *aulos* player in his speech against Patrocles [fr. 13 Kenyon]. It's amazing that the Athenians allowed a whore to be called by the name of the distinguished festival. It was forbidden to *hetaerae* (and slaves) to use such names, as Polemon says in his work *On the Acropolis*.

287. *Prostitutes. Athens, 4th cent. BC (Alexis, Fr. 103 PCG. G)*

First of all, they care about making money and robbing their neighbours. Everything else has second priority. They string up traps for everyone. Once they start making money they take in new prostitutes who are getting their first start in the profession. They remodel these girls immediately, and their manners and looks remain no longer the same. Suppose one of them is small; cork is sewn into her shoes. Tall? she wears thin slippers and goes around with her head pitched towards her shoulder; that reduces her height. No hips? she puts on a bustle, and the onlookers make comments about her nice bottom. They have false breasts for them like the comic actors'; they set them on straight out and pull their dresses forwards as if with punting poles. Eyebrows too light? They paint them with lamp-black. Too dark? she smears on white lead. Skin too white? she rubs on rouge. If a part of her body is pretty, she shows it bare. Nice teeth? then she is forced to keep laughing, so present company can see the mouth she's so proud of. If she doesn't like laughing, she spends the day inside, like the meat at the butcher's, when goats' heads are on sale; she keeps a thin slip of myrtle wood propped up between her lips, so that in time she will grin, whether she wants to or not.

288. *The famous trial of the hetaera Phryne of Thespiae. Athens, 4th cent. BC (Athenaeus 13.590e-591a = Hyperides, Fr. 178 Kenyon. G)*

Phryne had been charged with impiety, for leading disorderly and 'not altogether serious' religious processions of men and women in honour of an unrecognised god, Isodaites.[4] She was represented in court by the orator Hyperides.

Hyperides spoke in defence of Phryne, but his speech had not succeeded and the judges seemed ready to vote against her. So he brought her out where she could be seen, tore off her shift, and laid bare her breasts.[5] He concluded his speech with lamentations about her appearance, and made the judges superstitious about this servant and ministrant of Aphrodite and indulgent in their pity, so that they did not execute her.[6]

289. *The palace brothel. Rome, 1st cent. AD (Suetonius, Life of Gaius 40-1, excerpts. L)*

He [Caligula] imposed new and unheard of taxes.[7] At first they were collected by the tax-collectors, then, as these were earning too much, he sent centurions and praetorian tribunes to collect, and no person or thing was exempt. ... Porters had to pay an eighth of their earnings and prostitutes their usual fee for one act of intercourse. He made this law cover those who had married[8] as well as pimps and ex-pimps.

(41) ... Not wanting to neglect any source of income, he put a brothel in the Palace, where, he furnished decorously a number of cubicles and in them put matrons and freeborn boys. He then sent pages around the forums and basilicas inviting men, young and old, to pleasure. He loaned money with interest to any who were short of cash, while clerks took their names as though they were contributions to Caesar's revenue.

290. *The senate vs. Vistilia. Rome, AD 19 (Tacitus, Annals 2.85. L)*

In the same year the senate passed severe provisions to repress women's dissoluteness and prohibited prostitution for granddaughters, daughters, and wives of Roman knights. For Vistilia, a woman of a praetorian family, had made public, before the aediles, her practice of prostitution. This was done in keeping with a valid and venerable custom by which it is considered sufficient punishment for unchaste women to admit their shame publicly. The senate also wanted to know why Titidius Labeo, Vistilia's husband, had not carried out the punishment provided by law for his patently guilty wife. But he explained that the sixty days allowed for him to make up his mind what to do had not yet elapsed,[9] so the senate passed judgment only on Vistilia, who was relegated to the island of Seriphos.[10]

291. *Justinian*[11] *on pimps. Rome, 6th cent.* AD *(Justinian, Novellae 14 pr.-1. Tr. S.P. Scott, rev. L)*

The name and calling of pimp was so odious both to the ancient laws and to those of the Empire that many legal enactments have been published against persons committing offences of this description. We, ourselves, have already promulgated a constitution increasing the penalties against those who are guilty of such wicked deeds, and we have, in addition, supplied by other laws what our predecessors omitted, and have by no means lost sight of this matter, for we have very recently been informed of the evil consequences which such traffic has caused in this great city.

We are aware that certain people live illicitly, that they find opportunity for themselves for dishonourable wealth by cruel and hateful means. They travel around the provinces and many other places, and they deceive wretched girls promising them shoes and clothing. With these they buy them and lead them back to this most blessed city. They keep them in their homes, and give them wretched food and clothes and then hand them over to those desiring them for their pleasure. They themselves receive the shameful income earned from the bodies of the girls. They draw up agreements so that the girls will maintain this wicked and criminal occupation so long as their keepers wish. Some of the women also take sureties.

... houses of this kind exist in close proximity to holy places and religious establishments; and at the present time this wickedness is so prevalent that any persons who wish to withdraw these unhappy girls from the life that they are leading, and legally marry them, are not permitted to do so.

Some of these wretches are so unprincipled as to deliver over to corruption girls who have not yet reached their tenth year, and in order to ransom these unhappy beings for the purpose of contracting lawful marriage, great sums of money are exacted. Ten thousand means of effecting their ruin exist which are not susceptible of being described in words; and the resulting evil is so great, and the cruelty so widespread that, while it first was confined to the most remote parts of the capital, it now not only extends over the city itself but also over all its suburbs.

A certain person informed us in secret of this condition of affairs some time ago, and recently the most excellent Praetors have been directed by us to make inquiry concerning it, which they have done, and made their reports to us, and we immediately afterwards deemed it necessary to implore the assistance of God, and purge the city quickly of this iniquity.

(1) Therefore we direct all persons to live as chastely as possible, which, with confidence in God, can alone profit the souls of men. ... We absolutely forbid any women to be led by artifice, fraud, or compulsion to such debauchery; it is permitted to no one to support a prostitute or to prostitute them publicly, and to use the profits for any other business; we

forbid them to undertake agreements for this and to require sureties and to do any such thing which compels the wretched women unwillingly to destroy their chastity.

Nor shall it hereafter be lawful to deceive young girls, and induce them to prostitute themselves by promising them clothing, food and ornaments.

We strictly prohibit all these things; and, after having considered the subject carefully, we direct that any bonds which may have been executed to secure the performance of such contracts shall be of no effect; and that those who are guilty cannot recover any gifts which they may have made to the girls with whom the said contracts were made; and that they themselves shall be expelled from this most fortunate city as pestiferous persons, and destroyers of public morals, because of having reduced free women to slavery by requiring them to lead a licentious life and bringing them up for promiscuous debauchery.

Hence we decree that if anyone should hereafter remove a girl against her will, and compel her to remain with him, and, without providing her with sufficient food, to appropriate for himself the wages of her prostitution, he shall be arrested by the respectable Praetors of the People of this most blessed city, and condemned to death. We have already entrusted the Praetors of the People with the prosecution of persons guilty of pecuniary theft and robbery; and is there not much more reason for us to do so where crimes against chastity are concerned? If any owner of a house should rent it to a pimp for this purpose, and, knowing who he is, should not eject him; he shall be sentenced to pay a fine of a hundred pounds of gold, and shall risk losing his house. If anyone hereafter should draw up an agreement in writing as evidence of a contract of this kind, and receive a surety with reference the same, he is hereby notified that he will not be benefited in any way either by the obligation of the girl, or by that of her surety; for as her agreement is void in every respect, her surety will, under no circumstances, incur any liability. The guilty person shall, as we have already stated, undergo corporal punishment, and shall be expelled far from this great city. We exhort the women of our Empire to remain chaste, and not to allow themselves to be persuaded or compelled to embrace a life of debauchery; we absolutely prohibit pimping, and when it is committed, we shall punish it.

292. *Vibia Calybenis, the procuress. Beneventum, Imperial period. (CIL IX.2029 = ILS 8287. L)*

Vibia Chresta, freedwoman of Lucius, put up this monument for herself and her family and for Gaius Rustius Thalossus, freedman of Gaius, her son, and for Vibia Calybenis, freedwoman of Gaia, a freedwoman procuress, entirely with her own money, without fraud to others. This monument does not pass to the heirs.

293. *Graffiti. Pompeii, 1st cent.* AD *(CIL IV.2175, 2224, 2265, 8356, 10233, 10241. L)*

(2175)[12] Here I screwed many girls.
(2224) Felix (did it) with Fortunata.
(2265) Placidus with these (girls) screwed whomever he wanted.
(10233) Health to Hyginus. Hedone sucks off Pilades.

Two graffiti about the same woman

(8356) (*Found in the servants' quarters of the House of the Menander*) In Nuceria, near Porta Romana, in the district of Venus, ask for Novellia Primigenia.
(10241) (*On a tomb outside the Porta Nuceria*) Health to Primigenia of Nuceria. For just one hour I'd like to be the stone of this ring, to give to you who moisten it with your mouth, the kisses I have impressed on it.

294. *A runaway slave. Bulla Regia, Roman Africa. (ILS 9455. L)*

Inscription on a lead collar, such as worn by slaves.

Adulterous whore. Take me, because I ran away from Bulla Regia.

Women gladiators
'He had dwarfs fight against women'

Scattered brief references to women fighting publicly do not give a very satisfactory picture of this surprising activity. They tell us little more than that it was not an everyday occurrence but that the practice lasted for some centuries. Several of the mentions of women gladiators in ancient literature are in the context of the opening of the Flavian amphitheatre, better known as the Colosseum, begun by Vespasian in AD 69, after the death of Nero and year of the four emperors. It was dedicated during the brief reign of Vespasian's elder son, Titus (AD 79-81), but really got going under Domitian, Titus' successor and younger brother. See also Juvenal's sixth satire (no. 69).

295. *Freedom. Halicarnassus. (CIG 6855. G)*

A dedicatory offering of two women gladiators on the occasion of getting their freedom. The inscription is a caption to a relief carving showing two armed women in single combat (see plate 11).

Amazon and Achillia were set free.

296. *Lady gladiators. Rome, AD 63 (Tacitus, Annals 15.32.3. L)*

Not all female gladiators were professionals.

That same year he [the Emperor Nero] held gladiatorial shows as magnificent as those that went before; but many distinguished ladies and senators disgraced themselves in the arena.

297. *In the Colosseum. Rome, AD 81 (Suetonius, Life of Domitian 4.2. L)*

He put on hunts and gladiatorial shows even at night, by torchlight, in which women as well as men fought.

298. *Domitian's entertainment for the masses. Rome, AD 89 (Dio Cassius, History of Rome 67.8.4. Early 3rd cent. AD. G)*

Domitian often held games at night, and one time he had dwarfs fight against women.

Both the satirist Martial, whose first published poems were in celebration of the opening of the Colosseum, and Domitian's court poet Statius find women gladiators worthy of mythological allusion.

299. *Lion slayers. Rome, AD 80 (Martial, Liber spectaculorum 6, 6b. L)*

Warlike Mars serves you, Caesar, with his invincible arms. But that's not enough for you. You want Venus too.
    Fame sings of Hercules and the lion lying dead in the vast valley of Nemea.
    Let the old story rest: After the games you put on, Caesar, women [kill the lions] ...

300. *Amazons in the Colosseum. Rome, AD 92-96 (Statius, Silvae 1.6.51-6. L)*

With all the new thrills and extravagances the tenuous pleasure of watching goes quickly: the sex untrained in weapons recklessly dares men's fights! You would think a band of Amazons was battling by the river Tanais or the barbarous Phasis.

301. *Fans. Rome, 1st cent. AD (Petronius, Satyricon 45. L)*

The speaker is Echion the rag dealer.

Say, we're going have some gladiatorial show for the festival – three days long. And not with professional gladiators but with lots of freedmen. And our Titus is a generous sort, and an aficionado. You can say what you like, it's going to be a big deal. I'm a friend of his, and I can tell you he doesn't do things halfway. He'll put on the best swords, no running away, with a pile of bodies in the middle for the whole audience to see. He has the wherewithal to do it too. He inherited 30 million sesterces from his father who died prematurely. So if he spends 400,000 he doesn't feel the pinch at all. He already has some characters: a woman who fights from a chariot and Glyco's paymaster who got caught fooling around with the lady of the house. You'll see a real battle between the jealous men and the fond lovers. That tightwad Glyco turned over his paymaster to the beasts, airing his dirty linen in public. What fault was it of the slave? She made him do it. It's that bitch instead who should be tossed by a bull.

302. *Septimius Severus calls a halt. Rome, AD 193-211. (Dio Cassius, History of Rome, 76.16.1. Early 3rd cent. AD. G)*

At that time a gymnastic contest took place; so many athletes were compelled to assemble that we wondered how the stadium could accommodate them. And women also competed in this contest so fiercely that jokes about their conduct were also directed at other very prominent women. Because of that it was no longer permitted for any woman, whatever her origin, to fight in a gladiatorial contest.[13]

The arts and entertainment
'A woman who played the trumpet'

303. *An exceptional tumbler. Athens, 4th cent. BC (Xenophon, Symposium 2.9. G)*

I saw this dancer stand up and someone hand hoops to her. After that another woman played the *aulos* for her, and someone stood beside the dancer and one-by-one handed her twelve hoops. She took them and at the same time danced, and threw the hoops up spinning, estimating how high she had to throw them in order to catch them in time to the music.

Then Socrates observed: 'Like many other things, what this girl is doing demonstrates that the female nature is in no way inferior to the male, except that it lacks judgment and strength. So if any of you has a wife, he should confidently teach her whatever he wants her to be able to do.'

Antisthenes replied: 'Since you advise this, how come you don't educate your wife Xanthippe, who is one of the most difficult women of our own time, and also of times past and future?'[14]

304. *A tumbler. Athens, 2nd cent. BC (IG II².12583. G)*

Excellent Sanno, a good tumbler.

305. *Aglaïs the trumpet-player. Alexandria, 270 BC (Athenaeus 10.415ab = Posidippus, Supp. Hell. 702. G)*

There was also a woman, Aglaïs the daughter of Megacles, who played the trumpet in the first great procession in Alexandria, wearing a wig and a plume on her head, as Posidippus describes vividly in his epigrams. She used to eat 12 pounds of meat, four days' worth of bread and a whole jug of wine.[15]

306. *A harpist. Delphi, 86 BC (Pleket 6. G)*

An inscription honouring a Theban woman for her services to Delphi. In a succeeding paragraph, similar honours are awarded to her nephew Lycinus, who lived with her.

To the god. With good fortune. During the archonship of Habromachus, in the month Boucatios. Strategos, Cleon, Antiphilus, and Damon were serving as councillors for the first six-month period.

The city of Delphi has decreed: whereas Polygnota, daughter of Socrates, a Theban harpist having come to Delphi, at the appointed time of the Pythian games, which could not be held on account of the present war, began on that very day and gave a day's time and performed at the request of the archons and the citizens for three days, and won the highest degree of respect, deserving the praise of Apollo and of the Theban people and of our city – she is awarded a crown and 500 drachmas. With good fortune.

Voted: to commend Polygnota, daughter of Socrates, the Theban, for her piety and reverence towards the god and for her dedication to her profession; to bestow on her and on her descendants the guest-friendship of the city, the right to consult the oracle, the privileges of being heard first, of safety, of exemption from taxes, and of front seating at the games held by the city, the right of owning land and a house and all the other honours ordinarily awarded to other benefactors of the city; to invite her to the town hall to the public hearth, and provide her with a victim to sacrifice to Apollo. To the god. With good fortune.

307. *Women painters. 1st cent. AD (Pliny the Elder, Natural History 35.40, 147. L)*

Women, too, have been painters. Timarete, the daughter of Micon, painted a Diana on a panel of the very archaic painting in Ephesus. Irene, daughter and student of Cratinus, painted a girl at Eleusis, a Calypso, the old juggler Theodorus, and the dancer Alcisthenes. Aristarete, daughter and student of Nearchus, painted an Asclepius. Iaia of Cyzicus, who never married, worked in Rome during the youth of Marcus Varro.[16] She used both the painter's brush and, on ivory, the graving tool. She painted women most frequently, including a panel picture of an old woman in Naples, and even a self-portrait for which she used a mirror. No one's hand was quicker to paint a picture than hers; so great was her talent that her prices far exceeded those of the most celebrated painters of her day, Sopolis and Dionysius, whose works fill the galleries. A certain Olympias, too, was a painter. About her we know only that Autobulus was her student.

308. *An actress. From the theatre at Aquileia, 3rd cent.* AD *(Kaibel 609. G)*

The talents of actors and actresses may have been admired, but their low social status was maintained by law. See Chapter V.

In the past she won resounding fame in many towns and many cities for her various accomplishments in plays, mimes, and choruses, and (often) dances. But she did not die on the stage, this tenth Muse.

To Bassilla the actress Heracleides, the skilled speaker and biographer, set up this stone. Even though she is dead, she will have the same honour she had in life, when she made her body 'die' on the floor of the stage. This is what her fellow actors are saying to her: 'Bassilla farewell, no one lives forever.'

309. *A troupe of castanet-dancers. Philadelphia, Egypt,* AD *206 (Cornell papyrus 9. G)*

The dancers are presumably being hired for a wedding feast.

To Isidora the castanet-dancer from Artemisia of the town of Philadelphia. I wish to hire you along with two other castanet-dancers for a six-day engagement at our house from the 24th of the month Pauni (according to the old reckoning). You are to receive for each day 36 drachmas and for the whole engagement 4 artabas of grain and 20 double loaves of bread. All the cloaks and gold jewellery that you bring with you we undertake to keep safe. We will provide two donkeys for your journey here and two for your return. In the 14th year of Lucius Septimius Severus Pius Pertinax and Marcus Aurelius Antoninus Pius Augustus and Publius Septimius Geta Caesar Augustus, 16 Pauni.

310. *Menophila. Athens, 1st cent.* BC? *(Agora XVII no. 913. G)*

The tomb of Menophila [connected] with the theatre.

311. *A citharist. Rome, Imperial period (CIL VI.10125 = ILS 5244. L)*

To the gods of the dead. Gaius Cornelius Neritus made this for himself and for Auxesis the citharist, the best wife.

---

312. *Phoebe Vocontia. Rome, Imperial period (CIL VI.10127 = ILS 5262. L)*

An *emboliaria* was an actress who performed during interludes in the theatre.

Phoebe Vocontia, *emboliaria*, learned in all the arts. Fate suppressed her. She lived 12 years.
On the right: Publius Fabius Faustus, freedman of Publius and Gaia, (put this up) while he was still alive.
On the left: Pompeia Sabbatis, freedwoman of Gnaeus, (put this up) while she was still alive.

---

313. *Twin singers. Rome, outside the Porta Salaria (ILS 9347. L)*[17]

Thelxis Cottia; Chelys Cottia (still alive), beloved twin sisters, singers, both dear to their loved ones

---

314. *A musical family. Rome, imperial period. (CIL VI.10131 = ILS 5264 = CLE 1282. L)*

To the gods of the dead.
Here lie three, taken by an untimely death, a mother and her small twin charges. Pollia Saturnina, the mother, lived 30 years and shone forth as performer of learned songs. The boy Titius Philippus, her offspring snatched prematurely away, lived for 8 years, and a sister very dear to her sweet brother, went away a year older, nor did leaping or dancing prolong her life.

---

315. *A singer. Rome, Imperial period. (CIL VI.10132 = ILS 5231. L)*

To Paesuza, slave of Caesar, solo singer,[18] who lived 18 years, 8 months, Euchrestis put this up to his well-deserving wife.

---

316. *A lutenist. Rome. (CIL VI.10158 = ILS 5248. L)*

Licinia, freedwoman of Gaius, lutenist,[19] and attendant in the family.

Skilled labour
'By her handiwork and skill'

317. *Handiwork. Athens, after 350 BC (CEG 774 = IG II².4334. G)*

By her handiwork and skill, and with righteous courage, Melinna raised her children and set up this memorial to you, Athena, goddess of handiwork, a share of the possessions she has won, in honour of your kindness.

318. *Handiwork. Athens, after 350 BC (CEG 537 = IG II².12254. G)*

I worked with my hands; I was a thrifty woman, I, Nicarete who lie here.

319. *A weaver of gold. Rome (CIL VI.9213 = ILS 7691. L)*

Viccentia, sweetest daughter, a weaver of gold, who lived 9 years, 9 months.

320. *A reader. Rome (CIL VI.33473 = ILS 7771.[20] L)*

Derceto, reader of Aurelia the (Vestal) Virgin, wretched, I died in my twentieth year.

(*On the same stone:*) Sabina Helena, freedwoman of Gaia, lived 16 years.

321. *A dressmaker. Rome (CIL VI.9214 = ILS 7692. L)*

Sellia Epyre, dressmaker in gold[21] in the Via Sacra, (wife of) Q. Futus Olympicus.

Sales and services
'... the Women's Market'

All specific information about women in retail trade comes from Athens. Men dominated lucrative trades (armaments, books, animals); women handled only relatively small sums. Prostitution may have been an exception, but we lack data about prices and fees paid to owners or employers.

322. *A washerwoman. Athens, 6th cent. BC (IG II².473. G)*

Smikythe, a washerwoman, offered a tithe.

323. *A society of launderers. Athens, 4th cent. BC (IG II².2934. G)*

A tablet set up by a society of persons who washed clothes on the banks of the Ilissos river.

To the nymphs and all the gods, fulfilling a vow, the washers set up this tablet: Zoagoras the son of Zocyprus, Socyprus the son of Zoagoras,

Thallos, Leuce,[22] Socrates son of Polycrates, Apollopanes, Euporionus, Sosistratus, Manes, Myrrhine,[23] Sosias, Sosigenes, Midas.

324. *A grocer. Athens, 4th cent. BC (IG III.iii.87. G)*[24]

... Callias the grocer in the neighbour's street and his wife **Thraitta** ... Glycanthis whom they call Malthace ... Mania the (woman) grocer near the spring ...

325. *The women's market. 4th-3rd cent. BC (Pollux 10.18 = Menander 390 Koerte-Thierfelder. G)*

If you should want to call the place where they sell such things the Women's Market, you will find the name in Menander's play *Synaristosae*.[25]

326. *A bar-maid. Tibur (CIL XIV.3709 = ILS 7477. L)*

Women innkeepers, waitresses, and bar-maids frequently worked as prostitutes as well and were dealt with by the Roman jurists (see Chapter V). This woman, whose husband praises her virtue, was evidently at least one who did not.[26]

... sweet
... in this tomb lies Amemone, a bar-maid known [beyond the boundaries] of her own country, [on account of whom] many people used to frequent Tibur. [Now the supreme] god has taken [fragile life] from her, and a kindly light receives her spirit [in the aether]. I, ...nus, [put up this inscription] to my holy wife. [It is right that her name] remain forever.

Other records of women's employment
'Shepherdess. Scribe. Fuller.'

Papyri

The following two texts list some jobs held by women in Hellenistic and Roman Egypt.

327. *Egypt, 3rd cent. BC (BGU VI 129.11, Michigan papyrus iv. 23. G)*

Shepherdess. Scribe. Fuller.

328. *Egypt, Roman Imperial period (CPR XIII. G)*

Flute-player. Scribe. Olive-oil seller. Ibis-feeder. Barber. Wool-seller. Dancer.

Inscriptions

Nos. 330-2 are excerpted from inscriptions recording the completion of the process of manumission.

329. *Occupations of freedwomen. Athens, 4th cent. BC (Lewis, Hesperia 28 [1959] 208-38. G)*

(A.221) Onesime, sesame seed-seller ... (255) Lampris, wet-nurse ... (259) Eupeithe, her child, wet-nurse ... (328) Lyde, woolworker[27] ... (468) Rhodia, woolworker ... (472) Cordype, her child, woolworker ... (493) Thraitta, grocer ... (497) Itame, woolworker ... (505) Demetria, harpist ... (518) Olympias, woolworker ... (B.91) ...one,[28] horsetender ... (112) Atta, pulse vendor ... (114) Malthace, woolworker (with her three children) ... (212) ...rityra,[29] *aulos*-player ... (214) Echo, woolworker.

330. *Occupations of freedwomen. Athens, 4th cent. BC (Lewis, Hesperia 37 [1968] 368-80. G)*

(49.4-5) Elpis,[30] *aulos*-player ... (50.34) Habrosyne, perfume vendor.[31]

331. *Occupations of freedwomen. Athens, 4th cent. BC (IG II². 1561.22-7, 1570.73, 1576.15 ff., 1578.5 ff. G)*

(1561.22-7) Midas[32] sesame seed-seller and Soteris[33] sesame seed-seller *(from the same household)* ... (1570.73) Piloumene, honeyseller ... (1576.15ff.) Melitta, frankincense seller ... (1578.5ff.) shoe-seller[34]...

332. *Occupations of women, from inscriptions on gravestones. Athens, 4th cent. BC (IG².11647, 12387, 12559, 11254, 11688, 12073, 12996, 13065. G)*

(11647) Good Theoxene, wet-nurse ...
(12387) Good Paideusis, wet-nurse ...
(12559) Good Pynete, wet-nurse
(11254) Elephantis, cloak-seller ...
(11688) Thraitta, unguent-boiler ...
(12073) Melitta, salt-vendor ...
(12996) Philyra, wet-nurse
(13065) Choerile, wet-nurse[35]

333. *A storeroom attendant. Cape Zoster, near Athens, 56/5 BC (Kaibel 118 = Peek 1007. G)*

An epitaph by a mother for a daughter who worked for Cleopatra at the royal court of Alexandria.

Her mother, an Athenian woman, raised her to be an attendant of foreign storerooms. She too rushed for her child's sake to come to the palace of the king who had set her over his rich possessions. Yet still she could not bring her daughter back alive. But the daughter has a tomb in Athens instead of on Libyan sand.[36]

334. Women in the service of the imperial household.[37] Rome, 1st cent. AD (CIL VI.8947, 8949, 5201 [= ILS 1837], 4352, 9037 [= ILS 1788], 8958 [= ILS 1784], 5539 [= ILS 1786], 8959 [= ILS 1786a7], 8957. L)

These texts, funerary inscriptions found in Rome, record the death and the occupation in life of slaves and freedwomen who worked for the families of Julio-Claudian emperors. Carved alongside the servants' names on these modest marble plaques are some of the most famous names of Roman history.

(8947) [The tomb] of Antonia Thallusa, freedwoman of the emperor, a midwife.[38]

(8949) To Julia ... sia, freedwoman of the deified empress,[39] a midwife.

(5201) Gaius Papius Asclepiades, Papia, freedwoman of Eros, Julia Jucunda, nurse of Drusus and Drusilla.[40]

(4352) Prima, freedwoman of the emperor [Tiberius] and empress [Livia], nurse of Julia [Livilla], daughter of Germanicus.

(9037) Extricata, seamstress of Octavia, daughter of [Claudius] Augustus, lived 20 years.

(8958) To Juno. [The tomb] of Dorcas, hairdresser of Julia Augusta,[41] born a slave on Capri [in the imperial house]. Lycastus, polling-clerk, her fellow freedman, [put this up] for his dearest wife and for himself.

(5539) To Paezusa, hairdresser of Octavia, daughter of Caesar Augustus [Claudius], who lived 18 years. Philetus, silver-slave of Octavia, daughter of Caesar Augustus [Claudius], put this up for his dearest wife and for himself.

(8959) To the gods of the dead. To Telesphoris, who lived 25 years, 3 months, and 11 days, hairdresser of Domitia [wife] of the emperor Domitian. Theopompus [put this up] for his wife.

(8957) To the gods of the dead. Claudia Parata, freedwoman of the emperor, hairdresser. She lived 27 years. Tiberius Julius Romanus, Tiberius Claudius Priscus, and Nedimus, slave of the emperor,[42] her husbands,[43] put up [this altar] at their own expense.

335. Occupations of slaves and freedwomen in Italy.[44] Rome, 1st cent. BC–2nd cent. AD (CIL VI.9754, 6331, 9758, 33892 [= ILS 7760], 9523 [= ILS 7397], 9496, 9497, 9498, 6350, 9884 [= ILS 7567], 6357 [= ILS 7435b], 9980 [= ILS 7428], 9727 [= ILS

*7420], 9730 [= ILS 7419], 9732 [= ILS 7420a], 9801 [= ILS 7500],
9683 [= ILS 7488], 6326, 6336, 6395, 6362 [= ILS 7432b]. 6342 [=
ILS 7432c], 6346 [= ILS 7432d]. L)*

These texts, like those in no. 334, are epitaphs recording the job of the
deceased. Unless freed status is specifically noted, the women may be
assumed to be slaves. It was generally more common to name the
occupation of the deceased in the case of slaves than of freedmen and
women.

(9754) Gaius Sulpicius Venustus, freedman of Gaius, Sulpicia Ammia,
freedwoman of Gaius. Sulpicia Galbilla daughter of Gaius, [put this up]
for her pedagogues.

(6331) Statilia Tyrannis, freedwoman of Titus, pedagogue of Statilia.

(9758) Urbana, pedagogue. She lived 25 years.

(33892) Sacred to the gods of the dead. To Hapate, a Greek
stenographer, who lived 25 years. Pittosus put this up for his sweetest
wife.

(9523) Grapte, secretary of Egnatia Maximilla.[45] Gaius Egnatius
Arogus [dedicated this] to his dearest wife.

(9496) Crecusa, the wool-weigher.

(9497) To the gods of the dead. [The tomb] of Irene the wool-weigher.
She lived 28 years. Olympus put this up for his well-deserving wife.

(9498)[46] To the gods of the dead. [The tomb] of Julia Soter, a
wool-weigher. She lived 80 years. Marcus Julius Primus, Julia Musa,
Julia Thisbe, Julia Ampliata, and Julia Romana put this up.

(6350) Here lies Musa the seamstress.

(9884) Titus Thoranius Savius, freedman of Titus, [erected this
monument] for himself and for Matia Prima, freedwoman of Gaia,[47] his
wife, a seamstress from Six Altars.[48] She lived 46 years.

(6357) Phyllis, Statilia's seamstress, [dedicated this stone] to Sophrus,
her deserving husband.

(9980) To Italia, dressmaker of Cocceia Phyllis. She lived 20 years.
Acastus, her fellow slave, put this up because she was poor.

(9727)[49] To the gods of the dead. Polydeuces dedicated this to the
well-deserving Cypare, a hairdresser.

(9730) Gnome, handmaiden and hairdresser of Pieris, was buried on
28 January of the year of Caesar [Augustus'] thirteenth consulship,[50]
when Marcus Plautius Silvanus was his colleague.[51]

(9732) Psamate, Furia's hairdresser, lived 19 years. Mithridates, baker
of Thorius Flaccus, put up [this stone].[52]

(9801)[53] Aurelia Nais, freedwoman of Gaius, fishmonger in the
warehouses of Galba. Gaius Aurelius Phileros, freedman of Gaius, and
Lucius Valerius Secundus, freedman of Lucius, [dedicated this altar].

(9683) To the gods of the dead. To Abudia Megiste, freedwoman of
Marcus, most kindly, Marcus Abudius Luminaris, her patron and

husband, built [this tomb] for the well-deserving dealer in grains and vegetables from the middle staircase,[54] and for himself and for his freedmen and freedwomen and descendants and for Marcus Abudius Saturninus his son, of the senior body of the Esquiline tribe. He lived 8 years.

(6326) Optata Pasa, portress. Her friends put this up.

(6336) Posis, Statilia's attendant.

(6395) Hilara, slave of Hermia.[55] 14 years old.

From the tomb of the Statilii, Rome

(6362) The bones of Italia the weaver.

(6342) Italia, spinning girl. She lived 20 years. Scaeva, letter-carrier of Taurus, made this for his wife.

(6346) Urbana, veteran slave, a spinning girl. Here lie her bones.

336. *Occupations in Roman Athens. Athens, 2nd/3rd cent.* AD *(IG².11244 [= Kaibel 121], 11205, 11496 [= Kaibel 102]. G)*

(11244) Irene, salt vendor.

(11205) Dmois, worn out by her work; beloved by the household that raised her. When she died she received this tomb.

(11496) Eutychousa and Nais, unfortunate; sisters, both musical, both eloquent, both trained to play the harp and the lyre, here the earth covers them gently, O stranger.

337. *Jobs named on lead curse tablets. Patissia and Athens (IG III.iii.68, 69, excerpts. G)*

For lead curse tablets, see p. 298.

(68) Parthenia the grocer (her hands, feet) ... Arescusa the procuress (her hands, feet, tongue) ... Anyte the grocer (hands, feet, shop and everything in the shop) ... Lacaina Melas' concubine (her hands and feet) ... (69) Dionysius the helmet maker and his wife Artemeis the gilder (their household and workshop and work and livelihood) ...

IX. Medicine and anatomy

'There needs must be a female'

Philosophers observe nature
'A woman is an infertile male'

338. *Origins of the desire for procreation. Athens, 4th cent. BC (Plato, Timaeus 90e-91d. G)*

In this dialogue Plato attributes to a Pythagorean philosopher, Timaeus of Locri in Italy, an account of the creation of the universe. Timaeus, by comparing human genitalia to undomesticated animals, provides an aetiology for sexual desire and for female hysteria (cf. no. 346).

Of the men who were born in that generation, those who were cowardly and acted unjustly during their lifetimes, were (as required by logic) changed into women in the second generation.[1] For this reason at that time the gods created the passion for sexual intercourse, settling one living creature in us, and another in women. They made the two kinds in the following manner. They made the outlet for liquids, by which the drink goes through the lungs under the kidneys into the bladder, which receives it and expels it under pressure from air, and they drilled a channel for this outlet also into the marrow that is fixed from the head along the neck and through the back – the substance that we called the seed in our previous discussion. And this marrow, because it is alive and has acquired the power of respiration, ... produces in it a lively desire for emission, and so brings about the desire for begetting. For this reason in men the thing connected with the nature of the genitals is intractable and self-willed, like an animal that will not obey reason, and it tries to control everything because of its maddening desires.

It is the same for those things which are called mothering-places (*metrai*) and latter places (*hysterai*)[2] in women. They have an animal within them eager for conception, which whenever it goes without issue for a long time beyond its proper season, becomes angry and miserable, and wanders everywhere around the body, blocks the outlets for air, and prevents respiration, causing extreme helplessness and bringing on all sorts of other diseases, until the desire and passion of both the man and the woman bring them together, and as if they were picking fruit from a tree, they sow into the field that is the womb (*metra*) living beings that are too small to be seen and formless, and then again they separate out the large beings within [the womb] and nourish them, and after that bring them to the light and so complete the generation of animals. Thus women and the female race in general were created.

339. *The female role in generation. Athens, 4th cent. BC (Aristotle, On the Generation of Animals, 716a5-23, 727a2-30, 727b31-3, 728b 18-31, 765b8-20, 766a17-30, 783b26-784a12. Tr. A.L. Peck, LCL. G)*

Aristotle's explanation of the process of conception is deduced from external secretions: male semen has primary generative importance, female semen (i.e. menstrual fluid, which also sustains the developing embryo) purely nutritive value.

Male and female defined
(716a5) As far as animals are concerned, we must describe their generation just as we find the theme requires for each several kind as we go along, linking our account on to what has already been said. As we mentioned, we may safely set down as the chief principles of generation the male [factor] and the female [factor]; the male as possessing the principle of movement and of generation, the female as possessing that of matter. One is most likely to be convinced of this by considering how the semen is formed and whence it comes; for although the things that are formed in the course of Nature no doubt take their rise out of semen, we must not fail to notice how the semen itself is formed from the male and the female, since it is because this part is secreted from the male and the female, and because its secretion takes place in them and out of them, that the male and the female are the principles of generation. By a 'male' animal we mean one which generates in another, by 'female' one which generates in itself. This is why in cosmology too they speak of the nature of the earth as something female and call it 'mother', while they give to the heaven and the sun and anything else of that kind the title of 'generator', and 'father'.

Now male and female differ in respect of their logos in that the power or faculty possessed by the one differs from that possessed by the other; but they differ also to bodily sense, in respect of certain physical parts. They differ in their logos, because the male is that which has the power to generate in another (as was stated above), while the female is that which can generate in itself, i.e. it is that out of which the generated offspring, which is present in the generator, comes into being ...[3]

Male and female secretions
(727a2) This much is evident: the menstrual fluid is a residue, and it is the analogous thing in females to the semen in males. Its behaviour

shows that this statement is correct. At the same time of life that semen begins to appear in males and is emitted, the menstrual discharge begins to flow in females, their voices change and their breasts begin to become conspicuous; and similarly, in the decline of life the power to generate ceases in males and the menstrual discharge ceases in females. Here are still further indications that this secretion which females produce is a residue. Speaking generally, unless the menstrual discharge is suspended, women are not troubled by haemorrhoids or bleeding from the nose or any other such discharge, and if it happens that they are, then the evacuations fall off in quantity, which suggests that the substance secreted is being drawn off to the other discharges. Again, their blood vessels are not so prominent as those of males; and females are more neatly made and smoother than males, because the residue which goes to produce those characteristics in males is in females discharged together with the menstrual fluid. We are bound to hold, in addition, that for the same cause the bulk of the body in female vivipara[4] is smaller than that of the males, as of course it is only in vivipara that the menstrual discharge flows externally, and most conspicuously of all in women, who discharge a greater amount than any other female animal. On this account it is always very noticeable that the female is pale, and the blood-vessels are not prominent, and there is an obvious deficiency in physique as compared with males.

Now it is impossible that any creature should produce two seminal secretions at once, and as the secretion in females which answers to semen in males is the menstrual fluid, it obviously follows that the female does not contribute any semen to generation; for if there were semen, there would be no menstrual fluid; but as menstrual fluid is in fact formed, therefore there is no semen ...

(727b31) There are some who think that the female contributes semen during coition because women sometimes derive pleasure from it comparable to that of the male and also produce a fluid secretion. This fluid, however, is not seminal; it is peculiar to the part from which it comes in each several individual; there is a discharge from the uterus, which though it happens in some women does not in others. Speaking generally, this happens in fair-skinned women who are typically feminine, and not in dark women of a masculine appearance. Where it occurs, this discharge is sometimes on quite a different scale from the semen discharged by the male, and greatly exceeds it in bulk. Furthermore, differences of food cause a great difference in the amount of this discharge which is produced: e.g. some pungent foods cause a noticeable increase in the amount ...

(727b18) Further, a boy actually resembles a woman in physique, and a woman is as it were an infertile male; the female, in fact, is female on account of inability of a sort, viz. it lacks the power to concoct semen out of the final state of the nourishment (this is either blood, or its counterpart in bloodless animals) because of the coldness of its nature. Thus, just as lack of concoction produces in the bowels diarrhoea, so in the blood vessels it produces discharge of blood of various sorts, and especially the menstrual discharge (which has to be classed as a discharge of blood, though it is a natural discharge, and the rest are morbid ones).

Hence, plainly, it is reasonable to hold that generation takes place from this process; for, as we see, the menstrual fluid is semen, not indeed semen in a pure concoction, but needing still to be acted upon. It is the same with fruit when it is forming. The nourishment is present right enough, even before it has been strained off, but it stands in need of being acted upon in order to purify it. That is why when the former is mixed with the semen, and when the latter is mixed with pure nourishment the one effects generation, and the other effects nutrition ...

The role of heat

(765b8) Now the opinion that the cause of male and female is heat and cold, and that the difference depends upon whether the secretion comes from the right side or from the left, has a modicum of reason in it, because the right side of the body is hotter than the left; hotter semen is semen which has been concocted; the fact that it has been concocted means that it has been set and compacted, and the more compacted semen is, the more fertile it is. All the same, to state the matter in this way is attempting to lay hold of the cause from too great a distance, and we ought to come as closely to grips as we possibly can with the primary causes.

We have dealt already elsewhere with the body as a whole and with its several parts, and have stated what each one is, and on account of what cause it is so. But that is not all, for (1) the male and the female are distinguished by a certain ability and inability. Male is that which is able to concoct, to cause to take shape, and to discharge, semen possessing the 'principle' of the 'form'; and by 'principle' I do not mean that sort of principle out of which, as out of matter, offspring is formed belonging to the same kind as its parent, but I mean the proximate motive principle, whether it is able to act thus in itself or in something else. Female is that which receives the semen, but is unable to cause semen to take shape or to discharge it. And (2) all concoction works by means of heat. Assuming the truth of these two statements, it follows of necessity that (3) male animals are hotter than female ones, since it is on account of coldness and inability that the female is more abundant in blood in certain regions of the body. And this abundance of blood is a piece of evidence which goes to prove the opposite of the view held by some people, who suppose that the female must be hotter than the male, on account of the discharge of menstrual fluid.

When the 'principle' is failing to gain the mastery and is unable to effect concoction owing to deficiency of heat, and does not succeed in reducing the material into its own proper form, but instead is worsted in the attempt, then of necessity the material must change over into its opposite condition. Now the opposite of the male is the female, and it is opposite in respect of that whereby one is male and the other female. And since it differs in the ability it possesses, so also it differs in the instrument which it possesses. Hence this is the condition into which the material changes over. And when one vital part changes, the whole make-up of the animal differs greatly in appearance and form. This may be observed in the case of eunuchs; the mutilation of just one part of them results in such a great alteration of their old semblance, and in close approximation to the appearance of the female. The reason for this is that some of the body's parts are 'principles', and once a principle has been 'moved' (i.e. changed), many of the parts which cohere with it must of necessity change as well ...

(766a17) Also, the fact that the menstrual discharge in the natural course tends to take place when the moon is waning is due to the same cause. That time of month is colder and more fluid on account of the waning and failure of the moon (since the moon makes a summer and winter in the course of a month just as the sun does in the course of the whole year) ...

(783b26) So that if you reckon up (a) that the brain itself has very little heat, (b) that the skin surrounding it must of necessity have even less, and (c) that the hair, being the furthest off of the three, must have even less still, you will expect persons who are plentiful in semen to go bald at about this time of life.[5] And it is owing to the same cause that it is on the front part of the head only that human beings go bald, and that they are the only animals which do so at all; i.e. they go bald in front because the brain is there, and they alone do so, because they have by far the largest brain of all and the most fluid. Women do not go bald because their nature is similar to that of children: both are incapable of producing seminal secretion. Eunuchs, too, do not go bald, because of their transition into the female state, and the hair that comes at a later stage they fail to grow at all, or if they already have it, they lose it, except for the pubic hair: similarly women do not have the later hair, though they do grow the pubic hair. This deformity constitutes a change from the male state to the female.

340. *Menstruation. Athens, 4th cent.* BC *(Aristotle, On Dreams 459b-460a. G)*

An illustration of how the eye affects what it sees.

In the case of very clean mirrors, if a woman who is menstruating looks into the mirror, the mirror's surface becomes bloody-dark, like a cloud. It isn't easy to wipe off the stain if the mirror is new, but if it is old it is easier. The reason for this is that vision, as we have said, is not only affected by the air, but indeed it also affects and does something to it[6] ... Eyes are affected like any other part of the body when the monthly period occurs, since by nature they happen to be full of blood vessels. Accordingly during the monthly period, there is a difference [in the eyes] because of the disturbance and inflammation of the blood – invisible to us, but none the less there, for that is the effect of the seed and the menstrual period; the air is disturbed by them, and it has an effect on the air on the surface of the mirror, similar to how it itself has been affected, and the mirror's surface is affected accordingly ...

Writings of practising physicians
'If they become pregnant, they will be cured'

The Hippocratic Corpus

341. *Intercourse, conception and pregnancy. Cos, 4th cent. BC (Hippo-crates, On the Generating Seed and the Nature of the Child 4-7, 13, 30.4 = VII.474-80, 488- 92, 536-8 Littré. Tr. I.M. Lonie. G)*

Doctors, who were throughout antiquity with very few exceptions male (see below, p. 264), concerned themselves only with diseases. The normal female functions of menstruation, childbirth, nursing, menopause, were dealt with by women – midwives and wet-nurses. Hence few records exist of normal procedures and reactions.

(4) In the case of women, it is my contention that when during intercourse the vagina is rubbed and the womb is disturbed, an irritation is set up in the womb which produces pleasure and heat in the rest of the body. A woman also releases something from her body, sometimes into the womb, which then becomes moist, and sometimes externally as well, if the womb is open wider than normal. Once intercourse has begun, she experiences pleasure throughout the whole time, until the man ejaculates. If her desire for intercourse is excited, she emits before the man, and for the remainder of the time she does not feel pleasure to the same extent; but if she is not in a state of excitement, then her pleasure terminates along with that of the man. What happens is like this: if into boiling water you pour another quantity of water which is cold, the water stops boiling. In the same way, the man's sperm arriving in the womb extinguishes both the heat and the pleasure of the woman. Both the pleasure and the heat reach their peak simultaneously with the arrival of the sperm in the womb, and then they cease. If, for example, you pour wine on a flame, first of all the flame flares up and increases for a short period when you pour the wine on, then it dies away. In the same way the woman's heat flares up in response to the man's sperm, and then dies away. The pleasure

experienced by the woman during intercourse is considerably less than the man's, although it lasts longer. The reason that the man feels more pleasure is that the secretion from the bodily fluid in his case occurs suddenly, and as the result of a more violent disturbance than in the woman's case.

Another point about women: if they have intercourse with men their health is better than if they do not. For in the first place, the womb is moistened by intercourse, whereas when the womb is drier than it should be it becomes extremely contracted, and this extreme contraction causes pain to the body. In the second place, intercourse by heating the blood and rendering it more fluid gives an easier passage to the menses; whereas if the menses do not flow, women's bodies become prone to sickness.

(5) When a woman has intercourse, if she is not going to conceive, then it is her practice to expel the sperm produced by both partners whenever she wishes to do so. If however she is going to conceive, the sperm is not expelled, but remains in the womb. For when the womb has received the sperm it closes up and retains it, because the moisture causes the womb's orifice to contract. Then both what is provided by the man and what is provided by the woman is mixed together. If the woman is experienced in matters of childbirth, and takes note when the sperm is retained, she will know the precise day on which she has conceived.

Male and female sperm

(6) Now here is a further point. What the woman emits is sometimes stronger, and sometimes weaker; and this applies also to what the man emits. In fact both partners alike contain both male and female sperm (the male being stronger than the female must of course originate from a stronger sperm). Here is a further point: if (a) both partners produce a stronger sperm, then a male is the result, whereas if (b) they produce a weak form, then a female is the result. But if (c) one partner produces one kind of sperm, and the other another, then the resultant sex is determined by whichever sperm prevails in quantity. For suppose that the weak sperm is much greater in quantity than the stronger sperm: then the stronger sperm is overwhelmed and, being mixed with the weak, results in a female. If on the contrary the strong sperm is greater in quantity than the weak, and the weak is overwhelmed, it results in a male. It is just as though one were to mix together beeswax with suet, using a larger quantity of suet than of the beeswax, and melt them together over a fire. While the mixture is still fluid, the prevailing character of the mixture is not apparent: only after it solidifies can it be seen that the suet prevails quantitatively over the wax. And it is just the same with the male and female forms of sperm.

(7) Now that both male and female sperm exist in both partners is an inference which can be drawn from observation. Many women have borne daughters to their husbands and then, going with other men, have

produced sons. And the original husbands – those, that is, to whom their wives bore daughters – have as the result of intercourse with other women produced male offspring; whereas the second group of men, who produced male offspring, have with yet other women produced female offspring. Now this consideration shows that both the man and the woman have male and female sperm. For in the partnership in which the women produced daughters, the stronger sperm was overwhelmed by the larger quantity of the weaker sperm, and females were produced; while in the partnership in which these same women produced sons, it was the weak which was overwhelmed, and males were produced. Hence the same man does not invariably emit the strong variety of sperm, nor the weak invariably, but sometimes the one and sometimes the other; the same is true in the woman's case. There is therefore nothing anomalous about the fact that the same women and the same men produce both male and female sperm: indeed, these facts about male and female sperm are also true in the case of animals.

A spontaneous abortion

(13) As a matter of fact I myself have seen an embryo which was aborted after remaining in the womb for six days. It is upon its nature, as I observed it then, that I base the rest of my inferences. It was in the following way that I came to see a six-day-old embryo. A kinswoman of mine owned a very valuable danseuse, whom she employed as a prostitute. It was important that this girl should not become pregnant and thereby lose her value. Now this girl had heard the sort of thing women say to each other – that when a women is going to conceive, the seed remains inside her and does not fall out. She digested this information, and kept a watch. One day she noticed that the seed had not come out again. She told her mistress, and the story came to me. When I heard it, I told her to jump up and down, touching her buttocks with her heels at each leap. After she had done this no more than seven times, there was a noise, the seed fell out on the ground, and the girl looked at it in great surprise.[7] It looked like this: it was as though someone had removed the shell from a raw egg, so that the fluid inside showed through the inner membrane – a reasonably good description of its appearance. It was round, and red; and within the membrane could be seen thick white fibres, surrounded by a thick red serum; while on the outer surface of the membrane were clots of blood. In the middle of the membrane was a small projection: it looked to me like an umbilicus, and I considered that it was through this that the embryo first breathed in and out. From it, the membrane stretched all around the seed. Such then was the six-day embryo that I saw, and a little further on I intend to describe a second observation which will give a clear insight into the subject. It will also serve as evidence for the truth of my whole argument – so far as is humanly possible in such a matter.

(30) ... In fact it is impossible for pregnancy to last longer than ten months, and I shall explain why. The nutriment for growth which the mother's body provides is no longer sufficient for the child after ten months are up and it is fully grown. It is nurtured by drawing the sweetest part of the blood towards itself, although it is fed to some extent from the milk as well. Once these are no longer sufficient and the child is already big, in its desire for more nutriment than is there it tosses about and so ruptures the membranes. This occurs more frequently in women who are bearing their first child; with them, the supply of nutriment for the child tends to give out before the ten months are up. This is the reason: the menstrual flow of some women is sufficiently abundant, while with other women the flow is less. (If this is always the case it is the result of the constitution which the woman has inherited from her mother.) Now it is the women whose menses are small in quantity who also provide their infants with insufficient nutriment towards the end of their term when the infant is already large, and so cause it to toss about and bring on birth before ten months are up. The reason is their small flow of blood. Usually too these women cannot give milk; this is because they have a dry constitution and their flesh is densely packed.

342. *A contraceptive. Cos, 4th cent. BC (Hippocrates, Nature of Women 98 = VII.414 Littré. G)*

If a woman does not want to become pregnant, make as thick a mixture of beans and water as you can, make her drink it, and she will not become pregnant for a year.[8]

343. *Women's illnesses. Cos, 4th cent. BC (Hippocrates, Diseases of Women 1.1, 2, 6, 7, 21, 25, 33, 62 excerpts. = VIII.12-22, 30-4, 60-2, 64-8, 78, 126 Littré. Tr. A. Hanson. G)*

Problems with the female sexual organs were thought to affect the woman's organism as a whole. It was believed that normal conditions could be restored in the first instance by sexual intercourse and pregnancy, and then (if that were not possible) by manipulation of the affected areas and the insertion into the vagina of medicinal pessaries or fumigations, intended to expel accumulated blood or fluid and/or restore a displaced uterus to its proper position. Along with a wide range of vegetable substances, doctors employed strong drugs like Spanish fly and substances that they did not use with such frequency on their male patients, such as animal dung and urine.[9]

(1) The following concerns women's diseases. I say that a woman who has never given birth suffers more intensely and more readily from menstruation than a woman who has given birth to a child. For whenever a woman does give birth, her small vessels become more easy-flowing for

menstruation (because the birth process stretches the vessels and so makes menstruation easier). ...

I say that a woman's flesh is more sponge-like and softer than a man's: since this is so, the woman's body draws moisture both with more speed and in greater quantity from the belly than does the body of a man ...

And when the body of a woman – whose flesh is soft – happens to be full of blood and if that blood does not go off from her body, pain occurs, whenever her flesh is full and becomes heated. A woman has warmer blood and therefore she is warmer than a man. If the existing surplus of blood should go off, no pain results from the blood. Because a man has more solid flesh than a woman, he is never so totally overfilled with blood that pain results if some of his blood does not exit each month. He draws whatever quantity of blood is needed for his body's nourishment; since his body is not soft, it does not become overstrained nor is it heated up by fullness, as in the case of a woman. The fact that a man works harder than a woman contributes greatly to this; for hard work draws off some of the fluid.

(2) Whenever in a woman who has never given birth the menses are suppressed and cannot find a way out, illness results. This happens if the mouth of the womb is closed or if some part of her vagina is prolapsed. For if one of these things happens, the menses will not be able to find a way out until the womb returns to a healthy state. This disease occurs more frequently in women who have a womb narrow at the mouth or who have a cervix which lies far away from the vagina. For if either of these conditions exists and if the woman in question does not have intercourse and if her belly is more emptied than usual from some suffering, the womb is displaced.[10] The womb is not damp of its own accord (as, for example, in the case of a woman who does not have coitus) and there is empty space for the womb (as, for example, when the belly is more empty than usual) so that the womb is displaced when the woman is drier and emptier than normal.

There are also occasions when, after the womb is displaced, the mouth happens to be turned too far, such as in a case where the cervix lies far away from the vagina. But if her womb is damp from coitus and her belly is not empty, her womb is not easily displaced.

The following things also happen. For some women, when two months' menses are accumulated in quantity in the womb, they move off into the lungs whenever they are prevented from exiting. The woman suffers all the symptoms which have been mentioned in the discussion of phthisis[11] and she cannot survive ...

(6) If a woman is healthy, her blood flows like that from a sacrificial animal and it speedily coagulates. Those women who habitually menstruate for longer than four days and whose menses flow in great abundance, are delicate and their embryos are delicate and waste away. But those women whose menstruation is less than three days or is

meagre, are robust, with a healthy complexion and a masculine appearance; yet they are not concerned about bearing children nor do they become pregnant.

(7) If suffocation occurs suddenly, it will happen especially to women who do not have intercourse and to older women rather than to young ones, for their wombs are lighter. It usually occurs because of the following: when a woman is empty and works harder than in her previous experience, her womb, becoming heated from the hard work, turns because it is empty and light. There is, in fact, empty space for it to turn in because the belly is empty. Now when the womb turns, it hits the liver and they go together and strike against the abdomen – for the womb rushes and goes upward towards the moisture, because it has been dried out by hard work, and the liver is, after all, moist. When the womb hits the liver, it produces sudden suffocation as it occupies the breathing passage around the belly.

Sometimes, at the same time as the womb begins to go towards the liver, phlegm flows down from the head to the abdomen (that is, when the woman is experiencing the suffocation) and sometimes, simultaneously with the flow of phlegm, the womb goes away from the liver to its normal place and the suffocation ceases. The womb goes back, then, when it has taken on moisture and has become heavy ... Sometimes, if a woman is empty and she overworks, her womb turns and falls towards the neck of her bladder and produces strangury – but no other malady seizes her. When such a woman is treated, she speedily becomes healthy; sometimes recovery is even spontaneous.

In some women the womb falls towards the lower back or towards the hips because of hard work or lack of food, and produces pain.

Diseases of pregnant women
(21) Now I shall discuss the diseases of pregnant women. Some women conceive a child easily, but are not able to carry it full term; the children are lost through miscarriage in the third or fourth month – even though the woman has suffered no physical injury nor eaten the wrong kind of food. In such women the cause of the circumstances mentioned is especially when the womb releases matter which would make the embryo grow. The woman's bowels become upset: weakness, high fever, and lack of appetite affect them during the time in which they are aborting their children. The following is also a cause, namely if the womb is smooth – either naturally or due to the presence of lacerations in the womb. Now if the womb is smooth, sometimes the membranes which envelop the child are detached from the womb when the child begins to move – because these membranes are less a part of the womb than they ought to be, due to the fact that the womb is smooth. Anyone would know all these details if he would carefully ask about them. Insofar as the smoothness of the womb is concerned, let another woman touch the womb when it is empty,

for the smoothness is not immediately distinguishable. If the menses flow in these women, they come copiously. Occasionally some of these women carry their embryos to full term, and when such women are cared for, they have hope of a normal birth ...

(25) I say that if menses flow each month for a woman who is two or three months pregnant or more, she is necessarily thin and weak. Occasionally a fever grips her during the days until the menses flow. When the menstrual blood flows, she becomes pale, yet very little flows out. Her womb has come to gape open more than it ought to and it releases matter which would make the embryo grow. Blood comes down from all the body when a woman is pregnant and gradually enters the womb, encircling that which is inside it; the blood makes it grow. But if the womb gapes open more than it should, it releases the blood each month just as it has been accustomed to do in the past, and that which is in the womb becomes thin and weak. When such a woman is cared for, the embryo also is better and the woman herself is healthy. If she is not cared for, she loses her child and, in addition, she runs the risk of having a long-lasting disease ...

There are also many other dangers by which embryos are aborted; if, for example, a pregnant woman is sick and weak, and if she picks up a burden with all her bodily strength, or if she is beaten, or leaps into the air, or goes without food, or has a fainting spell, or takes too much or too little nourishment, or becomes frightened and scared, or shouts violently. Nurture is a cause of miscarriage, and so is an excessive drink. Wombs by themselves also have natural dispositions by which miscarriage can occur: wombs that are flatulent, for example, or tightly packed, loose, over large, over small, and other types which are similar.

If a pregnant woman feels distressed in her belly or in her lower back, one must fear lest the embryo bring on a miscarriage, since the membranes which surround it have been broken.

There are also women who lose their children if they eat or drink something pungent or something bitter contrary to their usual habits – if the child is in an early stage of its development. For whenever something happens to a child contrary to its usual habits, it will die when it is little, especially if the mother drinks or eats the kind of thing that strongly upsets her stomach when the child is in an early stage of development. For the womb perceives when a diarrhoetic flux comes down from the belly ...

(33) If in the case of a pregnant woman the time for birth is already past, if labour pains are present, and if for a long time the woman has been unable to bring forth the child without injury to herself, usually the child is coming in lateral or breech position – yet it is better for it to come out head-first. The pain involved is of the following sort: as if, for example, someone would throw an olive pit into a small-mouthed oil flask, the pit is not naturally suited to be taken out when it is turned on

its side. In this way, then, the birth of the embryo laterally presented is also a very painful experience for the woman; it just doesn't go out. The pains are even more difficult if the embryo proceeds feet-first; many times the women die, or the children, or even both. A major cause of the embryo not going out easily is if it is dead, or paralysed, or if there are two of them ...

62. All these diseases, then, happen more frequently to women who have not borne a child; yet they also happen to those who have. These diseases are dangerous, as has been said, and for the most part they are both acute and serious, and difficult to understand because of the fact that women are the ones who share these sicknesses. Sometimes women do not know what sickness they have, until they have experienced the diseases which come from menses and they become older. Then both necessity and time teach them the cause of their sicknesses. Sometimes diseases become incurable for women who do not learn why they are sick before the doctor has been correctly taught by the sick woman why she is sick. For women are ashamed to tell even of their inexperience and lack of knowledge. At the same time the doctors also make mistakes by not learning the apparent cause through accurate questioning, but they proceed to heal as though they were dealing with men's diseases. I have already seen many women die from just this kind of suffering. But at the outset one must ask accurate questions about the cause. For the healing of the diseases of women differs greatly from the healing of men's diseases.

344. *Displacement of the womb. Cos, 4th cent. BC (Hippocrates, Places in Human Anatomy 47 = V. 344-6 Littré. G)*

As for what are called women's diseases: the womb is responsible for all such diseases. For the womb, when it is displaced from its natural position, whether forward or back, causes diseases. When the neck of the womb has been moved back and does not bring its opening towards or touch the lips of the vagina, the problem is minor. But if the womb falls forward and brings its opening towards the lips, it first of all causes pain when it makes contact, and then because the womb is cut off and obstructed by the contact of its neck with the lips of the vagina, there is no so-called menstrual flow. This flow if retained causes swelling and pain. If the womb descends and is diverted so that it approaches the groin, it causes pain. If it ascends and is diverted and cut off, it causes illness through its compression. When a woman is ill because of this problem, she has pains in her thighs and her head. When the womb is distended and swollen, there is no flow, and it becomes filled up. When it is filled, it touches the thighs. When the womb is filled with moisture and distended, there is no flow, and it causes pain in both the thighs and the groin, something like balls roll through the stomach, and cause pain in the head, first in one part, and then in all of it, as the disease develops.

The treatment is as follows: if the womb has only moved forward and it is possible to apply ointment, use any foul-smelling ointment you choose, either cedar or myssoton, or some other heavy and ill-scented substance, and fumigate, but do not use a vapour-bath, and do not give food or a diuretic liquid during this time, or wash her in hot water. If the womb has turned upwards and is not obstructed, use sweet-smelling pessaries that are also inflammatory. These are myrrh, or perfume, or some other aromatic and inflammatory substance. Use these in pessaries, and from below apply fumigations with wine vapour, and wash with hot water, and use diuretics. It is clear that the womb is turned upwards and is not obstructed, because there is a flow.

If the womb is obstructed, then there is no so-called menstrual flow. This disease must be treated first with a vapour-bath; put wild figs into the wine, and heat it and put a gourd around the mouth of the vessel in which the wine is heated. Then do as follows: cut the gourd through the middle and hollow it out, and cut off a bit of its top, as if you were making a nozzle for a bellows, so that the vapour can go through its channel and reach the womb. Wash with hot water, and use pessaries made of inflammatory drugs. The following inflammatory drugs bring on menstruation: cow dung, beef bile, myrrh, alum, galbanum, and anything similar; use as much of these as possible. Evacuate from below by laxative drugs that do not cause vomiting, diluted, so that it does not become a purgative by being too strong. Use pessaries as follows, if you want them to be strong. Use half-cooked honey, and add some of the substances prescribed to bring on menstruation; after you have added them, make the pessaries like pellets used for the anus, but make them long and thin. Make the woman lie down, and elevate the feet of the bed towards her feet, insert the pessary, and apply heat either on a chamber-pot or on some other vessel, so that the pessary melts. If you want to make the pessary less strong, wrap it in linen. And if the womb is filled with fluid, with its mouth swollen, so that amenorrhoea results, heal it by bringing on menstruation with medicinal pessaries, using both inflammatory pessaries as described, as in the case of the preceding amenorrhoea. If there is an excessive flow, do not use hot water or any other kind, nor diuretics or laxative foods. Raise the foot of the bed higher, so that the inclination of the bed does not encourage the flow, and use astringent pessaries. The flow, if her period comes directly, is bloody, if it diminishes, it contains pus. Young women bleed more, and the so-called menstrual periods of older women contain more mucus.

345. *Hysterical suffocation. Cos, 4th cent.* BC *(Hippocrates, Diseases of Women 2.126, 123 = VIII. 271-3, 266 Littré. G)*

(126) When the womb remains in the upper abdomen, the suffocation is

similar to that caused by the purgative hellebore, with stiff breathing and sharp pains in the heart. Some women spit up acid saliva, and their mouths are full of fluid, and their legs become cold. In such cases, if the womb does not leave the upper abdomen directly, the women lose their voices, and their head and tongue are overcome by drowsiness. If you find such women unable to speak and with their teeth chattering, insert a pessary of wool, twisting it round the shaft of a feather in order to get it in as far as possible – dip it either in white Egyptian perfume or myrtle or bacchar or marjoram. Use a spatula to apply black medicine (the kind you use for the head) to her nostrils. If this is not available, wipe the inside of her nostrils with silphium, or insert a feather that you have dipped in vinegar, or induce sneezing. If her mouth is closed tight and she is unable to speak, make her drink castoreum in wine. Dip your finger in seal oil and wipe inside her nostrils. Insert a wool pessary, until the womb returns, and remove it when the symptoms disappear. But if, when you take the pessary out, the womb returns to the upper abdomen, insert the pessary as you did before, and apply beneath her nostrils fumigations of ground-up goat or deer horn, to which you have added hot ashes, so that they make as much smoke as possible, and have her inhale the vapour up through her nose as long as she can stand it. It is best to use a fumigation of seal oil: put the coals in a pot and wrap the woman up – except for her head. So that as much vapour as possible is emitted, drip a little fat on it, and have her inhale the vapour. She should keep her mouth shut. This is the procedure if the womb has fallen upward out of place ...

(123) When the womb moves towards her head and suffocation occurs in that region, the woman's head becomes heavy, though there are different symptoms in some cases. One symptom: the woman says the veins in her nose hurt her and beneath her eyes, and she becomes sleepy, and when this condition is alleviated, she foams at the mouth.

You should wash her thoroughly with hot water, and if she does not respond, with cold, from her head on down, using cool water in which you have previously boiled laurel and myrtle. Rub her head with rose perfume, and use sweet-scented fumigations beneath her vagina, but foul-scented ones at her nose. She should eat cabbage, and drink cabbage juice.

346. *Dislocation of the womb. Cos, 4th cent.* BC *(Hippocrates, Nature of Women 8, 3 = VII. 322-4, 314-16 Littré. G)*

(8) If her womb moves towards her hips, her periods stop coming, and pain develops in her lower stomach and abdomen. If you touch her with your finger, you will see the mouth of the womb turned towards her hip.[12]

When this condition occurs, wash the woman with warm water, make her eat as much garlic as she can, and have her drink undiluted sheep's milk after her meals. Then fumigate her and give her a laxative. After the laxative has taken effect, fumigate the womb once again, using a preparation of fennel and absinthe mixed together. Right after the fumigation, pull the mouth of the womb with your finger. Then insert a pessary made with squills; leave it in for a while, and then insert a pessary made with opium poppies. If you think the condition has been corrected, insert a pessary of bitter almond oil, and on the next day, a pessary of rose perfume. She should stop inserting pessaries on the first day of her period, and start again the day after it stops. The blood during the period provides a normal interruption. If there is no flow, she should drink four cantharid beetles[13] with their legs, wings and heads removed, four dark peony seeds, cuttlefish eggs, and a little parsley seed in wine. If she has a pain and irregular flow, she should sit in warm water, and drink honey mixed with water. If she is not cured by the first procedure, she should drink it again, until her period comes. When it comes, she should abstain from food and have intercourse with her husband. During her period she should eat mercury plant, and boiled squid, and keep to soft foods. If she becomes pregnant she will be cured of this disease ...

(3) When her womb moves towards her liver, she suddenly loses her voice and her teeth chatter and her colouring turns dark. This condition can occur suddenly, while she is in good health. The problem particularly affects old maids and widows – young women who have been widowed after having had children.

When this condition occurs, push your hand down below her liver, and tie a bandage below her ribs.[14] Open her mouth and pour in very sweet-scented wine; put applications on her nostrils and burn foul-scented vapours below her womb ...

347. *Dropsy in the womb. Cos, 4th cent. BC (Hippocrates, Nature of Women 2 = VII. 312-14 Littré. G)*

When there is a dropsy in her womb, her monthly periods become smaller and weaker, and then stop suddenly, and her stomach bloats up, and her breasts dry out, and everything else suffers, and she seems to be pregnant – this is how you know she has dropsy. A further indication is the condition of the mouth of the womb: when she touches it, it seems withered. Fever and swelling attack her. As time goes on, pain develops in her lower stomach and loins and abdomen. This disease is usually brought on by miscarriage, but there are other causes.

When swelling in the womb occurs, one should wash the woman with warm water and apply warm poultices where she has pain. One should make her drink a laxative. After the laxative, put her in a vapour bath made with cow dung, then insert a pessary made with cantharid beetle, and after three days a pessary made of bile. Leave this in for one day, and then after three days give her a vinegar douche. Then if her stomach becomes soft and her fever goes away, and her period comes, have her sleep with her husband. If not, follow the previous procedure over again, until her period comes, and have her use some suppositories. In the days between suppositories have her drink samphire bark and dark peony berries, and eat as much mercury plant as possible, and garlic both raw and cooked. Have her eat soft foods such as squid and other soft animals. If she gives birth, she will be cured.

348. *The dangerous first and sixth 40-day periods during pregnancy. Cos, 4th cent. BC (Hippocrates, On the Seventh-Month Child 3-4 = VII. 438-42 Littré. G)*

The author shows some impatience with women who do not seem to understand the logical medical explanation for miscarriages during the early stages of pregnancy and for still-births in the later stages.[15]

(3.1) At the age of seven months most foetuses, when the membranes relax, move to the yielding part of the body and get their nourishment there. There they spend the first 40-day period [after the move],[16] for better or for worse, because of the transition they have made from the places that had nourished them [previously], and because the umbilical cord is pulled and displaced, and because of the discomfort suffered by the mother. (3.2) When the membranes are stretched and the umbilical cord is pulled, it gives pain to the mother. The foetus, once released from its old binding, becomes heavier. Many women develop fevers when this happens, and others even die, along with their foetuses. All women agree on this point. For they say that during the eighth month[17] it is most difficult for them to carry their bellies, and they are correct. But this eighth month is not the only critical time; there are also the days that are added from the seventh month and the ninth month [to make up the 40-day period].

(3.3) But women do not talk about these [additional] days in the same way and do not know about them. They lose track because the period is not always the same, since sometimes a greater number of days from the seventh month are added to the 40-day period and sometimes from the ninth month. It all depends on when during the month and on the time of day that she happens to have conceived. The eighth month, however, is unambiguous, because this is the critical time, and the month is a unit among ten, so that it is easily remembered.

(4.1) You cannot disregard what women say about child-bearing. For they are talking about what they know and always inquiring about; they could not be persuaded either by deed or word that they do not know rather more [than you do] about what is happening in their own bodies. It is possible for those [doctors] who wish to say something different, but it is the women who make the judgments and who award the prize, and they always will inquire about this subject and will insist that they give birth to seventh-month and eighth-month and ninth-month and tenth-month and eleventh-month babies, and that the eighth-month babies do not survive, but the others do. (4.2) For they confirm that the majority of miscarriages occur in the first 40 days.[18]

When the membranes are broken in the seventh month, and the embryo descends, the discomfort begins that is said to arise around the time of eighth month and the sixth forty-day period. After that time has passed, in women for whom matters go well, the inflammation of the foetus and mother disappears, and the belly is softer. And the weight descends from the upper abdomen and the flanks to the lower region for its convenience in turning for birth. (4.3) During the seventh 40-day period, the foetus rests there for most of the time; there is a soft place for it, and its movements are easier and more frequent. Women carry their bellies in the last days of this 40-day period most easily until the foetus tries to turn. After this there are labour pains and discomfort until the mother is delivered of the child and the after-birth.

349. *Hysteria in virgins. Cos, 4th cent. BC (Hippocrates, On Virgins =*
    VIII.466- 70 Littré. G)

As a result of visions, many people choke to death, more women than men, for the nature of women is less courageous and is weaker. And virgins who do not take a husband at the appropriate time for marriage experience these visions more frequently, especially at the time of their first monthly period, although previously they have had no such bad dreams of this sort. For later the blood collects in the womb in preparation to flow out; but when the mouth of the egress is not opened up, and more blood flows into the womb on account of the body's nourishment of it and its growth, then the blood which has no place to flow out, because of its abundance, rushes up to the heart and to the lungs; and when these are filled with blood, the heart becomes sluggish, and then, because of the sluggishness, numb, and then, because of the numbness, insanity takes hold of the woman.[19] Just as when one has been sitting for a long time the blood that has been forced away from the hips and the thighs collects in one's lower legs and feet, it brings numbness, and as a result of the numbness, one's feet are useless for movement, until the blood goes back where it belongs. It returns most quickly when one stands in cold water and wets the tops of one's ankles. This numbness presents no complications, since the blood flows back quickly because the veins in that part of the body are straight, and the legs are not a critical part of the body. But blood flows slowly from the heart and from the phrenes.[20] There the veins are slanted, and it is a critical place for insanity, and suited for madness.

When these places[21] are filled with blood, shivering sets in with fevers. They call these 'erratic fevers'. When this is the state of affairs, the girl goes crazy because of the violent inflammation, and she becomes murderous because of the decay and is afraid and fearful because of the darkness. The girls try to choke themselves because of the pressure on their hearts; their will, distraught and anguished because of the bad condition of the blood, forces evil on itself. In some cases the girl says dreadful things: [the visions] order her to jump up and throw herself into wells and drown, as if this were good for her and served some useful purpose.[22] When a girl does not have visions, a desire sets in which compels her to love death as if it were a form of good. When this person returns to her right mind, women give to Artemis various offerings, especially the most valuable of women's robes, following the orders of oracles, but they are deceived. The fact is that the disorder is cured when nothing impedes the downward flow of blood. My prescription is that when virgins experience this trouble, they should cohabit with a man as quickly as possible. If they become pregnant, they will be cured. If they don't do this, either they will succumb at the onset of puberty or a little later, unless they catch another disease. Among married women, those who are sterile are more likely to suffer what I have described.

350. *Case histories. Cos, 4th cent.* BC *(Hippocrates, Epidemics 5.12 and 25 = V.212, 224 Littré. G)*

(12) In Pheres a woman for a long time had headaches and no one could help her at all, not even when she had her head drained. It was easier for her when her period passed easily. When she had a headache, scented pessaries in her womb were helpful, and she was drained [of the fluid in her head] somewhat. But when she became pregnant, her headaches disappeared.

(25) In Larissa a servant in Dyseris' household, when she was young, suffered severe labour pains whenever she had intercourse – otherwise she had no pains. She had never been pregnant. When she was 60, she felt labour pains in the middle of the day, as severe as if in childbirth. Before that she had eaten a large number of leeks. When a pain came that was more severe than any she had had before, she stood up and felt something rough in the mouth of her womb. Then, after she had fainted, another woman inserted her hand and squeezed out a rough stone, like the whorl of a spindle. And the woman recovered immediately and stayed well thereafter.

Galen

351. *Comparison of male and female anatomy. Pergamum, 2nd cent.* AD *(Galen, On the Usefulness of the Parts of the Body 14.6-7, excerpts. Tr. M.T. May. G)*

Galen, born and educated in Pergamum, the great Hellenistic seat of learning in Asia Minor, was philosopher, physician and eclectic dogmatist. He began his career as a gladiators' doctor, but eventually became physician to the Emperor Marcus Aurelius. His pathology was speculative and based on the doctrine that health depended on the balance of the four humours (black bile, yellow bile, blood and phlegm). His reliance on philosophical premise and astrological prognostication has little connection with modern scientific technique. Some of his anatomical conclusions are based on inaccurate comparisons between animals, which he dissected, and humans, whom he did not. But he made significant contributions to diagnosis and prognosis.[23]

The female is less perfect than the male for one principal reason, because she is colder, for if among animals the warm one is the more active, a colder animal would be less perfect than a warmer. A second reason is one that appears in dissecting ...

All the parts, then, that men have, women have too, the difference between them lying in only one thing, which must be kept in mind throughout the discussion, namely, that in women the parts are within [the body], whereas in men they are outside, in the region called the perineum.[24] Consider first whichever ones you please, turn outward the woman's, turn inward, so to speak and fold double the man's, and you will find them the same in both in every respect. Then think first, please, of the man's turned in and extending inward between the rectum and the bladder.

If this should happen, the scrotum would necessarily take the place of the uteri, with the testes lying outside, next to it on either side; the penis of the male would become the neck of the cavity that had been formed; and the skin at the end of the penis, now called the prepuce, would become the female pudendum [the vagina] itself. Think too, please of the converse, the uterus turned outward and projecting. Would not the testes [the ovaries] then necessarily be inside it? Would it not contain them like a scrotum? Would not the neck [the cervix], hitherto concealed inside the perineum but now pendent, be made into the male member? And would not the female pudendum, being a skinlike growth upon this neck, be changed into the part called the prepuce? It is also clear that in consequence the position of the arteries, veins, and spermatic vessels [the ductus deferentes and Fallopian tubes] would be changed too. In fact, you could not find a single male part left over that had not simply changed its position; for the parts that are inside in woman are outside in man. You can see something like this in the eyes of the mole, which have vitreous and crystalline humours and the tunics that surround these and grow out from the meninges, as I have said, and they have these just as much as animals do that make use of their eyes. The mole's eyes, however, do not open, nor do they project but are left there imperfect and remain like the eyes of other animals when these are still in the uterus ...

So too the woman is less perfect than the man in respect to the generative parts. For the parts were formed within her when she was still a foetus, but could not because of the defect in the heat emerge and project on the outside, and this, though making the animal itself that was being formed less perfect than one that is complete in all respects, provided no small advantage for the race; for there needs must be a female. Indeed, you ought not to think that our creator would purposely make half the whole race imperfect and, as it were, mutilated, unless there was to be some great advantage in such a mutilation.

Let me tell what this is. The foetus needs abundant material both when it is first constituted and for the entire period of growth that follows. Hence it is obliged to do one of two things; it must either snatch nutriment away from the mother herself or take nutriment that is left over. Snatching it away would be to injure the generant, and taking left-over nutriment would be impossible if the female were perfectly warm; for if she were, she would easily disperse and evaporate it. Accordingly, it was better for the female to be made enough colder so that she cannot disperse all the nutriment which she concocts and elaborates ... This is the reason why the female was made cold, and the immediate consequence of this is the imperfection of the parts, which cannot emerge on the outside on account of the defect in the heat, another very great advantage for the continuance of the race. For, remaining within, that which would have become the scrotum if it had emerged on the outside was made into the substance of the uterus, an instrument fitted to receive and retain the semen and to nourish and perfect the foetus.

Forthwith, of course, the female must have smaller, less perfect testes, and the semen generated in them must be scantier, colder, and wetter (for these things too follow of necessity from the deficient heat). Certainly such semen would be incapable of generating an animal, and, since it too has not been made in vain, I shall explain in the course of my discussion what its use is: the testes of the male are as much larger as he is the warmer animal. The semen generated in them, having received the peak of concoction, becomes the efficient principle of the animal. Thus, from one principle devised by the creator in his wisdom, that principle in accordance with which the female has been made less perfect than the male, have stemmed all these things useful for the generation of the animal: that the parts of the female cannot escape to the outside; that she accumulates an excess of useful nutriment and has imperfect semen and a hollow instrument to receive the perfect semen; that since everything in the male is the opposite [of what it is in the female], the male member has been elongated to be most suitable for coitus and the excretion of semen; and that his semen itself has been made thick, abundant, and warm ...

It is clear that the left testis in the male and the left uterus in the female receive blood still uncleansed, full of residues, watery and serous, and so it happens that the temperaments of the instruments themselves that receive [the blood] become different. For just as pure blood is warmer than blood full of residues, so too the instruments on the right side, nourished with pure blood, become warmer than those on the left ... Moreover, if this has been demonstrated and it has been granted that the male is warmer than the female, it is no longer at all unreasonable to say that the parts on the right produce males and those on the left, females. In fact, that is what Hippocrates meant when he said, 'At puberty, whichever testis appears on the outside, the right, a male, the left, a female.'[25] That is to say, when the generative parts first swell out and the voice becomes rougher and deeper – for this is what puberty is – Hippocrates bids us observe which of the parts is the stronger; for of course, those that swell out first and have a greater growth are the stronger.

352. *Psychological origins of hysteria. Pergamum, 2nd cent. AD (Galen, On Prognosis 6. Tr. A J. Brock. G)*

A rare case history of elegant deductive analysis; that the causes of hysteria are primarily psychological was not rediscovered until the twentieth century.[26]

I was called in to see a woman who was stated to be sleepless at night and to lie tossing about from one position to another. Finding she had no fever, I made a detailed inquiry into everything that had happened to her, especially considering such factors as we know to cause insomnia. But she either answered little or nothing at all, as if to show that it was useless to question her. Finally, she turned away, hiding herself completely by throwing the bedclothes over her whole body, and laying her head on another small pillow, as if desiring sleep.

After leaving I came to the conclusion that she was suffering from one of two things: either from a melancholy dependent on black bile, or else trouble about something she was unwilling to confess. I therefore deferred till the next day a closer investigation of this. Further, on first arriving, I was told by her attendant maid that she could not at present be seen; and on returning a second time, I was told the same again. So I went yet a third time, but the attendant asked me to go away, as she did not want her mistress disturbed. Having learned, however, that when I left she had washed and taken food in her customary manner, I came back the next day and in a private conversation with the maid on one subject and another I found out exactly what was worrying the patient. And this I discovered by chance.

After I had diagnosed that there was no bodily trouble, and that the woman was suffering from some mental uneasiness, it happened that, at the very time I was examining her, this was confirmed. Somebody came from the theatre and said he had seen Pylades dancing. Then both her expression and the colour of her face changed. Seeing this, I applied my hand to her wrist, and noticed that her pulse had suddenly become extremely irregular. This kind of pulse indicates that the mind is disturbed; thus it occurs also in people who are disputing over any subject. So on the next day I said to one of my followers that, when I paid my visit to the woman, he was to come a little later and announce to me, 'Morphus is dancing today.' When he said this, I found that the pulse was unaffected. Similarly also on the next day, when I had an announcement made about the third member of the troupe, the pulse remained unchanged as before. On the fourth evening I kept very careful watch when it was announced that Pylades was dancing, and I noticed that the pulse was very much disturbed. Thus I found out that the woman was in love with Pylades, and by very careful watch on the succeeding days my discovery was confirmed.

Similarly too I diagnosed the case of a slave who administered the household of another wealthy man, and who sickened in the same way. He was concerned about having to give an account of his expenses, in which he knew that there was a considerable sum wanting; the thought of this kept him awake, and he grew thin with anxiety. I first told his master that there was nothing physically wrong with the old man, and advised an investigation to be made as to whether he feared his master was about to ask an account of the sums he had entrusted to him and for this reason was worried, knowing that a considerable amount would be found wanting. The master told me I had made a good suggestion, so in order to make the diagnosis certain I advised him to do as follows: he was to tell the slave to give him back all the money he had in hand, lest, in the event of his sudden death, it should be lost, owing to the administration passing into the hands of some other servant whom he did not know: for there would be no use asking for an account from such a one. And when the master said this to him, he felt sure he would not be questioned. So he ceased to worry, and by the third day had regained his natural physical condition.

Now what was it that escaped the notice of previous physicians when examining the aforesaid woman and the aforesaid slave? For such discoveries are made by common inductions if one has even the smallest acquaintance with medical science. I suppose it is because they have no clear conception of how the body tends to be affected by mental conditions. Possibly also they do not know that the pulse is altered by quarrels and alarms which suddenly disturb the mind.

Aretaeus of Cappadocia

353. *The wandering womb. Cappadocia, 2nd cent.* AD *(Aretaeus, On the Causes and Symptoms of Acute Diseases 2, excerpts. Tr. F. Adams. G)*

Aretaeus of Cappadocia, a contemporary of Galen, accepts the basic Hippocratic doctrines about hysteria but adds dramatic analogy to his account.

In the middle of the flanks of women lies the womb, a female viscus, closely resembling an animal; for it is moved of itself hither and thither in the flanks, also upwards in a direct line to below the cartilage of the thorax, and also obliquely to the right or to the left, either to the liver or spleen; and it likewise is subject to prolapsus downwards, and, in a word, it is altogether erratic. It delights, also, in fragrant smells, and advances towards them; and it has an aversion to fetid smells, and flees from them; and, on the whole, the womb is like an animal within an animal.

When, therefore, it is suddenly carried upwards, and remains above for a considerable time, and violently compresses the intestines, the woman experiences a choking, after the form of epilepsy, but without convulsions. For the liver, diaphragm, lungs and heart are quickly squeezed within a narrow space; and therefore loss of breathing and of speech seems to be present. And, moreover, the carotids are compressed from sympathy with the heart, and hence there is heaviness of head, loss of sensibility, and deep sleep.

And in women there also arises another affection resembling this form, with sense of choking and loss of speech, but not proceeding from the womb; for it also happens to men, in the manner of catalepsy. But those from the uterus are remedied by fetid smells, and the application of fragrant things to the female parts; but in the others these things do no good; and the limbs are moved about in the affection from the womb, but in the other affection not at all. Moreover, voluntary and involuntary tremblings ... but from the application of a pessary to induce abortion, powerful congelation of the womb, the stoppage of a copious haemorrhage, and such like.

If, therefore, upon the womb's being moved upwards, she begins to suffer: there is sluggishness in the performance of her offices, prostration of strength, atony, loss of the faculties of her knees, vertigo (and the limbs sink under her), headache, heaviness of the head, and the woman is pained in the veins on each side of the nose.

But if they fall down they have heartburn ... in the hypochondriac regions; flanks empty, where is the seat of the womb; pulse intermittent, irregular, and failing; strong sense of choking; loss of speech and of sensibility; respiration imperceptible and indistinct; a very sudden and incredible death, for they have nothing deadly in their appearance; in colour like that of life, and for a considerable time after death they are more ruddy than usual; eyes somewhat prominent, bright, not entirely fixed, but yet not very much turned aside.

But if the uterus be removed back to its seat before the affection comes to a conclusion, they escape the suffocation. When the belly rumbles there is moisture about the female parts, respiration thicker and more distinct, a very speedy rousing up from the affection, in like manner as death is very sudden; for as it readily ascends to the higher regions, so it readily recedes. For the uterus is buoyant, but the membranes, its supporters, are humid, and the place is humid in which the uterus lies; and, moreover, it flees from fetid things, and seeks after sweet; wherefore it readily inclines to this side and to that, like a log of wood, and floats upwards and downwards. For this reason the affection occurs in young women, but not in old. For in those in whom the age, mode of life, and understanding is more mobile, the uterus also is of a wandering nature; but in those more advanced in life, the age, mode of living, understanding, and the uterus are of a steady character. Wherefore this suffocation from the womb accompanies females alone.

But the affections common to men happen also to the uterus, such as inflammation and haemorrhage, and they have the common symptoms, namely, fever, asphyxia, coldness, loss of speech. But in haemorrhage the death is even more sudden, being like that of a slaughtered animal.

354. *Inflammation of the womb. Cappadocia, 2nd cent. AD (Aretaeus, Therapeutics of Acute Diseases 2.11, excerpts. Tr. F. Adams. G)*

The uterus in women has membranes extended on both sides at the flanks, and also is subject to the affections of an animal in smelling; for it follows after fragrant things as if for pleasure and flees from fetid things as if for dislike. If, therefore, anything annoys it from above, it protrudes even beyond the genital organs. But if any of these things be applied to the os, it retreats backwards and upwards. Sometimes it will go to this side or to that – to the spleen and liver, while the membranes yield to the distension and contraction like the sails of a ship.

It suffers in this way also from inflammation; and it protrudes more than usual in this affection and in the swelling of its neck; for inflammation of the fundus inclines upwards; but if downwards to the feet, it protrudes externally, a troublesome, painful and unseemly complaint, rendering it difficult to walk, to lie on the side or on the back, unless the woman suffers from inflammation of the feet. But if it mounts upwards, it very speedily suffocates the woman, and stops the respiration as if with a cord, before she feels pain, or can scream aloud, or can call upon the spectators, for in many cases the respiration is first stopped, and in others the speech. It is proper, then, in these cases, to call the physician quickly before the patient dies. Should you fortunately arrive in time and ascertain that it is inflammation, you must open a vein, especially the one at the ankle, and pursue the other means which prove remedial in suffocation without inflammation: ligatures of the hands and feet so tight as to induce torpor; smelling of fetid substances – liquid pitch, hairs and burnt wool, the extinguished flame of a lamp, and castor, since, in addition to its bad smell, it warms the congealed nerves. Old urine greatly rouses the sense of one in a death-like state, and drives the uterus downwards. Wherefore we must apply fragrant things on pessaries to the region of the uterus – any ointment of a mild nature, and not pungent to the touch, nard, or Egyptian bacchar, or the medicine from the leaves of the malabathrum, the Indian tree, or cinnamon pounded with any of the fragrant oils. These articles are to be rubbed into the female parts. And also an injection of these things is to be thrown into the uterus. The anus is to be rubbed with applications which dispel flatus; and injections of things not acrid, but softening, viscid, and lubricant, are to be given to the expulsion of the faeces solely, so that the region of the uterus may be emptied – with the juice of marsh mallow, or of fenugreek, but let melilot or marjoram be boiled along with the oil. But, if the uterus stands in need of support rather than evacuation, the abdomen is to be compressed by the hands of a strong woman, or of an expert man, binding it round also with a roller, when you have replaced the part, so that it may not ascend upwards again. Having produced sneezing, you must compress the nostrils; for by the sneezing and straining, in certain cases, the uterus has returned to its place. We are to blow into the nostrils also some of the root of soapwort, or of pepper, or of castor. We are also to apply the instrument for dry cupping to the thighs, loins, the ischiatic regions, and groins, in order to attract the uterus. And, moreover, we are to apply it to the spine, and between the scapulae, in order to relieve the sense of suffocation. But if the feeling of suffocation be connected with inflammation, we may also scarify the vein leading along the pubes, and abstract plenty of blood ... Should the patient partially recover, she is to be seated in a decoction of aromatics, and fumigated from below with fragrant perfumes. Also before a meal, she is to drink of castor, and a little quantity of the hiera with the castor. And if relieved, she is to bathe, and at the proper season is to return to her accustomed habits; and we must look to the woman that her menstrual discharges flow freely.

Soranus

355. *Menstruation, conception, contraception and abortion. Rome, 1st cent. AD (Soranus, Gynaecology 1.24, 26, 34, 36, 39, 40, 60, 61, 62, 64. Tr. O. Temkin. G)*

Soranus, a Greek from Ephesus in Asia Minor who practised in Rome, approaches his topic with more sympathy and common sense than his colleagues, and, unlike other practitioners, includes in his account of gynaecology all aspects of the female reproductive system, normal as well as abnormal.

Menstruation

(24) One has to infer approaching menstruation from the fact that at the expected time of the period it becomes trying to move and there develops heaviness of the loins, sometimes pain as well, sluggishness, continual yawning, and tension of the limbs, sometimes also a flush of the cheeks which either remains or, having been dispersed, reappears after an interval; and in some cases approaching menstruation must be inferred from the fact that the stomach is prone to nausea and it lacks appetite. Menstruation which is about to occur for the first time must be inferred from the same signs but above all from the growth of the breasts which, broadly, takes place around the fourteenth year, and from the heaviness, irritation and pubescence in the region of the lower abdomen.

(26) In women who have already menstruated often, each must be allowed to do according to her own custom. For some habitually take a rest, while others go on with moderate activities. But it is safer to rest and not to bathe especially on the first day. But in women who are about to menstruate no longer, their time for menstruation having passed, one must take care that the stoppage of the menses does not occur suddenly. For in regard to alteration, even if the body be changed for the better, all abruptness disturbs it through discomfort; for that which is unaccustomed is not tolerated, but is like some unfamiliar malaise. The methods we employ at the approach of the first menstruation must now be marshalled forth during the time when menstruation is about to cease; for that which is able to evoke the as yet absent excretion is even more able to preserve for some time menstruation which is still present. In addition, vaginal suppositories capable of softening and injections which have the [same] effect should be employed, together with all the remedies capable of rendering hardened bodies soft. But if the menstruation is too much for the strength of the patient, or again, if it is impeded by abnormal factors, then there is need for therapeutic measures which we shall elaborate in the section on 'things abnormal'.

Conception

(34) One must judge the majority from the ages of 15 to 40 to be fit for conception, if they are not mannish, compact, and oversturdy, or too flabby and very moist. Since the uterus is similar to the whole [body], it will in these cases either be unable, on account of its pronounced hardness, easily to accept the attachment of the seed, or by reason of its extreme laxity and atony [let it fall again]. Furthermore they seem fit if their uteri are neither very moist or dry, nor too lax or constricted, and if

they have their catharsis regularly, not through some moisture or ichors of various kinds, but through blood and of this neither too much nor, on the other hand, extremely little. Also those in whom the orifice of the uterus is comparatively far forward and lies in a straight line (for an orifice deviated even in its natural state and lying farther back in the vagina, is less suited for the attraction and acceptance of the seed).

(36) The best time for fruitful intercourse is when menstruation is ending and abating, when urge and appetite for coitus are present, when the body is neither in want nor too congested and heavy from drunkenness and indigestion, and after the body has been rubbed down and a little food been eaten and when a pleasant state exists in every respect. 'When menstruation is ending and abating,' for the time before menstruation is not suitable, the uterus already being overburdened and in an unresponsive state because of the ingress of material and incapable of carrying on two motions contrary to each other, one for the excretion of material, the other for receiving.

(39) (2) In order that the offspring may not be rendered misshapen, women must be sober during coitus because in drunkenness the soul becomes the victim of strange fantasies; this, furthermore, because the offspring bears some resemblance to the mother as well not only in body but in soul ...

(40) (3) Together with these points it has already been stated that the best time is after a rubdown has been given and a little food been eaten. The food will give the inner turbulence an impetus towards coitus, the urge for intercourse not being diverted by appetite for food; while the rubdown will make it possible to lay hold of the injected seed more readily. For just as the rubdown naturally aids the distribution of food, it helps also in the reception and retention of the seed, yesterday's superfluities, as one may say, being unloaded, and the body thoroughly cleansed and in a sound state for its natural processes. Consequently, as the farmer sows only after having first cleansed the soil and removed any foreign material, in the same manner we too advise that insemination for the production of man should follow after the body has first been given a rubdown.

Contraception
(60) A contraceptive differs from an abortive, for the first does not let conception take place, while the latter destroys what has been conceived ... And an expulsive some people say is synonymous with an abortive; others, however, say that there is a difference because an expulsive does not mean drugs but shaking and leaping ... For this reason they say that Hippocrates, although prohibiting abortives, yet in his book *On the Nature of the Child* employs leaping with the heels to the buttocks for the sake of expulsion.[27] But a controversy has arisen. For one party banishes abortives, citing the testimony of Hippocrates who says: 'I will give to no

one an abortive'; moreover, because it is the specific task of medicine to guard and preserve what has been engendered by nature. The other party prescribes abortives, but with discrimination, that is, they do not prescribe them when a person wishes to destroy the embryo because of adultery or out of consideration for youthful beauty; but only to prevent subsequent danger in parturition if the uterus is small and not capable of accommodating the complete development, or if the uterus at its orifice has knobbly swelling and fissures, or if some similar difficulty is involved. And they say the same about contraceptives as well, and we too agree with them. And since it is safer to prevent conception from taking place than to destroy the foetus, we shall now first discourse upon such prevention.

(61) For if it is much more advantageous not to conceive than to destroy the embryo, one must consequently beware of having sexual intercourse at those periods which we said were suitable for conception. And during the sexual act, at the critical moment of coitus when the man is about to discharge the seed, the woman must hold her breath and draw herself away a little, so that the seed may not be hurled too deep into the cavity of the uterus. And getting up immediately and squatting down, she should induce sneezing and carefully wipe the vagina all round; she might even drink something cold. It also aids in preventing conception to smear the orifice of the uterus all over before with old olive oil or honey or cedar resin or juice of the balsam tree, alone or together with white lead; or with a moist cerate containing myrtle oil and white lead; or before the act with moist alum, or with galbanum together with wine; or to put a lock of fine wool into the orifice of the uterus; or, before sexual relations to use vaginal suppositories which have the power to contract and to condense. For such of these things as are styptic, clogging and cooling cause the orifice of the uterus to shut before the time of coitus and do not let the seed pass into its fundus. [Such, however, as are hot] and irritating not only do not allow the seed of the man to remain in the cavity of the uterus, but draw forth as well another fluid from it.

(62) And we shall make specific mention of some. Pine bark, tanning sumach, equal quantities of each, rub with wine and apply in due measure before coitus after wool has been wrapped around; and after two or three hours she may remove it and have intercourse. Another: Of Cimolian earth, root of panax, equal quantities, rub with water separately and together, and when sticky apply in like manner. Or: Grind the inside of fresh pomegranate peel with water, and apply. Or: Grind two parts of pomegranate peel and one part of oak galls, form small suppositories and insert after the cessation of menstruation. Or: Moist alum, the inside of pomegranate rind, mix with water, and apply with wool. Or: Of unripe oak galls, of the inside of pomegranate peel, of ginger, of each 2 drachms, mould it with wine to the size of vetch peas and dry indoors and give before coitus, to be applied as a vaginal suppository. Or:

Grind the flesh of dried figs and apply together with natron. Or: Apply pomegranate peel with an equal amount of gum and an equal amount of oil of roses. Then one should always follow with a drink of honey water. But one should beware of things which are very pungent, because of the ulcerations arising from them. And we use all these things after the end of menstruation ...

Abortion

(64) In order that the embryo be separated, the woman should have [more violent exercise], walking about energetically and being shaken by means of draught animals; she should also leap energetically and carry things which are heavy beyond her strength. She should use diuretic decoctions which also have the power to bring on menstruation, and empty and purge the abdomen with relatively pungent clysters; sometimes using warm and sweet olive oil as injections, sometimes anointing the whole body thoroughly therewith and rubbing it vigorously, especially around the pubes, the abdomen, and the loins, bathing daily in sweet water which is not too hot, lingering in the baths and drinking first a little wine and living on pungent food. If this is without effect, one must also treat locally by having her sit in a bath of a decoction of linseed, fenugreek, mallow, marsh mallow, and wormwood. She must also use poultices of the same substances and have injections of old oil, alone or together with rue juice or maybe with honey, or of iris oil, or of absinthium together with honey, or of panax balm or else of spelt together with rue and honey, or of Syrian unguent. And if the situation remains the same she must no longer apply the common poultices, but those made of meal of lupins together with ox bile and absinthium, [and she must use] plasters of a similar kind.

(65) For a woman who intends to have an abortion, it is necessary for two or even three days beforehand to take protracted baths, little food and to use softening vaginal suppositories; also to abstain from wine; then to be bled and a relatively great quantity taken away. For the dictum of Hippocrates in the Aphorisms, even if not true in a case of constriction, is yet true of a healthy woman: 'A pregnant woman if bled, miscarries.' For just as sweat, urine or faeces are excreted if the parts containing these substances slacken very much, so the foetus falls out after the uterus dilates. Following the venesection one must shake her by means of draught animals (for now the shaking is more effective on the parts which previously have been relaxed) and one must use softening vaginal suppositories. But if a woman reacts unfavourably to venesection and is languid, one must first relax the parts by means of hip-baths, full baths, softening vaginal suppositories, by keeping her on water and limited food, and by means of aperients and the application of a softening clyster; afterwards one must apply an abortive vaginal suppository. Of the latter one should choose those which are not too pungent, that they

may not cause too great a sympathetic reaction and heat. And of the more gentle ones there exist for instance: Of myrtle, wallflower seed, bitter lupins equal quantities, by means of water, mould troches the size of a bean. Or: Of rue leaves 3 drachms, of myrtle 2 drachms and the same of sweet bay, mix with wine in the same way, and give her a drink. Another vaginal suppository which produces abortion with relatively little danger: Of wallflower, cardamom, brimstone, absinthium, myrrh, equal quantities, mould with water. And she who intends to apply these things should be bathed beforehand or made to relax by hip-baths; and if after some time she brings forth nothing, she should again be relaxed by hip-baths and for the second time a suppository should be applied. In addition, many different things have been mentioned by others; one must, however, beware of things that are too powerful and of separating the embryo by means of something sharp-edged, for danger arises that some of the adjacent parts be wounded. After the abortion one must treat as for inflammation.

356. *Childbirth: instructions for the midwife. Rome, 1st cent.* AD *(Soranus, Gynaecology 1.67-9, excerpts. G and L)*

For normal childbirth have the following ready: oil for injections and cleansing, hot water in order to wash the affected area, hot compresses to relieve the labour pains, sponges for sponging off; wool for covering the woman's body, and bandages to swaddle the baby in, a pillow so that the infant may be placed on it below the mother until the afterbirth has been taken away; scents, such as pennyroyal, sparganium, barley groats and quince, and if in season citron, or melon and anything similar to these, for the recovery of the mother's strength; a birthing stool so that the mother may be arranged on it ... a wide space in a crescent shape must be cut out in it [of a size appropriate] ... to prevent the woman from being pulled down beyond her thighs because the opening is too great, and on the contrary to prevent her from having her vagina pressured by its being too narrow (which is a greater problem); ... two couches, the one made up with soft coverings for rest after giving birth, the other hard for lying down on between labour pains ... When the mouth of the womb is open, and the midwife has washed her hands with hot oil, she should put in her forefinger (with the nail cut) of her left hand, and by gently drawing it arrange the opening so that the accessible part of the amniotic sac falls forward, and with her right hand she should apply oil to the area ... When the amniotic sac takes the size of an egg beneath the mouth of the womb, if the mother is weak and tense, one must deliver her while she is lying down there because this method is less disturbing and frightening ... Three women should stay ready who are able gently to calm the fears of the woman who is giving birth, even if they do not happen to have experience in childbirth. Two should stand on the sides, and one behind her so that the mother does not lean sideways because of the pain. If no birthing stool is available the same arrangement can be made if she sits on a woman's lap ... Finally the midwife, with her dress belted up high in an orderly way should sit down below, beneath and opposite the mother.

The midwife should then sit holding her thighs apart and with her left thigh leaning to support her left hand, in front of the mother as previously specified ... Then it is good for the midwife to be able to see the face of the mother, so she can calm her fears and assure her that there is nothing to worry about and that the childbirth is going well ... The midwife should guard against holding her face towards the mother's lap, lest she in modesty pull her body up; instead she should circle round the mouth of the womb with her finger ... [28] She should order the other woman who is holding her from behind to hold the mother's anus with a linen cloth, lest it be pushed out with her straining. If indeed the amniotic sac remains unbroken for a long time, she should break it with her fingernails and put her fingers in it and little by little open it wider. She should take care that the infant not fall out at once ... the helpers standing on the side, without shaking her and with open hands should bring the uterus downwards. When the infant tries to come out, the midwife should have a cloth in her hands to pick him up.

357. *Treatment for hysterical suffocation. Cappadocia, 2nd cent. AD (Soranus, Gynaecology 3.26, 28, 29. Tr. O. Temkin. G)*

Unlike some of his medical colleagues, Soranus did not believe in the theory of the wandering womb; he prescribes instead reassuring attention and physical therapy with soothing medicaments.

(26) Hysterical suffocation has been named after both the affected organ and one symptom, viz. suffocation. But its connotation is: obstructed respiration together with aphonia and a seizure of the senses caused by some condition of the uterus. In most cases the disease is preceded by recurrent miscarriages, premature birth, long widowhood, retention of menses and the end of ordinary childbearing or inflation of the uterus. When an attack occurs, sufferers from the disease collapse, show aphonia, laboured breathing, a seizure of the senses, clenching of the teeth, stridor, convulsive contraction of the extremities (but sometimes only weakness), upper abdominal distention, retraction of the uterus, swelling of the thorax, bulging of the network of vessels of the face. The whole body is cool, covered with perspiration, the pulse stops or is very small. In the majority of cases they recover quickly from the collapse and usually recall what has happened; head and tendons ache and sometimes they are even deranged ...

(28) [The disease] is of the constricted and violent class and exists both in an acute and chronic form; therefore the treatment must be suitable to

these characteristics. During the initial stage one should lay the patient down in a room which is moderately warm and bright and, without hurting her, rouse her from the collapsed state by moving the jaw, placing warm compresses all over the middle of her body, gently straightening out all the cramped parts, restraining each extremity, and warming all the cool parts by the touch of [the] bare hands. Then one should wash the face with a sponge soaked in warm water, for sponging the face has a vitalising effect. If, however, the state of aphonia persists, we also use dry cupping over the groin, pubes and the neighbouring regions; then we put on covers of soft clean wool. We also moisten these parts freely with sweet olive oil, keeping it up for some time, and swathe each extremity in wool (for this conducts the relaxation from the extremities towards the centre). Then we instil warm water into the opened jaws, and afterwards honey water too, and prescribe movement in a hammock. When the initial stage has ended we bleed, provided that weakness does not prevent it, or it is not long since food was given. Afterwards we give an injection of warm, sweet olive oil, moisten the parts, offer warm water as a mouthwash and drink, and make her abstain from food until the third day. On this day we first rub the patient down and afterwards we offer gruel-like food and give this from now on, every second day, until the dangerous condition regarding the uterus has safely subsided. [But every day] we use poultices like those prescribed for women who suffer from painful menstruation and apply hot sponge baths and relaxing hip-baths, the material for which we have mentioned above, and suppositories made of fat, marrow, fenugreek, mallow, and oil of lilies or henna oil, and injections by means of a clyster of olive oil or oil mixed with water, particularly if faeces are retained (for the excrement bruises the adjacent uterus). When the condition has abated we make use of wax salves and suppositories of a relatively high emollient power, then we give varied food, later on a bath, and finally wine.

(29) But the majority of the ancients and almost all followers of the other sects have made use of ill-smelling odours (such as burnt hair, extinguished lamp wicks, charred deer's horn, burnt wool, burnt flock, skins and rags, castoreum with which they anoint the nose and ears, pitch, cedar resin, bitumen, squashed bedbugs, and all substances which are supposed to have an oppressive smell) in the opinion that the uterus flees from evil smells. Wherefore they have also fumigated with fragrant substances from below, and have approved of suppositories of spikenard and storax, so that the uterus fleeing the first-mentioned odours, but pursuing the last-mentioned, might move from the upper to the lower parts. Besides, Hippocrates[29] made some of his patients drink a decoction of cabbage, others asses' milk; and he, believing that the uterus is twisted as the intestines are in intestinal obstruction, inserted a small pipe and blew air into the vagina by means of a blacksmith's bellow, thus causing dilation. Diocles, however, in the third book *On Gynaecology*, pinches the

nostrils, but opens the mouth and applies a sternutative; moreover, with the hand he pushes the uterus towards the lower parts by pressing upon the hypochondriac region; and applies warm fomentations to the legs. Mantias gives castoreum and bitumen in wine to drink, and if the arousal is imminent he orders playing on the flute and drumming. Xenophon proposes torchlight and prescribes the making of greater noise by whetting and beating metal plates. And Asclepiades[30] applies a sternutative, constricts the hypochondriac region with bandages and strings of gut, shouts loudly, blows vinegar into the nose, allows sexual intercourse during remissions, drinking of water [and pouring cold water over the head]. We, however, censure all these men who start by hurting the inflamed parts and cause torpor by the effluvia of ill-smelling substances. For the uterus does not issue forth like a wild animal from the lair, delighted by fragrant odours and fleeing bad odours; rather it is drawn together because of the stricture caused by the inflammation. Also upsetting the stomach, which suffers from sympathetic inflammation, with toxic and pungent potions makes trouble. Forcing air by means of the smith's bellows into the vagina – this inflation makes the uterus even more tense, which is already rendered sufficiently tense by reason of the inflammation. Moreover, the use of sternutatives, through their shaking effects and the pungency of the drugs, produces a metasyncrisis in chronic conditions, thus aggravating the condition of the patient who during the initial stage needs not force but gentleness. Sounds and the noise of metal plates have an overpowering effect and irritate those who are made sensitive by inflammation. At any rate, even many healthy persons have been given headaches by such sounds. Vinegar blown in is also harmful, for just as external inflammations, so internal inflammations are increased by every astringent. Furthermore, it is injurious to constrict externally with strings or bandages the inflamed uterus which cannot even bear a poultice without feeling it burdensome, because of the intensification caused by the pressure. And drinking of water is not only not helpful but sometimes even noxious, since the patient needs strengthening, not metasyncrisis; moreover, metasyncrisis is produced again by switching to diluted wine. Intercourse causes atony in everybody and is therefore not appropriate; for without giving any advantage it affects the body adversely by making it atonic. Pouring cold water over the head in order to stop aphonia is obviously a technical mistake. For if the body is rendered dense by the cold, the arousal necessarily becomes more difficult to accomplish on account of the increased inflammation.

Writings on medical matters by laymen
'When the foetus is male, the mother has an easier delivery'

358. *The women of Miletus (a traditional story) (Plutarch, The Bravery of Women 11, Moralia 249b-d. 2nd cent. AD. G)*

One time the young women of Miletus were afflicted by a dreadful and irrational trouble, of uncertain origin. It was suggested that the atmosphere had become polluted with an ecstatic concoction and poisonous character and so caused them to lose control of their senses. For suddenly all of them were seized with a desire to commit suicide, and there was an insane rush to hang themselves, and many managed to hang themselves before they could be stopped.[31] Neither their parents' arguments nor tears nor their friends' advice got through to them, but they got round every plot and trick their watchers could devise in order to destroy themselves. The affliction appeared to have been sent by some god, and to be more than human ability could handle, until the time when a sensible man proposed an ordinance that the women who hanged themselves must be carried naked through the market-place in their funeral procession. This ordinance, once approved, not only prevented, but completely stopped the young women from hanging themselves. Precaution against ill repute is a clear indication of goodness and virtue, and the women who were not afraid of the most dreadful of all possibilities, death and suffering, could not bring themselves to bear the thought of the disgrace that would come to them after their deaths.

359. *Pregnancy. Rome, 1st cent. AD (Pliny the Elder, Natural History 7.38-43, 48-49. L)*

While pursuing the public career of a Roman knight, which culminated in command of the fleet at Misenum, Pliny wrote on many and varied subjects. His only surviving work, the *Natural History*, consists of thirty-six books on the arts and sciences. Pliny casts a wide net in gathering his scientific 'facts'. Here he draws heavily on Aristotle, adding his own examples for his Roman readership.

(38) Other animals have set times for mating and bearing young. Man, on the other hand, is born any time of year and after a variable gestation period – sometimes seven months, sometimes eight and sometimes it goes to the beginning of the eleventh month. Before the seventh month, the pregnancy is never viable. In the seventh month are born only those babies conceived on the day before or day after the full moon, or during the new moon. (39) In Egypt it is common for babies to be born in the eighth month, in Italy too such births are viable, contrary to the opinions of our ancestors.[32] Gestation periods vary greatly. Vistilia, wife of Glitius

and then of Pomponius and Orfitius, all distinguished citizens, gave birth four times by them always in the seventh month, then gave birth to Suillius Rufus in the eleventh month and Corbulo in the seventh – both of them later consuls – then Caesonia, wife of the Emperor Gaius (Caligula) in the eighth. (40) Eighth-month babies are in danger until the fortieth day of life, while for the mothers the fourth and eighth month are riskiest, and an abortion in those months lethal. Masurius[33] writes that Lucius Papirius as praetor in a suit brought by a secondary heir found against him, since the mother said she had been pregnant for 13 months and no fixed gestation period had been established.

(41) At the tenth day after conception begin headaches, dizziness, and darkened visions, nausea are the signs that a human being has begun to form. When the foetus is male, the mother has a better colour and an easier delivery; the foetus begins to move in the uterus on the fortieth day. Everything is the opposite with the other sex. The weight is unbearable. The legs and groin are slightly swollen. The foetus first moves after ninety days. (42) But for both sexes, the greatest weakness occurs when the foetus begins to grow hair and when the moon is full, which is a very bad time for babies already born too. The way in which the mother-to-be walks and every little detail are of utmost importance. If a woman eats food that is too salty, the baby will be born without nails. Breathing makes delivery more difficult.[34] Yawning can be lethal during delivery, just as sneezing after intercourse can cause abortion.[35]

(43) It makes one feel pity and shame at how precarious are the beginnings of the proudest of animals, if the smell of a freshly extinguished lamp really can cause abortion. ...

(48) With the exception of women, few other animals mate during pregnancy, and only one or two other species have superfoetation.[36] It is found in writings of physicians and other experts that twelve foetuses were expelled in a single abortion. (49) But when the interval between conceptions is brief, both are carried to term. This was the case of Hercules and Iphicles,[37] and of a women who bore twins, one resembling her husband, the other her adulterous lover. Then there was a maid in Proconnesus[38] who had intercourse twice in one day and bore twins, one of whom resembled her master, the other his steward. Finally, there are the examples of two women one of whom bore one child after the normal time and produced a fifth-month baby at the same time, while the other had a baby at seven months and some months later had twins.

360. *Treatments for diseases of the womb. Rome, 1st cent.* AD *(Celsus, On Medicine 4.27; 5.21. L)*

Celsus, an encyclopaedist and not a physician, attempted to put diverse Hippocratic ideas into decorous and precise Latin.[39]

(4.27) From the womb a violent illness arises and after the stomach it is the part that most afflicts the body and that in turn most affects it. Sometimes it so knocks the wind out of the woman that she is prostrated, as with epilepsy. But this case differs in that the eyes do not roll, nor is there frothing at the mouth nor nerve spasms but only stupor. In some women it recurs frequently and never goes away. Bleeding her, if she is strong enough, is helpful. If she is weak, nevertheless, cupping should be done at the groin. If she lies down for a long time or habitually did so at other times, hold an extinguished lamp wick up to her nose[40] or one of the other things I have listed as being particularly foul-smelling, to stimulate the woman. Pouring cold water over her is effective too. Rue chopped up in honey helps, or wax-salve of cyprus oil or some sort of hot, moist compresses held to the pubic region. The hips and knees should be rubbed at the same time. Then, when she has come to, she should be cut off from wine for a year, even if she does not have a relapse. She should have a daily rub-down of the whole body but especially the abdomen and knees. She should be given food of the middle category;[41] mustard should be rubbed on the stomach every three or four days until the skin gets red. If induration remains, a handy emollient seems to be bitter-sweet dissolved in milk, then minced and mixed with white wax and deer marrow in iris oil, or beef or goat suet mixed with rose oil. She should be given a drink of castory or git[42] or dill. If the womb is not quite clean, it should be purged with a squared reed. If it is actually ulcerated, make a wax salve with rose oil mixed with fresh pork fat and eggwhite and apply it; or eggwhite mixed with rose oil with chopped roses in powder. When there is pain, the womb should be fumigated underneath with sulphur. If the menstrual flow is too heavy and doing harm, the remedy is cupping and scarifying at the groin and under the breasts. If it is too weak, these medications will stimulate the flow of blood: costmary, pennyroyal, white violet, parsley, catmint and savoury and hyssop. A suitable diet would include: leeks, rue, cummin, onion, mustard and other sharp-tasting vegetables. If the blood that usually comes out down below should appear from the nose, the groin should be scarified and cupped every thirty days for three or four months. If you still see no blood, you may know she has pain in her head. Then let blood from the arm and she'll be fine right away.

(5.21) ... But other compositions are useful, such as those used on women below: the Greeks call them *pessoi*.[43] They have this property: they are absorbed into soft wool and the wool is inserted into the genitals.

To induce menstruation, use two Caunean figs mixed with 2/3 denarius[44] of soda; or garlic seeds ground with a little myrrh and mixed with an ointment of lilies; or the inner part of wild cucumber mixed with mother's milk.

To soften the womb, mix eggyolk and fenugreek and rose oil and saffron. Or 1/6 denarius each of elaterium and salt, and 6 denarii of black bryony berries mixed with honey.

The Boethus pessary is a mixture of 4 denarii each of saffron and turpentine resin, 1/3 denarius of myrrh, 1 denarius of rose-oil, 1 1/6 denarii of veal suet, and 2 denarii of wax.

But Numenius' concoction is best against inflammations of the womb; it is made of 1/4 denarius of saffron, 1 denarius of wax, 8 denarii of butter, 12 denarii of goose-fat, 2 boiled eggyolks, and less than 1 cyathus of rose-oil.[45]

To facilitate expulsion of a dead foetus, use pomegranate rind rubbed in water.

If a woman has fits as a result of disease of the genitals, burn snails with their shells, pound them together and add honey.

If a woman does not conceive, soften lion's fat with rose-oil.

361. *The dangers of sharing a bath with women (Plutarch, Fr. 97. 2nd cent. AD. G)*

Men should not cleanse their skin in the women's bath. Men must not be naked together with women. In addition to the indecency, certain effluvia issue from women's bodies and excretions which are defiling when absorbed by men: anyone who enters the same air or water partakes of them.

362. *Side effects of menstruation. Rome, 1st cent. AD (Pliny the Elder, Natural History 28.23, excerpts. L)*

A sampling of the phenomena recorded by Pliny caused by menstrual fluid and menstruating women.

Terrible things are told about the monstrous power of menses, whose magic I have already discussed,[46] of which I can repeat the following without embarrassment: if the female force begins to flow in a solar or lunar eclipse the harm will be irremediable, even if there is no moon, and sexual intercourse is pestiferous or fatal to the man; purple is contaminated by menstruating women, so much the greater is their force. But at other times during the menstrual period, if the women walk naked through a field, worms, beetles, and other pests fall down. Metrodorus of Scepsis says that this was discovered in Cappadocia during an infestation of cantharid beetles,[47] so women walk through the fields with their dresses hiked up above their buttocks.

Case histories from inscriptions
'I die in pain, escaping the pangs of childbirth'

363. *Epitaph for a woman who died while pregnant. Egypt, 2nd/1st cent.* BC *(Peek 1233. G)*

Dosithea, daughter of —— . Look at these letters on the polished rock. Thallo's son Chaeremon married me in his great house. I die in pain, escaping the pangs of childbirth, leaving the breath of life when I was 25 years old; from a disease which he died of before, I succumbed after. I lie here in Schedia. Wayfarers, as you go by, all of you, say: 'Beloved Dosithea, stay well, also among the dead.'

364. *Malpractice. Rome (CIL VI.25580 = CLE 94. L)*

Here lies Ephesia Rufria, a good wife, a good mother, who died of a malignant fever which outlasted the doctors' expectations. This is a consolation nor is the story of the alleged crime true: I think a woman so sweet died because she was thought more worthy of the company of the gods.

365. *Death in childbirth. Ain Kebira, Mauretania, Imperial period (CIL VIII, Suppl. 20288 = CLE 1834. L)*

Sacred to the gods of the dead.
  Rusticeia Matrona lived 25 years.
  The cause of my death was childbirth and malignant fate.
  But stop crying, beloved spouse, and take care of our son with love. For my spirit is now with the stars in the heavens.
  … to his well-deserving wife.

366. *Death in childbirth. Roman Carthage, Imperial period (CIL VIII.24734 = CLE 2115. L)*

Daphne, bride of Hermes, I've been freed; even though the master wanted to free Hermes first. Fate made me first, fate took me first. All that I bore, the tears I so often shed I leave to my husband, since I just had a baby, though the master did not want me to. Now who will feed him? Who will take care of him for the rest of his life? The Styx snatched me away to the gods.
  She lived a pious woman for 25 years. Here she lies.

367. *Taking the cure. Ischia, 1st cent.* AD *(CIL X.6787. L)*

A votive inscription found near the fountain known as Nitrodi, on the island of Ischia, in the Bay of Naples. The fountain, and the waters and mud of the island as a whole, were believed in antiquity, and are still today, to have therapeutic properties. Argenne evidently was cured of something, but we don't know what.

Argenne, freedwoman of the empress Poppaea, made a votive offering to Apollo and the Nymphs.

368. *Socratea. Paros, 2nd century AD (Kaibel 218 = Peek 1871. G)*

... Nicander was my father, my country was Paros, and my name Socratea. My husband Parmenion buried me when I died, granting me that favour so that my good conduct in life might be remembered also by future generations.

The cruel Fury of the newborn,[48] implacable, with a haemorrhage took me from my happy life. In my third decade of life I reached the sixth year. I left my husband male offspring: two for my father and for my spouse; for myself, because of the third, I got this grave.

Female medical practitioners
'Her experience in the healing art'

Physicians

369. *Antiochis. Tlos, Lycia, 1st cent. AD (Pleket 12. G)*

Antiochis, daughter of Diodotus of Tlos, awarded special recognition by the council and the people of Tlos for her experience in the healing art, has set up this statue of herself.

370. *Primilla. Rome, 1st/2nd cent. AD (CIL VI.7581 = ILS 7804. L)*

To my holy goddess. To Primilla, a physician, daughter of Lucius Vibius Melito. She lived 44 years, of which 30 she spent with Lucius Cocceius Apthorus without a quarrel. Apthorus built this monument for his best, chaste wife and for himself.

371. *Terentia Prima. Rome, 1st/2nd cent. AD (CIL VI.9619. L)*

To Terentia Nice, freedwoman of Terentia Prima the physician. Mussius Antiochus and Mussia Dionysia, her children, put this up for their well-deserving mother.

372. *Four doctors. Rome, 1st/2nd cent.* AD *(CIL VI.9614, 9615, 9617, 6851. L)*

(9614) Julia Pye, a doctor.
(9615) Minucia Asste, a doctor, freedwoman of Gaia.[49]
(9617) Venuleia Sosis, a doctor, freedwoman of Gaia.
(6851) Melitine, a doctor, [slave] of Appuleius.

373. *Panthia. Pergamum, 2nd cent.* AD *(Pleket 20. G)*

Farewell, lady Panthia, from your husband. After your departure, I keep up my lasting grief for your cruel death. Hera, goddess of marriage, never saw such a wife: your beauty, your wisdom, your chastity. You bore me children completely like myself; you cared for your bridegroom and your children; you guided straight the rudder of life in our home and raised high our common fame in healing – though you were a woman you were not behind me in skill. In recognition of this your bridegroom Glycon built this tomb for you. I also buried here the body of [my father] immortal Philadelphus, and I myself will lie here when I die, since with you alone I shared my bed when I was alive, so may I cover myself in ground that we share.[50]

374. *Domnina. Neoclaudopolis, Asia, 2nd/3rd cent.* AD *(Pleket 26. G)*

You rush off to be with the gods, Domnina, and forget your husband. You have raised your body to the heavenly stars. Men will say that you have not died but that the gods stole you away because you saved your native fatherland from disease. Goodbye, and rejoice in the Elysian fields. But you have left pain and eternal lamentations behind for your loved ones.

Midwives

375. *Qualities and training. Rome, 2nd cent.* AD *(Soranus, Gynaecology 1.3-4, abridged. Tr. O. Temkin. G)*

A unique account of the elaborate professional skill involved in an exclusively female occupation.

(3) ... A suitable person ... must be literate in order to be able to comprehend the art through theory too: she must have her wits about her so that she may easily follow what is said and what is happening: she must have a good memory to retain the imparted instructions (for knowledge arises from memory of what has been grasped). She must love work in order to persevere through all vicissitudes (for a woman who wishes to acquire such vast knowledge needs manly patience). She must

be respectable since people will have to trust their household and the secrets of their lives to her and because to women of bad character the semblance of medical instruction is a cover for evil scheming. She must not be handicapped as regards her senses since there are things which she must see, answers which she must hear when questioning, and objects which she must grasp by her sense of touch. She needs sound limbs so as not to be handicapped in the performance of her work and she must be robust, for she takes a double task upon herself during the hardship of her professional visits. Long and slim fingers and short nails are necessary to touch a deep-lying inflammation without causing too much pain. This skill, however, can also be acquired through zealous endeavour and practice in her work ...

(4) ... We call a person the best midwife if she is trained in all branches of therapy (for some cases must be treated by diet, others by surgery, while still others must be cured by drugs); if she is moreover able to prescribe hygienic regulations for her patients, to observe the general and the individual features of the case, and from this to find out what is expedient, not from the causes or from the repeated observations of what usually occurs or something of the kind. Now to go into detail: she will not change her methods when the symptoms change, but will give her advice in accordance with the course of the disease: she will be unperturbed, unafraid in danger, able to state clearly the reasons for her measures, she will bring reassurance to her patients, and be sympathetic. And it is not absolutely essential for her to have borne children, as some people contend, in order that she may sympathise with the mother, because of her experience with pain; for [to have sympathy] is not more characteristic of a person who has given birth to a child. She must be robust on account of her duties but not necessarily young as some people maintain, for sometimes young persons are weak whereas on the contrary older persons may be robust. She will be well disciplined and always sober, since it is uncertain when she may be summoned to those in danger. She will have a quiet disposition, for she will have to share many secrets of life. She must not be greedy for money, lest she give an abortive wickedly for payment; she will be free from superstition so as not to overlook salutary measures on account of a dream or omen or some customary rite or vulgar superstition. She must also keep her hands soft, abstaining from such wool-working as may make them hard, and she must acquire softness by means of ointments if it is not present naturally. Such persons will be the best midwives.

376. *A midwife and physician. Athens, 4th cent. BC (Kaibel 45 = Pleket 1. G)*

The memorial tablet represents two women, one seated, one standing, surrounded by infants of both sexes.

Phanostrate, a midwife and physician,[51] lies here. She caused pain to none, and all lamented her death.

377. *Epitaphs of midwives. Rome, 1st/2nd cent. AD (CIL VI.6325, 6647, 8192, 9720, 9721, 9722, 9723. L)*

The nomenclature and status-indications of midwives in the inscriptions suggest that they began their careers in slavery, but continued to practise, and to own slaves themselves, after receiving their freedom. Some of the stones were dedicated by the midwives' slaves.

(6325) Secunda, the midwife, [slave] of Statilia the Elder.

(6647) To Hygia [goddess of health]. [The tomb] of Flavia Sabina, midwife. She lived 30 years. Marius Orthrus and Apollonius [put this up] to [Apollonius'] dearest wife.

(8192) Quintus Sallustius Dioges, freedman of Dioga. Sallustia Athenais, midwife, freedwoman of Artemidorus.

(9720) To Claudia Trophima, midwife. Titus Cassius Trophimus, her son, to his most gentle mother, and Tiberius Cassius Trophimianus to his grandmother, and to their descendants, [put this up]. She lived 75 years and 5 months.

(9721) Gaius Grattius Plocamus, freedman of Hilara, the midwife from the Esquiline Hill.

(9722) To the gods of the dead. To Julia Veneria, the midwife, well-deserving. Julius He... put this up.

(9723) Poblicia Aphe, midwife, freedwoman of Gaia.[52] May your bones rest peacefully. She lived 21 years.

378. *Epitaph of a midwife. Puteoli, 2nd cent. AD (CIL X.1933. L)*

To the gods of the dead. To Coelia Hagne, midwife. Marcus Ulpius Zosimus (put this up) to his most holy wife.

Wet-nurses

These texts address principally the medical aspects of nursing. For the social aspects, see above nos. 250-3.

379. *A nurse. Athens, after 350 BC (CEG 571 = IG II².7873. G)*

[Epitaph for] Apollodorus the immigrant's[53] daughter, Melitta, a nurse.[54] Here the earth covers Hippostrate's good nurse; and Hippostrate still misses you. 'I loved you while you were alive, nurse, I love you still now even beneath the earth and now I shall honour you as long as I live. I know that for you beneath the earth also, if there is reward for the good, honours will come first to you, in the realm of Persephone and of Pluto.'

380. *Advice on hiring a wet-nurse. Rome, 1st cent.* AD *(Soranus, Gynaecology 2.18-20. Tr. O. Temkin. G)*

A physician's advice; as in the pseudo-Pythagorean treatise on this subject, the nurse is thought to pass her character on with her milk.

(18) ... To be sure, other things being equal, it is better to feed the child with maternal milk, for this is more suited to it, and the mothers become more sympathetic towards the offspring, and it is more natural to be fed from the mother after parturition just as before parturition. But if anything prevents it one must choose the best wet-nurse, lest the mother grows prematurely old, having spent herself through the daily suckling.[55] ...

(19) One should choose a wet-nurse not younger than twenty nor older than forty years, who has already given birth twice or thrice, who is healthy, of good constitution, of large frame, and of a good colour. Her breasts should be of medium size, lax, soft and unwrinkled, the nipples neither big nor too small and neither too compact nor too porous and discharging milk overabundantly. She should be self-controlled, sympathetic and not ill-tempered, a Greek, and tidy. And for each of these points the reasons are as follows:

She should be in her prime because younger women are ignorant in the rearing of children and their minds are still somewhat careless and childish; while older ones yield a more watery milk because of the atony of the body. In women in their prime, however, every natural function is at its highest. She should already have given birth twice or thrice, because women with their first child are as yet unpractised in the rearing of children and have breasts whose structure is still infantile, small and too compact; while those who have delivered often have nursed children often and, being wrinkled, produce thick milk which is not at its best.

[She should be healthy because healthful] and nourishing milk comes from a healthy body, unwholesome and worthless milk from a sickly one; just as water which flows through worthless soil is itself rendered worthless, spoiled by the qualities of its basin. And she should be of good constitution, that is, fleshy and strong, not only for the same reason, but also lest she easily become too weak for hard work and nightly duties with the result that the milk also deteriorates. Of large frame: for everything else being equal, milk from large bodies is more nourishing. Of a good colour: for in such women bigger vessels carry the material up to the breasts so that there is more milk. And her breasts should be of medium size: for small ones have little milk, whereas excessively large ones have more than is necessary so that if after nursing the surplus is retained it will be drawn out by the newborn when no longer fresh, and in some way already spoiled. If, on the other hand, it is all sucked out by other children or even other animals, the wet-nurse will be completely exhausted ...

The wet-nurse should be self-controlled so as to abstain from coitus, drinking, lewdness, and any other such pleasure and incontinence. For coitus cools the affection towards the nursling by the diversion of sexual pleasure and moreover spoils and diminishes the milk or suppresses it entirely by stimulating menstrual catharsis through the uterus or by bringing about conception.

In regard to drinking, first the wet-nurse is harmed in soul as well as in body and for this reason the milk also is spoiled. Secondly, seized by a sleep from which she is hard to awaken, she leaves the newborn untended or even falls down upon it in a dangerous way. Thirdly, too much wine passes its quality to the milk and therefore the nursling becomes sluggish and comatose and sometimes even afflicted with tremor, apoplexy, and convulsions, just as suckling pigs become comatose and stupefied when the sow has eaten drugs.

[She should be] sympathetic and affectionate, that she may fulfil her duties without hesitation and without murmuring. For some wet-nurses are so lacking in sympathy towards the nursling that they not only pay no heed when it cries for a long time, but do not even arrange its position when it lies still; rather, they leave it in one position so that often because of the pressure the sinewy parts suffer and consequently become numb and bad. Not ill-tempered: since by nature the nursling becomes similar to the nurse and accordingly grows sullen if the nurse is ill-tempered, but of mild disposition if she is even-tempered. Besides, angry women are like maniacs and sometimes when the newborn cries from fear and they are unable to restrain it, they let it drop from their hands or overturn it dangerously. For the same reason the wet-nurse should not be superstitious and prone to ecstatic states so that she may not expose the infant to danger when led astray by fallacious reasoning, sometimes even trembling like mad. And the wet nurse should be tidy-minded lest the odour of the swaddling clothes cause the child's stomach to become weak and it lie awake on account of itching or suffer some ulceration subsequently. And she should be a Greek so that the infant nursed by her may become accustomed to the best speech.

(20) At the most she should have had milk for two or three months. For very early milk, as we have said, is thick of particles and is hard to digest, while late milk is not nutritious, and is thin. But some people say that a woman who is going to feed a male must have given birth to a male, if a female, on the other hand, to a female. One should pay no heed to these people, for they do not consider that mothers of twins, the one being male and the other female, feed both with one and the same milk. And in general, each kind of animal makes use of the same nourishment, male as well as female; and this is [no] reason at all for the male to become more feminine or for the female to become more masculine. One should, on the

other hand, provide several wet-nurses for children who are to be nursed safely and successfully. For it is precarious for the nursling to become accustomed to one nurse who might become ill or die, and then, because of the change of milk, the child sometimes suffers from the strange milk and is distressed, while sometimes it rejects it altogether and succumbs to hunger.

381. *Two contracts for the services of wet-nurses for slave children. Alexandria, 13 BC (BGU 4.1106, 1107. G)*

The contracts appear to favour the slave-owners over the resident aliens who have been engaged to nurse their foundling slave babies. In the first contract, the foundling is specifically female (cf. no. 249), but in the second the sex of the child is not specified. Although repetitions in the phraseology indicate that such contracts were standard, the stiff penalties and exact specifications suggest that in previous instances both the slave-owners and wet-nurses had failed to keep their part of the bargain.

(1106) To Protarchus on the tribunal from Marcus Aemilius son of Marcus of the Claudian tribe and from Theodote the daughter of Dositheus, a Persian,[56] with her husband Sophron son of …archus, from the Persian expedition serving as her guardian and guarantor in regard to this contract. According to the agreement Theodote contracts for 18 months from Phamenoth of the present 17th year of the emperor Augustus to care for and nurse outside his home in her own home in the city with her own pure and unadulterated milk the foundling slave child that Marcus has entrusted to her as a nursling by the name of Tyche,[57] having taken from him for each month as pay for her milk and nursing care along with olive oil 8 drachmas.

Theodote has also received from Marcus by hand from his own house for the aforesaid 18 months for nine months' nursing 72 drachmas, and if during that time the child should experience a mortal calamity, Theodote agrees to care for another foundling child and to nurse her and to hand the child over to Marcus after nine months, receiving no additional wages at all, because she has undertaken to bring up a child irrespective of whether it dies or not, taking good care of her in all other respects month by month, and to give her the care she would give her own child, not ruining her milk or sleeping with her husband nor becoming pregnant or nursing another child. Whatever things she receives she shall keep safe and return when requested to, or pay back [to Marcus] the value of each unless it can be demonstrated that the child is dead; if this can be shown she is released from obligation. Moreover, she is not to abandon her nursing responsibilities during the time.

If she does not abide by the contract, she and her husband Sophron are liable to prosecution and to be held in custody until she has paid back the wages she has already received, and she is to pay what she has taken plus one half and the damages and expenses and 300 silver drachmas in addition. In the event of such a judgment, both parties are liable for restitution of the money and it may be taken from either one or the other, and from all their property, as if by court judgment, with all assurances that they may produce and all protection being invalid. But if she fulfils her contractual obligations, Marcus Aemilius is to pay Theodote her monthly wages for nursing for the remaining nine months and he shall not take away the child during that time unless he pays her the equivalent wages. Theodote is to come to Marcus three times per month in order that the child may be inspected by him. Theodote the daughter of Dositheus and her husband Sophron for the slave child Tyche and for 18 months have received 8 drachmas for 9 months, in the city.

(1107) To Protarchus from Isidora the daughter of Com... with her brother Eutychides son of Com... acting as guardian and from Didyme the daughter of Apollonius, a Persian, with her brother Ischyrion son of Apollonius of the Persian expedition acting as guardian. Didyme agrees to take care of and to nurse outside of his home at her home in the city with her own pure and unadulterated milk for 16 months from Pharmouthi of the current 17th year of Augustus Caesar, the foundling infant slave child that Isidora has entrusted to her as nursling. Didyme has received from the aforesaid Isidora wages for her milk and nursing care for each month ten drachmas of silver and two cotylae of oil. In return for these wages she contracts to take care of herself and not ruin her milk nor sleep with a man nor become pregnant nor nurse another child. Whatever belongings from the child she receives or is entrusted with, she shall keep safe and return when requested to, or to pay back the value of each unless it can be demonstrated that the child is dead; if this can be shown she is released from obligation.

Furthermore Didyme has received from Isidora by hand from her house oil for the first three months, Pharmouthi, Pachon, and Pauni. She is not to abandon her nursing during this time, but if she does not abide by the contract she must pay back the wages she has received and half of whatever she has received plus damages and expenses, and in addition she is to pay 500 drachmas and the prescribed fine. Isidora is to have right of execution on Didyme's person, and on all her possessions as if by court judgment, with all assurances that Didyme may produce and all protection being invalid. But if she fulfils all the conditions of the contract, Isidora is to provide her with the monthly wages for the remaining 13 months as specified above, and not to take the child away during that time, unless she pays her the equivalent wages. Didyme shall visit Isidora every month on four separate days taking the child with her to be inspected by her.

(*second hand*) I, Isidora, agree to abide by this contract as written. I, Eutychides, declare myself as guardian of my sister and have written for her because she does not know letters.

(*third hand*) I, Didyme agree to abide by this contract as written. I, Ischyrion, declare myself as guardian of my sister and have written for her because she does not know letters. (*first hand*) Isidora's contract. 17th year of Caesar's reign.

382. *Receipt of wages for nursing. Oxyrhynchus,* AD *187 (Oxyrhynchus papyrus 91. G)*

In this formal legal document an owner acknowledges the receipt from a child's mother of wages for the services of his slave.

Chosion, son of Sarapion, son of Harpocration, his mother being Sarapias of the city of Oxyrhynchus, to Tanenteris, daughter of Thonis, son of Thonis, her mother being Zoilous, of the same city, with her *kyrios* Demetrius son of Orion, his mother being Arsinoe, from the same city, greetings.

I acknowledge receipt from you through Heliodorus and his fellow overseers of the bank at the Sarapeion in the city of Oxyrhynchus, as promised by Epimachus, 400 drachmas of silver in Imperial coin for wages, oil, clothing, and other expenses incurred during the two years in which my slave Sarapias nursed your daughter Helene, known as her father's child[58] whom you received from her having been weaned and having received proper care. I acknowledge that I have no complaint nor shall I bring a complaint about this matter or about any other matter up to the present date. This receipt is valid. In the 27th year of the Emperor Caesar Marcus Aurelius Commodus Antoninus Pius Felix Augustus Armeniacus Medicus Parthicus Sarmaticus Germanicus Maximus Britannicus, Phaophi 15.[59]

(*written in a different hand*) I, Chosion, son of Sarapion, have received the 400 drachmas for the nursing and have no complaint to make, as previously stated. I, Tanenteris daughter of Thonion, with Demetrius, son of Orion, assent and have received my daughter as previously stated. I, Ploution, son of Hermes, have written the contract for them because they do not know letters.

X. Religion

'Maenadic rites and noble customs'

Dionysus/Bacchus
'Initiation in all the orgies'

The politically oppressed often turn to ecstasy as a temporary means of possessing the power they otherwise lack: orgiastic ritual, secret cults, trances and magic provided such outlets, especially for women, who could not justify meeting together for any other purpose.

383. *Imported Phrygian rituals. Athens, 4th cent. BC (Demosthenes, On the Crown 258-60. G)*

An excerpt from a passage in which Demosthenes seeks to discredit his opponent Aeschines by claiming that Aeschines as a young man helped his mother to run initiations and rituals to Dionysus Sabazius in Athens.

As a child you were raised in utter poverty ... when you became a man, you read the service while your mother performed the initiations and prepared the ritual equipment. At night you put the fawn-skins on the initiates and mixed the libations and cleansed the initiates by wiping them down with mud and bran, and you stood up after the lustration and proclaimed, 'I have escaped evil, and found a better way ...' During the day you led the sacred bands through the streets, with their heads wreathed in crowns of fennel and white poplar. As you went you squeezed the Asclepian snakes and raised them over your head shouting 'euhoe Saboi' and dancing 'hyes attés attes hyes'. You were greeted by old women as Conductor and Leader and Ivy-bearer and Carrier of the Winnowing Fan, and you were paid with sops, twisted rolls and new cakes.

384. *Rules of ritual. Miletus, 276/5 BC (Sokolowski, LSAM 48. Tr. A. Henrichs. G)*

Whenever the priestess performs the holy rites on behalf of the city ... , it is not permitted for anyone to throw pieces of raw meat [anywhere], before the priestess has thrown them on behalf of the city, nor is it permitted for anyone to assemble a band of maenads [*thiasos*] before the public *thiasos* [has been assembled] ...

... to provide [for the women] the implements for initiation in all the orgies ...

And whenever a woman wishes to perform an initiation for Dionysus Bacchius in the city, in the countryside, or on the islands, she must pay a piece of gold to the priestess at each biennial celebration.

385. *Epitaph for a priestess. Miletus, 3rd/2nd cent. BC (HSCP 82 [1978] 148. Tr. A. Henrichs. G)*

Bacchae of the City, say, 'Farewell you holy priestess.' This is what a good woman deserves. She led you to the mountain and carried all the sacred objects and implements, marching in procession before the whole city. Should some stranger ask for her name: Alcmeonis, daughter of Rhodius, who knew her share of the blessings.

386. *Authorisation by the Delphic oracle to establish a temple in Ionian Magnesia.[1] Delphi, Hellenistic. (I. Magn. 215[a].2440. Tr. A. Henrichs. G)*

Go to the holy plain of Thebes to fetch maenads from the race of Cadmean Ino. They will bring you maenadic rites and noble customs and will establish troops of Bacchus in your city.[2]

'In accordance with the oracle, and through the agency of the envoys, three maenads were brought from Thebes: Cosco, Baubo and Thettale. And Cosco organised the *thiasos* named after the plane tree, Baubo the *thiasos* outside the city, and Thettale the *thiasos* named after Cataebates. After their death they were buried by the Magnesians, and Cosco lies buried in the area called Hillock of Cosco, Baubo in the area called Tabarnis, and Thettale near the theatre.'

387. *Equipment for women's orgiastic rites. Egypt, c. 245 BC (Hibeh papyrus 54. G)*

Demophon to Ptolemaeus, greetings. Send us at your earliest opportunity the flautist Petoun with the Phrygian flutes, plus the other flutes. If it's necessary to pay him, do so, and we will reimburse you. Also send us the eunuch Zenobius with a drum, cymbals and castanets. The women need them for their festival. Be sure he is wearing his most elegant clothing. Get the special goat from Aristion and send it to us ... Send us also as many cheeses as you can, a new jug, and vegetables of all kinds, and fish if you have it. Your health! Throw in some policemen at the same time to accompany the boat.

388. *Senatus consultum de bacchanalibus. Rome, 186 BC (CIL I².581 =*
ILS 18 = ILLRP 511. Tr. ARS. L)

The worship of the god Dionysus spread through Italy from the Greek cities
of the south and was particularly popular among the lower classes and
slaves.[3] While the exaggerated reports of orgiastic rites were shocking to
conservative Romans, far more alarming was the organisational nature of
this new religion. Secret societies of any sort, and especially of the lower
classes, always held for the Romans the threat of sedition. The senate's
decree which follows applied to all Italy and placed strict limitations on the
worship of Bacchus, though it did not prohibit it entirely.

The consuls Quintus Marcius, son of Lucius, and Spurius Postumius, son
of Lucius, consulted the Senate on 7 October in the Temple of Bellona,
Marcus Claudius, son of Marcus, Lucius Valerius, son of Publius, and
Quintus Minucius, son of Gaius, assisted in drafting the decree.
Regarding the Bacchanalia the senators proposed to issue a decree as
follows to those who are allied with us: 'No one of them shall have a place
devoted to the worship of Bacchus: and if there are any who say that they
have a need for such a place, they shall appear in Rome before the urban
praetor; and when the pleas of these men have been heard, our Senate
shall make a decision regarding these matters, provided that not less
than 100 senators are present when the matter is discussed. No Roman
citizen or man of Latin rights or any one of the allies shall associate with
the Bacchae, unless they have appeared before the urban praetor and he
has given permission, in accordance with the opinion of the Senate,
delivered while not less than 100 senators were present when the matter
was discussed.'
The proposal passed.
'No man shall be priest of, nor shall any man or woman be master of,
such an organisation; nor shall any one of them have a common fund; nor
shall anyone appoint any man or woman to be master of such an
organisation or to act as master; nor hereafter shall anyone take common
oath with them, shall make common vows, shall make stipulations with
them; nor shall anyone give them surety or shall take surety from them.
No one shall perform their rites in secret; nor shall anyone perform their
rites in public, in private, or outside the city, unless he has appeared
before the urban praetor and he has given permission, in accordance with
the opinion of the Senate, delivered while not less than 100 senators were
present when the matter was discussed.'
The proposal passed.
'No one in a company of more than five persons altogether, men and
women, shall perform such rites; nor in that company shall more than
two men or three women be present, unless it is in accordance with the
opinion of the urban praetor and the Senate, as has been written above.'
You shall publish these decrees in public assembly for not less than

three market days, that you may know the opinion of the Senate. For the opinion of the senators is as follows:

'If there are any persons who act contrary to what has been written above, it is our opinion that a proceeding for a capital offence must be made against them'; and you shall inscribe this on a bronze tablet, for thus the Senate voted was proper; and you shall order it to be posted where it can be read most easily; and, as has been written above, you shall provide within ten days after these tablets have been delivered to you that those places devoted to the worship of Bacchus shall be dismantled, if there are any such, except in case something sacred is concerned in the matter.

389. *Rules in the cult of Dionysus. Physcus, Locris, 2nd cent.* AD *(IG IX.ii 670 = Sokolowski, LSCG 181.[4] Tr. A. Henrichs. G)*

With a Good Omen.

The Law of the *thiasos* of Amandus has been [ratified?] in two [meetings ?].

The [... ?] must pay to the association 14 obols and no less.

The association has to provide three lamps.

A Maenad must not get excited over another Maenad nor rail at her. Likewise a Cowherd must not get excited or rail. If someone does, he or she shall give to the association a fine of 4 drachmas for each word.

For someone who does not attend the meetings although he is in town, the same. Someone who does not join the others on the mountain shall pay 5 drachmas to the association. [If] a Maenad does [not] bring 15 [??] for the Holy Night, she shall pay 5 drachmas [to the association]. The same if (a Cowherd) does not bring ... *(The rest is lost.)*

390. *The festival of Agrionia (Plutarch, Moralia 299e-300a. 2nd cent.* AD. *G)*

As a historian, Plutarch had a keen interest in ancient practices of all kinds; but he reports this incident also as a pious believer in the traditional gods.[5]

The story is that the daughters of Minyas, Leucippe and Arsinoe and Alcathoe, went crazy.[6] They developed a craving for human meat and drew lots to choose among their children. Leucippe won and offered up her son Hippasos to be torn to pieces. Their husbands were called 'Psoloeis'[7] because in their pain and grief they were shabbily dressed. The daughters of Minyas were called Oleiae[8] because they were destructive.

Today the people of Orchomenus still call women in this family by that name. Every year at the festival of Agrionia the Oleiae flee and are pursued by the priest of Dionysus, sword in hand. If he captures one of the women he is permitted to kill her, and in my day the priest Zoilus did kill one. But the killing did the people of Orchomenus no good. Zoilus became sick as a result of a small wound he had, which became gangrenous, and eventually died. The people of Orchomenus were beset by suits for damages and adverse judgments. They took the priesthood away from Zoilus' family, and picked as new priest the best man in the city.

Hera
'The priestess placed a lighted torch near
the garlands and fell asleep'

391. *Chrysis, priestess of Hera. Argos, 5th cent. BC (Thucydides, History 2.2.1, 4.133.2-3. G)*

The list of priestesses at Argos was the oldest chronological record available to fifth-century historians. In other cities dates were reckoned by the (male) holders of public office.[9]

(2.2.1) In the fifteenth year of the 30 years' truce, when Chrysis had been priestess in Argos 48 years, Aenesias was Ephor in Sparta and Pythodorus had two months more as archon in Athens [*431 BC*] ...

(4.133.2) During the same summer [*423 BC*] the temple of Argos was destroyed by fire, when Chrysis the priestess placed a lighted torch near the garlands and fell asleep, so that she did not notice that everything had caught fire and had been burned. Then Chrysis fled immediately to Phlious in the middle of the night because she was afraid of the Argives. The Argives appointed another priestess according to their established custom, whose name was Phaeinis. Chrysis had been priestess for 8 years of the war and half of the ninth, when she went into exile.

392. *The cult of Hera. Olympia, 1st cent. AD (Pausanias, Guide to Greece 5.16.2-4. G)*

Every fourth year the Sixteen Women weave a robe for Hera and also hold the Heraean games. The games consist of foot-races for girls. The girls are not all from the same age-group (*helikia*), but the youngest run first, and after that the next youngest age-group, and finally the oldest group of girls runs. They run as follows: their hair hangs loose. Their tunics come just above the knee, and they leave their right shoulder bare above the breast. The stadium at Olympia is made available for them as well, but they shorten the length of course by about one-sixth. They give the winners crowns of olives and a portion of the cow sacrificed to Hera, and they set up statues of them with their names inscribed.[10] Married women administer for the Sixteen Women who preside over the games, since they themselves are married. The competition among the girls goes back to ancient times; they say that Hippodamia in gratitude to Hera for her marriage to Pelops assembled the Sixteen Women and founded the Heraea.

Demeter
'With their hearts in agreement they cheered their souls'

393. *The story of Persephone. 7th cent.* BC? *(Homeric Hymn to Demeter, vv. 370-95. G)*

Secret rites at Eleusis celebrated Persephone's return to her mother, Demeter, from Hades. Though no one knows exactly what happened at the Mysteries, the possibility of rebirth suggested by the story was represented also in the notion of the dead grain's becoming the live seed of the next year's crop. The *Homeric Hymn to Demeter* describes in detail how Hades, god of the underworld, stole Persephone, how her mother searched for her and hid the seed within the earth until she got her daughter back again. This excerpt describes how Persephone returns, but only for part of the year, because she ate seeds in the underworld and must now forever return to spend four months of the year with her husband.

So Aidoneus spoke, and wise Persephone was delighted, and in her joy swiftly rose up from the bed; but Aidoneus gave her to eat the sweet seed of a pomegranate, furtively, looking out for himself to keep her from spending all of her days here on earth with revered black-robed Demeter. And before them Aidoneus, ruler of many, got ready his immortal horses in his golden chariot. Persephone got into the chariot, and beside her strong Hermes took the reins and whip in his hands and drove out of the palace. The two horses flew on eagerly; they easily completed the long journey – neither the sea nor the water of rivers nor grassy valleys nor mountain peaks held back the horses' speed, but as they went they cut the steep air beneath them. Hermes stopped them and brought her where fair-crowned Demeter was waiting beside her fragrant temple [at Eleusis].

And when Demeter saw Persephone, she rushed like a maenad along the mountain shaded in forest; and Persephone opposite ... leaped down ... [Demeter asked ...] ... 'Child ... ? [You have not tasted food in the Underworld?] Tell me! Because if you refused it, you could live with me and your father, Zeus of the black clouds, honoured by all the immortals ... But if you have tasted food, you must live for a third part of the seasons [below] and for two parts with me and the other immortals. When the earth blooms with all kinds of fragrant spring flowers, then from the murky darkness you will come up once again and be a great wonder to gods and to mortal men. And with what trick did the strong Receiver of Many deceive you?'

Then beautiful Persephone addressed her in return: 'Then, Mother, I will tell you everything truthfully. When Hermes came as a messenger from my father Zeus and the other gods of Heaven to say I was to come from the Underworld, so you could see me with your own eyes and end your anger and cruel rage against the immortals, then in my joy I got up from the bed and he furtively put into me the seed of a pomegranate, sweet food; he compelled me to taste it by force, against my will. And I will tell you how Aidoneus carried me off because of my father's clever plan, and went and took me beneath the depths of the earth; I will relate everything in detail, as you request.

'We were playing, all of us, in the lovely meadow: Leucippe and Phaeno and Electre and Ianthe and Melite and Iache and Rhodeia and Callirhoe and Melobosis and Tyche and pretty Ocyrhoe and Chryseis and Ianeira and Acaste and Rhodope and Plouto and lovely Calypso and Styx and Urania and lovely Galaxaure and Pallas rouser of battles and Artemis shooter of arrows; and we were gathering lovely flowers in our arms, soft crocuses mingled with irises and hyacinths and rose blossoms and lilies, wondrous to see; and the narcissus which the broad earth made grow like a crocus. This I picked in my joy, and the earth parted beneath me, and there the strong lord, the Receiver of Many, leaped out. He came and took me away beneath the earth in his golden chariot, much against my will, and I cried out in a shrill voice. This, in my sorrow, is the whole truth that I tell you.'

So then with their hearts in agreement they cheered their souls and hearts by embracing each other, and their hearts had respite from their sorrows. They took and gave joyousness to one another. And Hecate with her bright headband came near them, and embraced many times the daughter of holy Demeter; since then she has been her guardian and attendant queen. And then far-seeing Zeus of the loud thunder sent them a messenger, fair-haired Rhea, to bring black-robed Demeter back to the family of the gods, and he promised to give her honours that she could choose for herself among the immortals. He agreed that her daughter should spend the third part of the circling year beneath the murky darkness, but two parts with her mother and the other immortals. This was what Zeus said, and Demeter did not disobey his message. But she rushed swiftly to the peaks of Olympus, and she came to the Rharian plain, which before had been the nourishing breast of the land, but now no longer nourishing, since it stood fallow and leafless; it hid the white barley because of slim-ankled Demeter's devising. But then as spring grew strong, she began to adorn the field with long stalks of grain, and the plain's rich furrows were laden with grain stalks, which were bound into sheaves. Here she went first of all from the barren air. And the goddesses were happy to see one another and rejoiced in their hearts.

Then Rhea of the shining headband spoke to her thus: 'Come here, my child; far-seeing Zeus of the loud thunder is calling you to come to the family of the gods, and he has promised to give you honours, which you could choose from among the immortals. He has agreed that your daughter should spend the third part of the year beneath the murky darkness, but two with you and the other immortals … He has nodded his head in confirmation. But come, my child, and obey them, and do not any longer be relentlessly angry at Zeus of the black clouds. Make a nourishing harvest grow for mortal men directly.'

So she spoke, and fair-crowned Demeter did not disobey her. Directly she sent up a harvest for the fields with their dark loam. And all the broad earth was laden with leaves and with flowers. And she came and showed the just kings Triptolemus and Diocles smiter of horses and mighty Eumolpus and Celeus leader of people the performance of her ritual and instructed them in her sacred mysteries, which one must never transgress or hear of or speak of, for great reverence for the gods holds back one's tongue. Happy the man who has seen these mysteries; but he who has not been initiated, and has not taken part in the ritual, does not share in the same rewards when he goes down beneath the broad darkness.

But when the bright goddess had taught them all her rituals, she went to Olympus to the company of the other gods. And there the two goddesses live beside Zeus who delights in thunder, awful and revered. Happy the man whom the goddesses willingly love; for directly they send as a guest to his great house Wealth who gives men riches. But now goddesses who protect the city of fragrant Eleusis, and sea-girt Paros and rocky Antron, queen Deo with your shining gifts, bringer of harvests, Mistress, you and your daughter beautiful Persephone willingly give me a good living in return for my song; and I shall remember you and another song also.

394. *Thesmophoria. Alexandria, 3rd cent. BC (Callimachus, Hymn 6.119-33. G)*

Women celebrated the annual festival of Demeter Thesmophoria (Lawgiver) to ensure the continued fertility of the earth. In this hymn the poet Callimachus tells how Demeter punished young Erysichthon when he cut down her sacred tree by giving him an insatiable appetite. The hymn concludes with a prescription for appropriate tribute to the goddess.

Sing, virgins, and mothers join the chorus: 'Demeter, all hail, nurse of many, giver of full measure.' And as four white horses pull the basket, so will the great goddess, the wide-ruler, come to us bringing white spring, and white summer, and winter and the season of withering. She will protect us through another year. As we walk through the city without sandals and with our hair unbound, so we shall have our feet and hands unharmed forever. And as the basket-bearers bring baskets full of gold, so may we taste boundless gold. The uninitiated women may process as far as the city hall; the initiated right to the goddess's temple – all who are younger than sixty. But women who are heavy, who stretch their hands to Eileithuia goddess of childbirth, or who are in pain – it's enough that they go as far as their legs can carry them. For these Deo (Demeter) will give all things full to the brim and let them come to her temple. Hail goddess, and keep this city safe in harmony and in prosperity. Bring all things from the fields in abundance. Nourish the cattle, bring us sheep, bring us grain, bring in the harvest, nourish peace also, so that he who sows may reap. Have mercy on me, thrice-prayed to, great queen among goddesses.

395. *Regulations for women attending the festival of Demeter. Patras, 3rd cent. BC (IG V.11390 = Sokolowski, LSCG 33A. G)*

At the festival of Demeter women should not wear gold in excess of one obol in weight, nor wear embroidered robes, nor purple, nor put white lead on their faces,[11] or play the *aulos*. If a woman disregards these rules, the sanctuary should be purified, on the grounds that she has been impious.

396. *The order of the procession at the Mysteries. Andania, 92 BC (Ditt. Syll. 2653 = Sokolowski LSCG 95.28-33. G)*

Women walk ahead of men in parts of the parade in this excerpt from a long inscription.

Rules for the procession. Mnesistratus [the hierophant] should lead the procession. Then the priest of the gods for whom the mysteries are being celebrated, after the priestess. Then the contest officials, the sacrifice officials, the *aulos* players. After this, the maiden initiates in the order determined by lot, bringing the chariots containing the boxes that hold the sacred mysteries. Then the officials of the feast of Demeter and the under-officials of the feast who have come forward, and then the priestess of Demeter at the sanctuary near the Hippodrome, and then the priestess of Demeter at the sanctuary in Aigila. Then the female initiates, one by one, in the order determined by lot, and then the male initiates in the order arranged by the Ten.

Athena
'Something useful for the city'

397. *Inscribed monument dedicated by a woman.*[12] *Athens, 520 BC (Raubitschek, DAA 348 = IG I² 756. G)*

Only three other such monuments exist.[13]

Callicrate placed me here as a dedication to Athena.

398. *The priestess and temple of Athena Nike. Athens, 450-445?* BC *(excerpt from IG I².24 = GHI 44. G)*

Although in most cases priestesses were selected from the aristocratic families that had the rights to certain cults, the priestess of this cult is to be chosen by lot from all Athenian women.

(*a man's name*) made the motion: a priestess to Athena Nike ... who is to be appointed from all Athenian women, and the temple precinct is to be provided with doors as Callicrates[14] shall prescribe. The Sellers[15] shall let out the contract during the prytany of the Leontis tribe. The priestess is to receive 50 drachmas [per year] and the legs and hides from public [sacrificial victims]. The temple and a stone altar are to be built as Callicrates prescribes ...

399. *The religious duties of aristocratic young girls. Athens, 5th cent.* BC *(Aristophanes, Lysistrata 638-47. Tr. H. Lloyd-Jones. G)*

We are setting out, all you citizens, to say something useful for the city, as we well may, because it reared me in splendid affluence. From the moment I was seven I served as arrhephoros;[16] then at ten I was a baker for Athena Archegetis; then I had my saffron robe (*krokotos*) and was a bear [for Artemis] at the Brauronia;[17] and then I was once a basket-carrier (*kanephoros*), a lovely girl with a bunch of figs.

400. *A procession. Delphi, 2nd cent.* BC *(IG II².1136. G)*

Inscription in the form of a letter from the people of Delphi to the people of Athens.

... Greetings. Whereas the people of Athens led a Pythian procession to Pythian Apollo in a grand manner worthy of the god and their particular excellence: the priestess of Athena, Chrysis daughter of Nicetes, also was present with the procession; she made the journey out and the return well, appropriately, and worthily of the people of Athens and of our own city. With good fortune, it was voted by the city of Delphi to praise Chrysis, daughter of Nicetes, and to crown her with the god's crown that is customary among the Delphians. It was voted also to give *proxenia* to her and to her descendants from the city, and the right to consult the oracle, priority of trial, safe conduct, freedom from taxes, and a front seat at all the contests held by the city, the right to own land and a house and all the other honours customary for *proxenoi* and benefactors of the City.

Artemis
'I see her as the sun'

Women of all ages were concerned to appease the goddess Artemis, killer of women; but young women reaching the age of puberty and women bearing children were particularly vulnerable. There may be a correspondence between the shedding of blood requisite for those stages of female life and the sacrifice of ritual victims on the altar.

401. *A puberty ritual. Sparta, 7th cent.* BC *(Alcman, Fr. 1.5-101. G)*

A chorus of young girls describe themselves and their ceremonial role in a special song. They appear to be offering a robe to a goddess, possibly Helen, who was worshipped in Sparta. Their erotic attraction to their leaders, Hagesichora and her friend Agido, recalls Sappho's world; perhaps Aenesimbrota was their teacher and trainer. Emphasis on the beauty of face and hair suggests that they are involved in a ritual that marks the transition (hence perhaps the references to battle) from girlhood to womanhood: the running of races is also a feature of puberty rites for Athena in Argos and Artemis in Brauron. Comparison to horses may suggest the imminence of marriage, which is often described in metaphors of taming and yoking. Doves frequently represent women's vulnerability.[18] The girls readily accept their leaders' pre-eminence. But in men's competition, success is ordinarily accompanied by strong expressions of envy and resentment.

I sing of Agido's light. I see her as the sun; Agido calls him to testify to us that he is shining. But our famous leader will not let me either praise or criticise her; for our leader seems to us to be supreme, as if one set a horse among the herds, strong, prize-winning, with thundering hooves – horse of the world of dreams. And don't you see: the race-horse is Venetic; but my cousin[19] Hagesichora's hair blooms like unmixed gold. And her silver face – why should I spell it out? Here is Hagesichora. And she who is second to Agido in looks, runs like a Colaxian horse to an Ibenian. For the Doves bring the robe to the Goddess of the Dawn for us; they rise like the dog star through the immortal night and fight for us. There is not enough purple to protect us, nor jewelled snake of solid gold, nor Lydian cap – adornment of girls with their dark eyes; nor Nanno's hair, no nor Areta who is like the gods; not Sylakis and Cleesisera. You wouldn't go to Aenesimbrota's house and say: let me have Astaphis; may Philylla look at me, and lovely Damareta and Vianthemis – no, it's Hagesichora who excites me. For Hagesichora of the fair ankles is near her; close to Agido ... she praises our festival. Yes, gods, receive [their prayer]. From the gods [comes] accomplishment and fulfilment. Leader, I could say – a young girl that I am; I shriek in vain from my roof like an owl, and I will say what will please Dawn most, for she has been healer of our troubles;

but it is through Hagesichora that girls have reached the peace they long for ...

402. *Excerpts from records of offerings to Artemis at Brauron. Brauron, Attica, 4th cent. BC (IG II².1514. G)*

The women's names indicate aristocratic rank; the list gives an idea of the variety of decoration and colour in their clothing.[20]

Archippe [dedicated] a dotted, sleeved tunic in a box during the year Callimachus was archon.[21] Callippe a short tunic, scalloped and embroidered; it has letters woven in. Chaerippe and Eucoline, a dotted tunic in a box. Philumene a silken tunic, in the year Theophilus was archon.[22] Pythias a dotted robe in the year Themistocles was archon.[23] There is an embroidered purple tunic; Thyaene and Malthace dedicated it. Phile [dedicated] a woman's girdle; Pheidylla a white woman's cloak[24] in a box. Mneso a frog-green garment. Nausis a woman's cloak, with a broad purple border in a wave design.[25]

403. *Records of dedications to Artemis Brauronia. Athens, early 4th cent. BC (IG II².1388. 78-80, 82-3; IG II².1400. 41-2, 46, 47. G)*

Five perforated earrings: these Thaumarete the wife of Timonides dedicated, in a wooden box ... An ivory lyre and wooden pick inlaid with ivory in a carved box, which Cleito daughter of Aristocrates, Cimon's wife, dedicated ... A seal with a gold ring; Dexilla dedicated it ... To Artemis Brauronia a punctured golden ornament with a golden chain, which Callion dedicated, weight 2 drachmas ... a silver bowl which Aristola dedicated ... A gold ring which Dorcas who lives in Peiraeus[26] dedicated to Artemis Brauronia ...

404. *Ritual procedures. Cyrene, 4th cent BC (SEG IX.72.13-16 = Sokolowski, LSCG Supp. 115, excerpts. G)*

(13) [If a bride comes to the dormi]tory,[27] she must sacrifice as a penalty to Artemis. She must not share a roof with her husband and must not be polluted; she must purify the temple of Artemis and as penalty sacrifice a full-grown victim, and then she should go to the dormitory. If she pollutes involuntarily, she must purify the temple.

(14) A bride must make a ceremonial visit to the bride-room at the temple of Artemis at the festival of Artemis, whenever she wishes, but the sooner the better. If she does not make her ceremonial visit, she must make the regular sacrifice to Artemis at the festival of Artemis as one who has made no visit, and she must purify the temple and sacrifice a victim as penalty.

(15) [A pregnant woman] shall make a ceremonial visit [before birth] to the bride-room in the precinct of Artemis and give the Bear priestess feet and head and skin of the sacrifice. If she does not make a ceremonial visit before giving birth she must make a visit afterwards with a full-grown victim. If she makes a ceremonial visit to the temple she must observe ritual purity on the seventh, eighth and ninth day, and if she does not make a visit, she must perform the rites on these days. If she is polluted, she must purify herself and the temple and sacrifice a full-grown victim as penalty.

(16) If a woman miscarries, if the foetus is fully formed, they are polluted as if by a death; if it is not fully formed, the household is polluted as if from childbirth.[28]

Aphrodite
'The goddess Cypris'

405. *Dedication of statues of women. Corinth, 5th cent. BC (Page, FGE xiv. G)*

Several versions survive of this epigram, explaining the dedication of statues of women in the temple of Aphrodite on Acrocorinth, the Acropolis of Corinth, after the war against Xerxes. The text does not make clear whether the supplication was made by cult prostitutes in the temple or by Corinthian wives (cf. Page, *ad loc.*).

These women stand here on behalf of the Hellenes and the courageous soldiers of their own city, after they made their sacred vows to the goddess Cypris. For divine Aphrodite contrived not to betray the acropolis of the Hellenes to the bow-carrying Medes.

Asclepius
'Cleo was pregnant for five years'

406. *Cures of women's diseases, from the shrine of Asclepius in Epidaurus. First half of 4th cent. BC (IG IV.².121-2, excerpts. G)*

From an inscription listing cures by Apollo and Asclepius, brought about as the result of 'incubation', or sleeping in the sanctuary.[29]

(1) Cleo was pregnant for five years. After she had been pregnant for five years she came as a suppliant to the god and slept in the sanctuary. As soon as she came out of the inner sanctuary and was outside the temple the enclosure she gave birth to a son. This son as soon as he was born washed himself in the spring and walked around with his mother. After this experience she put up a votive offering: 'Wonder not at the greatness

of this tablet but of the god, because he healed Cleo, after she had been pregnant and had carried the burden in her womb for five years, until she slept in the sanctuary.'

(2) A three-year pregnancy. Ithmonica of Pellene came to the sanctuary in order to have children. She fell asleep and saw a dream. She seemed to be asking the god that she become pregnant with a girl child, and that Asclepius said that she would become pregnant and told her that if she had any other request, he would grant it to her, but she said that she did not need anything. She conceived and was pregnant for three years, until she returned to the god as a suppliant, in order to give birth. After she went to sleep, she saw a dream. She thought that the god had asked if everything had not happened as she had asked and if she had not become pregnant. But she had not made any specific request about childbirth, and when he had inquired about this, and asked if she needed anything else, to say so, so that he could do that as well. But since she had come to him now about this matter, he said to tell him her request.[30] And after this when she went out of the sanctuary and left the temple enclosure, she gave birth to a daughter.

(21) Arata, a Spartan, suffering from dropsy. On her behalf her mother slept in the sanctuary while she stayed in Sparta. It seemed to her that the god cut off her daughter's head and hung her body with the neck downwards. After a considerable amount of water had flowed out, he released the body and put the head back on her neck. After she saw this dream she returned to Sparta and found that her daughter had recovered and had seen the same dream.

(23) Aristagora of Troezen. When she had a tapeworm in her stomach she slept in the sanctuary of Asclepius in Troezen and had a dream. She thought that since the god was not present, but rather in Epidaurus, his three sons cut off her head, but since they were not able to put it back again they sent a messenger to get Asclepius to come. Meanwhile daylight intervened and the priest saw her head removed from her body. The next night Aristagora had a dream. The god seemed to come from Epidaurus and replace her head on her neck, and after that he cut open her stomach and took out the tapeworm and sewed her up again, and after this she was cured.

(25) Sostrata of Pherae was pregnant with worms. When she was absolutely too weak to walk, she was brought into the sanctuary and slept there. When she did not see any clear dream, she went back home again. After that near Cornoi someone seemed to appear to her and her escort, a distinguished-looking man, who inquired about their misfortune; he told them to put down the litter on which they were carrying Sostrata. Then he cut open her stomach and removed a large multitude of worms, two washbasins full. Then he sewed up her stomach, and once he had cured her, Asclepius showed that it was he who had appeared, and ordered her to send votive offerings to Epidaurus.

(31) Andromache, from Epirus, for children. She fell asleep and saw a dream. It seemed to her that a handsome youth uncovered her, and after that the god touched her with his hand.[31] After this a son was born to Andromache, whose father was Arrybas.

(34) An anonymous woman from Troezen, for children. She fell asleep and saw a dream. The god seemed to say that she would bear children and asked her whether she wanted a boy or a girl. She said that she wanted a boy and after that within a year a son was born to her.

(39) Agameda of Ceos. She slept in the sanctuary, in order to have children and saw a dream. She thought that a snake lay on her stomach while she slept. After this five children were born to her.[32]

(40) Nicasiboula, a Messenian, slept in the sanctuary in order to have children and saw a dream. The god seemed to come to her carrying a snake that went towards her and that she had intercourse with the snake. After this she bore two male children within the year.

Serapis
'Twins who minister in the great Serapeum'

407. *A petition to Ptolemy and Cleopatra. Memphis, 163-162 BC (UPZ 19. Tr. G. Milligan. G)*

The cult of the Egyptian god Serapis grew out of the worship, at Memphis, of Apis, the sacred bull. Beginning under the first Ptolemy and continuing through the Roman Empire, Serapis came to combine features of Egyptian, Greek and Roman gods, namely Osiris, Zeus-Jupiter, Hades-Pluto, Asclepius, Helios and Dionysus. Incubation was associated with his cult as well as with that of Asclepius.

To King Ptolemy and Queen Cleopatra the sister, gods Philometores, greeting. We, Thaues and Taous are twins, who minister in the great Serapeum at Memphis. On a former occasion when you were in residence at Memphis and had gone up to the temple to sacrifice, we petitioned you, and gave in a petition, bringing before you our plea that we are not receiving the contribution of necessaries which it is fitting should be given to us both from the Serapeum and the Asclepeum. And having failed to receive them up to the present time in full, we have been compelled, under pressure of necessity, wasting away as we are through starvation, to petition you again, and in a few words to set before you the selfishness of those who are injuring us. For although you already from former times have proclaimed a contribution for the Serapeum and Asclepeum, and in consequence of this the twins who were there before us daily received what they required, to us also when we first went up to the temple straightway for a few days the impression was conveyed as if everything fitting would be done for us in good order, but for the remainder of the time this was not carried out. Wherefore we both sent repeatedly to the supervisors persons to petition on our behalf, and laid information on these matters before you, on the occasion of your visits to Memphis. And when those who had been appointed to the administration in the Serapeum and Asclepeum had insolently maltreated us, and were removing the privileges conferred on us by you, and were paying no regard to religious scruple, and when we were being crushed by our wants, we often made representations even to Achomarres the supervisor of the temple to give us [our rights]. And we approached the son of Psintaes the supervisor of the sacrifices, when we went up to the temple the day before yesterday, and gave him detailed information. And having called Achomarres to him, he strictly commanded him to give what was owing to us. And he, being by nature the most unfeeling of all mankind, promised us that he would perform what he had been directed to do, but no sooner had the son of Psintaes departed from Memphis than he took no further account of the matter. And not only this man, but also others connected with the Serapeum, and others connected with the Asclepeum in the administration, from whom it is usual for us to receive what we need, are defrauding, whose names and obligations, because they are numerous, we have decided not to record.

We beg you therefore, having as our one hope the assistance that lies in your power, to send away our petition to Dionysius Privy Councillor and *strategus*, that he may write to Apollonius the supervisor to compel them to render to us [what is owing], when he has received from us the written list of the necessaries owing to us and what further debts are due us along with the periods for which they have been owing and the persons who owe them, so that, when we have everything in order, we may be much better able to perform our regular duties to Serapis and to Isis, both for your own sakes and for the sake of your children. May it be given you to hold fast all the territory you desire. Farewell.

Vesta
'A Virgin who is seduced is buried alive'

408. *Vestal Virgins. Rome, 7th cent. BC (Plutarch, Life of Numa Pompilius 9.5-10.7, excerpts. 2nd cent. AD. G)*

The goddess of the hearth, Vesta, was served by six Virgins, whose duty it was to keep the sacred fire which took the place of a cult statue. Vesta's temple was a round building in the Roman Forum. Its institution was attributed to Numa Pompilius, the pious second king of Rome (715-673 BC), who succeeded the warlike Romulus.[33]

(10.1) At first they say that Gegania and Verenia were made priestesses by Numa, and next Canuleia and Tarpeia. Later Servius added two more, to bring the number up to what it has been since that time. The king set the term of service for the holy Virgins at thirty years; in the first decade they learn their duties, in the middle decade they do what they have learned, and in the third they teach others. (10.2) After that a Virgin is free to marry if she wishes to or to adopt another style of life, once her term of service has been completed. But few are said to have welcomed this opportunity, and matters did not go well for those who did, but rather because they were afflicted by regret and depression for the rest of their lives they inspired pious reverence in the others, so that they remained constant in their virginity until old age and death.

(10.3) Numa gave them significant honours, one of which is the right to make a will during their father's lifetime and to conduct their other business affairs without a guardian, like the mothers of three children.[34] When they go out they are preceded by lictors with the fasces, and if they accidentally happen to meet a criminal being led to execution, his life is spared. The Virgin must swear that the meeting was involuntary and accidental and not planned. Anyone who goes underneath a Vestal's litter when she is being carried is put to death. (10.4)

The Virgins' minor offences are punished by beating, which is administered by the Pontifex, with the offender naked, and in a dark place with a curtain set up between them. A Virgin who is seduced is buried alive near what is known as the Colline gate. At this place in the city there is a little ridge of land that extends for some distance, which is called a 'mound' in the Latin language.[35] (10.5) Here they prepare a small room, with an entrance from above. In it there is a bed with a cover, a lighted lamp, and some of the basic necessities of life, such as bread, water in a bucket, milk, oil, because they consider it impious to allow a body that is consecrated to the most holy rites to die of starvation.[36] They put the woman who is being punished on a litter, which they cover over from outside and bind down with straps, so that not even her voice can be heard, and they take her through the Forum. Everyone there stands aside silently and follows the litter without a word, in serious dejection. There is no other sight so terrifying, (10.7) and the city finds no day more distasteful than that day. When the litter is borne to the special place, the attendants unfasten her chains and the chief priest says certain secret prayers and lifts his hands to the gods in prayer because he is required to carry out the execution, and he leads the victim out veiled and settles her on the ladder that carries her down to the room. Then he, along with the other priests, turns away. The ladder is removed from the entrance and a great pile of earth is placed over the room to hide it, so that the place is on a level with the rest of the mound. That is how those who abandon their sacred virginity are punished.

409. *Vestal Virgins. Rome (Aulus Gellius, Attic Nights 1.12. 2nd cent AD. L)*

The Vestal Virgin, at what age and from what sort of family and by what ritual and ceremonies and rites and under what title she is taken by the Pontifex Maximus, and what rights she has as soon as she is taken; and that, as Labeo[37] says, by law she cannot be heir of an intestate person nor can anyone be her heir if she dies intestate.

Those who have written about the taking of a Virgin, of whom the most diligent was Labeo Antistius, say that it is unlawful to take a girl younger than six or older than ten, or to take a girl whose father and mother are not living, or who has a speech or hearing defect, or any other bodily imperfection. She must not have been freed from her father's power, even if her father is alive and she is in the power of her grandfather; likewise, neither of her parents must ever have been slaves nor held lowly occupations. But they say that she is exempt if her sister was elected to the priesthood; likewise if her father is a flamen or augur or one of the Fifteen in charge of the Sibylline Books,[38] one of the Seven of the banquets, or a Salian priest (of Mars).[39] Also exempt are girls who are betrothed to a pontifex or daughters of priests of the tubilustrium. Moreover, Ateius Capito writes that the daughter of a man who does not have a residence in Italy cannot be chosen, and the daughter of a man who has three children is to be excused.

As soon as a Vestal Virgin is taken and brought to the atrium of Vesta[40] and handed over to the pontifices, from that moment she leaves her father's power without being emancipated and without diminution of her rights and gains the right to make a will.

As to the custom and ritual of taking a Virgin, we do not possess ancient writings, except that the first one was taken by Numa when he was king. But we find the Papian law, according to which under the direction of the Pontifex Maximus twenty girls are to be chosen from among the people and one of these chosen by lot in an assembly and the Pontifex Maximus takes the winner who now belongs to Vesta. But the lottery of the Papian law is usually not needed nowadays. For if a man of respectable birth goes to the Pontifex Maximus and offers his daughter for the priesthood, insofar as it can be done in keeping with the religious observations, he is given exemption from the Papian law by the senate.

The word 'taken' is used, so it seems, because the Pontifex Maximus literally takes her by the hand and leads her away from the parent in whose power she is, as though she had been captured in war. In his first book, Fabius Pictor gives the words the Pontifex Maximus must say when he takes a Virgin. They are: 'I take you, Amata, to be a Vestal priestess, who will carry out sacred rites which it is the law for a Vestal priestess to perform on behalf of the Roman people, on the same terms as her who was a Vestal on the best terms.'[41]

Many think that the term 'taken' should apply only to Vestal Virgins, but also the *flamines Diales*, and pontiff and augurs were said to be 'taken'. Lucius Sulla wrote in book two of his autobiography: 'Publius Cornelius, who was the first to receive the cognomen Sulla, was taken as *flamen Dialis*.' Marcus Cato, writing on the Lusitanians, accused Servius Galba: 'Nevertheless they say he wanted to revolt. I now want to know pontifical law as well as possible; does that mean I am to be "taken" as pontiff? If I want to know augury, should I be "taken" for an augur?'

Moreover, in Labeo's *Commentaries on the Twelve Tables*, he wrote: 'A Vestal Virgin is neither heir to an intestate person nor is anyone her heir if she dies intestate, but her estate passes to the public treasury. It is not certain what the law meant.'

The Pontifex Maximus calls the girl 'Amata' when he takes her because that is the traditional name of the first Vestal Virgin to be taken.

410. *Augustus and the Vestal Virgins. Rome, 27 BC-AD 14 (Suetonius, Life of Augustus 31.4. L)*

He increased the numbers and the dignities, and likewise the privileges of the priests, and especially of the Vestal Virgins. Once, when a Virgin died and had to be replaced and many parents tried to keep their daughters from being picked by lot, he swore that if one of his granddaughters had been of the right age, he would have offered her.

411. *Inscription to the chief Vestal. Rome, AD 215 (?) (CIL VI.2144 = ILS 4927. L)*

This inscription, from the Atrium Vestae in the Roman Forum, was carved on the base of a statue of the chief vestal, by her brother and his wife and nephew. It is one of several dedications found to the same chief vestal.[42]

To Terentia Flavula, Chief Vestal Virgin, his sister, Terentius Gentianus, *flamen Dialis, vir clarissimus, praetor tutelarius*,[43] with his wife Pomponia Paetina and Lollianus Gentianus, the son of his brother (put this up).

Bona Dea
'The goddess whom the Romans call "Good" '

412. *A divine portent. Rome, 63 BC (Plutarch, Life of Cicero 19.3, 20.1-2. 2nd cent. AD. G)*

Plutarch records a story which demonstrates how Cicero had divine support in his prosecution of the Catilinarian conspirators.

(19.3) It was now evening and a crowd had gathered. Cicero came forward and told the citizens what had happened. He was then escorted to the house of a friend and neighbour; his own was occupied by women who were celebrating the secret rites of the goddess whom the Romans call 'Good' (*Agathe*, i.e. in Latin, *Bona*) and the Greeks the 'Women's Goddess' (*Gynaikeia*). Sacrifice is offered to this goddess annually in the house of the consul by his wife or mother, in the presence of the Vestal Virgins. Cicero went to his friend's house, and began to deliberate with himself (since he had only a small entourage with him) how he should deal with the conspirators ... (20.1) While he still did not know what to do, a sign was given to the women holding the sacrifice. Although the fire on it seemed to have died out, a large bright flame shot forth from the ash and burnt bark on the altar. The rest of the women were frightened, but the Vestals told Cicero's wife Terentia to go to her husband as quickly as possible and tell him to do what he had decided to do on behalf of his country, because the goddess had sent a light to him to lead him to salvation and glory. Terentia – who was not meek or fearful by nature, but a particularly ambitious woman, as Cicero himself says, who was inclined to take a share in his political concerns rather than involve him in household affairs[44] – gave him the message and strengthened his determination against the conspirators.

413. *Desecration of the rites of the Bona Dea. Rome, 62 BC (Plutarch, Life of Caesar 9-10. 2nd cent. AD. G)*

> In this 'unfortunate incident' during Caesar's praetorship Clodius managed to spy on the secret rites.

(9.1) Publius Clodius was a man of noble birth and notable for his wealth and reputation, but not even the most notorious scoundrels came close to him in insolence and audacity. Clodius was in love with Caesar's wife Pompeia, and she was not unwilling. But a close watch was kept on the women's apartment, and Caesar's mother Aurelia followed the young wife around and made it difficult and dangerous for the lovers to meet.[45]

(9.3) The Romans have a goddess whom they call Good, whom the Greeks call the Women's Goddess. The Phrygians say that this goddess originated with them, and that she was the mother of their king Midas. The Romans say that she was a Dryad nymph who married Faunus, and the Greeks say that she was the Unnameable One among the mothers of Dionysus. For this reason the women who celebrate her rites cover their tents with vine-branches, and a sacred serpent sits beside the goddess on her throne, as in the myth. It is unlawful for a man to approach or to be in the house when the rites are celebrated. The women, alone by themselves, are said to perform rites that conform to Orphic ritual during the sacred ceremony.

(9.4) As a result, when the time for the festival comes, and a man is consul or praetor or general, he goes away and takes every male with him, and his wife takes over the house and decorates it for the festival. Most of the rites are celebrated at night, and with great amounts of festivity in the revels and music as well.

(10.1) At the time [that the incident occurred] Pompeia was celebrating this ritual; Clodius did not yet have a beard and for this reason thought that he would escape detection if he were dressed up as a lyre-player, and went into the house looking like a young woman. He found the doors open and was led in without difficulty by a slave-woman who was in on the plot; this woman went to Pompeia and told her, and some time passed, but Clodius could not bear to wait, and as he was wandering around the large house and trying to avoid the lights, one of Aurelia's attendants got hold of him, and asked him to play with her, as one woman might with another, and when he refused, she dragged him before the others and asked who he was and where he came from.

(10.3) Clodius said that he was waiting for Pompeia's slave Abra (which happened to be the woman's name), and gave himself away by his voice. The attendant dashed away from him towards the lights and the crowd, shouting that she had caught a man. The women were terrified, and Aurelia called a halt to the rites of the goddess and hid the sacred objects; she ordered the doors to be shut and went around the house with torches, looking for Clodius. He was found in the room that belonged to the girl where he had gone in an attempt to escape. When he was discovered, he was taken through the doors by the women and thrown out of the house. That night the women went right off and told their husbands about the affair, and during the day the story spread through the city that Clodius had been involved in sacrilege and had committed injustice against not only those he had insulted, but the city and the gods.

(10.5) Clodius was indicted for sacrilege by one of the tribunes, and the most influential senators joined forces against him and testified about other dreadful outrages he had committed and his incest with his sister, who was married to Lucullus.[46] But the common people strenuously opposed these senators' efforts, and defended Clodius, and the mob helped him considerably by terrifying and frightening the jury.

(10.6) Caesar immediately divorced Pompeia, but when he was summoned as a witness in the trial said that he knew nothing about the accusations against Clodius. The prosecutor asked him about the apparent contradiction: 'Why then did you divorce your wife?' He answered, 'Because I thought my wife should be above suspicion.' Some say that that was what Caesar really thought; others that he was eager to save Clodius in order to gratify the common people. Clodius was acquitted because most of the jurors handed in their opinions in illegible writing, so that they would not endanger themselves with the common people by voting against him, or disgrace themselves with the nobility by letting him off.

Witchcraft
'I will sing to Hecate underground'

Many papyri and tablets survive to testify to a pervasive faith, among all strata of society, in the efficacy of magic. Although both men and women were practitioners, sexual motives were considered particularly unnatural in females, who are portrayed in such works as Apuleius' *Golden Ass* as capable of murdering children and husband to attain their evil desires. Such things at least were believed to have happened in real life: cf. the epitaph for Iucundus (*CIL* VI.19747 = *ILS* 8522, Rome, c. AD 20): 'As I was approaching my fourth birthday I was seized and put in the ground, when I could have been sweet to my mother and father. A magic hand (*saga manus*) stole me away, everywhere cruel. While she is on earth she can also harm you and your children; guard them, parents, lest sorrow be driven into your hearts.' Horace composed a dramatic poem about a similar event: a young boy is killed to provide ingredients for a love charm to bring back Varus, the lover of the witch Canidia; the text is given in no. 417.

414. *Medea (Apollonius of Rhodes, Argonautica 3.838-67. Alexandria, 3rd cent BC. G)*

A poet's account of how the young Medea found the drug she needed to protect Jason.

Medea called to her maidservants – there were twelve in all; they slept in the porch of her fragrant bedchamber, of the same age as she; they had not yet shared their beds with husbands – swiftly to yoke the mules to the wagon, so they might bring her to the beautiful temple of Hecate. Then the maidens got the chariot ready. And meanwhile Medea took from a hollow casket the drug that men say is called Prometheian. If a man should wet his body with this drug and appease Persephone with sacrificial offerings by night, he would not be wounded by blows from bronze weapons nor would he yield to blazing fire, but on that day he would be superior in valour and power. The drug first sprang up when the savage eagle let drop to earth in the valleys of Caucasus bloody ichor from Prometheus in his agony.[47] Its flower came out as high as a cubit above the ground, in colour like the Corycian crocus, rising on twin stems. In the ground its root was like new-cut flesh. Its juice, dark like a beech tree in the mountains, Medea collected in a shell from the Caspian sea to use as a drug; she washed it seven times in flowing water, and seven times called on Brimo protectress of children. Brimo who travels by night, from the underworld, queen of the dead, in the murky night, in black clothes. And the dark earth shook beneath and groaned as the root of the Titan god was cut, and Prometheus himself cried out in pain in his heart's agony. Medea now took out this drug and put it underneath the fragrant band that was fastened below her divine breasts.

415. *A love potion. Alexandria, 3rd cent.* BC *(Theocritus, Idyll 2, excerpts. G)*

A dramatic representation of a courtesan's attempt to win back a handsome lover.

Where are my bay-leaves? Go get them, Thestylis. And where are my drugs? Put a wreath of crimson wool round the bowl, so I can bind my dear lover, who is cruel to me. It's now the twelfth day that the beast hasn't even come near me and he doesn't know if I'm dead or alive; cruel man, he hasn't knocked on my door. I'm sure that Love has gone off with his fickle heart elsewhere, and so has Aphrodite. I'll go to Timagetus' wrestling-ring tomorrow, so I can see him, and I'll complain about how he is treating me.

But today I will bind him with what I burn here. Now, Moon, shine brightly, and I will sing to you softly, goddess, and to Hecate underground, before whom even dogs tremble as she comes from the graves of the dead and their black blood. Hail, Hecate unapproachable, and guide me until I am finished; make these drugs of mine in no way inferior to Circe's or Medea's or blonde Perimede's.

Magic wheel, draw that man to my house.

First barley melts on the fire. Sprinkle them on, Thestylis. Fool, where have your wits flown to? You curse, do you also think you can make fun of me? Sprinkle it on and say as follows: 'I sprinkle the bones of Delphis.'

Magic wheel, draw that man to my house.

Delphis has hurt me. So I burn this bay on Delphis. As they catch fire, crackle loudly and are consumed in an instant and I can't even see their ashes, so may Delphis' flesh be consumed in flames.

Magic wheel, draw that man to my house.

Now I'll burn the bran. Artemis, you can move the power of Death and anything else that is immovable – Thestylis, dogs all round the city are barking; the goddess is at the crossroads. As quick as you can, clash the cymbals.

Magic wheel, draw that man to my house.

Now the sea is still; the winds are still, but the pain in my heart is not still, but the whole of me burns for him; instead of a wife, he has made me miserable, a fallen woman, no longer a virgin.

Magic wheel, draw that man to my house.

As I melt this wax with the goddess's assistance, so may Delphis from Myndus melt with desire. As this bronze wheel of Aphrodite's spins, so may Delphis spin in front of my door.

Magic wheel, draw that man to my house.

I shall pour three libations and say three times as follows, 'O goddess: whether a woman lies beside him or whether a man does, let him forget that person as fast as they say Theseus once forgot fair-haired Ariadne on Naxos.'

Magic wheel, draw that man to my house.

Coltsfoot is a herb that grows in Arcadia, and for it all the colts run mad through the mountains, and the swift mares. May I see Delphis like that; may he rush to this house like a madman, from the glistening wrestling-ring.

Magic wheel, draw that man to my house.

Delphis lost this, the fringe of his cloak. I now shred it and throw it in the wild fire. Ai ai, painful Desire, why have you drunk the black blood from my flesh, all of it, like a marsh leech stuck to me?

I'll grind up a lizard and bring it tomorrow for him to drink. Now, Thestylis, take these flowers and knead them over his threshold, while it's still night, and say in a whisper, 'I knead the bones of Delphis.'

Magic wheel, draw that man to my house.

416. *Bitto's curse. Athens, 3rd/2nd cent. BC (Kaibel 1136. G)*

A curse inscribed on a lead tablet; at the end the name of the author Bitto and her victim Sosiclea are written upside-down.

I shall bind Sosiclea and her possessions and her actions and her thoughts. May she become hateful to her friends. I shall bind her beneath empty Tartarus in cruel bonds, and with the aid of Hecate under the earth. Sosiclea. Bitto. Dedicated to the Maddener[48] Furies.

417. *Ingredients for a love charm. Rome, 1st cent. BC (Horace, Epodes 5. L)*

'Oh, by all the gods in the sky who rule earth and the human race, what does this noise mean, why are all of you looking at me savagely? I beg you, by your children, if you ever called on Lucina[49] and she came to bring you successful childbirth – by this purple band on my toga, insignia of innocent childhood; by Jupiter, who will not approve of this – why are you looking at me like a stepmother, like a wild animal facing a spear?'

This is what the boy said in protest, with his lips trembling. He stood there (they had torn off his children's insignia), a young body, the sort that would soften the sacrilegious heart of a Thracian. Canidia, who had twined little snakes in her dishevelled hair, gave orders to burn in her witch's fire wild fig trees uprooted from tombs and funeral cypresses, eggs dipped in the blood of foul frogs, a night owl's feather, herbs from Iolchus[50] and Spain with its rich poisons, and bones torn from the mouth of a hungry bitch.

Now Sagana, with her skirts tied up, sprinkles water from Lake Avernus[51] through the whole house, with her rough hair standing on end, like a sea-urchin or some bristling wild boar. Vera, who lacks any conscience, had been digging up the ground with thick hoes, groaning with the effort, so the boy could be placed in the ditch and die from watching, throughout the long day, meals brought in two and three times – only his face would remain unburied, like a swimmer hanging in water by his chin. All this so his marrow could be cut out and his liver dried, to make a love charm, once his eyeballs had melted away from staring at the food.

Folia of Ariminum was there also, with her man's lust – so the resort town of Naples and all the neighbouring towns believed – she can bring down the stars and the moon from the sky with her Thessalian incantations. Then Canidia, gnawing her nails – what did she say (or not say?):

'Oh faithful witnesses to my deeds, Night and Diana, you who rule the silent time, when the secret rites are enacted, come to me now, and turn your divine anger on my enemy's house. While wild beasts lie hidden in the treacherous woods, relaxed in sweet slumber, that old man, whom everyone laughs at, my lover Varus – have Subura's[52] dogs bark at him – he has been rubbed with an ointment, the most perfect my hands have yet made. What has happened? Why do barbarian Medea's poisons work less well [for me], the poisons she used when she went into exile, after taking revenge on her royal rival, high Creon's daughter, when the robe she prepared, a gift steeped in poison, carried off the new bride in fire? No herb, no root hidden in inaccessible places has escaped me. He is lying asleep on his couch, forgetting all of his lovers. But no! He's free to move around, thanks to an incantation by some more knowledgeable poisoner! No, Varus, I won't use ordinary potions. You'll regret what you've done; you'll come back to me, and your devotion to me will return with no help from Marsian spells.[53] I'll prepare a stronger potion, made stronger because you disdain me. You'll see heaven sinking beneath the sea, below the earth's surface, before you'll fail to burn with love for me, just like pitch in dark flames.'

After she said this the boy stopped trying (as he had earlier) to mollify the sacrilegious women with kind words and, uncertain how he should break the silence, he threw out Thyestean curses: 'Your magic poisons don't have the power to invert right and wrong, to stop a man's vengeance. I'll pursue you with curses; no sacrifice can atone for my angry curse. No, when I die the death you have determined, I'll come as a Fury by night,[54] as a shade I'll find your face with my hooked talons, the gods of the Dead[55] have this power, and I'll sit on your restless hearts and drive your sleep off in terror. People will pursue you in turn and hit you with stones, you dirty old hags, and the wolves and the birds on the Esquiline hill[56] will scatter your unburied remains – a sight my parents (who alas will survive me)[57] will not fail to enjoy.'

418. *Epitaph with a curse. Rome, 1st cent.* AD *(CIL VI.20905 = CLE 95. Tr. R. Lattimore. L)*

An epitaph set up by a father to his daughter, with a curse added against the girl's mother, Acte, who had left him.

To the gods of the dead, the tomb of Junia Procula, daughter of Marcus. She lived eight years, eleven months, five days. She left in sorrow her unhappy father and mother. Marcus Junius Euphrosynus put up this altar for himself and the (*name erased*).

You, may your daughter's bones and your parents' rest together without you. Whatever you have done to us, may you get the same yourself. Believe me, you will be witness to your [fate]: here are inscribed the marks of eternal shame of Acte, a freedwoman, a treacherous, tricky, hard-hearted poisoner. [I leave her] a nail and a hempen rope to fasten about her neck, and burning pitch to sear her evil heart. Manumitted gratis, she went off with an adulterer, cheated her patron, and took away his servants, a maid and a boy, as he lay in bed, leaving him a lonely, despoiled man, broken-hearted. And the same curse [is laid upon] Hymnus and those who went away with Zosimus.

Defixiones ('bindings') usually give the names of the victim and the author of the curse (cf. no. 337, although the authors' names are omitted here) and list the parts of the body to be affected by the malediction. The reason for the curse is not always given.

419. *A comprehensive curse. Rome, late 2nd/3rd cent.* AD *(ILS 8751. L)*

This text, written on a thin sheet of lead, was discovered in a cinerary urn in a tomb at Mentana, north of Rome, along with the cremated woman's remains.

Rufa Pulica: her hands, her teeth, her eyes, her arms, her belly, her tits, her chest, her bones, her marrow, her belly, her legs, her mouth, her feet, her forehead, her nails, her fingers, her belly, her navel, her cunt, her womb, her groin; I curse Rufa Pulica on these tablets.

420. *A curse against Aristo. Athens, Roman period. (IG III.iii.97.34-41. G)*

I take Aristo and bind her hands and feet and soul; may she not utter an evil word about Philo, but may her tongue become lead and you [the daimon] bite her tongue!

421. *A curse against Aristocydes. Athens, 4th cent. AD (IG III.iii.78. G)*

Aristocydes and the women who accommodate him; may he never marry another woman; nor a boy either.

422. *A remedy for induration of the breasts. Egypt, 3rd-4th cent. AD (PGM VII. 208-9 = Preisendanz Henrichs 2 11, p. 9. Tr. J. Scarborough. G)*

[*A remedy*] against induration[58] of the breasts: take a fine linen rag and write on it in black ink: THERTTHARTHRL.[59]

423. *A remedy for ascent of the womb. Egypt. 3rd-4th cent. AD (PGM VII. 260-71 = Preisendanz Henrichs 2 11, p. 12. G)*

[A remedy] against ascent of the uterus: 'I swear to you, Womb of the Origin of the World, by him who has been set over the underworld, before Heaven and Earth and Sea came into being, who created the angels, from whom first (magic words: amichamchou kai chochao cheroei oueiacho odou proseionges); by him who sits with the Cherubim and who bears his appointed throne; return again back to your seat, [and] do not bite into the heart like a dog, but stop and remain in your proper place; do not rage; as long as I swear to you by him who in the Beginning created the heaven and earth and all that is in them. Hallelujah. Amen.' Write that on a plate [or strip] of tin and clothe it in seven colours.[60]

424. *Women alchemists: Mary the Jewess and Cleopatra. Egypt, 2nd cent. AD? (Berthelot, Coll. II 102. G)*

Alchemy was the 'divine science and art' that purported to enable its practitioners to turn base metals into gold; but at the same time it was also a mystical religion concerned with prolonging and even creating human life, and hence of great interest to philosophers and rulers.[61] Early treatises about alchemy quote the aphorisms of Mary the Jewess, who was said to have invented the 'bain-marie', or double-boiler, and record the mystical pronouncements of Cleopatra, who is said to have invented the ambix, or beaker.[62] But since their names also occur in the New Testament and the sayings attributed to them survive only in quotation, it seems probable that they are fictions, like Socrates' instructor in Plato's *Symposium*, Diotima.[63]

(1) Sayings of Mary the Jewess: (p. 102) 'Join the male and the female and you will find what you seek; without the association of this union, nothing can be done right. The one nature seeks the other ...' (p. 103) 'Do not seek to touch them with your hands; you are not of the race of Abraham, and [you cannot touch it] unless you are from our race.' (p. 201) 'Do not try to touch them with your hands, because the fiery element is a drug.' (p. 382)

'If you dip bronze seven times, you find a paradox.'

(2) Cleopatra's response to the philosophers' questions about how the dead may be brought to life, from 'the account of Comarus, priest and philosopher, of the holy Cleopatra and the sacred art of the philosopher's stone'. (p. 404) The Hebrew prophetess cried out loud: 'The one becomes two, and two three, and the one from three four; in two there is one.'

(pp. 293-4) 'The waters waken the bodies and the spirits that are locked up and weak, for again', she said, 'the waters apply pressure and again surround the dead, and little by little they come to life and rise up and put on varied and remarkable colours, like the flowers in spring, and the spring itself is glad and rejoices in the beauty with which it is surrounded. I speak to those of you who understand. When you take up plants and elements and stones from their places, they seem both to be beautiful and not beautiful, when the fire tests them. But when they take on the glory of the fire and their radiant colour, there you will see them become larger in their hidden glory, and you will see their intense beauty, and their earthly nature transformed into a divine nature, because they are nursed by the fire, as a foetus nursed in the womb grows quickly, when the ordained time approaches, nothing prevents it from coming out. That is how this remarkable art survives. Swelling waters and waves coming one after the other in Hades and in the tomb in which the waters lie wound our art. But when the tomb is opened, the waters leave Hades, as when a baby comes from the womb. The philosophers admire the art's beauty, as a loving mother who admires the child that she has borne. Then the philosophers seek where they may put the child to nurse, like a baby, with waters instead of milk. The art is like a baby, and when the baby takes shape, and when it is grown up among the other elements, behold the mystery that was sealed.

(11) 'After this I will tell you plainly where the elements and plants lie hidden. I shall begin by speaking in riddles. Go to the highest roof, to the dense mountain among the trees, and behold rocks on the height, and from the rocks take arsenic ("the male element"); there too is its partner, in which it becomes one, with which it rejoices. And the nature of the one rejoices in the nature of the other and without it it cannot be made whole ...'

Priestesses
'They burn all kinds of incense'

425. *Mamia. Pompeii, 1st cent. AD (CIL X. 816, 998 = ILS 6369. L)*

From a small temple on the side of the Portico of Concord:

Mamia, daughter of Publius, public priestess, [built this] to the genius of Augustus on her own land and with her own money.

From a monumental tomb on the Street of Tombs:

To Mamia, daughter of Publius, public priestess, the place of burial was given by decree of the decurions.[64]

426. *Priestesses at the sanctuary of Hilaeira and Phoebe, daughters of Apollo. Amyclae (near Sparta), 1st cent., AD (Pausanias, Guide to Greece 3.16.1-2. G)*

Their priestesses are unmarried girls, called Leucippides, like the goddesses themselves. One of the images was adorned by a priestess of the goddesses called Leucippis, who painted its face in modern style instead of the ancient one, but a dream forbade her to paint the other one as well. There is an egg in the temple hung from the rafters by ribbons. According to the story, this is the egg that Leda bore.[65] Each year the women in Amyclae weave a tunic for Apollo.

427. *The priestesses of Eileithyia and of Zeus Sosipolis at Olympia. Olympia, Elis, 2nd cent. AD (Pausanias, Guide to Greece 6.20.2-3. G)*

There is a sanctuary of Eileithyia[66] between the treasuries and Mount Cronion, and in the temple there is a cult of the local Eleian divinity Sosipolis [Saviour of the Polis]. Eileithyia has the cult title Olympia, and they appoint a priestess to her cult on a yearly basis. The old woman tends the cult of Sosipolis, lives in celibacy according to an Eleian custom and herself brings the god's bathwater and makes barley cakes for him mixed with honey. In the front of the sanctuary (for it is built in two parts) there is an altar to Eileithyia and a public entrance. But the cult of Sosipolis is in the inner part of the temple, and no one can enter there except for the god's attendant, with her head and face covered with a white veil. Young girls and women remain in the sanctuary of Eileithyia and sing a hymn; they burn all kinds of incense to Sosipolis, but it is not the custom to pour libations of wine.

428. *Flavia Ammon. Phocaea, 1st cent. AD (Pleket 11. G)*

The tribe of the Tethades to Flavia Ammon, daughter of Moschus, who is called Aristion, high priestess of the temple of Asia in Ephesus, president, twice stephanephoros, priestess of Massilia, president of the games, wife of Flavius Hermocrates, for her excellence and decorous life and her holiness.[67]

429. *The priestess Lalla. Lycia, 1st cent. AD (Pleket 13. G)*

The people of Arneae and vicinity, to Lalla daughter of Timarchus son of Diotimus, their fellow citizen, wife of Diotimus son of Vassus; priestess of the emperor's cult and gymnasiarch out of her own resources, honoured five times, chaste, cultivated, devoted to her husband and a model of all virtue, surpassing in every respect. She has glorified her ancestors' virtues with the example of her own character. [Erected] in recognition of her virtue and good will.

> **430.** *Tullia, priestess of Hestia. Ephesus, 1st cent. AD (Inscr. Eph. 1063-4. G)*

Votive offerings in verse.[68]

(1063) (*In dactylic hexameters*) Hestia, oldest of the gods,[69] you who watch over the immortal fire, to you Zeus the ruler has given the right to control the eternal flame for the city. You who were born before the other gods, grant to Tullia – since she has fulfilled her term of office without blemish in your temple – grant her children like in all respects to herself, and who think the way she does.[70] Grant her this wish, I pray, because of her unblemished chastity and her wisdom, because she has surpassed in these respects all mortals, both in the past and those who were born in our own time.

(1064) (*In iambic trimeters*) O goddess of the excellent and wise city founded by Androclos,[71] Hestia, eternal virgin, and Artemis, you who have the greatest name among the gods, be helpers to Tullia in all respects, because she served as your prytanis eagerly and willingly and generously provided her wealth for every purpose.

> **431.** *The priestess Alexandria. Rome, 2nd cent. AD (?) (ILS 4414. L and G)*

A young pastophorus (acolyte of Isis, who carried her cult statue in processions) is depicted on the side of the tombstone.

(*In Latin verse*) Here lies the famous priestess of the god Bacchus the Ancient, chaste pastophorus of the Nile goddess, whose name was Alexandria. She had barely attained the bloom of youth when the notorious envy of the fates took her away to Dis [the god of the Dead]. (*In Greek verse*) Here lies the maiden Alexandria, priestess of Dionysus, pastophorus of the goddess of the Nile, holy Isis, having fulfilled in her time twenty years ...

> **432.** *Tata. Aphrodisias, 2nd cent. AD (Pleket 18. G)*

The council and the people and the senate honour with first-rank honours Tata, daughter of Diodorus son of Diodorus son of Leon, reverend priestess of Hera for life, mother of the city, who became and remained

the wife of Attalus son of Pytheas the stephanephorus, herself a member
of an illustrious family of the first rank, who, as priestess of the imperial
cult a second time, twice supplied oil for athletes in hand-bottles, filled
most lavishly from basins for the better part of the night as well [as in the
day], who became a stephanephorus, offered sacrifices throughout the
year for the health of the imperial family, who held banquets for the
people many times with couches provided for the public, who herself, for
dances and plays, imported the foremost performers in Asia and
displayed them in her native city (and the neighbouring cities could also
come to the display of the performance), a woman who spared no expense,
who loved honour, glorious in virtue and chastity.

433. *Cassia Victoria. Misenum, late 2nd cent.* AD *(Unpublished.*[72] L)

An inscription from a shrine of the Augustales, a college of freedmen who
kept the emperor's cult.

Cassia Victoria, daughter of Gaius,[73] priestess of the Augustales,
dedicated in her own name and in that of her husband, Lucius Laecanius
Primitivus, a pronaos with columns and epistyle,[74] because of [the
Augustales'] extraordinary good will towards them. She gave a banquet
and to each man twelve sesterces.

434. *Theano the arrhephoros. The acropolis in Athens, 2nd cent.* AD *(A
dedicatory inscription in verse; Kaibel 861 = IG II² 3634. G)*

Little girls, 'carriers of dew' (*arrhephoroi*) brought a robe and basket to
Athena in an an ancient rite. This little girl appears deliberately to have
been named for a Homeric priestess.[75]

Revered goddess, my father Sarapion and my mother Chresime and my
five brothers and sisters have dedicated me, Theano as your arrhephoros.
Grant that they may reach maturity, and that my parents reach old age.

435. *Thesmophane. Athens, 2nd cent.* AD *(IG II².11674 = Peek 1029. G)*

My dear father and mother as well[76] gave me the name Thesmophane
before I met my sad death. For me the fates spun seven complete years
with their threads and then cut them off. And indeed my renowned father
lavished on me all the good things that belong to the noblest children. He
did not omit libations or anything owed to the gods of the dead for my life.
The priests of Eumolpus made a sacred branch for me and gave me great
honour. The *thiasotai* of Dionysus wove me a crown, and I was initiated
into the mysteries of torch-bearing Demeter. I won a good honour, since

the saying is true that children the gods love die.[77] Therefore, good father, do not distress your dear heart longer in sorrow.

436. *A priestess of Demeter at Eleusis. Athens, 2nd cent.* AD *(Kaibel 863. G)*

I am Marcianus' mother and Demetrius' daughter; my own name may not be spoken. I locked it away when the Athenians made me sacred priestess of Demeter, and myself hid it in the unconquerable depths. I did not initiate [into the Eleusinian mysteries] the children of Spartan Leda, nor Asclepius who discovered cures that healed diseases, nor Heracles who completed by his efforts all twelve labours for Eurystheus; [instead I initiated] the ruler of the wide earth and sea, the sovereign of innumerable mortals, Hadrian, who lavishes the cities with his boundless wealth, and above all these the famous land of Cecrops.[78]

437. *Berenice. Syros, 2nd/3rd cent.* AD *(Pleket 25. G)*

The resolution of the prytaneis approved by the council and the people: Whereas Berenice, daughter of Nicomachus, wife of Aristocles son of Isidorus, has conducted herself well and appropriately on all occasions, and after she was made a magistrate, unsparingly celebrated rites at her own expense for gods and men on behalf of her native city, and after she was made priestess of the heavenly gods and the holy goddesses Demeter and Kore and celebrated their rites in a holy and worthy manner, has given up her life – meanwhile she had also raised her own children. Voted to commend the span of this woman's lifetime, to crown her with the gold wreath which in our fatherland is customarily used to crown good women. Let the man who proposed this resolution announce at her burial: 'The people of Syros crown Berenice daughter of Nicomachus with a gold crown in recognition of her virtue and her good will towards them.'

438. *Flavia Vibia Sabina. Thasos, late Empire (Pleket 29. G)*

With good fortune. The senate honours Flavia Vibia Sabina, most noteworthy high priestess, and because of her ancestors uniquely mother of the council: she is the only woman, first in all time to have honours equal to those of the senators.

439. *Paulina, priestess of several mystery cults. Rome,* AD *384 (CIL VI.1779, 1780, 2145 = ILS 1259-61. L)*

Wife of Vettius Agorius Praetextatus, an important imperial official and leader of the pagans in the senate, a devout adherent of traditional religion.[79] Cf. nos. 427-37.

(1779) To the gods of the dead. Vettius Agorius Praetextatus, augur, priest of Vesta, priest of the Sun, quindecemvir,[80] curialis of Hercules, initiate of Liber and the Eleusinian [mysteries], hierophant, neocorus, tauroboliatus, father of fathers.[81] In public office imperial quaestor, praetor of Rome, governor of Tuscia and Umbria, governor of Lusitania, proconsul of Achaia, praefect of Rome, senatorial legate on seven missions, prefect of the praetorian guard twice in Italy and Illyrica, consul ordinarius elect,[82] and Aconia Fabia Paulina,[83] initiate of Ceres and the Eleusinian [mysteries], initiate of Hecate at Aegina, tauroboliata, hierophant. They lived together for 40 years.

On the right side of the tomb: Vettius Agorius Praetextatus to his wife Paulina. (*In verse*) Paulina, conscious of truth and chastity, devoted to the temples and friend of the divinities, who put her husband before herself, and Rome before her husband, proper, faithful, pure in mind and body, kindly to all, helpful to her family gods ...

On the left side: Vettius Agorius Praetextatus to his wife Paulina. (*In verse*) Paulina, the partnership of our heart is the origin of your propriety; it is the bond of chastity and pure love and fidelity born in heaven. To this partnership I entrusted the hidden secrets of my mind; it was a gift of the gods, who bind our marriage couch with loving and chaste bonds. With a mother's devotion, with a wife's charm, with a sister's bond, with a daughter's modesty; with the great trust by which we are united with our friends, from the experience of our life together, by the alliance of our marriage, in pure, faithful, simple concord; you helped your husband, loved him, honoured him, cared for him.

On the back of the monument. Paulina is speaking, in verse: My parents' distinction did nothing greater for me than that I even then seemed worthy of my husband. But all glory and honour is my husband's name, Agorius. You, descended from noble seed, have at the same time glorified your country, senate, and wife with your mind's judgment, your character and your industry, with which you have reached the highest pinnacle of excellence. For whatever has been produced in either language by the skill of the sages to whom the gate of heaven is open, whether songs that poets composed or writings in prose, these you make better than when you took them up to read.[84] But these are small matters; you as pious initiate conceal in the secrecy of your mind what was revealed in the sacred mysteries, and you with knowledge worship the manifold divinity of the gods;[85] you kindly include as colleague in the rites your wife, who is respectful of men and gods and is faithful to you. Why should I speak of your honours and powers and the joys sought in men's prayers? These you always judge transitory and insignificant, since your title to eminence depends on the insignia of your priesthood. My husband, by the gift of your learning you keep me pure and chaste from the fate of death; you take me into the temples and devote me as the servant of the gods. With you as my witness I am introduced to all the mysteries; you, my pious consort, honour me as priestess of Dindymene and Attis with sacrificial rites of the taurobolium;[86] you instruct me as minister of Hecate in the triple secret and you make me worthy of the rites of Greek Ceres. On account of you everyone praises me as pious and blessed, because you yourself have proclaimed me as good through the whole world; though unknown I am known to all.[87] For with you as husband how could I not be pleasing? Roman mothers seek an example from me, and think their offspring handsome if they are like yours.[88] Now men, now women want and approve the insignia that you as teacher have given me. Now that all these have been taken away I your wife waste away in sorrow; I would have been happy, if the gods had given me a husband who had survived me, but still I am happy because I am yours and have been yours and will now be yours after my death.

(1780) To Fabia Aconia Paulina, daughter of Aco Catullinus formerly prefect and consul, wife of Vettius Praetextatus prefect and consul elect, initiate at Eleusis to the god Iacchus, Ceres and Cora, initiate at Lerna to the god Liber and Ceres and Cora,[89] initiate at Aegina to the two goddesses, tauroboliata, priestess of Isis, hierophant of the goddess Hecate, and initiate in the rites of the Greek Ceres.[90]

(2145) In honour of Coelia Concordia, chief Vestal Virgin, Fabia Paulina arranged that a statue be made and set up first on account of her distinguished chastity and celebrated holiness concerning the divine cult, and chiefly because [Coelia Concordia] first had set up a statue to [Paulina's] husband Vettius Agorius Praetextatus, who was a man in all ways exceptional and deserving of honour even by Virgins and by priestesses of this [high] rank.[91]

440. *Umbria Matronica. Constantine, Algeria, Imperial period (CIL VIII.7604 = CLE 1613. L)*

To the spirits of the dead
Here lies Marcus Mundicius Saturninus who lived 95 years; may he rest in peace.

To the spirits of the dead
Umbria Matronica
That which for the other is maturity, for me was only prolonged service of the divinity I served for 80 years. Even barefoot, observing chastity and modesty, I went about earnestly to all the cities of the earth and for this my reward is that the earth receives me with benevolence.
She lived 115 years. Here she lies; may she rest in peace.

Christianity
'If they cannot control themselves, let them marry'

Christianity was, for the Romans, another foreign religion (in this case an offshoot of Judaism) to be regarded with suspicion. Like the cult of Bacchus, the Christian religion brought members of the lower classes together in assemblies, which was particularly worrisome to the authorities. Christians were also victims of wildly exaggerated stories and false accusations based upon misinterpretation: incest and cannibalism, for example. Still, the Roman concern was for security of the state; the opposition to Christianity was not theological.

441. *Teachings of Paul of Tarsus on women. Ephesus, c. AD 51-54 (I Corinthians 7.1-16, 25-40, 11.2-16, 14.33b-5. G)*

The teaching of Paul of Tarsus about women follows Jewish tradition more closely than notions of female behaviour in other early texts that came to be regarded as apocryphal or heretical. In his first epistle to the Corinthians Paul characterises marriage primarily as a vehicle for sexual satisfaction and as a financial burden. He recommends celibacy highly, for both men and women.

(7.1) About the matters you have written me about: it is a good idea for men not to lay hands on women. But rather than resort to prostitutes, every man ought to have relations with his own wife. The husband ought to give his wife her due, and likewise the wife ought to give her husband his. A woman does not have authority over her own body; it belongs to her husband. Likewise the husband does not have authority over his own body; it is his wife's. Do not deprive yourselves of one another, unless in a temporary agreement so that you have time to devote yourselves to prayer; then come together again, so that Satan does not tempt you with inability to control yourselves. I say this in order to be understanding, but not as a directive. I would prefer that all human beings be as I am myself,[92] but each person has his own blessing from God, some one thing, others another.

(7.8) I say to the unmarried and the widows, that it is better for them if they remain as I am. But if they cannot control themselves, let them marry, for it is better to marry than to be consumed with desire. To those who are married I proclaim – no, not I, but rather the Lord – that a wife should not be separated from her husband. If she is separated, let her remain unmarried or be reconciled with her husband, and the husband must not divorce his wife. To the rest of you I (not the Lord) say: if a Brother[93] has an unbelieving wife, and she prefers to live with him, let him not divorce her. And if a wife has an unbelieving husband, and she prefers to live with him, let her not divorce her husband. For the unbelieving man is sanctified by his wife, and the unbelieving wife by the

Brother. Since your children are unclean, now they are sanctified. If however an unbeliever wishes to divorce, let him be divorced. In these cases the Brother or Sister is not bound. God has summoned you in peace. For who knows, wife, if you will be your husband's salvation, and who knows, husband, if you will be your wife's salvation?

(7.25) About virgins I do not have the Lord's instructions, but I offer my advice as one of the faithful thanks to the mercy of the Lord. I believe that it is well in the present time of crisis for a person to be as he or she is. Are you married to a wife? Do not seek to be divorced. Are you divorced? Do not look for a wife. But if you do marry, you will not be committing a sin. If a virgin marries, she is not committing a sin. But such people will have afflictions in bodily life, and I wish to spare you. I assure you of this, brothers. The present time is limited. During what remains of it, those of you who are married to wives should be as if they were not, and those of you who are weeping as if they were not, and those of you who are rejoicing as if they were not, and those of you who purchase as if they had nothing and those of you who use the world as if they did not use it, for the whole frame of this world is passing away.[94] I wish you to be free from care. The unmarried man cares for the Lord's business, his concern is to please the Lord. The man who is married thinks about the business of the world, and how he may please his wife, and he divides his concern between them. The unmarried woman and the virgin care about the business of the Lord, and how they may be pure in body and in soul. The married woman cares about the business of this world, and how she may please her husband. I say this for your own benefit, and not to put a halter around your neck, but rather for your own good and for you to serve the Lord without distraction.

(7.36) If a man thinks that he is behaving improperly towards his virgin companion,[95] if he happens to be overwrought, and it ought to happen, let him do as he wants. He is not committing a sin. Let them get married. The man who is steadfast in his own heart, and is under no compulsion, but has control of his own will and has decided in his own heart to respect his virgin, does well to do so. So too the man who marries his own virgin does well, but the one who does not marry her does better. A wife is bound to her husband as long as he lives. If he dies, she is free to marry whomever she wishes, so long as it is a Christian marriage. But she is more blessed if she remains unmarried, in my opinion, and I believe that I have the spirit of God.

(11.2) I commend you because you remember all that I have told you and follow the advice that I gave you. I wish you to know that the head of every man is Christ, the head of every woman is her husband, and the head of Christ is God.[96] A man who prays or speaks out with his head covered disgraces his head. But every woman who offers a prayer or who prophesies without her head covered disgraces her head. For it is the same as if her head were shaven. If a woman's head is not covered, it may as well be shaven. For a man ought not to cover his head, since he is the image and glory of God. A woman is the glory of her husband. For man was not created from woman, but woman from man. And man was not created for woman's sake, but woman for the sake of man.[97] For this reason a woman ought to have authority on her head, for the sake of the angels.[98] None the less in the Lord there can be no woman without man nor man without woman. Just as woman was created out of man, man is born from woman. All things come from God. Judge for yourselves: is it proper for a woman to pray to God without a covering on her head? Does not nature herself teach us that while long hair is a disgrace to a man, it is the glory of a woman, because hair was given to her as a wrapping? If some of you want to start an argument, we do not have such a custom, nor do the congregations of God.

(14.33b) In all the churches of the faithful, let women be silent in the congregation, for it is not appropriate for them to speak. They should be obedient, as the law states. If they want to learn something, they should ask their own husbands at home, for it is a disgrace for a woman to speak out in the congregation. You must not think that you can direct the word of God, or that he speaks only to you.[99]

442. *Teachings about women attributed to Paul. As from Macedonia, 1st. cent.* AD *(I Timothy 2.8-15, 5.3-16. G)*

This pastoral letter, although attributed to St Paul, is written in a different style and almost certainly by a different author, probably within a few decades of his death. The writer's strictures are evidence that women continued to hope to be active in the church, and that there was at least at one time and one place an organisation of widows without families who depended upon the church for their support.[100]

(2.8) It is my wish that in every setting men should pray by raising pious hands without anger and contention; likewise women should adorn themselves in fitting dress with modesty and chastity and not with braids and gold jewellery or pearls or rich garments, but clothing fitting for women who profess piety, through good works.[101] Let a woman learn in silence in all obedience. I do not permit a woman to teach, nor to boss her husband around, but she should keep silent. For Adam was made first, and then Eve.[102] And Adam was not deceived, but his wife was deceived and became involved in transgression. A woman will be saved by child-bearing, if she remains constant in faith and love and piety, with chastity.

(5.3) Show respect for widows who really are widows.[103] But in the case of widows who have children or grandchildren, let them learn first to do their duty to their own household and to repay their debt to their ancestors, for this is acceptable in the sight of God. The true widow has put her hope in God and remains constant day and night in entreaty and prayer. The widow who lives in luxury dies a living death. Publicise these views, so that the widows will be beyond reproach. If a widow does not think first of her own affairs and particularly of her family, she is denying her faith and is worse than an unbeliever.

(5.9) A woman should not be enrolled as a widow unless she is over sixty years of age, the wife of one man,[104] attested for her good works. If she has raised her children, if she has been hospitable, if she has washed the feet of the saints, if she has come to the aid of the afflicted, and been active in every kind of good work. But refuse the younger widows, for when they show an affected devotion to Christ, they want to get married, since they are subject to condemnation because they have broken their first pledge. It is also true that they learn slowly, because they are busy with their households, not only are they slow, but frivolous and preoccupied, and they talk about unimportant matters. I want the younger widows to marry, bear children, run their households, and not to allow the Anti-Christ any opportunity to criticise them for their abuses; for some already have turned back to Satan. If a believing woman has widows [in her house], let her take care of them; that way the church will not be burdened, and will be able to look after the true widows.

443. *The conversion of Lydia and the exorcism of a slave-girl. Philippi, Macedonia,* AD *49 (Acts of the Apostles 16.12-18,40. G)*

(12) After we had spent several days in that city, on the Sabbath we went outside the city gates to the river where we thought there was a place of prayer,[105] and we sat down there to talk with some women who had gathered there. A woman, called Lydia, who was a seller of purple dye in Thyatira, a worshipper of God,[106] listened to us, and the Lord opened her heart to pay heed to the teachings of Paul. Then she was baptised, and her household as well, and she addressed us, saying 'if you have judged me to be faithful to the Lord, come to my house and stay there'. And we went to stay with her.

(16) As we were going to the place of prayer it happened that a slave girl met us. She was inhabited by a prophetic spirit, and because of her prophecies provided her masters with a good income.[107] This woman followed Paul and ourselves, prophesying and saying, 'these men are slaves of the Lord on high, who are proclaiming to us the way of salvation'. She kept this up for many days. Paul became tired of it and turned on the spirit and said, 'I order you in the name of Jesus Christ to leave her', and the spirit left her at that time.

The slave's owners persecute Paul, and he and his followers are jailed and flogged, but later released with an apology, because they are Roman citizens.

(40) After they had been let out of prison they went to Lydia, and when they saw their brothers [in Christ] they encouraged them, and then they left Philippi.

444. *St Thecla's devotion to St Paul and mission as a celibate teacher. Asia Minor, 3rd cent. (?) AD (Acts of Paul and Thecla 7-9, 18-20, 25, 34-5, 40-1. G)*

The Acts of Paul has been compared to ancient pagan novels that describe the adventures of a couple who are separated but after many dangerous escapades are reunited; in this Christian story, however, both partners remain chaste. One of the most popular documents to come from the earlier church, copies were circulated widely and translated into Latin, Syriac, Slavic, Arabic, Coptic and Ethiopic. But the notion of independent women teachers (i.e. outside monasteries) was not accepted by the later church.[108]

(7) As Paul was speaking in the midst of the congregation in Onesiphorus' house, a certain Thecla, a virgin, whose mother was Theocleia and who was engaged to be married to Thamyris, sat in the window near the house and listened night and day to what Paul was saying about chastity. She did not leave the window, but she was led onward by her faith, and rejoiced greatly. And then, when she saw many women and virgins going into the house to see Paul, she herself determined to stand face to face with Paul and to hear the word of Christ. For she had not yet seen Paul's face, but had only heard what he said.

(8) When she did not leave the window, her mother sent for Thamyris. He came eagerly, in order to take her as his bride. Then Thamyris said to Theocleia, 'Where is my Thecla?' And Theocleia said: 'I have news for you, Thamyris. Thecla has not stirred for three days and three nights from the window, not even to eat or to drink, but she is intent as if on a joyous festival, she is so intent on the deceitful and tricky speeches of a stranger who is lecturing, that I am amazed that her maidenly modesty can be so compromised. (9) Thamyris, that person is disturbing the city of Iconium, and Thecla even more. All the women and young people are going to see him, and being taught by him that (as he says) "you must revere one god alone and live chastely". And still my daughter is attached to the window like a spider overpowered by the man's speeches with a new and terrible passion. She hangs on what he says, and the virgin is seduced. You come and talk to her, since she is engaged to you.'

Thecla refuses to speak to her mother or to Thamyris, and Thamyris arranges that Paul be put in prison.

(18) But at night Thecla took off her bracelets and gave them to the doorkeeper, and when the door was opened for her went into the prison. Then she gave the guard a silver mirror and went to see Paul, and sat at

his feet to hear of the glory of God. And Paul was not frightened, but acted like a free man because of God's encouragement. And Thecla's faith increased, when she kissed his chains. (19) Meanwhile Thecla was being sought by her family and by Thamyris, and hunted through the streets as if she were lost, until one of the doorkeeper's fellow slaves told them what had happened during the night. They confronted the doorkeeper, and he told them that she had gone to the stranger inside the prison. And they went as he had told them and found Thecla imprisoned (as it were) by her affection for Paul. So they went out and gathered crowds and told the governor. (20) The governor demanded that Paul be led before the tribunal, but Thecla rolled herself on the ground where Paul had spoken to her when he was sitting in the prison.

> Paul is beaten and driven out of town and Thecla is sentenced to be burned, but God sends a storm to quench the fire, and Thecla escapes and finds Paul praying with Onesiphorus and his family in an open tomb outside Iconium.

(25) There was much affection in the tomb, with Paul rejoicing, and Onesiphorus, and all of them. They had five loaves of bread and vegetables and water and salt, and they rejoiced at the holy works of Christ. And Thecla said to Paul, 'I shall cut my hair off and follow you wherever you go.' But he said, 'The time is not right, and you are very beautiful, I am afraid lest another temptation get hold of you worse than the first one, and that you will not remain faithful but will lose your courage.' Thecla said, 'Just give me the seal of Christ, and temptation will have no hold on me.' And Paul said, 'Thecla, be patient, and you shall be baptised.'

> Thecla goes to Antioch, is wooed by Alexander and rejects him. She is sentenced to be thrown to the beasts, but a lioness licks her feet and she is adopted by the queen Tryphaena. The women of the city protest when she is once again thrown to the beasts.

(34) Then they threw in many wild beasts, but Thecla stood there and stretched out her hands and prayed. When she stopped praying, she turned and saw a big pit full of water, and she said, now the time has come for me to be baptised. So she threw herself in saying, 'I baptise myself in the name of Jesus Christ on the last day.' And behold, the women and the whole crowd wept, saying, 'Don't throw yourself in the water', so that even the governor began to cry, that such beauty would be devoured by seals. But Thecla threw herself into the water in the name of Jesus Christ, and the seals when they saw the lightning flash were dead in the water. And about her there was a cloud of fire, so that none of the beasts touched her and no one saw her naked. (35) When other more fearful beasts were thrown in the women shouted, and some threw

garlands, and others nard, cassia and balsam, so that there was the scent of many different perfumes, and all the beasts that had been thrown in stopped as if in sleep and did not touch her.

Thecla survives and is honoured by the governor, and Tryphaena takes her into her home.

(40) But Thecla longed for Paul and searched for him, sending in all directions. She was told that he was in Myra. She took with her some young men and female slaves, and hitched up her dress[109] and sewed her mantle into a cloak that looked like a man's, and went to Myra; she found Paul speaking the word of God and she stood near him. He was amazed when he saw her and the crowd with her, and wondered if some other temptation had come to her. When she saw him she said, 'I have taken the baptism, Paul; for He who works with you to spread the gospel has worked with me to baptise me.' (41) And Paul took her hand and led her to Hermeias' house and heard everything that had happened to her. Paul was amazed, and those who heard were confirmed and prayed for Thecla. And Thecla stood up and said to Paul, 'I am going to Iconium.' And Paul said, 'Go and teach the word of God.' Tryphaena had given her much clothing and sent much money with her, and she left this with Paul for his ministry to the poor.

445. *The martyrdom of St Perpetua. Carthage, AD 203 (Acts of the Christian Martyrs 8.2-10. Tr. H. Musurillo. L)*

In 203 Septimius Severus banned conversion to either Judaism or Christianity, and as a result of this ban, St Perpetua was martyred in Carthage. Greek and Latin versions of her story were circulated; the account is atypical (and thus perhaps authentic) because it contains a long narrative attributed to Perpetua herself.[110]

A number of young catechumens were arrested, Revocatus and his fellow slave Felicitas, Saturninus and Secundulus, and with them Vibia Perpetua, a newly married woman of good family and upbringing. Her mother and father were still alive and one of her two brothers was a catechumen like herself. She was about twenty-two years old and had an infant son at the breast. Now from this point on the entire account of her ordeal is her own, according to her own ideas and in the way that she herself wrote it down.

While we were still under arrest, she said, my father out of love for me was trying to persuade me and shake my resolution.

'Father,' said I, 'do you see this vase here, for example, or waterpot or whatever?'

'Yes, I do,' said he.

And I told him: 'Could it be called by any other name than what it is?' And he said: 'No.'

'Well, so too I cannot be called anything other than what I am, a Christian.'

At this my father was so angered by the word 'Christian' that he moved towards me as though he would pluck my eyes out. But he left it at that and departed, vanquished along with his diabolical arguments.

For a few days afterwards I gave thanks to the Lord that I was separated from my father, and I was comforted by his absence. During these few days I was baptised, and I was inspired by the Spirit not to ask for any other favour after the water but simply the perseverance of the flesh. A few days later we were lodged in the prison; and I was terrified, as I had never before been in such a dark hole. What a difficult time it was! With the crowd the heat was stifling; then there was the extortion of the soldiers; and to crown all, I was tortured with worry for my baby there.

Then Tertius and Pomponius, those blessed deacons who tried to take care of us, bribed the soldiers to allow us to go to a better part of the prison to refresh ourselves for a few hours. Everyone then left that dungeon and shifted for himself. I nursed my baby, who was faint from hunger. In my anxiety I spoke to my mother about the child, I tried to comfort my brother, and I gave the child in their charge. I was in pain because I saw them suffering out of pity for me. These were the trials I had to endure for many days. Then I got permission for my baby to stay with me in prison. At once I recovered my health, relieved as I was of my worry and anxiety over the child. My prison had suddenly become a palace, so that I wanted to be there rather than anywhere else.

Then my brother said to me: 'Dear sister, you are greatly privileged; surely you might ask for a vision to discover whether you are to be condemned or freed.'

Faithfully I promised that I would, for I knew that I could speak with the Lord, whose great blessings I had come to experience. And so I said: 'I shall tell you tomorrow.' Then I made my request and this was the vision I had.

I saw a ladder of tremendous height made of bronze, reaching all the way to the heavens, but it was so narrow that only one person could climb up at a time. To the sides of the ladder were attached all sorts of metal weapons: there were swords, spears, hooks, daggers, and spikes; so that if anyone tried to climb up carelessly or without paying attention, he would be mangled and his flesh would adhere to the weapons.

At the foot of the ladder lay a dragon of enormous size, and it would attack those who tried to climb up and try to terrify them from doing so. And Saturus was the first to go up, he who was later to give himself up of his own accord. He had been the builder of our strength, although he was not present when we were arrested. And he arrived at the top of the staircase and he looked back and said to me: 'Perpetua, I am waiting for you. But take care; do not let the dragon bite you.'

'He will not harm me,' I said, 'in the name of Christ Jesus.'

Slowly, as though he were afraid of me, the dragon stuck his head out from underneath the ladder. Then, using it as my first step, I trod on his head and went up.

Then I saw an immense garden, and in it a grey-haired man sat in shepherd's garb; tall he was, and milking sheep. And standing around him were many thousands of people clad in white garments. He raised his head, looked at me, and said: 'I am glad you have come, my child.'

He called me over to him and gave me, as it were, a mouthful of the milk he was drawing; and I took it into my cupped hands and consumed it. And all those who stood around said: 'Amen!' At the sound of this word I came to, with the taste of something sweet still in my mouth. I at once told this to my brother, and we realised that we would have to suffer, and that from now on we would no longer have any hope in this life.

A few days later there was a rumour that we were going to be given a hearing. My father also arrived from the city, worn with worry, and he came to see me with the idea of persuading me.

'Daughter,' he said, 'have pity on my grey head – have pity on me your father, if I deserve to be called your father, if I have favoured you above all your brothers, if I have raised you to reach this prime of your life. Do not abandon me to be the reproach of men. Think of your brothers, think of your mother and your aunt, think of your child, who will not be able to live once you are gone. Give up your pride! You will destroy all of us! None of us will ever be able to speak freely again if anything happens to you.'

This was the way my father spoke out of love for me, kissing my hands and throwing himself down before me. With tears in his eyes he no longer addressed me as his daughter but as a woman. I was sorry for my father's sake, because he alone of all my kin would be unhappy to see me suffer.

I tried to comfort him saying: 'It will all happen in the prisoner's dock as God wills; for you may be sure that we are not left to ourselves but are all in his power.'

And he left me in great sorrow.

One day while we were eating breakfast we were suddenly hurried off for a hearing. We arrived at the forum, and straight away the story went about the neighbourhood near the forum and a huge crowd gathered. We walked up to the prisoner's dock. All the others when questioned admitted their guilt. Then, when my turn came, my father appeared with my son, dragged me from the step, and said: 'Perform the sacrifice – have pity on your baby!'

Hilarianus the governor, who had received his judicial powers as the successor of the late proconsul Minucius Timinianus, said to me; 'Have pity on your father's grey head; have pity on your infant son. Offer the sacrifice for the welfare of the emperors.'

'I will not', I retorted.

'Are you a Christian?' said Hilarianus.

And I said: 'Yes, I am.'

When my father persisted in trying to dissuade me, Hilarianus ordered him to be thrown to the ground and beaten with a rod. I felt sorry for father, just as if I myself had been beaten. I felt sorry for his pathetic old age.

Then Hilarianus passed sentence on all of us: we were condemned to the beasts, and we returned to prison in high spirits. But my baby had got used to being nursed at the breast and to staying with me in prison. So I sent the deacon Pomponius straight away to my father to ask for the baby. But my father refused to give him over. But as God willed, the baby had no further desire for the breast, nor did I suffer any inflammation; and so I was relieved of any anxiety for my child and of any discomfort in my breasts.

Some days later when we were all at prayer, suddenly while praying I spoke out and uttered the name Dinocrates. I was surprised; for the name had never entered my mind until that moment. And I was pained when I recalled what had happened to him. At once I realised that I was privileged to pray for him. I began to pray for him and to sigh deeply for him before the Lord. That very night I had the following vision. I saw Dinocrates coming out of a dark hole, where there were many others with him, very hot and thirsty, pale and dirty. On his face was the wound he had when he died.

Now Dinocrates had been my brother according to the flesh; but he had died horribly of cancer of the face when he was seven years old, and his death was a source of loathing to everyone. Thus it was for him that I made my prayer. There was a great abyss between us: neither could approach the other. Where Dinocrates stood there was a pool full of water; and its rim was higher than the child's height, so that Dinocrates had to stretch himself up to drink. I was sorry that, though the pool had water in it, Dinocrates could not drink because of the height of the rim. Then I woke up, realising that my brother was suffering. But I was confident that I could help him in his trouble; and I prayed for him every day until we were transferred to the military prison. For we were supposed to fight with the beasts at the military games to be held on the occasion of the Emperor Geta's birthday. And I prayed for my brother day and night with tears and sighs that this favour might be granted me.

On the day we were kept in chains, I had this vision shown to me. I saw the same spot I had seen before, but there was Dinocrates all clean, well dressed, and refreshed. I saw a scar where the wound had been, and the pool that I had seen before now had its rim lowered to the level of the child's waist. And Dinocrates kept drinking water from it, and there above the rim was a golden bowl full of water. And Dinocrates drew close and began to drink from it, and yet the bowl remained full. And when he had drunk enough of the water, he began to play as children do. Then I awoke, and I realised that he had been delivered from his suffering.

Some days later, an adjutant named Pudens, who was in charge of the prison, began to show us great humour, realising that we possessed some great power within us. And he began to allow many visitors to see us for our mutual comfort.

Now the day of the contest was approaching, and my father came to see me overwhelmed with sorrow. He started tearing the hairs from his beard and threw them on the ground; he then threw himself on the ground and began to curse his old age and to say such words as would move all creation. I felt sorry for his unhappy old age.

The day before we were to fight with the beasts I saw the following vision. Pomponius the deacon came to the prison gates and began to knock violently. I went out and opened the gate for him. He was dressed in an unbelted white tunic, wearing elaborate sandals. And he said to me: 'Perpetua, come; we are waiting for you.'

Then he took my hand and we began to walk through rough and broken country. At last we came to the amphitheatre out of breath, and he led me into the centre of the arena.

Then he told me: 'Do not be afraid. I am here, struggling with you.' Then he left.

I looked at the enormous crowd who watched in astonishment. I was surprised that no beasts were let loose on me; for I knew that I was condemned to die by the beasts. Then out came an Egyptian against me, of vicious appearance, together with his seconds, to fight with me. There also came up to me some handsome young men to be my seconds and assistants.

My clothes were stripped off, and suddenly I was a man. My seconds began to rub me down with oil, as they are wont to do before a contest. Then I saw the Egyptian on the other side rolling in the dust. Next there came forth a man of marvellous stature, such that he rose above the top of the amphitheatre. He was clad in a beltless purple tunic with two stripes, one on either side, running down the middle of his chest. He wore sandals that were wondrously made of gold and silver, and he carried a wand like an athletic trainer and a green branch on which there were golden apples.

And he asked for silence and said: 'If this Egyptian defeats her he will slay her with the sword. But if she defeats him, she will receive this branch.' Then he withdrew.

We drew close to one another and began to let our fists fly. My opponent tried to get hold of my feet, but I kept striking him in the face with the heels of my feet. Then I was raised up into the air and I began to pummel him without as it were touching the ground. Then when I noticed there was a lull, I put my two hands together linking the fingers of one hand with those of the other and thus I got hold of his head. He fell flat on his face and I stepped on his head.

The crowd began to shout and my assistants started to sing psalms. Then I walked up to the trainer and took the branch. He kissed me and said to me: 'Peace be with you, my daughter!' I began to walk in triumph towards the Gate of Life.[111] Then I awoke. I realised that it was not with wild animals that I would fight but with the Devil, but I knew that I would win the victory. So much for what I did up until the eve of the contest. About what happened at the contest itself, let him write of it who will.

446. *Persecution under Diocletian. Rome, AD 303 (Acts of the Christian Martyrs 22. Tr. H. Musurillo. G)*

When the Emperor Diocletian became ill in 303, a sacrifice for his health was required of all citizens, and those who did not cooperate were executed.

Since the advent and the presence on earth of our Lord and Saviour Jesus Christ, the greater the grace of the men of old, so much the greater was the victory of holy men. For instead of those visible enemies, we have now begun to crush enemies that cannot be seen with bodily eyes, and the invisible substance of the demons has been handed over to the flames by pure and holy women who were full of the Holy Spirit. Such were the three saintly women who came from the city of Thessalonica, the city that the inspired Paul celebrated when he praised its faith and love, saying, Your faith in God has gone out to every place.[112] And elsewhere he says, Of charity for your brothers I have no need to write to you; for you yourselves have learned from God to love one another.[113]

When the persecution was raging under the Emperor Maximian, these women, who had adorned themselves with virtue, following the precepts of the Gospel, abandoned their native city, their family, property, and possessions because of their love of God and their expectation of heavenly things, performing deeds worthy of their father Abraham. They fled the persecutors, according to the commandment, and took refuge on a high mountain. There they gave themselves to prayer: though their bodies resided on a mountain top, their souls lived in heaven.[114]

At any rate, they were here captured and brought to the official who was conducting the persecution, that, by thus fulfilling the rest of the divine commands and loving their Master even unto death, they might weave for themselves the chaplet of immortality. Of these girls one had preserved the shining purity of her baptism according to the holy prophet who said: *You will wash me and I shall be whiter than snow*,[115] and she was called Chione [Snow]. The second girl possessed the gift of our God and Saviour within herself and manifested it to everyone according to the word, *My peace I give you*,[116] and she was called Irene [Peace] by everyone. The third girl possessed the perfection of the Gospel, loving God with her whole heart and her neighbour as herself, in accord with the holy Apostle who says, *The aim of our charge is love*,[117] and she was appropriately named Agape [Love]. When these three girls were brought before the magistrate and refused to sacrifice, he sentenced them to the fire, in order that thus by a short time in the fire they might overcome those that are devoted to fire, that is, the Devil and all his heavenly host of demons, and, attaining the incorruptible crown of glory, they might endlessly praise along with the angels the God who had showered this grace upon them. The record that was taken down in their case is the material of our account.

The prefect Dulcitius was sitting on the tribunal, and the court clerk Artemisius spoke: 'With your permission, I shall read the charge which was sent to your genius by the guard here present, in connection with the parties in court.'

'You may read it,' said the prefect Dulcitius. And the charge was duly read: 'To you, my lord, greetings from Cassander, staff-officer. This is to inform you, sir, that Agatho, Irene, Agape, Chione, Cassia, Philippa, and Eutychia refuse to eat sacrificial food, and so I have referred them to your genius.'

'What is this insanity,' said the prefect Dulcitius, 'that you refuse to obey the order of our most religious emperors and Caesars?' And turning to Agatho, he said: 'When you came to the sacrifices, why did you not perform the cult practices like other religious people?'

'Because I am a Christian,' said Agatho.

The prefect Dulcitius said: 'Do you still remain in the same mind today?'

'Yes,' said Agatho.

The prefect Dulcitius said: 'What do you say, Agape?'

'I believe in the living God,' replied Agape, 'and I refuse to destroy my conscience.'

'What do you say, Irene?' asked the prefect Dulcitius. 'Why did you disobey the command of our lords the emperors and Caesars?'

'Because of my fear of God,' said Irene.

'What do you say, Chione?' asked the prefect.

'I believe in the living God,' replied Chione, 'and I refuse to do this.'

The prefect said: 'And how about you, Cassia?'

'I wish to save my soul,' said Cassia.

The prefect said: 'Are you willing to partake of the sacrificial meat?'

'I am not,' said Cassia.

The prefect said: 'And what say you, Philippa?'

'I say the same,' said Philippa.

'What do you mean, the same?' said the prefect.

Said Philippa: 'I mean, I would rather die than partake.'

'Eutychia,' said the prefect, 'what do you say?'

'I say the same,' said Eutychia; 'I would rather die.'

The prefect said: 'Do you have a husband?'

'He is dead,' said Eutychia.

'When did he die?' asked the prefect.

'About seven months ago,' said Eutychia.

The prefect said, 'How is it then that you are pregnant?'

Eutychia said: 'By the man whom God gave me.'

The prefect said: 'But how can you be pregnant when you say your husband is dead?'

Eutychia said: 'No one can know the will of almighty God. So God willed it.'

The prefect said: 'I urge Eutychia to cease this madness and to return to sound reason. What do you say? Will you obey the imperial command?'

'No, I will not,' said Eutychia. 'I am a Christian, a servant of almighty God.'

The prefect said: 'Since Eutychia is pregnant, she shall be kept meanwhile in jail.' Then he added: 'What say you, Agape? Will you perform all the actions which religious persons perform in honour of our lords the emperors and Caesars?'

Agape replied: 'It is not at all in Satan's power. He cannot move my reason; it is invincible.'

The prefect said: 'What say you, Chione?'

Chione said: 'No one can change my mind.'

The prefect said: 'Do you have in your possession any writings, parchments, or books of the impious Christians?'

Chione said: 'We do not, sir. Our present emperors have taken these from us.'

'Who was it who gave you this idea?' asked the prefect.

'God almighty,' said Chione.

The prefect said: 'Who was it who counselled you to commit such folly?'

'It was almighty God,' answered Chione, 'and his only begotten Son, our Lord Jesus Christ.'

The prefect Dulcitius said: 'It is clear to all that you are all liable to the crime of treason against our lords the emperors and Caesars. But seeing that you have persisted in this folly for such a long time, in spite of strong warnings and so many decrees, sanctioned by stern threats, and have despised the command of our lords the emperors and Caesars, remaining in this impious name of Christian, and seeing that even today when you were ordered by the soldiers and officials to deny your belief and signify this in writing, you refused – therefore you shall receive the punishment appropriate for you.'

Then he read the sentence written on a sheet: 'Whereas Agape and Chione have with malicious intent acted against the divine decree of our lords the Augusti and Caesars, and whereas they adhere to the worthless and obsolete worship of the Christians which is hateful to all religious men, I sentence them to be burned.' Then he added: 'Agatho, Irene, Cassia, Philippa and Eutychia, because of their youth are to be put in prison in the meanwhile.'

After the most holy women were consumed in the flames, the saintly girl Irene was once again brought before the court on the following day. Dulcitius said to her: 'It is clear from what we have seen that you are determined in your folly, for you have deliberately kept even till now so many tablets, books, parchments, codices, and pages of the writings of the former Christians of unholy name; even now, though you denied each time that you possessed such writings, you did show a sign of recognition when they were mentioned. You are not satisfied with the punishment of your sisters, nor do you keep before your eyes the terror of death. Therefore you must be punished.

'It would not, however, seem out of place to show you some measure of mercy: if even now you would be willing to recognise the gods you will be released from all danger and punishment. Now what do you say? Will you do the bidding of our emperors and Caesars? And are you prepared to eat the sacrificial meats and to sacrifice to the gods?'

'No,' said Irene, 'I am not prepared, for the sake of the God almighty who has created heaven and earth and the seas and all that is in them.[118] For those who transgress the word of God there awaits the great judgment of eternal punishment.'

The prefect Dulcitius said: 'Who was it that advised you to retain those parchments and writings up to the present time?'

'It was almighty God,' said Irene, 'who bade us to love him unto death. For this reason we did not dare to be traitors, but we chose to be burned alive or suffer anything else that might happen to us rather than betray the writings.'

The prefect said: 'Was anyone else aware that the documents were in the house where you lived?'

'No one else,' said Irene, 'saw them, save almighty God who knows all things. But no stranger. As for our own relatives, we considered them worse than our enemies, in fear that they would denounce us. Hence we told no one.'

'Last year,' said the prefect, 'when this edict of our lords the emperors and Caesars was first promulgated, where did you hide?'

'Wherever God willed,' said Irene. 'We lived on the mountains, in the open air, as God is my witness.'

'Whom were you living with?' asked the prefect.

Irene answered. 'We lived out of doors in different places among the mountains.'

The prefect said: 'Who supplied you with bread?'

Irene answered: 'God, who supplies all men.'

'Was your father aware of this?' asked the prefect.

Irene answered: 'I swear by almighty God, he was not aware; he knew nothing at all about it.'

'Were any of your neighbours aware of this?' asked the prefect.

Irene answered: 'Go and question our neighbours, and inquire about the area to see whether anyone knew where we were.'

The prefect said: 'Now after you returned from the mountain where you had been, as you say, were any persons present at the reading of these books?'

Irene answered: 'They were in our house and we did not dare to bring them out. In fact, it caused us much distress that we could not devote ourselves to them night and day as we had done from the beginning until that day last year when we hid them.'

Dulcitius the prefect said: 'Your sisters, in accordance with my commands in their regard, have received their sentence. Now you were guilty even before you ran away and before you concealed these writings and parchments, and hence I do not wish you to die immediately in the same way. Instead I sentence you to be placed naked in the brothel with the help of the public notaries of this city and of Zosimus the executioner; and you will receive merely one loaf of bread from our residence, and the notaries will not allow you to leave.'

And so, after the notaries and the slave Zosimus, the executioner, were brought in, the prefect said: 'Be it known to you that if ever I find out from the troops that this girl was removed from the spot where I have ordered her to be even for a single instant, you will immediately be punished with the most extreme penalties. The writings we have referred to, in the cabinets and chests belonging to Irene, are to be publicly burned.'

After those who were put in charge had taken the girl off to the public brothel in accordance with the prefect's order, by the grace of the Holy Spirit which preserved and guarded her pure and inviolate for the God who is the lord of all things, no man dared to approach her or so much as tried to insult her in speech. Hence the prefect Dulcitius called back this most saintly girl, had her stand before the tribunal, and said to her: 'Do you still persist in the same folly?'

But Irene said to him: 'It is not folly, but piety.'

'It was abundantly clear from your earlier testimony,' said the prefect Dulcitius, 'that you did not wish to submit religiously to the bidding of the emperors; and now I perceive that you are persisting in the same foolishness. Therefore you shall pay the appropriate penalty.'

He then asked for a sheet of papyrus and wrote the sentence against her as follows: 'Whereas Irene has refused to obey the command of the emperors and to offer sacrifice, and still adheres to a sect called the Christians, I therefore sentence her to be burned alive, as I did her two sisters before her.'

After this sentence had been pronounced by the prefect, the soldiers took the girl and brought her to a high place, where her sisters had been martyred before her. They ignited a huge pyre and ordered her to climb up on it. And the holy woman Irene, singing and praising God, threw herself upon it and so died. It was in the ninth consulship of Diocletian

Augustus, in the eighth of Maximian Augustus, on the first day of April, in the kingship of our Lord Jesus Christ, who reigns for ever, with whom there is glory to the Father with the Holy Spirit for ever. Amen.

447. *Gnostic ritual. Lugdunum, 2nd cent.* AD *(Irenaeus, Against Heresies 1.13.1-4, excerpts. L)*

Irenaeus, a second-century bishop of Lugdunum (Lyon), in describing the initiation of a woman into a Gnostic sect, emphasises as the most dangerous aspects of this heretical cult its appeal to women and the priest Marcus' use of magic tricks. The important role played by a female essence (grace) in the ritual, a characteristic of Gnostic Christian belief, is significantly absent from the conversion literature of the 'right-thinking' or orthodox church in this period.[119]

There is another one of those Gnostics who prides himself on having improved on his teacher. His name is Marcus. He is skilled in the art of false magic, and has used it to deceive many men and not a few women and to convert them to his cult, on the grounds that he is the most knowledgeable and has the greatest access to hidden and indescribable places. One could call him the One before the Antichrist (if such a person existed).[120] ... He pretends to say grace over a cup with wine in it; while he strings out his prayer at great length, he makes the wine turn red and purple, so that they will believe that the true Grace of the Company of the Most High is letting her blood drop into his cup during his prayer, and that those present should strongly desire to taste of that cup so that into them too Grace would drop, because she is summoned by that magician.[121] Again, he gives women cups full of wine and orders them to say grace in his presence. When this is done he offers another cup much larger than the one over which the deceived woman has said grace; he then pours from the smaller cup (over which the woman said grace) into the much larger one which he has brought forward; at the same time he says as follows: 'May grace who is before all things, who cannot be known or imagined, fill your inner person and multiply in you her understanding, sowing her mustard seed in good soil.'[122] By saying this sort of thing he makes the poor woman insane, while he appears to be working wonders, since the bigger cup is filled up by the smaller cup, so that it spills over. By performing other tricks like that he has destroyed many people, and steals them for his cult ...

He spends his time mainly with women, and particularly with those who come from good families and who have fine clothes and are very rich. He frequently deceives them with flattery, and seduces them by saying: 'I want you to share in my grace, since the Father of All always sees your angel before his face.[123] The place of your greatness is in us; it is right that we come together into one being. Take grace first from me and through me. Prepare yourself as a bride to receive your bridegroom so that you may be what I am, and I be what you are. Set in your bridal chamber the seed of light. Receive from me your bridegroom, take him, and be taken in him. Behold grace descends on you. Open your mouth and prophesy.' But when the woman answers, 'I have never prophesied and I have nothing to prophesy,' he offers new prayers, to the bewilderment of the woman who is being deluded: 'Open your mouth and speak whatever comes to you, and you will prophesy.' And she in her delusion, excited by what has already been said, her courage stimulated by the notion that she can prophesy, with her heart pounding harder than it should, takes the chance, and speaks in her delirium, and all sorts of things come out, foolishly and brazenly ... From that time on she thinks she is a Prophetess and gives thanks to Marcus because he shared his grace with her. She offers to pay him, not only by giving him her possessions (by which means he has amassed a huge amount of wealth) but also by intercourse with her body, and in addition she seeks to be united with him in everything so that she may enter with him into the One ... This same Marcus uses love potions and aphrodisiacs so that he can inflict violence on the bodies of some women – not of all. Those who return to the Church of God very often confess that not only have their bodies been corrupted by him but that they were passionately in love with him ...

448. *Drinking parties. Alexandria (?), late 2nd-early 3rd cent.* AD *(Clement of Alexandria, Christ the Educator [Paedagogus] 2.33.1-4. G)*

A church father warns about the licentious behaviour of women at drinking parties.

(1) As far as women are concerned, it is undoubtedly because they wish to be attractive that they do not drink from wide-mouthed drinking-cups[124] because they might cut their lips when opening their mouths wide, and so they drink out of narrow perfume-bottles that fit precisely in their mouths. When they drink they tilt back their heads in an unseemly fashion, and reveal their bare necks indecorously, as it seems to me, and they stretch out their throats to gulp down the drinks, as if to show everything they can to the other guests, and bring up belches like men, or rather like slave-men, and ruin themselves by such indulgences.

(2) It is not appropriate for a reasonable man to make a noise while drinking, and even less appropriate for a woman; it brings only disgrace to a woman who has some idea of who she is. 'A drunken woman is a cause for anger', says the Bible,[125] since a woman who debauches herself in drink is a source of irritation to God. Why? Because 'such a woman does not hide her shamelessness'. For a woman quickly can be lured into disorderly behaviour, if she has only an inclination to licentiousness.

(3) I do not forbid women to drink from perfume-bottles, but I condemn the desire to drink from these vessels exclusively. I advise the use of whatever vessels one has to hand, in order to put a stop to these desires before they can develop.

(4) The passage of the air that gives rise to belching should be managed in silence. In no way should women be permitted to show any part of their bodies naked, lest both parties fall into sin, the men because they are excited by the sight, and the women because they attract the men's attention to themselves.

449. *Celibacy. Palestine, 4th cent.* AD *(St Jerome, Against Jovinianus 47. Tr. W.H. Fremantle. L)*

In the process of marshalling evidence against marriage (and women) the priest Jerome, who often appears to be more concerned with making an effective case than with historical accuracy, cites an otherwise unknown treatise on marriage by Aristotle's successor Theophrastus (fourth century BC). Such treatises had been in circulation since the late fifth century BC and it is interesting that even in the context of Christian theology Greek and Roman misogyny did not lose its currency.

A book *On Marriage*, worth its weight in gold, passes under the name of Theophrastus.[126] In it the author asks whether a wise man marries. And after laying down the conditions – that the wife must be fair, of good character, and honest parentage, the husband in good health and of ample means, and after saying that under these circumstances a wise man sometimes enters the state of matrimony, he immediately proceeds thus: 'But all these conditions are seldom satisfied in marriage. A wise man therefore must not take a wife. For in the first place his study of philosophy will be hindered, and it is impossible for anyone to attend to his books and his wife. Matrons want many things, costly dresses, gold, jewels, great outlay, maid-servants, all kinds of furniture, litters and gilded coaches. Then come lectures the livelong night: she complains that one lady goes out better dressed than she; that another is looked up to by all: "I am a poor despised nobody at the ladies' assemblies." "Why did you ogle that creature next door?" "Why were you talking to the maid?" "What did you bring from the market?" "I am not allowed to have a single friend, or companion." She suspects that her husband's love goes the same way as her hate. There may be in some neighbouring city the wisest of teachers; but if we have a wife we can neither leave her behind, nor take the burden with us. To support a poor wife is hard: to put up with a rich one is torture.

'Notice, too, that in the case of a wife you cannot pick and choose: you must take her as you find her. If she has a bad temper, or is a fool, if she has a blemish, or is proud, or has bad breath, whatever her fault may be –

all this we learn after marriage. Horses, asses, cattle, even slaves of the smallest worth, clothes, kettles, wooden seats, cups, and earthenware pitchers, are first tried and then bought: a wife is the only thing that is not shown before she is married, for fear she may not give satisfaction. Our gaze must always be directed to her face, and we must always praise her beauty: if you look at another woman, she thinks that she is out of favour. She must be called my lady, her birthday must be kept, we must swear by her health and wish that she may survive us, respect must be paid to the nurse, to the nursemaid, to the father's slave, to the foster child, to the handsome hanger-on, to the curled darling who manages her affairs, and to the eunuch who ministers to the safe indulgence of her lust: names which are only a cloak for adultery.

'Upon whomsoever she sets her heart, they must have her love though they want her not. If you give her the management of the whole house, you must yourself be her slave. If you reserve something for yourself, she will not think you are loyal to her; but she will turn to strife and hatred, and unless you quickly take care, she will have the poison ready. If you introduce old women, and soothsayers, and prophets, and vendors of jewels and silken clothing, you imperil her chastity; if you shut the door upon them, she is injured and fancies you suspect her. But what is the good of even a careful guardian, when an unchaste wife cannot be watched, and a chaste one ought not to be? For necessity is but a faithless keeper of chastity, and she alone really deserves to be called pure, who is free to sin if she chooses. If a woman be fair, she soon finds lovers; if she be ugly, it is easy to be wanton. It is difficult to guard what many long for. It is annoying to have what no one thinks worth possessing. But the misery of having an ugly wife is less than that of watching a comely one. Nothing is safe, for which a whole people sighs and longs. One man entices with his figure, another with his brains, another with his wit, another with his open hand. Somehow, or sometime, the fortress is captured which is attacked on all sides.

'Men marry, indeed, so as to get a manager for the house, to solace weariness, to banish solitude; but a faithful slave is a far better manager, more submissive to the master, more observant of his ways, than a wife who thinks she proves herself mistress if she acts in opposition to her husband, that is, if she does what pleases her, not what she is commanded. But friends, and servants who are under the obligation of benefits received, are better able to wait upon us in sickness than a wife who makes us responsible for her tears (she will sell you enough to make a deluge for the hope of a legacy); who boasts of her anxiety, yet drives her sick husband to the distraction of despair. But if she herself feels ill, we must fall sick with her and never leave her bedside. Or if she be a good and agreeable wife (how rare a bird she is!), we have to share her groans in childbirth, and suffer torture when she is in danger.'[127]

A wise man can never be alone. He has with him the good men of all time, and turns his mind freely wherever he chooses. What is inaccessible to him in person he can embrace in thought. And, if men are scarce, he converses with God. He is never less alone than when alone.

450. *St Macrina, her mother Emmelia, and their community of celibate women. Annesi, Asia Minor, 4th cent. AD (Gregory of Nyssa, Life of St Macrina pp. 371.24-375.5, 375.21-377.7, 381.15-382.2, 382.15-18, 388.7-389.10, 398.23-399.9, 401.2, 401.23-402.6, 407.4-14 Woods Callahan. G)*

Macrina was the oldest daughter of a large landowning family. Given a Christian education by her mother, she influenced the careers of two younger brothers, St Basil the Great and St Gregory of Nyssa, and founded a monastery on her family estate. In these excerpts from his biography of his sister, Gregory describes Macrina's lifelong devotion to her mother and her religion, her celibacy and asceticism.[128]

(371.24) The baby was named Macrina, because in the past there had been a famous Macrina in the family, who had been our father's mother and who at the time of the persecutions had like an athlete undergone confessions on behalf of Christ, and it was in honour of her that the child was named by her parents. But this name was only what she was called in public by her acquaintances; she was called by another secret name in private, which she was called by before she was she was brought to birth on account of a certain vision.

Macrina's mother[129] was so committed to virtue that she was at all times obedient to the will of god, and she had particular affection for the pure and unsullied conduct of life, so that she chose marriage only with reluctance. But since she had lost both her parents and her body had reached a perfect maturity and the reputation of her beauty had attracted many suitors, there was a risk that if she did not pick a husband of her own choice, she might suffer as a result of an insult some fate that she did not wish, at the hands of the suitors who were inflamed by her beauty and preparing to abduct her. Because of this she chose as her husband a man known for his piety and committed to Christianity, in order to have him as a guardian of her life, and with her first labour-pains became the mother of Macrina.

When the time had come in which she would be released from the labour-pains by giving birth, she fell asleep and thought she was holding in her hands the baby she was in the process of bearing, and someone more majestic in form and dress than a human being appeared to her and addressed the baby she was holding by the name of Thecla – that Thecla who had the great reputation among the Virgins.[130] After he did this and bore witness to it three times the vision disappeared from her eyes and brought release to her labour, so that she woke up from her sleep and saw

the dream had come true. This was the child's secret name. I think that
the vision told her not so much to give the child a name as to provide guidance for the child, and to predict the young girl's future life and to hint at
the similar manner of life the child would lead by the use of Thecla's
name.

The child was then brought up, and although she had her own nurse,
for the most part the child was nursed in her mother's arms. She
surpassed the children of her own age with her facility in learning
children's lessons, and her nature led her to excel in whatever lesson her
parents chose for her. Her mother was determined to educate her child,
not however with an ordinary or common education, in which the
teaching during the first years of childhood consists mainly of learning
poetry. For she considered it disgraceful and inappropriate that she be
taught either the tragic passions that arise from women and give the
poets the starting points and plots, or the disorder of comedy or the
disgraces of the evils in Troy or that her child's tender and plastic nature
be defiled in some way by the unholy treatment of women.

Instead her mother taught her the holy writings that she thought were
readily understood by young children, and these were what the child
studied, particularly the Wisdom of Solomon, and more particularly the
sections that had bearing on ethical life. There was no section of the book
of psalms that she did not know, and at specified times she would recite
each section of the Psalter. When she rose from bed, when she began her
household duties, when she rested, when she took nourishment, when
she rose from table, when she went to bed, and when she rose up to pray,
she always had the Psalter as a kind companion that never abandoned
her at any time.

Fortified by these pursuits and her household duties, and practising
her wool-working with diligence,[131] Macrina reached the age of twelve,
the time in which the bloom of adolescence begins to flourish. Here it is
worth remarking that the young girl's beauty could not remain hidden,
and in all that region there was nothing wonderful in comparison with
her beauty and her elegance ... But her father (for he was a sensible man
and considered to be a good judge) chose from the rest a young man of the
family who was well respected and known to be sensible, who had just
completed his education; it was he that the father decided should
be his daughter's bridegroom, when she was old enough. In the meantime
they had high hopes for the young man, who brought to Macrina's father
his skill in speaking as one of his wedding gifts, since he had already
demonstrated his power in the law courts on behalf of those who had been
wronged. But Envy cut off these high hopes by snatching him from life at
a pitifully young age.

Macrina resolves to stay faithful to her intended husband by remaining
unmarried and refuses to consider another match.

(375.21) In order to reject the arguments of all those who tried to persuade her that she should marry, she decided on a single safeguard for her good resolution: not to be separated from her mother even for a moment of time. As a result her mother often said of her, that she bore her other children at particular times, but Macrina she was pregnant with and in a manner of speaking carried for all time. But her daughter's companionship was not burdensome or useless for her mother. Instead of having many servants she had the services of her daughter, and the benefit was reciprocal for both parties. For the mother took care of her daughter's soul, and the daughter looked after the mother's body, and in other respects undertook to perform the services that her mother required, and often prepared her mother's food with her own hands.[132] Not that this was her principal task; but after she had anointed her hands for religious rituals (for she thought that she ought to concentrate on this in the conduct of her life), in the time she had left she provided nourishment for her mother by her own labours. Not only this, but she participated with her in all her responsibilities. For her mother had four sons and five daughters and paid taxes to three governors, because her property was spread over three districts. For this reason her mother was variously preoccupied with these responsibilities, since her father had already departed from life. In all these matters she was her mother's partner, sharing the responsibilities with her and lightening the weight of her sorrows. And on account of her mother's stewardship she kept her own life blameless in her mother's eyes, through her mother's guidance and observation, while at the same time she offered her mother the example of her own life with an eye towards the same goal, I mean philosophy, leading her little by little towards the immaterial and the simpler life.[133]

(381.15) When the mother had ceased being responsible for childcare and involved in the children's education and development, and most of the demands of the physical life had been divided up among the children,[134] then, as I said, the daughter's life served as a guide for the mother in the conduct of a philosophical and immaterial existence; the mother gave up everything she was accustomed to in order to attain the same degree of humility, and she put herself on terms of equality with the group of Virgins, so that she shared with them the same table and beds and all the necessities of life, abandoning all distinctions between them in her manner of existence.[135] Such was the organisation of their lives and so great was the height of their philosophy and so holy their community in its conduct both by day and by night, that it is impossible to describe it in words ... (382.15) Their existence consisted solely of the worship of God, and unremitting prayer and ceaseless singing of hymns, which was carried out equally at all times both by day and by night, so that this was their work and their rest from work.

Around AD 389 the mother died, and Gregory returned home to find
Macrina on her deathbed.

(388.7) When I reached the actual place (word had already reached the
Brothers of my arrival), the whole organisation of men came from the
men's quarters to meet me, for it was customary for them to honour their
loved ones by meeting them. The community of women remained
modestly in the women's quarters near the church awaiting my arrival.
When the prayers and blessing were over and the women had respectfully
bowed their heads after the blessing had been given, they returned to
their quarters, and none of them was left with us. I guessed the reason
why, that their Teacher was not among them. Someone led me to a house
where the great Macrina was, and opened the door, and I went into that
holy place. She was severely ill, and was resting not on a bed or a couch,
but on the floor. A board had been covered with a sack and another board
was supporting her head, constructed so as to serve in place of a pillow,
slanting in order to support the tendons in her neck and holding her neck
comfortably.

When I was inside the door, she raised herself on her elbow but was not
able to come up to me, since her strength had been reduced by fever. But
by placing her hands on the floor and stretching her body forward from
her pallet she paid the respect due to my rank.[136] I rushed forward and
lifted her, and raised her face from the ground and put her down again in
her customary resting position.

Excerpts from Gregory's description of Macrina's death and funeral.

(398.23) After this at evening time when the light was brought in, she
opened her eyes wide and looked at the light, and clearly wanted to sing
the Thanksgiving at the lighting of the lamps. Although she had lost her
voice she accomplished her wishes with her heart and the movement of
her hands, and fulfilled her desire by moving her lips. As she completed
the Thanksgiving, she brought her hand to her face in the sign of the
Cross, signalling the end of the prayer; she drew a deep breath, and
with her prayer brought her life to an end.

(401.2) The women who called her mother and nurse were more
afflicted with grief than the others, for these were the women that she
had taken up when they were cast out by the roadside in time of famine,
and had nursed and cared for and led towards the pure and imperishable
life ... (401.23) I asked certain women to remain whose services she
welcomed in life. Among these was a woman from a wealthy and
distinguished family, who had been famous when young for her beauty
and general distinction. She had been married to a man of great merit,
but after she had been married a short time, she had been while still
young released from that marriage, and took the great Macrina as the

guardian and guide of her widowhood, and spent most of her time with the Virgins, learning the life of virtue from them. Her name was Vestiana; her father Araxius was in the council for the consulate.

> Vestiana explains Macrina's wish for a simple burial. A dark cloak that had belonged to Emmelia is chosen as a shroud, and an all-night vigil held.

(407.4) Although I was sick at heart because of her loss, at the same time I determined that none of the actions fitting for such a funeral be omitted. I divided the crowd that rushed in by sex , putting the women with the choir of Virgins, and the crowd of men in the ranks of the monks, so that I was able to provide from both singing of the psalms in good rhythm and harmony as if by a choir, all blended in unison singing ...

Late pagan 'saints'
'She surpassed by far the philosophers of her time'

451. *The martyrdom of the pagan philosopher Hypatia. Alexandria, AD 415 (Socrates, Ecclesiastical History VII.15, Migne, PG vol. 67, col. 768-9; Suda, s.v. Hypatia, Y166 I.4 644-5 Adler = Damascius Fr. 163-4 Zintzen. G)*[137]

There was a woman in Alexandria named Hypatia. She was the daughter of the philosopher Theon. She had progressed so far in her education that she surpassed by far the philosophers of her time, and took over the Neoplatonic school that derived from Plotinus, and set forth every philosophical approach to those who wanted to learn them. Accordingly people from all over who wanted to study philosophy rushed to her side. Because of the dignified reputation that derived from her education, she began (with due modesty) to address even the rulers. And she had no hesitation about being in the company of men, since they all respected her more because of her extraordinary chastity.

Then she became the subject of envy. Because she was frequently in the company of Orestes, people in the church began to slander her, as if that were what was preventing Orestes from making friends with the bishop. Some hot-headed men who agreed with this, who were led by a certain Peter the Reader, were on the lookout for the woman when she returned to her house from wherever she had been. They threw her out of her carriage, and dragged her to the church known as Caesarion. They tore off her clothing, and killed her with potsherds. When they had torn her apart limb from limb, they took the pieces of her body to the place called Cinaron, and burned them.

This act did no small amount of damage to Cyril and to the Church at Alexandria. For murder and fighting, and everything of that sort, are totally alien to those who believe in Christ. These events took place after

Cyril had been bishop for four years, and Theodosius for ten [c. AD 415], in the month of March, during Lent.

Hypatia: daughter of Theon the geometrician, the Alexandrian philosopher; she was also a philosopher herself and widely known. She was the wife of Isidorus the philosopher. Her prime occurred when Arcadius was on the throne. She wrote a commentary on Diophantus, the astronomer Kanon, and a commentary on the Conic Sections of Apollonius. She herself was torn to shreds by the Alexandrians, and her savaged remains scattered throughout the city. She suffered this fate because of envy and her extraordinary learning, and particularly because of what she knew about astronomy. Some say that she was killed by Cyril, others say that she died because of the violence and disorder characteristic of the Alexandrians. For they did this also to many of their own bishops, for example, George and Proterius.

About Hypatia the philosopher. An illustration of how disorderly the Alexandrians are. She was born and raised and educated in Alexandria. She inherited her father's extraordinarily distinguished nature, and was not satisfied with the training in mathematics that she received from her father, but turned to other learning also in a distinguished way. Although she was a woman she put on a man's cloak and made her way into the centre of the city and gave to those who wanted to listen public lectures about Plato or Aristotle or about some other philosophers. In addition to her teaching she also excelled in the practical arts, being just and chaste, she remained a virgin, though she was so beautiful to look at that one of her pupils fell in love with her. When he was no longer able to control his passion, he let her know how he felt about her. The uneducated stories have it that Hypatia told him to cure his disease through the study of the arts. But the truth is that he had long since given up on culture; instead, she brought in one of those women's rags and threw it at him, revealing her unclean nature, and said to him, 'This is what you are in love with, young man, and not with the Beautiful,' and in shame and wonder at this ugly display his soul was converted and he became more chaste.

That (according to this account) is what Hypatia was like, skilled in debate and dialectic, intelligent in her conduct and politically adept. The other citizens understandably were fond of her and accorded her the greatest respect, and the current magistrates of the town always went first to her, as used to happen also in Athens. For even though the practice had died out, the name of philosophy still seemed distinguished and impressive to the people who had primary charge of the city. It then happened that the man in charge of the opposing sect, Cyril, passed by Hypatia's house and saw a large crowd in front of the door, consisting of both men and horses, some arriving, some leaving, and some waiting there. He asked what the gathering was, and why there was commotion in front of the house, and learned from his followers that the philosopher Hypatia was giving a lecture and that this was her house. And when he learned this he was very upset and soon planned her murder, the most unholy of all murders. As she was going out to lecture, as was her custom, a group of bestial men attacked her, true ruffians, who had no respect for god and no concern for men's indignation; they killed the philosopher and brought the greatest pollution and disgrace on their fatherland ...

452. *Sosipatra the philosopher. Sardis, mid-4th cent.* AD *(Eunapius, Lives of the Philosophers, 466-70, excerpts. G)*

In this idealised portrait, a pagan 'saint' is praised for her inspiration and clairvoyance. She appears to have been skilled in theurgy, a form of religion that employed magic in the course of ritual and that incorporated Neoplatonic notions of the life after death.[138]

So the renowned philosopher Eustathius[139] married Sosipatra, who by the excellence of her own wisdom made her husband seem simple and insignificant in comparison to herself. This woman deserves to be mentioned even at some length in a catalogue of wise men, so wide was her renown. She was born in the region of Asia near Ephesus that is called after the river Cayster which rises there and flows through it. Her ancestors and family were fortunate and wealthy. But when she was a little child, she made everything prosper, such beauty and respect illumined her childhood ...

When she was 5, two old men who turned out to be skilled in theurgy came to the farm and in return for his hospitality promised her father that they would in five years educate her so that his daughter would have a mind 'not like a woman's or a mere mortal's'.

The old men (who may have been heroes or divine beings or even gods) initiated her into no one knows what mysteries, and it was unclear even to those who were eager to learn in what religious rites she had been consecrated ... Her father did not recognise his daughter because of her height, and the strange beauty that shone down from her, and she hardly recognised her father. He saluted her as one would a divinity, so different did she look to him. Her teachers were with her and the table was set out, and they said, 'Ask the girl any question you wish.' But she interrupted and said, 'No, father, instead ask me what happened to you on your way to the farm.' When he told her to tell him ... she related everything, including his words and threats and fears, just as if she had been driving the chariot alongside him. Her father was so overcome with admiration that he was not simply amazed, but struck dumb, and believed that she was a goddess ...

The old men went away to their secret destination, and her father took his daughter from them initiated and (although decorously) inspired; he allowed her to live as she wished and did not interfere in any of her business, and was only disappointed at her silence. When she had reached maturity, although she had no other teachers, she had the works of the poets and philosophers and orators on her lips, and she could discourse with ease about matters which it was possible to know with difficulty and dimly after long labour and struggling. When it seemed to her time to marry, it was clear that of all men only Eustathius was worthy of the match. So she said to him and the assembled company: 'Listen to me, Eustathius, with the others as witness. I shall bear three children to you, all of whom will not attain what is thought to be human happiness, but each will win the happiness of the gods. You will go away before me, having obtained a beautiful and appropriate sphere, but I will probably obtain something better. Your home will be around the moon, and you will not serve here nor philosophise longer than five years, for thus your Image tells me, but you shall go in good and easily controlled motion to a place under the moon. And I wish to tell you my own fate.' She was silent for a brief time and then said 'No, my god will not let me.' Then she married Eustathius, for so the Fates had decreed, and her words were no different from a fixed decree of an oracle, since everything happened and came out exactly as she had predicted.

I must record what happened after these events. After Eustathius' passing away, Sosipatra returned to her own estate and lived in Asia in the ancient city of Pergamum. The great Aedesius[140] looked after her, and educated her sons. She taught philosophy in her own home, and after the students had listened to Aedesius, they went to her house. There was none among them who did not approve and admire the accuracy of Aedesius' discourse, but they worshipped and revered Sosipatra's inspiration ...

Once when they all had gathered at her house but Philometor[141] was not present but visiting in the country, the topic under discussion was the soul. After much heated argument, Sosipatra began to speak, and little by little destroyed propositions by her arguments, and then began to describe the descent of the soul and what part of it is punished and what part immortal, when she suddenly interrupted her bacchic and inspired talk and became silent; after a short time she said, 'What is this?' and shouted to the others, 'My kinsman Philometor is riding in a carriage, and the carriage is being overturned by an obstacle in the road and his legs are in danger – but his slaves have pulled him out alive, except that he has some wounds to his ankles and his arms, but even these are not serious. He is being carried on a litter, groaning.' That is what she said and so it happened and everyone knew that Sosipatra was everywhere, and that she was present at all events, as the philosophers say about the gods. And she died leaving the three sons.

Notes

I. Women's Voices

1. Cole 1981, 219-45.

2. On women writers, cf. esp. Snyder 1989.

3. Aphrodite's promise resembles the type of binding formula used in magical incantations. See Preisendanz, I, 112-14.

4. In the Greek there is more emphasis on imagination – the 'I' of the poem (a female, but not necessarily Sappho herself) says 'he seems to me to be like one of the gods'. See Lefkowitz 1981a, 66-7.

5. Sappho's simile describes not just the moon's beauty but its sustaining effect on whatever its light touches. The implication is that her absent friend will similarly beautify and nourish everyone in her new environment. Cf. Alcman, Fr. 1.39-43 (below, no. 401), where the sun is used simply as a metaphor of pre-eminence, stressing physical appearance.

6. On the dramatic situation of this ode, see especially Burnett 1979.

7. An *aulos* was a pipe, although it is sometimes translated as 'flute', but in sound it more closely resembled an oboe.

8. On interpretation, see especially Pomeroy 1978a and Pomeroy 1977.

9. A bogey-woman who was believed to kill children because she had lost her own.

10. Another island; her birthplace may be mentioned because she died away from home.

11. Miletus was sacked in 277 BC. An epigram (*AP* VII.493) by Antipater of Thessalonica describes how a mother killed herself and her daughter when the Romans sacked Corinth in 146 BC. Cf. Polyxena's willingness to sacrifice herself in Euripides, *Hecuba* 345-78.

12. For a female, death before marriage was considered particularly wasteful. For other examples in extant inscriptions, see Lattimore, 189-92.

13. A likeness of the deceased was carved on the tombstone. Cf. FH 60 and p. 137.

14. Syracuse.

15. The Greeks admired verisimilitude. Cf. what the women say about the tableau of Adonis and Aphrodite in Theocritus 15 (no. 229). The two women in Herodas 4 are equally effusive.

16. Cf. *Inscr. Eph.* nos. 508, 1012.

17. Merkelbach suggests that the comparison of springs of water and fire may attempt to reflect the thought of the fifth-century pre-Socratic philosopher Heraclitus, Fr. 22 B 31 D-K.

18. The idea of drinking (*pion*) is suggested by the mountain's name.

19. Cf. West 1978, 101-15.

20. The language of the poem is deliberately archaic and 'poetic'.

21. Cf. Lefkowitz 1981, 89-90.

22. Although usually the sex of the priest matched the sex of the god, at the oracle of Apollo at Delphi a woman priestess, the Pythia, delivered the god's messages, in the presence of his priests; many quotations of such oracles survive, often in hexameter verse. Unfortunately a coherent picture cannot be derived from surviving information about the precise nature of the priestess's utterance, and presumably the procedure of consultation changed over time. Cf. Parke and Wormell 1956, 17-45.

23. At Dodona priestesses called 'Doves' delivered oracles in response to questions submitted on folded lead tablets.

24. Cf. Agamemnon's assertion in *Od.* 24.200-2, that because Clytemnestra murdered her husband, 'people will sing an evil song about women, and she will give a bad reputation to women, even the ones who do good', and Hippolytus' tirade, no. 61.

25. On the authorship and date, see Bühler 1963.

26. In order to preserve the family property, fathers (or guardians) had the right to determine whom their daughters should marry; cf. no. 52. The plot of Menander's *Epitrepontes* concerns a similar situation.

27. On the presumption that the male is naturally more intelligent, see Schaps 1979, 92.

II. Men's Opinions

1. Tyrant of Athens, 527-510 BC, son of Pisistratus.

2. Cf. Sophocles, *Oedipus the King* 873-80.

3. *Domiseda*.

4. The numeral one.

5. I.e. died in his arms. It was the Roman custom for the nearest relative to kiss the dying person on the mouth at the last possible moment in order to capture the soul as it left the body.

6. Cf. Horsfall 1985.

7. Evidently Allia was supported by two lovers, one of whom was probably Aulus Allius himself, her patron. Cf. no. 90, para. 29, where Neaera is owned by two lovers simultaneously.

8. A play on the word *potestas*, which means 'power'. A very plausible explanation of this unusual name is that it is merely the Latin translation of the Greek word and name *Dynamis*, also meaning power. It would not be at all surprising if she were Greek or of Greek descent.

9. In Aeschylus' *Agamemnon* (416-19) the chorus comments on the inadequacy of a statue as substitute for Menelaus' real wife Helen. Admetus, in Euripides' *Alcestis*, promises his dying wife that he will put a likeness of her in his bed, so that he can embrace and caress it and hold it in his arms, 'so that I will seem to hold my dear wife in my arms even though I am not holding her' (348-54), a speech that illustrates how much emphasis he places on her physical presence. Compare Anyte's epitaph for Thersis, above, no. 14. A Roman sarcophagus lid in the Terme Museum, Rome, shows a man reclining, Etruscan-style, with his arm around not his wife but a bust of her.

10. Probably best understood in Christian terms: because of her death she has won eternal freedom in the next world. Cf. no. 444.

11. A reference to the story of the Amazon Penthesileia, who came to defend Troy but was killed in battle by Achilles, who fell in love with her when he saw her dead body.

12. Ptolemy VI Philometor, king of Egypt 181-146 BC.

13. Mother of the Gracchi; see nos. 259, 260 and index.

14. 191 BC. Cf. Plutarch's suggestion that a wife should see respect for herself in her husband's turning to another woman for debauchery (*Moralia* 140b).

15. Cf. no. 167.

16. 42 BC

17. 42 BC

18. From 'all' (*pantes*) and 'gift' (*doron*).

19. I.e. your neighbours will laugh because she is unfaithful. Cf. Semonides, no. 57, and Archilochus, no. 234.

20. See Lloyd-Jones 1976.

21. Cf. also the enigmatic Roman inscription at no. 276.

22. Cf. no. 276.

23. Presumably, since money was left in sanctuaries not only for safekeeping, but in the expectation of divine favour, a richer man might hope to buy from the god a better child, since he could leave a larger sum.

24. Hippolytus assumes that no woman is capable of *homonoia*, 'same-mindedness', agreeing with one's husband about what ought to be done. Cf. no. 57; a good wife does what her husband tells her to do. Cf. no. 267.

25. For the same thought, cf. the comic poet Aristophon, Fr. 6 PCG, perhaps from a common source?

26. On conventional attitudes towards women in the fourth century, see Dover 1974, 95-102.

27. The practice was widespread enough to be a good subject for social comedy; see Schaps 1979, 76. Apuleius in his *Apology* (second century AD) offers a spirited defence of why he married a rich widow, older than himself. Cf. also Plutarch's Amatorius.

28. In the Latin translation by Caecilius (third century BC), the husband emphasises how badly he will be disgraced if people find out that his wife has such great power over him (Aulus Gellius 2.23).

29. Cf. Cole 1981, 246 n. 118.

30. For female gladiators, see below, nos. 295-302.

31. The infamous Empress Messalina, mother of Octavia and Britannicus. She was later put to death for conspiracy against Claudius.

32. See no. 233 for an account of the rape of the Sabines.

33. The 'triumphs' are those of her father Scipio Africanus, the hero of the Second Punic War. Cf. no. 52.

34. Cf. no. 178, Valerius Maximus on Gaia Afrania.

35. At the Floralia, a particularly joyous festival in honour of the goddess Flora, celebrated from April 28 to May 3. See Ovid, *Fasti* 5.331ff.

36. Cf. no. 173, p. 142.

37. Queen of Carthage, lover of Aeneas. She committed suicide when he abandoned her.

38. Eclipses of the moon, thought by some to be caused by witchcraft, were met with loud noises to dispel the accompanying evil spirits.

39. A reference to the short tunic worn by men.

40. Forbidden to women.

41. Palaemon, a freedman, was a grammarian of the early first century AD.

42. See Geffcken 1973 on Cicero's use of ridicule to discredit Clodia.

43. This is the 'Lesbia' of Catullus. She was the sister of Publius Clodius Pulcher, Cicero's bitter enemy. Her husband was Quintus Caecilius Metellus Celer (consul in 60 BC).

44. Gnaeus Domitius Calvinus, the praetor who presided over the trial.

45. Appius Claudius Caecus ('blind'), consul in 307 and 296 BC. An aristocrat, he championed the lower classes and, as censor in 312 BC, built the first aqueduct in Rome, the Aqua Claudia, parts of which still stand, and the first of the great roads, the Via Appia.

46. Quintus Caecilius Metellus Celer, consul in 60 BC, died suddenly in 59, giving rise to the suspicion that he had been poisoned by his wife.

47. A spa on the Bay of Naples known for luxury and loose living. 'The mere mention of Baiae [in the *Pro Caelio*] contributed effectively to the impression of Clodia's immorality which Cicero was striving to establish' (D'Arms 1970).

48. The translation of the couplet is by R.Y. Hathorn. Cicero is quoting a comic playwright, perhaps Caecilius Statius (*c.* 168 BC).

III. Philosophers on the Role of Women

1. Sophocles, *Ajax* 293.

2. 369 BC.

3. The contrast with Athenian women is striking, see Schaps 1979, 88.

4. At the time of the Theban invasion.

5. On *Resp.* 5, cf. now Vlastos 1989; Lefkowitz 1989, 481, 484; Lefkowitz 1990, 801-15.

6. I.e. Socrates, who is represented as the narrator of the dialogue.

7. Cf. no. 98. Ordinarily, women exercised in public only in the company of other women and at religious festivals: girls ran races at Brauron (in 5th cent.; cf. no. 399), at the Heraea at Olympia (no. 392), and in the Roman period women's races were added to the games at Delphi (no. 206) and to the Capitoline games at Rome (Suetonius, *Life of Domitian* 4.4). Cf. Lee 1984, 46.

8. A quotation from the renowned fifth-century poet Pindar (Fr. 209 Maehler).

9. I.e. the end (guardianship) justifies the means (women's gymnastics).

10. Perhaps Glaucon makes no objection because he was used to Socrates' theories of eugenics from other discussions; cf. no. 97, and Xenophon's commentary on Theognis 183-4 (Greek text in Marchant 1900). Cf. also Aristotle Fr. 92 Rose, and Euripides Fr. 95N; *Andromache* 1279-82.

11. The metrical pattern of the phrase indicates that it is a quotation from a poem, but we do not know which; Plato implies that males will produce better children when they are sexually less active.

12. Plato does not question the ancient belief that premature babies who survive are 'seven-months children'; cf. no. 348.

13. Lutz 1947, 3-147. Cf. de Ste. Croix 1981, 110.

14. *Od.* 4.392.

15. Cf. no. 267.

16. A Socratic notion; cf. Plato, *Crito* 49c.

17. Cf. nos. 251, 253.

18. Cf. nos. 39 and 47.

19. This analogy is attributed to Socrates by Plato, *Republic* 451d-e (no. 73).

20. 'Hateful Eriphyle, who took valuable gold in exchange for her husband' (*Od.* 11.326-7) was frequently cited as an example of the treacherous wife.

21. Cf. no. 125.

22. Cf. nos. 267 and 47.

23. I.e. the quality of being 'manly' (*andreios*) cannot be acquired simply by being a man (*aner*).

24. Perhaps Musonius had in mind Odysseus' characterisation of an ideal marriage, 'May the gods grant your heart's desire, a husband and household, and may they grant that you are of one mind. For there is nothing stronger or better than when a husband and wife are of one mind and share a household. They bring pain to their enemies, and joy to their friends. And they themselves know it best' (*Od.* 11.180-5).

IV. Legal Status in the Greek World

1. Cf. Willetts 1967; Sealey 1990, 50-81.

2. A free man, but not a citizen, perhaps roughly equivalent in status to the Attic *metoikos*, 'resident alien', who had more rights than a slave but fewer than a citizen.

3. Here and elsewhere in the Code, if oaths are sworn by both sides, the oath that has precedence wins by default; presumably, the oath was not merely an asseveration that one is telling the truth, but a solemn demand that the gods punish the swearer for lying.

4. Special provisions were made for daughters when no brothers were available to inherit.

5. The father's kinship group, sometimes translated 'tribe' or 'clan'.

6. Cf. Plutarch, *Life of Solon* 21. On the political reasons for the legislation and modern analogues, cf. Alexiou 1974, 21-3.

7. The women in the household washed the corpse and laid it out for burial.

8. For similar regulations, cf. Demosthenes 43.62.

9. Apparently legislation against customs intended to remove death-pollution by catching it in a cup of water and by interring all traces of dirt in the house along with the corpse. Cf. Parker 1983, 35-6. Probably the additional five women were relations by marriage; at the end of the *Iliad* Hector is mourned formally by his mother Hecuba, his wife Andromache and his sister-in-law Helen. Cf. Parker 1983, 40.

10. Pasion was originally a resident alien (or metic) himself, but had been granted Athenian citizenship by special decree. Sealey 1990, 18-19; Carey 1991, 84-9.

11. The Greek *gyne* can signify both 'wife' and 'woman'.

12. For interpretation, see de Ste. Croix 1970, 274-5; Harrison 1968, 110; Schaps 1979, 10-11, 14.

13. Cf. esp. Lacey 1968, 148-9; Humphreys 1983, 106.

14. Aristotle dedicated the *Nicomachean Ethics* to this son, who was named after Aristotle's father.

15. Cf. MacDowell 1990, 43-7.

16. For interpretation, cf. de Ste. Croix 1970; Harrison 1968, 110; Schaps 1979, 10-11; Sealey 1990, 44.

17. The property would, however, be managed by a guardian (*kyrios*); see de Ste. Croix 1970, 273-8; Schaps 1979, 48-60; Sealey 1990, 36-8.

18. The four classes of Athenian society at this time were: (1) Pentacosiomedimni, '500-measure men', who had an income of 500 measures of grain or wine. (2) Knights, who were able to bring a horse to the army and had an income of 300

measures. (3) Zeugitae, 'yoke men', who could own a yoke of oxen and had an income of 200 measures. (4) Thetes, 'serfs', who had either no land or an income of less than 200 measures.

19. On this 'law', see Schaps 1979, 28-9.

20. Presumably the household was split up when Diogeiton remarried, and he moved from the house in Collytus, north of the Acropolis, to the house of Phaedrus (a friend of Socrates and admirer of Lysias, a character in several Platonic dialogues).

21. On the interpretation of this 'law', see especially de Ste. Croix 1970, 274.; Schaps 1979, 52.

22. 305/4 BC.

23. 303/2 BC.

24. Cf. Schaps 1977, 323-30.

25. Cf. no. 394.

26. I.e. until 365/4 or 364/3.

27. Cf. the 'law' cited in Demosthenes 23.53: 'If a man involuntarily kills another in the course of competing in an athletic contest or in apprehending a thief on a road, or when he does not recognise [him] in war, or if [he catches] him with his wife or mother or sister or daughter or with a concubine whom he keeps for the purpose of begetting legitimate children; in the event of any of these the murderer is not prosecuted.'

28. 373/2 BC, thirty years or more before the present trial.

29. The next year.

30. Until it could be determined whether she was slave or free. The polemarch was the archon in charge of suits involving foreign residents.

31. The Thesmothetae were magistrates in charge of courts and juries.

32. On these texts see de Ste. Croix 1970, 275-6; Finley 1951; Schaps 1979, 85.

33. Hooker 1988, 136.

34. The late fourth-century BC philosopher Cleanthes wrote a treatise on this subject. Cf. also no. 303.

35. Note that while husbands can decide what to do with their wives, wives do not have a choice about what to do with themselves or their husbands; as in the *Republic*, they are regarded in Lycurgus' legislation as vehicles for the production of children.

36. Cf. Hodkinson in Powell 1988, 90: 'Both monogamy and polyandry can be interpreted as practices designed to limit the number of legitimate offspring a man sired and hence the division of the inheritance.'

37. Cf. no. 72.

38. The poet Theocritus (third century BC) imagines that Helen as a young woman took part in such races on the banks of the river Eurotas, along with 240 other young girls. In Aristophanes, *Lysistrata* 82 a Spartan woman, Lampito, says she gets exercise by kicking her buttocks when she dances. According to the second-century AD encyclopaedist Pollux (4.102) both boys and girls participated in this dance, known as the *bibasis*, at athletic competitions (cf. Lawler 1964, 121). But there is no other evidence for girls' athletic competitions at Sparta (cf. Gow 1965, II 354). On girls' races elsewhere, see p. 338 n. 7.

39. Cf. the ceremony at Brauron in Attica during which girls shed the *krokotos*, no. 399. Cf. Sourvinou-Inwood 1988, 66. The philosopher Zeno (333-261 BC), founder of Stoicism, suggested that in his utopia wives should be shared and that men and women dress alike, covering no part of the body completely (Diogenes Laertius 7.33).

40. The pre-Lycurgan Spartan maiden-songs that survive describe the mythic past and concentrate on women. Cf. no. 401.

41. Cf. nos. 72, 99.

42. Cf. Plato, *Republic* 458d, no. 73.

43. Women wore a belt or girdle (*zone*) just above their hips; removing it is a euphemism for sexual intercourse; cf. Homer, *Odyssey* 11.245.

44. A *lesche* was a public building or meeting-place, here probably the tribe's headquarters. Cf. the legitimisation ritual in Athens, no. 87.

45. I.e. the 'putting away' place.

46. An Athenian general of noble birth and notorious character, who in 415 BC, during the Peloponnesian war, defected to Sparta.

47. Cf. Aristotle's complaints about the freedom allowed to Spartan women in no. 72.

48. I.e. in the event of his death; he was killed in the battle in 480 BC.

49. On Etruscan women, see Bonfante Warren 1984. Cf. no. 166, the story of Lucretia, in which the Roman matron works virtuously at her wool while the Etruscan princesses enjoy a dinner party.

50. A 'Persian' originally meant a member of the Persian military settlement or their descendants, but starting in the first century BC it seems to have also been used to designate a legal status that required the person designated as Persian to be personally liable for any fault in a contract. Cf. Fraser 1972, 58-9.

51. Both Greek and Egyptian names are frequently given, with the formula 'also known as' or 'also called', when two languages or cultures are involved, but unfortunately from the end of the third century BC, names in the papyri are not reliable indications of origin. See Turner 1968, 82-3.

52. Cf. Euripides, *Supplices*, 40-1: 'Women can usually get everything through men, if they are clever.'

53. In a fragment of another papyrus, *POxy* 315, dated AD 37, Tryphon complains that Demetrous and her mother assaulted his pregnant wife.

V. Legal Status in the Roman World

1. *Confarreatio*. See below, no. 132.

2. Probably a reference to contraception and abortion. Divorce on grounds of sterility appears to have been first allowed in 235 BC (Aulus Gellius, *Attic Nights* 17.21.44). Complex laws concerning the disposition of the dowry – such as deductions for children or bad behaviour – operated to prevent ill-considered divorce.

3. In the later Republic and the Empire, either spouse – or father, if a spouse was still in his power – could divorce the other by simple notification.

4. Twenty-five was the age of majority for both women and men. A woman remained subject to either her father's power (*potestas*) or her husband's (*manus*) or, lacking both, that of a tutor. See below, nos. 115-17, on guardianship, and on Vestal Virgins, no. 408.

5. Agnatic relationships are traced through the male line and can include artificial relationships, as through adoption; cognatic relationships are traced through the female line and are confined to blood relations.

6. Boys 7-14, girls 7-12, and women who were not under a father's or husband's power. This law, for which there is no surviving text, is derived from Gaius, *Institutes* 1.155.

7. This law too is derived from the *Institutes* of Gaius 1.111 (below, no. 132), where the jurist explains that the institution had become obsolete by his day.

8. In Romulus' day.

9. Consul in 166 BC.

10. Consul in 268 BC.

11. 235 BC.

12. Marcus Porcius Cato 'Censorius' – Cato the Elder (234-149 BC). He was the quintessential conservative and champion of traditional morality. Among his acts as censor in 184 BC was the taxation of luxury. He deplored and fought vainly against the acceptance of anything Greek into Roman life.

13. On the prohibition see Bettini, forthcoming.

14. The magistrate whose jurisdiction included public morals and the leasing of public buildings and spaces.

15. Except where indicated otherwise, translations from the *Corpus Iuris Civilis* are by S.P. Scott, edited and revised with considerable help, graciously offered and gratefully accepted, from Professors T. Honoré and S.D. Martin, who, of course, bear no responsibility for errors that remain. Material for the introduction to and notes on the jurists was provided by S.D. Martin.

16. On the jurists see Schiller 1978, Watson 1967, Berger 1953 and Nicholas 1962.

17. Translates *propter animi levitatem*, literally 'on account of lightness of the mind'.

18. *Potestas*.

19. On Paul, see below, no. 118.

20. I.e. sexually mature.

21. Of the life of Aelius Marcianus, very little is known. He wrote sixteen books of *Institutes* and was probably active in the early third century AD.

22. See below, no. 118.

23. Translates *fructus*.

24. For an interesting fictional account of Julia's exile and the events which led to it, see Williams 1972.

25. This portion of the speech is preserved by Aulus Gellius (1.6.2), who mistakes this Metellus (Macedonicus, cos. 143 BC) for Metellus Numidicus (cos. 109 BC). Cf. Holford-Strevens 1988, 65 n.20, 228.

26. Cf. Aristophanes, *Lysistrata* 1038-9: 'A true saying and well-said: you can't live with the cursed creatures or without them.'

27. I.e. his great-grandchildren, the children of Germanicus and his grand-daughter Agrippina.

28. To postpone marriage and the birth of children.

29. Not because it is prohibited but in the sense that sexual relations with such women are not considered adultery.

30. Aemilius Papinianus, Papinian, had a career in the imperial bureaucracy. In AD 198 he took over the office *a libellis* (for Petitions) under Septimius Severus (AD 193-211) and Caracalla (AD 211-217). He was Praetorian Prefect from 205 to 211 with Paul and Ulpian acting as his clerks. He was executed in 212, perhaps in the aftermath of Caracalla's murder of his brother Geta.

31. 'A matron, *materfamilias*, is a decent or respectable free woman, whether married or a mother or widowed or not,' Honoré 1991.

32. On concubinage, see McGinn 1991, Rawson 1974 and Treggiari 1981.

33. Or outsider, stranger: *extraneus*.

34. Because fidelity was expected of a fiancée.

35. The Latin is *stuprum*.

36. Primarily a teacher and writer (no mention is made of his holding an imperial post), Sextus Pomponius lived in the mid-second century AD and wrote influential commentaries on Q. Mucius, Sabinus and the Praetor's Edict.

37. Little is known of Aemilius Macer other than that he was active in the early third century AD and was a member of a senatorial family.

38. For the freedwoman, the reverse is the case.

39. A correspondent, hence contemporary, of the jurist Proculus, thus active in the first half of the first century AD.

40. 'Marriage in the later Republic and Empire was always consensual, that is, by agreement. It existed if the man and woman intended their relationship to be a marriage (and had the necessary parental consent, etc.), symbolised usually by the husband carrying her over the threshold of his house or flat. It ended when one or both of them ceased to have this (firm) intention. Notification (*repudium*) meant telling the other party that the notifier no longer had the intention to be married, whereupon divorce took effect without more formality. Divorce (*divertere*) means going one's own way, and since if one spouse goes his or her own way, they are no longer going the same way, either spouse could divorce the other (and originally either spouse's father could do so if the child remained in his power). There was no requirement of mutual consent to divorce, and it made no legal difference' (Honoré 1991).

41. Herennius Modestinus was the last classical jurist of consequence. Ulpian alludes specifically to him as a student in responding to a letter Modestinus wrote to him from Dalmatia (*Digest* 47.2.52.20). He was *praefectus vigilum* at Rome sometime between AD 224 and 244. Among other works, he wrote ten books of *Rules*.

42. Generally regarded as one of the most brilliant of the classical jurists, Publius Salvius Julianus, consul in AD 148, enjoyed a distinguished career that spanned the reigns of Hadrian, Antoninus Pius and Marcus Aurelius. Hadrian entrusted to him the task of producing the final edition of the Praetor's Edict. He wrote a number of works and is much cited in the *Digest*.

43. Prominent as a legal thinker in his day, Publius Iuventius Celsus was praetor in AD 106 or 107 and consul for the second time in 128. He also served as governor of Asia and on Hadrian's council. His major work was the *Digests* in thirty-nine books.

44. Some scholars believe that Justinian changed the text from 'she is *taken* to disagree' to 'she is *free* to disagree'.

45. 'So even a woman in her husband's power could compel him to release her from power and then divorce him. This principle proved durable even in the Christian empire, though, for example, Constantine (*Codex Theodosianus* 3.16.1, AD 331) prescribed financial penalties and even deportation for those spouses who divorced without proper grounds, of which he listed three (the grounds and penalties were, however, different for the two sexes)' (Honoré 1991).

46. Marital subordination translates *quae in manu nostra sunt*.

47. Respectively *usus, confarreatio* and *coemptio*.

48. By this method, the woman did not free herself from the power of her husband but avoided entering it at all and instead remained in the power of her father, at his command, or, if she had been emancipated or her father was dead, her own.

49. Jupiter Farreus.

50. Spelt.

51. *Rex sacrorum*.

52. *In mancipio*.

53. *Sui iuris.*

54. *Contubernium*, the cohabitation of slaves who are forbidden from marrying; cf. below no. 142.

55. That is, she is an exclusive partner like a wife (which is why a man could not have both a wife and a concubine) but is not *regarded* as a social equal.

56. There is a contrast between actually handing over the property, declaring unilaterally that it will be handed over, and making a formal agreement to that effect.

57. Translates *ob violatum contubernium*.

58. A jurist active in the late first and early second centuries AD. His works are not excerpted in the *Digest*, and his opinions appear only in citations of other jurists.

59. Ulpius Marcellus, who served on the councils of both Antoninus Pius (AD 138-161) and Marcus Aurelius (AD 161-180), wrote a work called the *Digests* in thirty-one books.

60. *Materfamilias*; see above, n. 31.

61. I.e. the exchequer.

62. I.e. a woman possessing Latin rights, halfway between those of aliens and those of citizens.

63. Cf. no. 154.

64. 'As to making a will ... women not only had to have guardian's authorisation but, until Hadrian, also had to go through a complicated rigmarole of changing guardians by *coemptio*' (Crook 1967, 120). Cf. above, p. 342, n. 17.

65. Prefect of Egypt *c.* AD 84-85.

66. For a translation of the formal legal agreement, see *P. Fam. Tebt.* 22, pp. 76-7.

67. Sijpesteijn 1979.

68. The Latin name of Isidorus.

69. The name of a male guardian was regularly given in Greek-language contracts made by women, but not consistently in documents written in Egyptian demotic, at least in the Hellenistic age (cf. e.g. *P.Adl.* Gk. 7, 8 with *P.Adl.* dem. 3 in the late 2nd cent. BC, but guardians in both the demotic text and Greek subscription in *P.Mich* 253 in AD 30).

70. A close friend of the family.

71. The equivalent of 24 drachmas, a very favourable price.

72. A century later literate women could act on their own behalf without a *kyrios*, under the *ius trium liberorum*; see no. 154.

73. Cf. also Worp 1980, dated AD 348.

74. Such literacy appears to have been relatively rare; also despite its practical value, it had no legal significance. Cf. Cole 1981, 236.

75. Presumably it is because her husband is away from home that Tarmouthis appears without a guardian. Cf. Milligan 1910, 74.

76. Keys were bolts of wood or metal, sometimes substantial in size.

77. An insulting reference to the petitioner.

78. Literally, 'a woman of the city', *politike*. Cf. *P. Grenf.* II.73.

VI. Public Life

1. 494 BC; cf. Herodotus 6.77-83; Pausanias 2. 20. 8-10.

2. The historian Socrates of Argos, 310 *FGrHist* F6.

3. Plutarch omits the oracle (Parke and Wormell 1956, no. 85) that is said to have predicted the women's victory, which begins: 'But when the female conquers the male and drives him out and wins great glory in Argos, she will cause many women in Argos to tear their cheeks [in mourning]'; is the whole story an *aetion*, or fictional narrative explanation, for the ritual and the strange law about women with beards? Cf. Snyder 1989, 59-63. Transvestism is also associated with *rites de passage*, such as Plutarch's account of the origin of the Athenian festival Oschophoria (*Life of Theseus* 7).

4. The similarities between the stories about the armed women and the festivals at Argos and Tegea suggest that they may derive from ritual rather than history. But they suggest that the Greeks both knew that women could fight and applauded them for it. Cf. Farnell 1909, 5.405.

5. Charillus was king of Sparta at the time of Lycurgus. Cf. no. 98

6. According to the third-century BC historian Deinias of Argos (306 *FGrHist* F4) her first name was Perimede.

7. Only a few scraps of her poetry survive, the longest of which is two lines about Artemis fleeing from the river god Alpheus, 717 *PMG*.

8. For the sources that mention the statue, see Pollitt 1983.

9. Reggio Calabria.

10. Cf. Horsfall 1983.

11. 49 BC.

12. A fictitious purchase. See above, p. 343, n. 47.

13. Power. See above, p. 343, n. 48.

14. Or 'you resorted to supplications which were the expression of your devotion'.

15. Nero's wife, whom he persecuted, exiled and finally had put to death; her fate is described in the *Octavia*, a *fabula praetextata* or political drama attributed to Seneca.

16. Nero's prefect, who was responsible for many executions.

17. This refers particularly to purple, a very expensive dye obtained from certain shellfish. It was a sign of luxury. The togas of magistrates and wealthy youths (*togae praetextae*) were adorned with a purple stripe.

18. See above, no. 111.

19. Cato's history of early Rome.

20. Tarn 1934, 111.

21. Pelling 1988, 17-18.

22. 'My salad days, when I was young and green', Shakespeare, *Antony and Cleopatra*, I.v.73-4. Now she was 28.

23. Vergil's description of Dido's effect on Aeneas in Aeneid, book 1, has many interesting similarities to this scene; cf. Pelling 1988, 190.

24. Like most educated people of the Mediterranean after the conquest of Alexander, the royal family of Egypt, the Ptolemies, spoke a 'universal' (*koine*) form of Greek; originally they came with Alexander from Macedonia, in the north of Greece, which like most regions of that country had a distinct dialect.

25. Cf. Pelling 1988, 196-7. According to Plato, *Gorgias* 462c-466a, the four are sophistic, rhetoric, pastry-cooking, and cosmetics. Cf. also Plutarch, *How to tell a Flatterer* 55a, who emphasises the flatterer's need for artifice and contrivances.

26. Such petitions to the ruler's womenfolk became standard practice in the Empire; cf. no. 180.

27. Hortensia implies that women voluntarily cooperated with the provisions of the Oppian Law of 215, which was repealed in 195, see no. 173. Cf. Balsdon 1962, 31.

28. Cf. Suetonius, *Life of Vespasian* 3, 'After his wife's death, Vespasian took as his consort Caenis, Antonia's freedwoman and amanuensis, of whom he was very fond, and whom he treated almost like a wife even after he became emperor.'

29. She appears to have been named for the mythological character who was loved by Poseidon; when the god asked what she wanted in return, she asked to be changed into a man, Caeneus; cf. Ovid, *Metamorphoses* 12.189-209, 451-535.

30. Caenis apparently had written the letter on a waxed tablet.

31. In 77 BC.

32. Cf. *Digest* 3.1.1.5.

33. 48 BC.

34. Quintus Hortensius Hortalus (114-50 BC), consul in 69 BC, was one of the Republic's most famous orators and a great forensic rival of Cicero.

35. 42 BC. The triumvirs Octavian, Antony, and Lepidus levied this tax to help pay for the war against Brutus and Cassius.

36. Semiramis and Nitocris were legendary queens of Babylon.

37. Plautianus, prefect of the Praetorian Guard, had extraordinary power under Severus, until he was assassinated in 205.

38. The adopted grandsons of Augustus, who died before they could succeed to the throne. Cf. Tacitus, *Ann.* 1.3.

39. On this inscription and, briefly but with bibliography, the question of the women's curia, see Donati 1971.

40. Possibly Tigrides, as Mommsen suggests ad loc., and certainly a name of humble origin.

41. Three groups receive grants in this text, the Ciarnenses, the Herclanenses and 'the women'. The names of the men's groups may denote cult associations and the women's a burial society like the *collegium* in the document above. The Herclanenses were probably devoted to Hercules and the Ciarnenses (a name which occurs nowhere else) to a local deity. We are grateful to Professor S. Panciera for giving us the benefit of his singular expertise about this unique inscription.

42. Festivals of the dead. Other grants to women: *CIL* IX.4697, X.5853, XIV.2110.

43. Julia Domna; cf. no. 180.

44. The wife of Hadrian, who built in the first place whatever Julia restored.

45. *Conventu matronarum.*

46. No other evidence has been found for earlier rituals of this sort; but 'precedent' was often sought for new practices established in the late Empire. See Gagé 1963, 101f., n. 1. See also Straub 1966.

47. The word, a diminutive of senate, is impossible to translate in English, except perhaps as 'mini-senate'; it goes nicely into Italian, however, as *senatino*.

48. *Conventus matronalis.*

49. His mother, Julia Soaemias Bassiana, niece of Julia Domna.

50. A special magistrate who had the right to wear a crown (*stephanos*).

51. Cf. Fornara 1977, no. 45; among Ionian women at Persepolis *c.* 500 BC, mothers of boys received twice the allotment of women who had girls.

52. In Lycia.

53. Technically, a magistrate who supervised the town gymnasia; but by this period the office had become honorific, providing an opportunity for financial contribution to the municipality.

54. Cf. Rogers 1991 and van Bremen 1983.

55. The wording suggests that she could have owned the horses herself; see no. 72, 1270a15 ff.

56. She won again in 264, and was made a goddess as well!

57. None is from Athens.

58. An important Ptolemaic official, governor of Cyprus.

VII. Private Life

1. Cf. also the letter of Perictione on the 'harmonious woman', quoted in Pomeroy 1975, 134-6. Dr D. Monserrat has shown that portions of this and other Neopythagorean treatises were copied out in Egyptian schools in the 3rd and 4th centuries AD; e.g. Kraus 1919, 122-8; *P.Haun.* II.13.

2. Seventeen women (about 7 per cent) are included in an ancient list of members of the Pythagorean community (58 A D-K, I 448); writings also survive by women who do not appear in the list: Pythagoras' daughter Arignote, Melissa, Perktione (incidentally, also the name of Plato's mother) and Phintys.

3. For a translation of Perktione's treatise on women's duties, see Pomeroy 1975, 134-6.

4. Two letters about coping with mistresses are attributed to Pythagoras' wife Theano: no. 3 contains the sober advice: 'Tragedy teaches you to control you jealousy, through the examples of the dramas, in which Medea disobeys the law.' Cf. Snyder 1989, 108-13.

5. The ultimate proof. Cf. Glycon's praise for his wife Panthia (below, no. 373), 'You bore me children completely like myself': Lattimore, p. 277.

6. Cf. Cicero's emphasis on the luxury of Clodia's household, above, no. 71.

7. But even religious festivals could provide opportunity for misconduct. Thus Simaetha, below, no. 415, meets Delphis at the Thesmophoria of Artemis.

8. Cf. the Athenian law against excessive mourning (above, no. 77) and the public reaction to Dionysiac ritual (below, no. 388).

9. He practised what he preached. At 73.3, Suetonius says the emperor wore clothing woven by his sister, wife, daughter and granddaughters.

10. The young man can, however, be forgiven for thinking the rules were different at Baiae; see n. 47, p. 338.

11. To celebrate his appointment as Pontifex Maximus.

12. Ten a.m.

13. The parents/masters of this household are P. Larcius Nicia and Saufeia Thalea, both former slaves themselves. They had two sons, L. Larcius Rufus and P. Larcius Brocchus. The 'I' in the inscription is Horaea, a former slave in the household, who married Brocchus. She took the family name Larcia not when she married but when she received her freedom.

14. Nicknamed Sapiens, the wise. Laelius was a hero of the Third Punic War and consul in 140 BC. Cf. no. 223.

15. Cf. above no. 176.

16. Fr. 44 Wehrli.

17. Cf. no. 73.

18. Speusippus and Menedemus were a pupils of Plato; Hippobotus a Hellenistic writer about philosophers.

19. Her brother Metrocles was also a philosopher. Cf. Magnilla (no. 221).

20. Two of Plato's women disciples were said to have worn men's clothing; see above, no. 216. Usually the only women at men's dinner parties were courtesans, e.g. Neaera, no. 90.

21. Cf. how the prefect sentences the scholarly Irene to a brothel, below, no. 446.

22. Agave's boast to her father in Euripides, Bacchae 1326, when she returns

from the hunt, thinking she has caught a lion; but the head she is carrying turns out to be her son's.

23. An ancient encyclopaedia.

24. Demo, a woman grammarian, is said to have written an allegorical commentary on Homer (Cramer, *Anec. Graeca* iii, p. 189); Agallis, daughter of Agallias of Corcyra, a pupil of Aristophanes of Byzantium (third century BC) also wrote on Homer (*Suda*, s.v.).

25. Pornographic works are also attributed to the courtesans Astyanassa and Elephantine. A fragment survives of a manual by Philaenis of Samos (fourth century BC, above, p. 174), with advice on how to flatter women (Oxyrhynchus papyrus 2891; see Tsantsanoglou 1973). But it was claimed in antiquity that her work was written by a man (Aeschrion, *AP* IX.518); see West 1977.

26. The emperor Tiberius.

27. I.e. all the arts and disciplines governed by the Muses.

28. I.e. Medea.

29. In 10.38 Martial congratulates Sulpicia's husband Calenus on their fifteen years of blissful matrimony.

30. Cf. Halperin 1990, 123- 4.

31. *Hetaera*.

32. A clear indication of her profession – Philaenis was a noted courtesan, who is said to have written pornographic books (see above n. 25).

33. Testimony to the problems of getting round growing suburbs. Cf. Theocritus, *Idyll* 15, below, no. 229.

34. Also the name of Xenophon's son, who was a war hero.

35. In the Eleusinian myth of the Hellenistic period, the name of the hostess, otherwise called Iambe or Baubo, who persuaded Demeter to break her fast of mourning for Persephone (Cf. *Homeric Hymn to Demeter*, no. 393).

36. Other *hetaerae*, for whom she will now try to get offers.

37. A late Latin word derived from Hebrew for a cloth used as a covering.

38. A woman's sexual misbehaviour makes the husband a laughing-stock in nos. 55 and 57.

39. Cf. Plutarch, no. 270.

40. Apparently the blond (pubic) hair mentioned in the last line; he suggests that he will penetrate but the withdraw before ejaculation.

41. Since Neobule was said to have been Archilochus' fiancée, the 'I' of the poem may represent the poet.

42. Cf. the cuckold who is a joy to his neighbours in Semonides' poem, 110-11, above, p. 25, and Hesiod above, p. 25.

43. Cf. no. 225.

44. Aeschines the Socratic, in his dialogue Aspasia (now lost) Fr. 8 Krauss.

45. In the *Menexenus* Socrates delivers a speech which he claims Aspasia composed for him: 'She happens to be an accomplished teacher of rhetoric, who has trained many other distinguished orators, one of whom is the most important man in Greece, Pericles the son of Xanthippus' (235e). Cf. no. 225.

46. Hermippus T 2 *PCG*; but Plutarch or his source appears to have misunderstood the context, since this information almost certainly comes from a scene in a comedy and not from an actual trial. Cf. Schwarze 1971, 101-9

47. Aeschines, Fr. 11. Cf. Antisthenes the Socratic, fr. 35 Decleva Caizzi 1965, 13.589d.

48. The revolt against the Thirty in 403 BC.

49. Cf. Euripides, *Alcestis* 304-8.

50. Perhaps the only instance in extant Greek literature where the three words for love (*erao*, denoting sexual passion; *phileo*, love for family and friends; *agapao*, affection) 'recur at such short intervals, in each case referring to love between a man and a woman, and indeed between a husband and a wife' (Lloyd-Jones 1963, 28).

51. Similarly *CIL* IV.7024 and 7080.

52. The jackdaw put on peacock's feathers and tried to join a flock of peacocks, but the peacocks plucked them off; Phaedrus, *Fable* 1.3.

53. A reference to *Iliad* 6.429, where Andromache tells Hector 'But to me you are father and mother and brother, and you are my strong husband.'

54. The Gnomon of the Idiologue (no. 148), makes provision for the inheritance rights of male foundlings, or 'children from the dung-heap' (sects. 41, 107); no provisions are made for female children, who presumably were not given dowries but kept as slaves (cf. no. 381). Heraclas, a boy foundling who died while being nursed is mentioned in *POxy.* 37. i.7 and 38.7.

55. Brother or sister often denotes any close relationship.

56. Cf. the similar advice in Plutarch, *Moralia* 3e.

57. Pomeroy 1975, 166.

58. The doctrine of the superiority of the natural mother and emphasis on family ties is characteristic of the second century; Favorinus' friend Plutarch wrote a treatise on the subject (now lost); cf. Holford-Strevens 1988, 79. Cf. also nos. 251 and 253.

59. Cf. the modern emphasis on 'bonding' of parent and child.

60. If the letter is authentic (and nothing in its style precludes it), Cornelia writes in a formal manner, like an orator, without the diminutive forms characteristic of women's speech. But even if the letter is a forgery, it is clear that no one doubted that Cornelia could have written such a letter; Cicero thought that it was genuine. Cf. Gratwick 1982.

61. For Cornelia, see nos. 69, 223, 261.

62. Gaius Aurelius Cotta, the orator, was exiled from Rome but returned with Sulla (the dictator) and became consul in 75 BC.

63. This Helvidius was Fannia's stepson, her husband's son by his first wife. An ex-consul, he was condemned to death, possibly for his associations, in AD 93, by the Emperor Domitian.

64. See pp. 102 ff.

65. Compare the remark of Theodore Roosevelt that he could preside over the United States or control his daughter (Alice Roosevelt Longworth) – but not both.

66. The formidable empress Livia, second wife of Augustus, was Julia's stepmother. When Julia's first husband, Agrippa, died and Julia was obliged to marry the future emperor Tiberius, Livia became her mother-in-law as well.

67. If, in fact, this woman – whose name is not mentioned – is the same wife of Ischomachus (Chrysilla) whose daughter married Callias. Chrysilla seduced her son-in-law, drove out her daughter, and had a son by her son-in-law Callias, whom Callias later tried to have enrolled as his legal heir (cf. Euctemon's machinations in no. 87). Andocides, *Myst.* 124-7. Cf. MacDowell 1962, 151-2; Anderson 1974, 174 n.1; Harvey 1984, 68-70; Nais 1985.

68. Cf. esp. de Ste. Croix 1981, 557 n. 30; Murnaghan 1988, 9-22, esp. 16-18.

69. A joke: Ischomachus assures Socrates that people are interested in him not for his good character but for his money.

70. In Homer a housekeeper supervised the slave women's weaving, e.g. *Od.* 22.422-3, *Homeric Hymn* 5.144.

71. According to Hesiod, producing children is the best reason for marriage:

'The man who escapes marriage and the baneful works of women by preferring not to marry, comes to a deadly old age for want of someone to tend him in old age' (no. 56).

72. In the Pseudo-Platonic dialogue *Axiochus* (371e), this task is specifically assigned to the Danaids in Tartarus, as punishment for murdering their husbands.

73. Ischomachus implies that he would be her 'slave' within the context of the household, but not in other respects. A wife's concern that her husband will neglect her in favour of other younger and more beautiful women is expressed in many myths, where the husband brings home a concubine, e.g. Cassandra in Aeschylus' *Agamemnon*, Iole in Sophocles' *Women of Trachis*; hence, probably, Ischomachus' wife's attempt to put on make-up, below.

74. The word *basilissa* (perhaps with a diminutive connotation, like 'mini-queen'?) occurs for the first time here; the ordinary word is *basileia*.

75. In Aeschylus' *Agamemnon* Clytemnestra has 'a heart that plans like a man's' (*androboulon kear*, 11); cf. also ll. 348, 590-3.

76. Women ordinarily put on make-up when they wanted to make an impression; cf. nos. 88 and 90.

77. I.e. like an actor, as Aristophanes is said to have done when taking the role of Cleon in the ancient *Life of Aristophanes*, 11, or Demetrius the Besieger in 290 BC, in an attempt to impress the population of Athens, Duris of Samos 76 *FGrHist* F10.

78. Contrast with this prescription for exercise within the household, Plato's female athletics programme in *Republic* 5, no. 73.

79. For the purpose of entry into a more privileged class.

80. A prolific scholar of the first century BC, whose works are now lost.

81. Cf. Bowman and Thomas 1987, 137-40.

82. The mother's name is ordinarily omitted in archaic inscriptions. Cf. McClees 1920, 3, 35. But cf. FH 32: 'Her father Cleodamus son of Hyperanor and her mother Corona placed me here as a monument to Thessalia, their daughter' (late sixth century, Oloosson in Thessaly).

VIII. Occupations

1. The tomb of Naevoleia Tyche outside the Herculaneum Gate. See Will 1979.

2. *Ius quattuor liberorum*, which provided tax incentives and certain privileges to mothers of four children in the case of freedwomen and three (*ius trium liberorum*) for freeborn women. Claudius evidently saw potential entrepreneurs among freedwomen. Cf. ch. V no. 121.

3. See also nos. 90, 143, 155, 181.

4. Cf. Harpocration, *Lex.* s.v. Isodaites (Dindorf p. 163). One of the charges against Socrates was that he did not believe in the gods the city of Athens believed in, but rather in new [i.e. unauthorised, *kaina*] divinities; Plato, *Apol.* 24b. Cf. Winiarczyk 1984. In the 2nd cent. AD Isodaites was associated with Dionysus; Plu., *Mor.* 389a. Cf. Farina 1959, 68-9.

5. The gesture is meant to arouse pity rather than sexual desire. It is possible that Hyperides may have had in mind the passage in Euripides' *Hecuba* (557-65) where Hecuba's daughter Polyxena courageously bares her breast as she is about to be offered as a human sacrifice: 'She revealed breasts and chest as beautiful as a statue's.'

6. Athenaeus adds that after Phryne was acquitted a law was passed forbidding

orators to utter lamentations in court or to put defendants of either sex on display. Phryne served as the model for the painting of Aphrodite Anadyomene by the painter Apelles and for the statue of Aphrodite of Cnidos by Praxiteles. This statue was so beautiful that someone made love to it at night, and left a stain on it (Pliny, *N.H.* 36.20). Praxiteles also made a statue of Phryne herself, which Pausanias saw at Delphi (9.27.5).

7. On why the tax was introduced, how it was collected, and what this passage implies about the economic importance of prostitution and the emperor's attitude towards it, see McGinn 1989.

8. I.e. and no longer in business.

9. By the *lex Iulia de adulteriis*. Cf. p. 102 f.

10. A deserted island in the Cyclades used for the purpose.

11. On Justinian, see above, p. 98.

12. Found in vico del Lupanare, where the brothel was located.

13. Cf. Gardner 1986, 247-8.

14. Cf. Antisthenes, Fr. 72 n. Decleva Caizzi; the same thought is attributed to Alcibiades by Diogenes Laertius 2.37 and Aulus Gellius 1.17.

15. The poet Posidippus may have been making fun of Aglaïs, since Athenaeus mentions her in a discussion of large appetites, but not in his description of the great procession in 197c. Cf. Rice 1983, 48-9 n.39.

16. 116-27 BC. A scholar and politician whose extant writings are on agriculture and the Latin language. On women artists, see Baldwin 1981, 18-21.

17. See *AJP* 1910, p. 32. Cf. *CIL* VI 5014, 19365.

18. The Latin word is *monodiar(iae)*.

19. The Latin word is *psaltria* (misspelled *spaltria* on the stone).

20. Cf. VI.34270, 33830.

21. The Latin is *auri vestrix*. Evans 1991 proposes 'embroiderer in gold thread'.

22. Woman's name.

23. Woman's name.

24. From a bronze curse tablet.

25. Cf. Herfst 1922, 36-40. The Women's Market is also mentioned in Theophrastus' *Characters* 2.9, 22.10

26. On Roman bar-maids and waitresses, see Evans 1991, 133-7.

27. All woolworkers listed are female.

28. The word-ending indicates a female name.

29. See above, n. 27.

30. Set free by her master under arrangements similar to those made for Neaera, above, no. 90.

31. Her owner was a resident alien.

32. Male.

33. Female.

34. See above, n. 28.

35. 12812-16 state only wet-nurse, without proper name.

36. The desirability of burial at home is a common motif in epitaphs. Cf. Hoffleit 1948 and Peek 1955.

37. On this subject, see Treggiari 1974, 76-104.

38. The deceased was evidently named after Antonia, wife of Drusus.

39. Livia, wife of Augustus and mother of Tiberius. She was deified by Claudius in AD 41.

40. Children of Germanicus and Agrippina. Drusus was born in AD 7, Drusilla about ten years later.

41. Again Livia. She received the name Julia Augusta by order of Augustus' will in AD 14, so this inscription must date between 14 and 41.

42. Probably Claudius.

43. See Treggiari 1974, 6, who suggests that the three men are Claudia's divorced husbands, evidently friendly enough, listed in order of manumission.

44. On this subject, see Treggiari 1971, 196-8, 241-55; Treggiari 1969.

45. Grapte's mistress is herself noteworthy. According to Tacitus (*Ann.* 15.71), she accompanied her husband, Glitius Gallus, into the exile imposed on him by Nero. She possessed a large personal fortune, which was subsequently taken away from her, both of which circumstances, Tacitus says, 'increased her glory'.

46. Everyone mentioned in this inscription is freed.

47. The designation Gaia (abbreviated C) refers to any woman, regardless of her actual name; 'C l(liberta)' could be translated 'freedwoman of a woman'.

48. An unspecified area of the city.

49. This marble plaque is decorated with a roughly carved comb and hairpin.

50. A consular date on the tombstone of a slave is extremely rare.

51. 2 BC.

52. The stone is Augustan. Thorius Flaccus was proconsul of the province of Bithynia under Augustus.

53. The inscription is in rather finely cut lettering on a marble funerary altar decorated with an oak wreath, or *corona civica*, in relief. What that motif has to do with Aurelia Nais is not explained by the inscription, and it may be that the stone is reused.

54. Another obscure topographical reference.

55. Hilara is called *vicaria*, a generic term for a slave of a slave.

IX. Medicine and Anatomy

1. As in no. 267, it is presumed that women are naturally more fearful than men.

2. The Greek words *metrai* ('matrix') and *hysterai* ('womb') almost always appear in the plural; until the Hellenistic age, when dissection was practised, it was generally believed that humans had a bicornuate uterus like larger mammals. See A. Guttmacher's note in Ellinger 1952, 113-17.

3. Cf. Apollo's argument in Aeschylus, *Eumenides* 658-61, which helps win the case for Orestes: 'She who is called the child 's mother is not its begetter, but the nurse of the newly sown conception. The begetter is the male, and she as a stranger for a stranger preserves the offspring, if no god blights its birth' (tr. H. Lloyd-Jones).

4. Animals that give birth to live offspring, as opposed to those that lay eggs.

5. In the Hippocratic Corpus (*On the Nature of the Child* 20), baldness is also attributed to excess fluid.

6. Cf. Pliny the Elder, *NH* 28.23.82: this effect can be counteracted if the woman looks at the back of the mirror or carries a red mullet. For other effects of menstruation, see no. 362.

7. The flute-girl's gymnastics would not have aborted a healthy pregnancy, but they helped eject more quickly an early defective embryon (or 'blood mole') that would soon have been miscarried in the normal course of events. The embryon was of course much older than six days. See A. Guttmacher's note in Ellinger 1952, 113-17.

8. The idea is to induce a substitute pregnancy by using the Egyptian beans the Pythagoreans would not eat because they believed that they could house human souls.

9. On the medicinal use of excrement, cf. von Staden 1989, 18-19.

10. Womb here translates the plural in Greek. Since human dissection was not practised, doctors inferred that the human uterus was similar to the bicornuate uterus of domestic animals. See A. Guttmacher's note in Ellinger 1952, 113-17.

11. I.e. wasting away or atrophy.

12. In recent times women's backaches, pains and depression were sometimes attributed to a 'tipped' uterus, though now these symptoms can usually be traced to other causes. Pessaries and/or surgical suspension are now used to alleviate symptoms traceable to a malpositioned uterus.

13. According to Pliny the Elder, *Natural History* 29.95, ground-up cantharid beetles were used to induce menstruation (and presumably also abortion), and also as a diuretic. This dangerous medicine, known as 'Spanish fly', has been used in small quantities as an aphrodisiac in modern times, though apparently not in antiquity. Cf. Davies and Kathirithamby 1986, 93.

14. Simon 1978, 239, compares the 'ovary compressor' used by J.-M. Charcot in the 19th century, cf. Veith 1965, 232.

15. Cf. Hanson 1987; Garland 1990, 41-4.

16. On the significance of the number 40, cf. Parker 1983, 48-9.

17. As usual in ancient texts, calculations are based on lunar months of 28 days; hence a normal birth would occur in the tenth month.

18. Cf. the third-century AD Roman writer Censorinus: 'In Greece they treat fortieth days as important. For the pregnant woman does not go out to a shrine before the fortieth day' (*On Days of Birth* 11.7). Cf. Parker 1983, 48.

19. Cf. H. King in Cameron & Kuhrt 1983, 113-15.

20. The 'mind', located in or near the lungs.

21. The heart and the *phrenes*.

22. Cf. Io's behaviour in Aeschylus, *Prometheus* 645-9; Simon 1978, 563-608.

23. See below, no. 352, and Scarborough 1977. Cf. Jackson 1988, 86-111.

24. This notion may go back to the third-century BC doctor Herophilus of Alexandria; Galen, *On Seed* 2.1 = F 61 von Staden 1989.

25. *On Common Diseases* 6.6.21.

26. On the history of this 'disease', see especially Veith 1965 and Simon 1978.

27. See above, p. 232.

28. Since the Greek text is defective here, the description of bringing the baby out is taken from the sixth-century Latin summary by Muscio, 1.66a.

29. Cf. no. 345.

30. First century BC, a theoretical rather than experimental physician; virtually nothing is known about Mantias or about Xenophon of Cos.

31. Cf. the suicidal tendencies in virgins with the onset of menarche described in no. 349; H. King in Cameron & Kuhrt 1983, 118.

32. I.e. Aristotle, his principal source.

33. Masurius Sabinus, a famous jurist under the Emperor Tiberius.

34. I.e. as opposed to holding the breath.

35. Cf. Soranus' suggestion of sneezing as a contraceptive measure, no. 355, sec. 61.

36. The fertilisation of more than one egg at different times, resulting in embryos of different ages in the uterus at the same time.

37. In Greek mythology, the hero Heracles (Hercules) was the son of Alcmene

and Zeus, while his 'twin' brother Iphicles was the son of Alcmene and her mortal husband, Amphytrion.

38. Marmora.

39. Cf. von Staden 1991, 271-96.

40. The lamp wick recurs at no. 354 as an abortive.

41. The list of ingredients (in another context, 3.20.1) consists of: burning pitch, unscoured wool, pepper, hellebore, castoreum, vinegar, garlic, and onion.

42. *Nigella sativa*, melanthium, melanospermum or black cumin. Its seeds were used both as a spice and as a medication for various ills.

43. Pessaries.

44. The *denarius*, or dram, was a measure of weight equal to one-seventh of an *uncia* (one-twelfth of a Roman pound). The pound equalled about 333 metric grams, the *denarius* about 4 grams.

45. The *cyathus* was a liquid measure equivalent to about 42 cc.

46. At 7.64.

47. See above, n. 13.

48. In revenge, as if murdered by his next-of-kin, cf. Euripides, *Medea* 1389.

49. See above, p. 352, n. 47.

50. Kaibel 590 expresses many of the same sentiments of affection, but without so much self-praise.

51. See Pomeroy 1978.

52. See above, p. 352, n. 47.

53. Literally, the Isoteles' daughter, referring to a favoured class of metics.

54. Kaibel 47 is a fourth-century epitaph for a nurse who came from the Peloponnesus.

55. Cf. the similar advice in Plutarch, *Moralia* 3c-d.

56. Cf. no. 101.

57. I.e. 'Luck'; when Oedipus he was adopted as foundling, he states 'I shall regard myself as Tyche's child' (Sophocles, *Oedipus the King* 1080).

58. The scribe appears not to have known or not to have filled in the father's name.

59. I.e. Commodus, AD 180-192.

X. Religion

1. The verse inscription is followed by a prose postscript confirming the transfer.

2. *HSCP* 82 (1978) 123-4; this oracle is considered 'legendary' by Fontenrose 1978, 409-10.

3. See also Livy 39.8-18.

4. Cf. Dionysiac rituals, nos. 384-7.

5. Cf. Russell 1973, 83.

6. Cf. the description of the women worshippers of Dionysus in Euripides' *Bacchae* (especially 134-66), rushing through the mountains, freed from the constraints of home and domestic life.

7. 'Sooty'.

8. 'Destroyers'.

9. Cf. Hellanicus, 4 *FGrHist* 74-84; Wiedemann 1983.

10. Statues and inscriptions were always put up for male victors.

11. Cf. elaborate dress and/or heavy make-up as a sign of impropriety in nos. 88, 208, 267.

12. Cf. nos. 204-7.

13. *IG* I² 744 = *DAA* 232; IG I² 425.

14. The architect of the Parthenon, Plutarch, *Life of Pericles* 159e.

15. *Poletae*, commissioners in charge of collecting and distributing public revenues.

16. Cf. Lloyd-Jones 1983; also below, no. 434.

17. There was an ancient cult of Artemis at Brauron, with a precinct on the Acropolis; festivals were held at five-year intervals in which girls from five to ten years of age danced to the goddess dressed as bears. Cf. Simon 1983, 83-8; Burkert 1985, 263, Sourvinou-Inwood 1988, 25-6.

18. See especially Calame 1977.

19. Perhaps the term is metaphorical, signifying only that they are members of the same social group; Calame 1977, 84-5.

20. On offerings to Artemis, see Linders 1972.

21. 349/8 BC.

22. 348/7 BC.

23. 347/6 BC.

24. Cf. the offering referred to in the Hippocratic treatise *On Virgins*, no. 349.

25. Cf. the Pythagorean admonition that women should wear white, no. 208.

26. A resident alien.

27. The restoration is uncertain. Apparently Cyrenaean girls were required before marriage to spend a night in a dormitory in the precinct of Artemis.

28. A woman in childbirth pollutes everyone who enters the house for three days.

29. Cf. Edelstein 1945, no. 423.

30. A demonstration of the god's superior understanding, since mortals and even gods do not always know what they need to ask for; in the myth the goddess Dawn asks Zeus to grant immortality to her mortal lover Tithonus, but forgets to ask for eternal youth; *Homeric Hymn to Aphrodite* 217-38.

31. In the myth, Zeus restores Io's sanity by touching her with his hand (Aeschylus, *Prometheus Bound* 847-8).

32. The god's sacred snakes were kept in the sanctuary and effected many different kinds of cures.

33. See Beard 1980.

34. On the privilege of the *ius trium liberorum*, cf. 154.

35. The Latin word is *agger*.

36. Creon orders similar arrangements to be made for Antigone in Sophocles' play, also in order not to incur pollution, 772-6.

37. A jurist.

38. The Sibylline books, which contained prophecies by the Sibyl of Cumae, were guarded by a special ten-man priesthood and consulted in emergencies of state.

39. Other priesthoods.

40. The headquarters of the priesthood, in the Roman Forum.

41. I.e. 'with all a Vestal's entitlements'. See Holford-Strevens 1988, 221 n. 38.

42. See Calabi Limentani 1991, 236-237.

43. Priest of Jupiter, member of the senatorial class, and praetor in charge of guardians.

44. Unfortunately Cicero's own description of Terentia does not survive.

45. Compare no. 88, where the husband trusts his wife, and her lover is able to gain entry into the women's quarters.

46. The youngest of his three sisters; in no. 71 (56 BC) Cicero accuses him of committing incest with his second sister, the wife of Q. Metellus Celer.

47. Prometheus was punished by Zeus for disobedience by having his liver eaten each day by Zeus' eagle.

48. A word used only here. Cf. Aeschylus, *Eumenides* 326.

49. An epithet of Juno as goddess of childbirth.

50. A town in Thessaly known for witchcraft. Cf. *Odes* 1.27.21.

51. A volcanic lake near the Bay of Naples, believed in antiquity to be the entrance to the underworld.

52. The Subura was a crowded, dirty section of Rome between the Viminal and Esquiline Hills. Though it was notorious as a red-light district, it also contained respectable merchants and residents.

53. The Marsi inhabited the mountains east of Rome. They practised magic, but it was, apparently, not strong enough for Canidia.

54. That is, an avenger.

55. The Manes, spirits of the dead or gods of the underworld invoked on tombstones.

56. The land outside the Esquiline Gate (on the east side of the city) was used as a cemetery for paupers. Although cremation was the usual practice in Rome in this period, these bodies were inhumed, hence the reference to limbs. It was not far from the villa of Maecenas, Horace's patron: cf. Horace, *Satires* 1.8.

57. The conventional conclusion to a dying victim's curse (e.g. Dido's at *Aeneid* 4.620). Throughout antiquity crucial significance was attached to burial procedures and places by pagan and Christian, rich and poor.

58. Hardening.

59. A series of magic letters.

60. The tin strip or plate would be worn on the arm like an amulet.

61. Cf. Luck 1985

62. Cf. Taylor 1937.

63. Cf. Jesus' mother Mary and Mary of Clopas (or in Greek, Kleopatros; John 19.25). Cf. Berthelot 1885, 173

64. The local senate.

65. According to the myth, Zeus mated with Leda in the form of a swan, and Helen was born from the egg.

66. The goddess of childbirth.

67. Cf. Rogers 1991, 107-9.

68. Cf. also no. 1064; Merkelbach 1980.

69. Hestia was the oldest child of Cronus and Rhea, and Zeus the youngest, but since Cronus swallowed all of his children except for Zeus, he became the oldest by default, since Hestia was the last to be 'reborn'.

70. A significant variation on the man's wish for children who resemble himself, cf. nos. 57, 208, 373.

71. According to Greek myth, the founder of Ephesus, his worship under the Roman Empire served as a reminder to the Greeks in Ephesus of their national identity. Cf. Rogers 1991.

72. For the archaeological context of the inscription, see de Franciscis 1970. We are indebted to Professor J.H. D'Arms for bringing the inscription to our attention.

73. This indicates free birth. Her husband, however, was a freedman.

74. On which this inscription is carved.

75. On the ritual, cf. Burkert 1966, 1-25; on the name, Nagy 1979, 261.

76. Usually the father named the child. As in the case of Theano (no. 434), her name indicates that her parents may have wanted her to become a priestess, in this case of Demeter, for whom the festival of Thesmophoria was celebrated.

77. Menander's line 'Those whom the gods love die young' (Fr. 111 Koerte) had become proverbial by the second century BC.

78. Attica.

79. See esp. Bloch 1945.

80. The last three titles signify that Praetextatus was a member of three out of the four ancient priestly colleges; priest of the Sun could refer to the cult either of Mithras (cf. *ILS* 4152) or Sol Invictus; for Praetextatus (as for the Emperor Julian) the Sun represented the Twelve Gods (Macrobius, *Sat.* 1.xvii, 1-xxiv.1).

81. These titles refer respectively to the cult of the oriental gods Serapis, Magna Mater and Mithras. In the ritual of the taurobolium a bull (*tauros*) was slaughtered over the head of the initiate while he/she stood below in a pit. Through the shower of blood the initiate was reborn for eternity (e.g. *ILS* 4152). Cf. the metaphorical rebirth of Christians through drinking the wine that represents the blood of the Saviour.

82. Praetextatus was proconsul of Achaea in 362 under the philhellenic pagan Emperor Julian the 'Apostate', a particular honour. He was prefect of Rome in 367 under the Emperor Valentinian, when Christian factions were disputing the papacy. During this period he restored the Portico of the Twelve Gods with its statues in the Roman Forum. He was prefect of the Praetorian guard when he died in 384, and consul elect for 385, the year of his wife's death.

83. She has the honorary title of 'woman of distinction'.

84. Praetextatus translated Themistius' paraphrases of Aristotle's *Prior and Posterior Analytics*, but Paulina's words suggest that he also had better editions prepared of works of Latin literature.

85. See above, n. 82, on the Twelve Gods.

86. Dindymene, i.e. the Magna Mater. Praetextatus showed an unusual concern for the religious education of his wife; see Brown 1972. Cf. *ILS* 4154, an inscription on an altar set up in 340 by Caecina Lolliana and her son Ceionius Rufus Volusianus; his sister Sabina was an initiate of some of the same mystery cults as Paulina.

87. The reverse of Clodia's situation; see no. 71.

88. A variation on the usual praise of close resemblance of father and son; see nos. 208, 373.

89. As governor of Achaea Praetextatus had protected these cults against the Christian government.

90. I.e. the Magna Mater; with Isis, this represents her participation in Oriental cult; cf. above n. 81.

91. This action had been opposed by the prefect of Rome of 385, the prominent pagan Symmachus, on the grounds that it was untraditional to bestow such honours on men (Symm. *Ep.* 2.36). In general see esp. Bloch 1963.

92. Paul was celibate.

93. I.e. in Christ, a Christian.

94. Like many other founders of the new religion, Paul believed that the kingdom of the Lord was about to come and do away with the world as he knew it.

95. Presumably Paul has in mind her celibate partnerships among the faithful.

96. In this discussion, the head has importance as a symbol of rank; therefore women should cover their heads, as a sign of submission and modesty. Cf. Thompson 1988.

97. A reference to the story of how God created woman from Adam's rib in Genesis 2-3.

98. Presumably the covering will ward off bad angels and show respect to the good ones.

99. Here Paul appears to be concerned with some local deviation from standard practice that required women to remain silent in church; he makes a distinction, however, between asking questions about scripture (as here) and prophesying (above, 11.5), presumably because in prophecy she would be thought to be inspired by the Holy Spirit.

100. Harvey 1970, 660-71.

101. Cf. the similar restrictions advised for the Neopythagorean community, no. 208.

102. Cf. above, I Cor. 11:9, no. 441.

103. I.e. women who are bereft and needy.

104. Cf. the special epithet *univira*, 'married to one husband only' in Latin epitaphs.

105. I.e. not a regular synagogue.

106. Apparently Lydia is a convert to Judaism. Purple dye was a luxury, so profession would have made her a rich woman. She is head of her own household. Cf. Meeks 1983, 62

107. As in no. 382, the owners get the profits from the slave's work.

108. Cf. Lefkowitz 1986, 130-1.

109. Presumably because men wore their tunics shorter than women.

110. See especially Dodds 1965, 47-53.

111. Arenas had two gates, the Porta Sanavivaria (Gate of Life), for gladiators who survived, and the Porta Libitina (Gate of Death). On the political significance of Perpetua's death, see Lefkowitz 1981a, 57-8, Lefkowitz 1986, 105, and de Ste. Croix 1963.

112. I Thessalonians 1:8.

113. I Thessalonians 4:9.

114. Cf. Matthew 10:23. In Euripides' *Bacchae* the women's being 'on the mountain' is also construed as a serious social threat (e.g. 217-20).

115. Psalms 51:7.

116. John 14:27.

117. I Timothy 1:5.

118. Acts 4:24.

119. On the role of women in Gnostic cults, see Pagels 1979, 48-69; on women in orthodox practice, Cameron 1980.

120. As if he were John the Anti-Baptist.

121. Cf. the conversion language used by Jesus in the Gnostic *Gospel of Thomas*: 'He who will drink from my mouth will become as I am' (50.28).

122. Cf. Mark 4:31.

123. Matthew 18:10.

124. The kylix, or drinking cup, was shallow and wide with two handles, more like a modern saucer than a cup.

125. Clement quotes directly from the Septuagint Greek text of the (apocryphal) Ecclesiasticus (Wisdom of Jesus son of Sirach) 26.8.

126. The fragment of 'Theophrastus' has also been attributed to Seneca (Fr. 13, 47ff.) The anthologist Stobaeus preserves some theoretical abstracts from ethical treatises for and against marriage by Antiphon the Sophist (fifth century BC, 87 B D-K), and the Hellenistic Neophythagoreans (collected in Thesleff), and the Stoics

Antipater (first century BC) and Hierocles (first century AD).

127. Cf. Antiphon (see n. 126): 'Is it not clear that a wife, if she is to his mind, gives her husband no less cause for love and pain than he does to himself, for the health of two bodies, the acquisition of two livelihoods, and for respectability and honour? Suppose children are born: then all is full of anxiety, and the youthful spring goes out of the mind, and the countenance is no longer the same' (tr. Freeman 1957, 149-50).

128. Cf. Momigliano 1985, 331-9.

129. In this biography Gregory never refers to his mother by her name.

130. Gregory uses the term Virgins (*parthenoi*) to denote communities of celibate women.

131. From earliest times (e.g. Homer, *Odyssey* 2.116) wool-working was a valued female skill even in aristocratic families; e.g. Claudia, no. 39, Murdia, no. 43, and the family of the Emperor Augustus, no. 210.

132. Women of Macrina's rank did not ordinarily perform such menial tasks.

133. Gregory regards philosophy, i.e. the attainment of true knowledge, as virtually synonymous with the religious life.

134. In other words, the family estates had been divided up among the grown children.

135. Gregory does not say when and by whom this community came into existence, but when he returns home it is clear that the monastery, with separate dwellings for men and for women, had been established on the family estate.

136. The egalitarianism of the early church had long since been replaced by a carefully structured hierarchy; Gregory had been bishop of Nyssa since 372.

137. Discussion and bibliography in Lefkowitz 1986, 107-12.

138. Cf. Lloyd 1967, 276-9.

139. A member of the court of the Emperor Constantius, AD 324-61.

140. Aedesius, a pupil of the Neoplatonist philosopher Iamblichus, taught the Emperor Julian (332-63) briefly before sending him on to the younger and more energetic Maximius.

141. Sosipatra had discovered that Philometor, who was in love with her, had put her under a spell, but Maximius had contrived to break it.

Abbreviations

Adler = A. Adler, *Suidae Lexicon* (Stuttgart 1928-38).

AP = W.R. Paton, ed., *Greek Anthology* (Cambridge, Mass., 1916).

ARS = A.C. Johnson, P.R. Coleman-Norton & F.C. Bourne, *Ancient Roman Statutes* (Austin, Texas, 1961).

Bernand = A. & É. Bernand, *Les inscriptions grecques et latines du colosse de Memnon* (Paris, Institut Français d'Archéologie Orientale, 1960).

Berthelot = M. Berthelot, *Collection des anciens alchimistes grecs* (Paris, 1888).

BGU = *Ägyptische Urkunden aus den Museen zu Berlin: Griechische Urkunden* (Berlin, 1863-).

CEG = P.A. Hansen, ed., *Carmina Epigraphica Graeca* (Berlin, 1983-).

CIL = *Corpus Inscriptionum Latinarum* (Berlin, 1863-1959).

CLE = F. Buecheler, *Carmina Latina Epigraphica* (Leipzig, 1895-97).

CIG = *Corpus Inscriptionum Graecarum*, 4 vols (1828-77).

CPR = C. Wessely, ed., *Corpus Papyrorum Raineri* (Vienna, 1895).

DAA, see Raubitschek, *DAA*.

Decleva Caizzi = F. Decleva Caizzi, *Antisthenis Fragmenta* (Milan, 1965).

D-K = H. Diels & W. Kranz, *Die Fragmente der Vorsokratiker* (Berlin, 1956).

Ditt. *Syll.* = W. Dittenberger, *Sylloge Inscriptionum Graecarum*, 3rd ed. (Leipzig, 1915).

FGE = D.L. Page, ed., *Further Greek Epigrams* (Cambridge, 1981).

FGrHist = F. Jacoby, *Die Fragmente der griechischen Historiker* (Berlin, 1923-57).

FH = P. Friedländer, with H.B. Hoffleit, *Epigrammata: Greek Inscriptions in Verse* (Berkeley, Calif., 1948).

FHG = C. Müller, ed., *Fragmenta Historicorum Graecorum* (1841-70).

Finley = M.I. Finley, *Studies in Land and Credit in Ancient Athens, 500-200 BC* (New Brunswick, N.J., 1951).

FIRA = S. Riccobono et al., *Fontes Iuris Romani Antejustiniani*[2] (Florence, 1940-43).

Fouilles de Delphes = École française d'Athènes, *Fouilles de Delphes* (Paris, 1902-).

GHI = R. Meiggs & D. Lewis, *A Selection of Greek Historical Inscriptions* (Oxford, 1969).

GLP = D.L. Page, ed., *Select Papyri III* (Cambridge, Mass., 1941).

HCSP = *Harvard Studies in Classical Philology*.

I. Magn. = O. Kern, *Die Inschriften von Magnesia am Maeander* (Berlin, 1900).

IG = *Inscriptiones Graecae* (Berlin, 1873-).

IG III.3 = *IG* III.3. *Defixionum Tabellae*, ed. R. Wuensch (1897).

ILA = R. Cagnat, A. Merlin & L. Chatelain, *Inscriptions Latines d'Afrique* (Paris 1923).

ILLRP = A. Degrassi, *Inscriptiones Latinae Liberae Rei Publicae* I² (Florence 1965), II (Florence 1963).

ILS = H. Dessau, *Inscriptiones Latinae Selectae* (Berlin, 1892-1916).

Inscr. Creticae = Inscriptiones Creticae, ed. M. Guarducci (Berlin, 1935-50).

Inscr. Eph = H. Engelmann, D. Knibbe & R. Merkelbach, eds., *Die Inschriften von Ephesos* (Bonn, 1980).

JEA = Journal of Egyptian Archaeology.

JÖAI = Jahreshefte des Österreichischen Archäologischen Instituts

Kaibel = G. Kaibel, *Epigrammata Graeca ex lapidibus conlecta* (Berlin, 1878).

Kenyon = F.G. Kenyon, ed., *Classical Texts from Papyri* (London, 1891).

Kock = T. Kock, ed., *Comicorum Atticorum Fragmenta* (Leipzig, 1880).

LCL = Loeb Classical Library.

Malcovati = E. Malcovati, ed., *Oratorum Romanorum Fragmenta* (Turin, 1955).

Migne = J.-P. Migne. *Patrologiae cursus completus (series graeca)* (Paris 1928-36).

Nauck = A. Nauck, ed., *Tragicorum Graecorum Fragmenta*² (1889).

P. Adl. = E.N. Adler et al., *The Adler Papyri* (Oxford, 1939).

P. Cattaoui = B.P. Grenfell & A.S. Hunt, 'Papyrus Cattaoui', *Archiv für Papyrusforschung* (1903-6) 3: 55ff.

P. Corn. = W.L. Westermann & C.J. Kramer, Jr., eds., *Greek Papyri in the Library of Cornell University* (New York, 1926).

P. Eleph. = O. Rubensohn, *Elephantine-Papyri* (*BGU*, Sonderheft).

P. Fam. Tebt. = B.A. van Groningen, *Papyrologica Lugduno-Batava* (Leiden, 1950).

P. Giessen = O. Eger, E. Kornemann, & P.M. Meyer, ed., *Griechische Papyri im Museum des oberhessischen Geschichtsvereins zu Giessen* (Leipzig-Berlin, 1910-12).

P. Grenf. I = B.P. Grenfell, ed., *An Alexandrian Erotic Fragment* ... (Oxford, 1896).

P. Hamb. = P.M. Meyer, *Griechische Papyrustudien der hamburger Staatsurkunden und Universitätsbibliothek* (Leipzig-Berlin, 1911-24).

P. Haun. = T. Larsen, ed., *Papyri Graecae Haunienses*, fasc. 1 (Copenhagen, 1942).

P. Hibeh = B.P. Grenfell & A.S. Hunt, *The Hibeh Papyri*, pt. I (London, 1906).

P. Lond. = F.G. Kenyon & H.I. Bell, eds., *Greek Papyri in the British Museum* (London, 1903-17).

P. Mich. = J.G. Winter, *Papyri in the University of Michigan Collection* (Ann Arbor, 1936).

P. Oxy. = B.P. Grenfell & A.S. Hunt, *The Oxyrhynchus Papyri* (1896).

P. Tebt. = B.P. Grenfell, A.S. Hunt et al., *The Tebtunis Papyri* (London, 1902-35).

PCG = R. Kassel & C. Austin, eds., *Poetae Comici Graeci*. (Berlin, 1983-).

Peek = W. Peek, *Griechische Vers-Inschriften* I, *Grab-epigramme* (Berlin, 1955).

PGM = K. Preisendanz, *Papyri Graecae Magicae* (Leipzig, 1928).

Pleket = H.W. Pleket, *Epigraphica II: Texts on the Social History of the Greek World* (Leiden, 1969).

PMG = D.L. Page, ed., *Poetae Melici Graeci* (Oxford, 1962).

Preisendanz Henrichs = K. Preisendanz, ed., *Papyri Graecae Magicae*, 2nd ed. A. Henrichs (Stuttgart, 1973).

PSI = G. Vitelli et al., *Papiri della Società Italiana* (1912-32).

Raubitschek, *DAA* = D.E. Raubitschek, *Dedications from the Athenian Acropolis* (Cambridge, Mass., 1949).

SB = F. Preisigke et al., *Sammelbuch griechischer Urkunden aus Ägypten*

(Strassburg et al., 1915-).

SEG = *Supplementum Epigraphicum Graecum* (Leiden, 1923-).

Sokolowski, *LSAM* = F. Sokolowski, *Lois sacrées de l'Asie Mineure* (Paris, 1955).

Sokolowski, *LSCG* = F. Sokolowski, *Lois sacrées des cités grecques* (Paris, 1969).

Sokolowski, *LSCG, Supp.* = F. Sokolowski, *Lois sacrées des cités grecques, Supplément* (Paris, 1962).

Supp. Hell. = H. Lloyd-Jones & P. Parsons, eds., *Supplementum Hellenisticum* (Berlin, 1983).

Syll. = W. Dittenberger, *Sylloge Inscriptionum Graecarum* (Leipzig, 1915-24).

Tab. Vindol. = A.K. Bowman and J.D. Thomas, *Vindolanda: The Latin Writing Tablets* (London, 1984).

Thesleff = H. Thesleff, ed., *The Pythagorean Texts of the Hellenistic Period* (Abo, 1965).

UPZ = U. Wilcken, *Urkunden der Ptolemäerzeit (ältere Funde)* (Berlin-Leipzig, 1927-).

West = M.L. West, *Iambi et Elegi Graeci* (Oxford, i, 1989; ii, 1972).

Zintzen = C. Zintzen, ed., *Damascii Vitae Isidori Reliquiae* (Hildesheim, 1967).

Bibliography

Alexiou, M. (1974) *The Ritual Lament in Greek Tradition.* Cambridge.

Anderson, J.K. (1974) *Xenophon.* London.

Baldwin, B. (1981) *Classical News and Views* 25: 18-21.

Balsdon, J.P.V.D. (1962) *Roman Women.* London.

Beard, M. (1980) 'The Sexual Status of Vestal Virgins'. *JRS* 70: 12-27.

Berger, A. (1953) *Encyclopedic Dictionary of Roman Law (Trans. Am. Philos. Soc. n.s. 43.2).* Philadelphia.

Berthelot, M. (1885) *Les origines de l'alchimie.* Paris.

Bettini, M. (forthcoming) *Il vino stuprum: il bacio parentale e la purezza delle donna romana.* Paper read at conference 'In vino veritas', British School at Rome, March 1991.

Bloch, H. (1945) 'The last pagan revival in the West'. *Harvard Theological Review* 38: 199-244.

Bloch, H. (1963) 'The pagan revival in the West at the end of the fourth century'. In A. Momigliano, ed., *The Conflict between Paganism and Christianity in the Fourth Century*, 193-218. Oxford.

Bonfante Warren, L. (1984) 'The Women of Etruria'. In J.P. Sullivan, ed., *Women in the Ancient World*, 229-239. Albany, N.Y.

Bowman, A.K. & J.D. Thomas (1987) 'New Texts from Vindolanda'. *Britannia* 18: 137-40.

Brown, P. (1972) *Religion and Society in the Age of Augustine.* London.

Bühler, W. (1963) *Hermes* 91: 351.

Burkert, W. (1966) 'Kekropidensage und Arrhephoria'. *Hermes* 94: 1-25.

Burkert, W. (1985) *Greek Religion.* Oxford.

Burnett, A.P. (1979) *Classical Philology* 74: 16-27.

Calabi Limentani, I. (1991) *Epigrafia Latina*[4]. Milan.

Calame, C. (1977) *Les Choeurs de jeunes filles en Grèce archaïque II: Alcman.* Rome.

Cameron, A. (1980) *Greece and Rome* 27: 60-8.

Cameron, A. & A. Kuhrt, eds. (1983) *Images of Women in Antiquity.* Detroit.

Carey, C. (1991) 'Apollodorus' Mother'. *CQ* 41: 84-9.

Cole, S.G. (1981) 'Could Greek Women Read and Write?'. In H.P. Foley, ed., *Reflections of Women in Antiquity.* New York. 236ff.

Crook, J.A. (1967) *Law and Life of Rome.* London and Ithaca.

D'Arms, J.H. (1970) *Romans on the Bay of Naples.* Cambridge, Mass.

Davies, M. & J. Kathirithamby (1986) *Greek Insects.* London.

de Franciscis, A. (1970) In ed., *Atti del decimo convegno di studi sulla Magna Grecia*, 447-9. Taranto.

de Ste. Croix, G.E.M. (1963) *Past and Present* 26: 6-37.

de Ste. Croix, G.E.M. (1970) *CR* 20: 274-5.

de Ste. Croix, G.E.M. (1981) *The Class Struggle in the Ancient Greek World*. London.

Decleva Caizzi, F. (1965) *Antisthenis Fragmenta*. Milan.

Dodds, E.R. (1965) *Pagan and Christian in an Age of Anxiety*. Cambridge.

Donati, A. (1971) 'Sull'iscrizione lanuvina della curia mulierum'. *Rivista storica dell'antichità* 1: 235-7.

Dover, K.J. (1974) *Greek Popular Morality*. Oxford.

Edelstein, E.J.a.L. (1945) *Asclepius: A Collection and Interpretation of Testimonies*. Baltimore.

Ellinger, T.H. (1952) *Hippocrates on Intercourse and Pregnancy*. New York.

Evans, J.K. (1991) *War, Women and Children in Ancient Rome*. London.

Farina, A. (1959) *Il processo di Frine*.

Farnell, L.R. (1909) *The Cults of the Greek States*.

Finley, M.I. (1951) *Studies in Land and Credit in Ancient Athens, 500-200 BC*. Reissue 1973. New Brunswick, N.J.

Fontenrose, J. (1978) *The Delphic Oracle*. Berkeley.

Fornara, W. (1977) *Archaic Times to the End of the Peloponnesian War*. Baltimore.

Fraser, P.M. (1972) *Ptolemaic Alexandria*. Oxford.

Freeman, K. (1957) *Ancilla to the Pre-Socratic Philosophers*. Cambridge, Mass.

Friedländer, P. & Hoffleit, P.B. (1948) *Epigrammata: Greek Inscriptions in Verse*. Berkeley.

Gagé, J. (1963) *Matronalia: essai sur les dévotions et les organisations culturelles des femmes dans l'ancienne Rome, Collection Latomus*, 60. Brussels.

Gardner, J.F. (1986) *Women in Roman Law and Society*. London.

Garland, R. (1990) *The Greek Way of Life*. London and Ithaca.

Geffcken, K.A. (1973) *Comedy in the Pro Caelio*. Leiden.

Gow, A.S.F. (1965) *Theocritus*, 2 vols. Cambridge.

Gratwick, A.S. (1982) In *Cambridge History of Classical Literature*, 146-7. Cambridge.

Halperin, D. (1990) *One Hundred Years of Homosexuality*. London.

Hanson, A. (1987) *Bull. Hist. Med.* 61: 589-602.

Harrison, A.R.W. (1968) *The Law of Athens: the Family and Property*. Oxford.

Harvey, A.E. (1970) *Companion to the New Testament*. Oxford/Cambridge.

Harvey, F.D. (1984) 'The Wicked Wife of Ischomachus'. *EMC* 3.1.

Herfst, P. (1922) *Le Travail de la femme dans la Grèce Ancienne*. Utrecht.

Holford-Strevens, L. (1988) *Aulus Gellius*. London.

Honoré, T. (1991) Personal communication.

Hooker, J.T. (1988) In A. Powell, ed., *Classical Sparta*. Norman, Okla.

Horsfall, N. (1983) 'Some Problems in the "Laudatio Turiae" '. *Bull. Inst. Clas. Stud.* 30: 85-98.

Horsfall, N. (1985) '*CIL* VI 37965 = *CLE* 1988 (Epitaph of Allia Potestas): A Commentary'. *ZPE* 61: 251-72.

Humphreys, S.C. (1983) *Women, the Family, and Death*. London.

Jackson, R. (1988) *Doctors and Diseases in the Roman Empire*. Norman, Okla.

Kraus, H. (1919) *Zeitschrift des deutschen Vereins für Buchwesen und Schrifttum, Suppl. I*. Leipzig.

Lacey, W.K. (1968) *The Family in Classical Greece*.

Lattimore, R. (1942) *Themes in Greek and Latin Epitaphs*. Urbana.

Lawler, L.B. (1964) *The Dance in Ancient Greece*. London.

Lee, H.M. (1984) 'Athletics and the Bikini girls from Piazza Armerina'. *Stadion* 10: 45-76.

Lefkowitz, M.R. (1981) *The Lives of the Greek Poets*. London/Baltimore.

Lefkowitz, M.R. (1981a) *Heroines and Hysterics*. London.

Lefkowitz, M.R. (1986) *Women in Greek Myth*. London.

Lefkowitz, M.R. (1989) 'Only the best girls get to'. *TLS* 5/5-11: 481, 484.

Lefkowitz, M.R. (1990) 'Should Women Receive a Separate Education'. *New Literary History* 21.4: 801-15.

Levick, B. (1983) 'The Senatusconsultum from Larinum'. *JRS* 73: 97-115.

Linders, T. (1972) *Studies in the Treasure Records at Artemis Brauronia*. Stockholm.

Lloyd, A.C. (1967) 'The Later Neo-Platonists'. In ed., *The Cambridge History of Later Greek and Early Medieval Philosophy*. Cambridge. 272-325.

Lloyd-Jones, H. (1963) *JHS* 83: 75-99.

Lloyd-Jones, H. (1976) *Females of the Species*. London.

Lloyd-Jones, H. (1983) *JHS* 102: 92.

Luck, G. (1985) *Arcana Mundi*. Baltimore.

Lutz, C.E. (1947) *Yale Classical Studies* 10: 3-147.

MacDowell, D.M. (1962) *Andokides On the Mysteries*. Oxford.

MacDowell, D.M. (1990) *Demosthenes: Against Meidias*. Oxford.

Maiuri, A. (1965) *Pompeii*[7]. Rome.

Marchant, E.D., ed. (1900) *Xenophon, Opuscula*.

McClees, H. (1920) *A Study of Women in Attic Inscriptions*. New York.

McGinn, T.A.J. (1989) 'The Taxation of Roman Prostitutes'. *Helios* 16: 79-110.

McGinn, T.A.J. (1991) 'Concubinage and the Lex Iulia on Adultery'. *Transactions of the American Philological Association* 121: 335-74.

Meeks, W.A. (1983) *The First Urban Christians*. New Haven.

Merkelbach, R. (1980) 'Der Kult der Hestia im Prytaneion der griechischen Städte'. *ZPE* 37: 90.

Milligan, G. (1910) *Selections from the Greek Papyri*. Cambridge.

Momigliano, A. (1985) 'Macrina, una santa aristocrata'. In G. Arrigoni, ed., *Le Donne in Grecia*. Rome-Bari.

Murnaghan, S.B. (1988) 'How a woman can be more like a man: the dialogue between Ischomachus and his Wife in Xenophon's Oeconomicus'. *Helios* 15: 9-22

Nagy, B. (1979) *Classical Journal* 74: 261.

Nais, D. (1985) 'The Shrewish Wife of Socrates'. *EMC* 4.1: 97-9.

Nicholas, B. (1962) *An Introduction to Roman Law*. Oxford.

Pagels, E.H. (1979) *The Gnostic Gospels*. New York.

Parke, H.W. & D.E.W. Wormell (1956) *The Delphic Oracle*. Oxford.

Parker, R. (1983) *Miasma*. Oxford.

Peek, W. (1955) *Griechische Vers-Inschriften*. Berlin.

Pelling, C.B.R. (1988) *Plutarch: Life of Antony*. Cambridge.

Pollitt, J.J. (1983) *The Art of Rome c. 753 BC–AD 337: Sources and Documents*. Cambridge.

Pomeroy, S.B. (1975) *Goddesses, Whores, Wives and Slaves*. New York.

Pomeroy, S.B. (1977) 'Technikai kai Mousikai'. *AJAJ* 2: 51-68.

Pomeroy, S.B. (1978) *AJP* 99: 499-500.

Pomeroy, S.B. (1978a) 'Supplementary Notes on Erinna'. *ZPE* 32: 17-22.

Powell, A., ed. (1988) *Classical Sparta*. Norman, Okla.

Preisendanz, K. (1928) *Papyri Graecae Magicae*. Leipzig.

Rawson, B. (1974) 'Roman concubinage and other *de facto* marriages'. *TAPA* 104: 279-305.

Rice, E.E. (1983) *The Grand Procession of Ptolemy Philadelphus*. Oxford.
Rogers, G.M. (1922) 'The Constructions of Women at Ephesos'. *ZPE* 90: 215-23.
Rogers, G.M. (1991) *The Sacred Identity of Ephesos*. London.
Russell, D.A. (1973) *Plutarch*. London.
Scarborough, J. (1977) *The Historian* 39: 213-27.
Schaps, D.M. (1977) *Classical Quarterly* 27.
Schaps, D.M. (1979) *Economic Rights of Women in Ancient Greece*. Edinburgh.
Schiller, A.A. (1978) *Roman Law: Mechanisms of Development*. The Hague.
Schwarze, J. (1971) *Die Beurteilung des Perikles durch die attische Komödie*. Munich.
Sealey, R. (1990) *Women and Law in Classical Greece*. Chapel Hill.
Sijpesteijn, P.J. (1979) *Zeitschrift für Papyrologie und Epigrafik* 34: 119-22.
Simon, B. (1978) *Mind and Madness in Ancient Greece*. Ithaca, N.Y.
Simon, E. (1983) *Festivals of Attica*. Madison, Wisc.
Snyder, J.M. (1989) *The Woman and the Lyre*. Carbondale, Ill.
Sourvinou-Inwood, C. (1988) *Studies in Girls' Transitions*. Athens.
Straub, J. (1966) 'Senaculum, id est mulierum senatus'. In ed., *Bonner Historia Augusta Colloquium 1964-65*. Bonn. 221-40.
Tarn, W.W. (1934) *Cambridge Ancient History*, vol. 10. Cambridge.
Taylor, F.S. (1937) 'The Origins of Greek Alchemy'. *Ambix* 1: 30-47.
Thompson, C.L. (1988) 'Hairstyles, Head-coverings, and St. Paul'. *Biblical Archaeologist* 96-115.
Treggiari, S. (1969) *Roman Freedmen During the Late Republic*. Oxford.
Treggiari, S. (1971) 'Libertine ladies'. *Classical World* 64: 196-8.
Treggiari, S. (1974) *Women in Domestic Service in the Early Roman Empire*. Cambridge, Mass.
Treggiari, S. (1981) 'Concubinae'. *PBSR* 49: 59-81.
Tsantsanoglou, K. (1973) *ZPE* 12: 183-95.
Turner, E.G. (1968) *Greek Papyri*[2]. Princeton.
van Bremen, R. (1983) 'Women and Wealth'. In A. Cameron & A. Kuhrt, eds., *Images of Women in Antiquity*. Detroit.
Veith, I. (1965) *Hysteria*. Chicago.
Vlastos, G. (1989) 'Was Plato a Feminist?' *Times Literary Supplement* 3/17-23: 276, 288-9.
von Staden, H. (1989) *Herophilus: The Art of Medicine in Early Alexandria*. Cambridge.
von Staden, H. (1991) '*Apud nos foediora verba*: Celsus' reluctant construction of the female body'. In *Le Latin Médical*. St.-Étienne.
Watson, A. (1967) *The Law of Persons in the Later Roman Republic*. Oxford.
West, M.L. (1977) *ZPE* 25: 118.
West, M.L. (1978) 'Die griechischen dichterinnen der Kaiserzeit'. In *Kyklos (Festschrift R. Keydell)*. Berlin. 101-15.
Wiedemann, T.E.J. (1983) *Greece and Rome* 30: 168.
Will, E.L. (1979) *Women in Pompeii*. New York. 34-43.
Willetts, R.F. (1967) *The Law Code of Gortyn*. Berlin.
Williams, J. (1972) *Augustus*. New York.
Winiarczyk, M. (1984) 'Wer galt in Altertum als Atheist?' *Philologus* 128: 176.
Worp, K.A., ed. (1980) *Das Aurelia Charite Archiv*. Zutphen.

Concordance of Sources

The numbers in **bold** type refer to the document numbers in the text.

Greek and Latin texts

Achilles Tatius, *Leucippe and Clitophon* 2.37.5-9, 38.1-3, **241**
Acts of Paul and Thecla 7-9, 18-20, 25, 34-5, 40-1, **444**
Acts of the Christian Martyrs 8.2-10, **445**; 22, **446**
Aeschylus, *Seven Against Thebes* 181-202, **59**
Alcman, Fr. 1.5-10, **401**
Alexis, Fr. 103 *PCG*, **287**; Fr. 150 *PCG*, **64**
Amphis, Fr. 1 *PCG*, **65**
Anon., *Tract. de Mulieribus* 11, **163**
Antipater of Thessalonica, *AP* VII.413, **218**
Antiphon, *Prosecution of a Stepmother*, 1-4, 14-20, 25-7, **89**
Antisthenes, Fr. 72 Decleva Caizzi, **96**
Anyte, *AP* VII.486, **15**; 490, **13**; 492, **12**; 649, **14**; *AP* XIII.16, **202**
Apollodorus (= 'Demosthenes'), *Against Neaera* 59.18-42, 45-60, 72-3, 78-9, 85-7, 110-14, 122, **90**; *Against Stephanus* 45.29, **78**
Apollonius of Rhodes, *Argonautica* 3.838-67, **414**
Appian, *Civil War* 4.32-4, **176**; 4.39-40, **167**
Archilochus, Fr. 196a West, **234**
Aretaeus, *On the Causes and Symptoms of Acute Diseases* 2, exc., **353**; *Therapeutics of Acute Diseases* 2.11, exc., **354**
Aristophanes, *Lysistrata* 638-47, **399**
Aristotle, *On Dreams* 459b-460a, **340**; *On the Generation of Animals*, 716a5-23, 727a2-30, 727b31-3, 728b18-31, 765b8-20, 766a17-30, 783b26-784a12, **339**; *Politics* 1254b2-10; 1259a37-b17; 1260a9-24, 29-33; 1262a19-24; 1269b12-70a31; 1277b18-25; 1313b32-9, 1335a7-17, **72**
Artemidorus, *On the Interpretation of Dreams* 1.80, **231**
Athenaeus 10.415ab, **305**; 517d-518a, **100**; 13.587c, **286**; 13.590e-591a, **288**
Aulus Gellius, *Attic Nights* 1.12, **409**; 10.23, **111**; 12.1, exc. **239**; 17.21.44, **110**
Bernand 31, **26**; 83, **27**; 92-4, **25**
Berthelot, Coll. II 102, **424**
Callimachus, *Hymn* 6.119-33, **394**
Carcinus II, *Semele*, *TGrF* Fr. 70, **62**
Celsus, *On Medicine* 4.27, 5.21, **360**
Cicero, *Brutus* 58.211, **223**; *Pro Caelio* 13-16, **71**
Clement of Alexandria, *Christ the Educator* [*Paedagogus*] 2. 33.1-4, **448**
Corinna, 654 *PMG*, **7**; 664 *PMG*, **8**

Isaeus, 3.39, **84**; 3.64, **81**; 6.17-24, **87**; 8.18-20, **86**; 10.10, **83**

Justinian, *Codex* 5.1.1, 5.4.14, 8.38.2, **131**; 9.9.1, 8, 11, 17 pr.-1, **124**; 9.9.20, **147**;
    9.9.22, 23 pr., 24, 26, 28, **142**; 9.10.1, **115**; 9.11.1 pr., **144**; 9.12.1, **139**; *Institutes*
    1.9. pr.-3, **114**; *Novellae* 14 pr.-1, **291**

Juvenal, *Satire* 6, exc., **69**

Livy, *History of Rome* 1.9, **233**; 1.57.6-58, **166**; 2.13.6-11, **165**; 27.37.8-9, **187**; 34.1,
    exc., **173**

Lysias, *Against Diogeiton* 32.11-18, **82**; *On the Murder of Eratosthenes* 6-33,
    37-50, **88**

Macrobius, *Saturnalia* 2.5.1-10, **266**

Malcovati, Fr. 6, **120**

Martial, *Epigrams* 1.13, **171**; 8.12, **68**; 9.30, **70**; 10.35, **224**; *Liber spectaculorum* 6,
    6b, **299**

Menander, Fr. 333 Koerte-Thierfelder, **66**; Fr. 390, **325**; P. Antinoöp. 15, ed.
    Sandbach, p. 327, **238**; *P. Didot* I, ed. Sandbach, p. 328, **35**; *Synkrisis* I, 209-10,
    ed. Jäkel, **67**

Musonius Rufus, 3, 4, 13A, **75**

New Testament: I Corinthians 7:1-16, 25-40, 11:2-16, 14:33b-5, **441**; I Timothy
    2:8-15, 5:3-16, **442**; *Acts of the Apostles* 16:12-18, **443**

Nossis, *AP* VI.265, **16**; *AP* VI.273, **18**; *AP* VI.275, **17**; *AP* VI.332, **19**; *AP* IX.604, **20**;
    AP IX.605, **21**

Paul, *Opinions* 2.19.1-2, **135**; 2.21A.1-4, **146**; 2.24.1-9, **118**; 2.26.1-8, 10-12, 14-17,
    123

Pausanias, *Guide to Greece* 2.20.8, **162**; 3.16.1-2, **426**; 5.16.2-4, **392**; 6.20.2-3, **427**;
    8.48.4-5, **161**

Petronius, *Satyricon* 45, **301**

Plato, *Laws* 6.780e-781d, 7.804c-06c, 8.838a-39b, **74**; *Meno* 71e, **95**; *Republic*
    5.451c-452d, 454d-e, 455c-456b, 457a-b, 457c-e, 458c-59a, 459d-61e, **73**;
    Timaeus 90e-91d, **338**

Plautus, *Cistellaria* 22ff. **181**

Pliny the Elder, *Nat. Hist.* 7.38-43, 48-9, **359**; 28.23, exc., **362**; 35.40, **307**

Pliny the Younger, *Letters* 3.16, **170**; 4.19, **243**; 4.21, **262**; 5.16, **263**; 6.4, **224**; 6.7,
    245; 7.5, **246**; 7.19, **172**; 8.10, **247**

Plutarch, *Lives: Caesar* 9-10, **413**; *Cicero* 19.3, 20.1-2, **412**; *Gaius Gracchus* 4.3,
    19.1-3, **51**; *Lycurgus* 14-16, exc., **98**; *Mark Antony* 25.5-28.1, 29, **175**; *Numa*
    Pompilius 9.5-10.7, exc., **408**; *Pericles* 24.1-6, 32.1-2, **235**; *Tiberius Gracchus*,
    1.2-5, **52**; *Moralia* 138a-146a, exc., **242**; 240c-242d exc., **99**; 245c-f, **160**; 249b-d,
    358; 276d-e, 289a-b, **270**; 299e-300a, **390**; Fr. 97, **361**; Pseudo-Plutarch,
    Moralia 14b-c, **215**

Pollux 10.18, **325**

Posidippus, *Supp.Hell.* 702, **305**

Praxilla 747, 757 *PMG*, **9**

Quintilian, *Institutes of Oratory* 1.1.6, **213**

Sallust, *Conspiracy of Catiline* 24.3-25, **174**

Sappho, Fr. 1, **1**; Fr. 16, **3**; Fr. 31, **2**; Fr. 44, **6**; Fr. 94, **4**; Fr. 96, **5**

Semonides, *On Women*, **57**

Seneca, *On Benefits* 6.32.1, **265**; *On Consolation* 16, **261**

Socrates, *Ecclesiastical History* VII.15, Migne, PG vol. 67, col. 768-9, **451**

Sophocles, *Tereus*, Fr. 585 Radt, **32**; *Women of Trachis* 141-52, **31**

Soranus, *Gynaecology* 1.3-4, **375**; 1.24, 26, 34, 36, 39, 40, 60, 61, 64 **355**; 1.67-9,
    exc., **356**; 2.18-20, **380**; 3.26, 28, 29, **357**

St Jerome, *Against Jovinianus* 47, **449**
Statius, *Silvae* 1.6.51-6, **300**
Suda, s.v. Hypatia, Y166 I.4 644-5, **451**
Suetonius, *Augustus* 31.4, **410**; 34, **122**; 44.5-7, **211**; 64.4-5, **210**; *Claudius* 19, **284**;
    Domitian 4.2, **297**; *Gaius* 40-1, exc. **289**; *Galba* 5.1, **188**
Supp. Hell. 401, **10**
Sulpicia, ap. Tibullum 3.13, **23**; 3.14, **22**; 3.15, 3.16, 3.17, 3.18, **23**
Tacitus, *Annals* 2.85, **290**; 4.53, **220**; 15.32.3, **296**; *Dialogue* 28, exc., **258**
Theocritus, *Idylls* 2, exc., **415**; 15, exc., **229**
Theopompus, *Histories* 115, *FGrH* F204 **100**
Thesleff, pp. 123-4, **250**; pp. 151-4, **208**
Thucydides, *History* 2.2.1, 4.133.2-3, **391**; 6.59, **36**
Ulpian, *Rules*, 5.8-10, **133**; 6.1-2, 4, 6-7, 10, 12-13, **137**; 7.2, **141**; 11.1, **117**
Valerius Maximus, *Memorable Deeds and Sayings* 4.4 pr., **259**; 6.3.9-12, **109**;
    6.7.1-3, **53**; 8.3, **178**
Xenophon, *Constitution of the Lacedaemonians* 1, **97**; *Memorabilia* 2.7, **236**; 2.36,
    225; *Oeconomicus* 3.15, **225**; 6.17-10, exc., **267**; *Symposium* 2.9, **303**

Greek and Latin inscriptions

Agora XVII no. 913, **310**
CEG 2, **273**; 97, **226**; 153, **274**; 167, **37**; 526, **275**; 530, **237**; 537, **318**; 571, **379**; 774,
    317
CIG 6855, **295**
CIL I². 581, **388**; 1211, **39**; 1214, **40**; 1221, **239**; 1570, **212**; IV.171, **179**; 207, **179**;
    913, **179**; 1083, **179**; 2175, **293**; 2224, **293**; 2265, **293**; 3291, **179**; 3527, **179**;
    3678, **179**; 3684, **179**; 6610, **179**; 8356, **293**; 10231, **240**; 10233, **293**; 10241, **293**;
    V.2072, **185**; 7453, **280**; VI.997, **186**; 1779, 1780, **439**; 2144, **411**; 2145, **439**;
    3482, **285**; 4352, **334**; 5201, **334**; 5539, **334**; 6325, **377**; 6326, **335**; 6331, **335**;
    6336, **335**; 6342, **335**; 6346, **335**; 6350, **335**; 6357, **335**; 6362, **335**; 6395, **335**;
    6593, **45**; 6647, **377**; 6851, **372**; 7581, **370**; 8192, **377**; 8947, **334**; 8949, **334**;
    8957, **334**; 8958, **334**; 8959, **334**; 9037, **334**; 9213, **319**; 9214, **321**; 9496, **335**;
    9497, **335**; 9498, **335**; 9499, **239**; 9523, **335**; 9614, **372**; 9615, **372**; 9617, **372**;
    9619, **371**; 9683, **335**; 9720, **377**; 9721, **377**; 9722, **377**; 9723, **377**; 9727, **335**;
    9730, **335**; 9732, **335**; 9754, **335**; 9758, **335**; 9801, **335**; 9884, **335**; 9980, **335**;
    10125, **311**; 10127, **312**; 10131, **314**; 10132, **315**; 10158, **316**; 10230, **43**; 10423,
    184; 15346, **39**; 16631, **264**; 19128, **251**; 19747, p. 294; 20905, **418**; 22560, **281**;
    25580, **364**; 29149, **276**; 29580, **49**; 33473, **320**; 33892, **335**; 33898, **222**; 37965,
    47; 38605, **282**; VIII.2756, **278**; 7604, **440**; 8123, **256**; 9491, **255**; 23888, **199**;
    24734, **366**; VIII, Suppl. 20288, **365**; IX.2029, **292**; X.810, **196**; 813, **196**; 816,
    425; 998, **425**; 1933, **378**; 6009, **212**; 6328, **195**; 6787, **367**; XI.1491, **277**;
    XIV.2120, **183**; 3709, **326**
CLE 52, **39**; 56, **212**; 94, **364**; 95, **418**; 151, **255**; 959, **239**; 1030, **45**; 1282, **314**;
    1287, **256**; 1578, **280**; 1613, **440**; 1834, **365**; 1988, **47**; 2115, **366**
Ditt. *Syll.* 1218, **77**; 2653, **396**
FH 152, **227**; 177m, **207**
Finley 8, **93**; 9, **91**; 130, **94**; 155, **92**
Fouilles de Delphes 4, 79, **192**
GHI 44, **398**
HSCP 82 (1978) 148, **385**
I. Magn. 215 [a]. 2440, **386**

IG I².24, **398**; 756, **397**; II².473, **322**; 1136, **400**; 1388.78-80, 82-3, **403**; 1400.41-2, 46, 47, **403**; 1514, **402**; 1561.22-7, **331**; 2313.9-15, 60, **205**; 2314.50, 924, **205**; 2679, **85**; 2934, **323**; 3634, **434**; 4334, **317**; 7873, **379**; 10954, **226**; 11162, **38**; 11205, **336**; 11244, **336**; 11254, **332**; 11496, **336**; 11647, **332**; 11674, **435**; 11688, **332**; 12067, **237**; 12073, **332**; 12254, **318**; 12335, **275**; 12387, **332**; 12559, **332**; 12583, **304**; 12996, **332**; 13065, **332**; III.iii.68, 69, exc., **337**; 78, **421**; 87, **324**; 97.34-41, **420**; IV.2.121-2, exc., **406**; V.11390, **395**; IX.ii.526.19-20, **204**; 670, **389**

ILA, p. 54, no. 175, **279**

ILLRP 511, **388**; 793, **239**; 803, **40**; 971, **254**; 973, **39**; 977, **212**

ILS 18, **388**; 324, **186**; 840, **41**; 1030, **264**; 1259-61, **439**; 1784, **334**; 1786, **334**; 1786a, **334**; 1788, **334**; 1837, **334**; 3785, **196**; 4414, **431**; 4927, **411**; 5213, **40**; 5231, **315**; 5244, **311**; 5248, **316**; 5262, **312**; 5264, **314**; 6199, **183**; 6278, **195**; 6368, **196**; 6369, **425**; 6408a, **179**; 6414, **179**; 6415, **179**; 6431a, **179**; 7397, **335**; 7419, **335**; 7420, **335**; 7420a, **335**; 7428, **335**; 7432b, **335**; 7432c, **335**; 7432d, **335**; 7435b, **335**; 7459, **285**; 7472, **239**; 7477, **326**; 7488, **335**; 7500, **335**; 7567, **335**; 7691, **319**; 7692, **321**; 7760, **335**; 7771, **320**; 7783, **222**; 7804, **370**; 8287, **292**; 8393, **168**; 8394, **43**; 8403, **39**; 8450, **49**; 8461, **277**; 8522, p. 294; 8751, **419**; 9347, **313**; 9455, **294**

Inscr. Creticae 4.72, cols. ii.3-27, ii.45-iv.54, v.1-9. vi.31-46, vi.56-vii.2, vii.15-viii.19, xi. 18-19, **76**

Inscr. Eph. 1062, **24**; 1063-4, **430**

JEA 4 (1917) 253f., **182**

JÖAI 43 (1956) 22-3, **201**

Kaibel 45, **376**; 102, **336**; 118, **333**; 121, **336**; 176, **48**; 218, **368**; 609, **308**; 727, **50**; 861, **434**; 863, **436**; 1136, **416**

Lewis, *Hesperia* 28 (1959) 208-38, **329**; 37 (1968) 368-80, **330**

Maiuri, 1965, p. 83, **196**

Peek 1007, **333**; 1029, **435**; 1164, **50**; 1233, **363**; 1243, **46**; 1871, **368**; 1881, **42**

Pleket 1, **376**; 5, **194**; 6, **306**; 8, exc., **197**; 9, **206**; 10, **44**; 11, **428**; 12, **369**; 13, **429**; 14, **193**; 15, **191**; 18, **432**; 19, **198**; 20, **373**; 25, **437**; 26, **374**; 29, **438**; 30, **221**; 31, **200**

Raubitschek, *DAA* 348, **397**

SEG IX.72.13-16, **404**

Sokolowski, *LSAM* 48, **384**

Sokolowski, *LSCG* 33A, **395**; 95.28-33, **396**; 181, **389**

Sokolowski, *LSCG Supp.* 115, exc., **404**

Tab. Vindol. Inv. No. 85/87, **272**

Documentary papyri

BGU IV.22, **157**; 1024.6-8, exc., **155**; 1104, **102**; 1106, 1107, **381**; 1210, **148**; VI. 129.11, **327**

CPR XIII, **328**

P.Cattaoui 3, 4, **151**

P.Corn. 9, **309**

P.Eleph. 3.25, **103**

P.Fam.Tebt. 21, **149**

P.Giessen 80, 95, **214**

P.Grenf. I.53, **232**

P.Hamb. 86, **269**

P.Hibeh 54, **387**
P.Lond. 951 verso, **252**
P.Mich. 6551, **150**; iv.23, **327**
P.Oxy. 91, **382**; 111, **271**; 281, **122**; 282, **106**; 528, **248**; 744, **249**; 903, **159**; 930, **257**;
    1467, **154**; 1647, **283**; 2082, **203**; 2758, **156**; 3048, **153**; 3644, **158**
P.Tebt. 776, **104**; I 104, **101**
PGM VII. 208-9, **422**; 260-71, **423**
PMG 747, 757, **9**
Preisendanz Henrichs 2 11, p. 9, **422**; 2 11, p. 12, **423**
PSI 1080, **268**
SB X.10756, exc., **152**
UPZ 19, **407**

Concordance with the First Edition

The numbers in **bold** type refer to the documents in this edition; those in ordinary type refer to the first edition.

1/1	37/66	70/83	105/236
2/2	38/35	71/84	106/267
3/3	39/160	72/85	107/208
4/4	40/164	73/86	108/230
5/5	41/207	74/87	109/228
6/6	42/227	75/88	110/229
7/7	43/217	76/89	111/250
8/8	44/202	77/90	112/249
9/10	45/203	78/91	113/384
11/12	46/204	79/92	114/385
12/13	47/205	80/93	115/386
13/14	48/194	81/94	116/387
14/15	49/42	82/101	117/393
15/16	50/322	83/102	118/394
16/17	51/323	84/103	119/397
17/18	52/376	85/104	120/398
18/19	53/287	86/72	121/400
19/20	54/379	87/73	122/401
20/21	55/317	88/74	123/402
21/273	56/318	89/98	124/403
22/36	57/324	90/99	125/404
23/37	58(i)/329	91/338	126/405
24/274	58(ii)/330	92/339	127/406
25/226	58(iii)/331	93/341	128/407
26/237	59/332	94/342	129/414
27/275	60/304	95/340	130/415
28/54	61/310	96/343	131/416
29/55	62/333	97/345	132/22
30/57	63/306	98/346	133/23
31/58	64/76	99/347	134/39
32/32	65/77	100/349	135/40
33/33	66/78	101/350	136/254
34/63	67/79	102/363	137/239
35/64	68/80	103/358	138/212
36/238	69/81	104/234	139/43

140/44	175/373	202/152	237/186
141/368	176/375	203/174	238/187
142/46	177/377	204/223	239/188
143/47	178/380	205/178	240/189
144/48	179/381 (part)	206/176	241/190
145/259	180/382	207/168	242/408
146/52	181/307	208/167	243/388
147/51	182/334	209/172	244/390
148/261	183/335	210/179	245/389
149/258	184/336	211/351	246/412
150/170	185/337	212/359	247/413
151/262	186/308	213/355	248/417
152/263	187/107	214/356	249/418
153/53	188/108	215/353	250/419
154/180	189/111	216/354	251/420
155/71	190/109	217/357	252/421
156/175	191/173	218/360	253/422
157/69	192/121	219/352	254/423
158/197	193(i)/123	220/213	255/196
159/429	193(ii)/124	221/215	256/425
160/193	193(iii)/125	222/283	257/433
161/191	194/113, 132	223/269	258/428
162/198	195(i)/143, 115, 116	224/257	259/432
163/199	195(ii)/117, 133	225/268	260/434
164/200	196(i)/135	226/243-7	261/435
165/201	196(ii)/139, 134, 138, 140	227/242	262/436
166/219	196(iii)/137	228/68	263/437
167/220	197(i)/138	229/70	264/438
168/221	197(ii)/119, 145	230/270	264a/439
169/206	198/148	231/21	265/441
170/369	199/149	232/195	266/445
171/374	200/150	233/182	267/446
172/370	201/151	234/183	268/447
173/371		235/184	269/449
174/372		236/185	

Index of Women and Goddesses

General Index

abortion, 88, 188, 254-5, 260; spontaneous, 232-3, 235, 236-7; drugs to induce, 34, 252-3, 266; pessary to induce, 248
Achilles, 11
Acilius, wife of, 134
actresses, 102, 110, 217-18
Adonis, 5, 7
adoption, in Greek law, 58, 99-100; in Roman law, 99-100
Adriatic Sea, 31
adultery, 13, 36, 133, 192; in Greek law, 52, 55, 69, 70, 76, 80-1; in Roman law, 94, 97, 100-9, 114, 116-18, 195, 254, 327
Africa, 134, 160, 183, 206, 213. *See also* names of towns
afterbirth, 255
agnates, 95-6
agriculture, women working in, 48, 209
Agrionia, festival of, 276
Agrippa, 195-6
Ain Kebira, Mauretania, 263
Alcaeus, 1
alchemists, women, 299-300
Alcibiades, 87
Alexander Severus, 101, 105, 112
Alexander the Great, 89
Alexandria, 31, 90, 125, 149, 172, 187, 221, 270, 280; texts from, 91, 119-22, 217, 280, 294-5, 324, 331-3; women's club at, 155
alimentary grants, 159
amenorrhea, 234, 239
amniotic sac, 255-6
Amorgos, 25, 82-3, 206
Amyclae, 301
anatomy, comparison of male and female, 243-6
Andania, 281
Annesi, Asia Minor, 327
Antistius Rusticus, 34
Antistius Vetus, Q., 96
Antius, wife of, 134
Antoninus, 107. *See* Caracalla
Antony, Mark, 135, 146-9, 150
apetairos, 55

Aphrodisias, 302
Apollo, 169, 216, 264, 285, 301
Apollonia, Mysia, 169
Apothetae, 87
Appius Claudius Caecus, 35-6
apprenticeship, of girl, 208
Apuleius, wife of, 134
Aquileia, 217
Ardea, 132
Areopagus, 70
Ares, 40, 129, 130
arete, 84
Arezzo, 8
Argos, 129, 130, 162, 277, 283
Aristotle, 38, 59, 60, 84, 259, 332
arrhephoroi, 282, 303
Asclepius, 285-7
Asia Minor, 130, 160, 244, 250, 265, 311, 327, 333-4. *See also* names of towns
ass, woman compared to, 26
assault, 125, 126
Athens, 58, 73, 75-7, 80, 82-3, 277, 332; Ceramicus, 65; Acropolis, 303; texts from, 10-14, 16, 20, 28-31, 38, 41, 47, 59-62, 64-6, 71, 162, 167, 170, 178-80, 196, 215-22, 224-6, 229, 266-7, 273, 281-2, 284, 296, 298-9, 303-4
athletics, women's, 33, 43, 46-8, 53, 85. *See also* gymnastics, gladiators
Attica, 284
Augustales, priestess of, 303
Augustus, 137, 150, 165, 291, 300; marriage legislation of, 102-3, 105, 143; and family, 165, 191, 195-6. *See also lex Julia*, Julia
aulos-playing, 209, 215, 221, 281
Aurelian, 157

babies. *See* breast-feeding, wet-nurses, infanticide
Bacchic rites, 80, 275-6. *See also* Bacchus, Dionysus
Bacchus, 169, 272-6, 302, 307. *See also* Dionysus
Baiae, 36, 165

sexual intercourse, 50; purpose of wives, 82; desire for, 225
procuress, 65, 212, 224
Prometheus, 23
property, of women, in marriage, 54, 90, 92-3, 183, 198; in Greek law, 55-7, 62, 64, 81, 83, 85, 92; in Roman law, 94-5, 100, 115-17, 119-23
prostitutes, prostitution, 183, 187, 209-12, 220, 232, 307; in Greek law, 65, 73-7, 81-2; in Roman law, 111, 117-19, 125; organization of, 155; public, 125. *See also* brothels, pimps, procuresses
prytanis, female, 9, 302
puberty, 13, 24, 99, 101, 114, 243, 246, 283; ritual, 283
pubic hair, 178, 229
pulse vendor, 221
Puteoli, 267
Pythian games, 158, 162, 216
Pythion, 18

rape, 55, 70, 100, 119; of Lucretia, 132-3; of the Sabine women, 176-8
reader, 220
repudiation, of wife, 95, 106, 110, 115. *See also* divorce
Rheginus, wife of, 134
right of life and death, 69, 97, 104
rituals, 204, 274
rivalry, male-female, 5
Rome, texts from, 8, 16-17, 19, 20-2, 31-4, 50, 94-119, 133-58, 164-6, 168-9, 176-7, 181, 184, 188, 190-1, 194-5, 207, 210-11, 214-15, 217-19, 222-4, 250, 259-68, 275, 288-92, 294-5, 298, 302, 303, 318; Aqua Claudia, 36; Aventine Hill, 146, 156-7; Capitoline Hill, 143, 156; Colline Gate, 33; Colosseum, 213-14; Forum of Trajan, 156; Forum Romanum, 195, 288-9, 291; Porta Salaria, 218; Quirinal Hill, 157; Six Altars, 223; Via Appia, 36
Romulus, 94, 145, 177, 288

Sabine women, 32, 176-8, 205
Salamis, 130-1
salt vendors, 221, 224
Sardis, 17, 333
Sarmatian women, 48
Scipio Africanus, 21-3
scribe, 220
seamstresses, 222-3
secretary, 223
seed (semen), female, 226-9, 245
Sempronius Sophus, P., 96
senaculum, 157-8
senate, women's, 157-8

Senatus consultum de bacchanalibus, 275-6
Septimius Severus, 101, 107, 215
Serapis, 287-8
Seriphos, 210
sesame seed-seller, 221
sexual intercourse, 80, 258; promiscuous, 26; with animal, 13, 287; as prize, 45; between husband and wife, 84, 86; pleasure during, 230-1; in public, 89; unnatural, 49-50; unlawful, in Roman law, 104, 106-10, 117-18; desire for, 225, 252; 'labour' pains during, 243; physicians on, 230-5, 240, 252-3, 258, 260, 262. *See also* adultery, homosexuality, marriage, prostitution
shepherdess, 220
Sicyon, 5, 64, 162
silver-slave, 222
singing, 4, 6, 85, 109, 295, 301, 318, 322, 328, 331. *See also* music
slaves, and women compared, 39
Solon, 58, 69-70, 108, 182
Sosipolis, 301
sow, woman compared to, 25
Spanish fly, 233
Sparta, 11, 277; women of, 39, 48-9, 83-9, 183, 286; texts from, 161, 283, 301; war with, 75-6, 129-30
sperm, female, 231-2. *See also* seed
spinning girl, 224
spinning, 48, 52-3, 165, 173, 197, 215
statues, commemorative, of women, 21, 61, 132, 156, 158-61, 205, 264, 285, 291, 306; of goddesses, 7, 56, 130, 288, 302
stenographer, 223
sterility, 34, 96-7, 243
Stoics, 49-53, 140, 192
storeroom attendant, 221
stuprum. See rape
suicide, 34, 88, 133, 140-1, 259
sumptuary laws, 58, 103, 141. *See also* luxury
Syros, 188, 304

Tanagra, 4
Tarracina, 159
taxes, on prostitution, 210; for women, 103, 150-2, 329; exemption from, 216, 282
Tebtunis, 89, 120-1
Tegea, 6, 130
Telos, 5
temetum, 97. *See also* wine
Thasos, 18, 304
Thebes, 4, 28, 274
Thesmophoria, 64-5, 280-1, 303-4
Thessaly, 130, 170, 296